EMBRACING
REALITY

EMBRACING REALITY

THE INTEGRAL VISION OF KEN WILBER

*A Historical Survey and
Chapter-by-Chapter Guide
to Wilber's Major Works*

BRAD REYNOLDS

JEREMY P. TARCHER/PENGUIN
a member of Penguin Group (USA) Inc.
New York

Most Tarcher/Penguin books are available at special quantity discounts for bulk purchase for sales promotions, premiums, fund-raising, and educational needs. Special books or book excerpts also can be created to fit specific needs. For details, write Penguin Group (USA) Inc. Special Markets, 375 Hudson Street, New York, NY 10014.

Jeremy P. Tarcher/Penguin
a member of
Penguin Group (USA) Inc.
375 Hudson Street
New York, NY 10014
www.penguin.com

Library of Congress Cataloging-in-Publication Data

Reynolds, Brad.
Embracing reality : the integral vision of Ken Wilber : a historical survey and chapter-by-chapter guide to Wilber's major works / by Brad Reynolds.
p. cm.
Includes bibliographical references and index.
ISBN 1-58542-317-3
1. Wilber, Ken. I. Title
BF109.W54R49 2004 2004047887
191—dc22

Printed in the United States of America
1 3 5 7 9 10 8 6 4 2

BOOK DESIGN BY MAUNA EICHNER AND LEE FUKUI

This book is lovingly dedicated to my father:

CORBIN D. REYNOLDS
(October 14, 1926–August 9, 1996)

Contents

Wilber/Phase-1

THE SPECTRUM OF CONSCIOUSNESS
(1973–1977)

Wilber/Phase-2

THE EVOLUTION REVOLUTION
(1978–1983)

Wilber/Phase-5

INTEGRAL AQAL APPROACH

(NEW MILLENNIUM)

Bodhisattva Enlightenment

To Return to the Source it is not necessary to destroy and annihilate the lower levels. It is necessary only to transcend them, to cease identifying exclusively with them. . . . In true and unobstructed evolution, we take all the lower levels with us, out of love and compassion, so that all levels eventually are reconnected to the Source.

To negate everything is to preserve everything; to transcend all is to include all.

We must go whole-bodily to God; failing that, we fall into dissociation, repression, inner fragmentation. Ultimate transcendence is thus not ultimate annihilation of the levels of creation, but rather their ultimate inclusion in Spirit.

The Final Transcendence is the Final Embrace.

To me, the beauty of the twin concepts of evolution and compound individuality is this: my very existence today, although not reducible to or derivable from lower levels, nonetheless depends and rests upon the lower levels, whose early struggles and successes paved the way for my emergence. For that, I am grateful to them. Likewise, they are thankful to me, for in my own compound individuality, the mineral, the plant, and the animal participate in, or are a part of, higher mental consciousness, something they could never achieve on their own.

Ultimately, in the compound individuality of the sage, all the lower levels are allowed to participate in absolute Enlightenment and bathe in the glory of Spirit. The mineral, as mineral, the plant, as plant, and the animal, as animal, could never be enlightened—but the Bodhisattva takes all manifestation with him to Paradise, and the Bodhisattva vow is never to accept Enlightenment until all things participate in Spirit. There is, to my mind, no nobler conception than that.

Thus, at ultimate Enlightenment or Return to Spirit, the created world can still exist; it just no longer obscures Spirit, but serves it. All the levels remain as expressions of Atman, not substitutes for Atman.

—Ken Wilber, *Up From Eden*

Foreword

Brad Reynolds has done an extraordinary job of reading, categorizing, and explaining my work to date. I am deeply appreciative of the time and loving effort he has put into this project, and I am sure many people interested in my work will find it of great value.

There are now numerous books, articles, and postings that attempt to explain my work. I decided that, given their proliferation, the only fair stance was to respectfully decline to endorse or edit any of them. Once I started down that road, alas, it would be endless, having to check each sentence in each presentation for accuracy. Since I cannot do that for all, I have decided it is only fair to do it for none.

Thus, I have endorsed no work—including this one—as being a correct presentation of my integral approach. I have not read the chapters in this book for accuracy, except for a version of the introduction, where I tried to help with some biographical information. But until I can sit down with a team of scholars and hammer out some introductory texts, there remains no introduction to my work that I endorse. I must therefore warn critics that I cannot respond to their assertions if based on anything other than quotes from my books themselves, at least at this time.

That said, Brad's book is certainly meticulous and carefully presented. Brad has a profound and abiding interest in integral studies in all of its facets; he is deeply dismayed by the sad state of what usually passes for integral studies; and he shares a desire to help advance more encompassing, caring, and conscious approaches to the integral field itself.

All truly integral approaches are based on one major assumption: *everybody is right.* That is, all the various fields and disciplines—traditional, modern, and postmodern—have something incredibly important to tell us, and all of them should be acknowledged, honored, and incorporated in a more comprehensive, balanced, and integrated approach in both theory and practice.

Exactly how to bring them all together under one umbrella is the difficult and delicate task. My own version of this integral umbrella—called AQAL—is the most recent phase of my work, and, in a sense, all of my previous books have led up to this integral approach. If you want to see my own attempted "popular" introduction to this model, you might try *A Brief History of Everything* as well as check out www.integralinstitute.org. Brad's book covers this AQAL model, of course, as well as the books leading up to it, and thus ends up being a type of historical survey of the precursors to the present.

My hope is that Brad's labor of love will be of help to any and all who would like to pursue a more integral and holistic approach in their own fields, in their spiritual practices, or simply in their personal lives in general.

There is a fire in the integral, a passion that sooner or later awakens in the depths of the hidden heart and roars outwardly with flames of searing wonder. The fire that is the integral is almost impossible to capture in words—unless you are a Hölderlin, a Wordsworth, a Basho—and so sometimes all us poor academics have left are shadows and shells, arid abstractions, vaporous concepts that somehow attempt to hint, to point, to urge one on in the direction of one's own radiant soul and spirit—the ground and goal of all that is, and all that was, and all that ever shall be.

Thus, the final purpose of any integral approach is simply to give a framework to a series of living, vivid, electrifying experiences that catch the ego totally off guard and reduce it to nothingness through the enlightening jolt of spirit's unguarded shout. The shout can be heard but never written, so you will not find spirit in any of my books—or anybody else's books, either. You will instead find spirit as the very witness of this page, the very reader of these words, the very feeling of is-ness that you already are. My books, Brad's books, all of them are just reminders, after the fact, that if you would truly like to live an integral life, then awaken the Seer, feel into the Feeler, know the Knower, and let that Freedom expand into a Fullness that outshines the separate self entirely, reduced already to nothingness in the wonder of the present, only to embrace the entire universe in the outstretched palm of its hand, moment to nothing-special moment, just like *this*. . . . When wonder fades into infinity and the now captures eternity, the true meaning of integral will dawn with shocking familiarity, like coming home, really home, after the worst nightmare you could ever imagine. And there we will all find each other, radiant sparks of the same spirit, smiling in eternity, whispers of what we are.

—Ken Wilber
Denver, Colorado
Fall 2002

The Task of Philosophy

The task of philosophy, as it were, is not simply to clarify the maps and *correct* their deviations from reality, but to *elucidate* these deeper currents from which thought couldn't deviate even if it wanted to!

 In Zen there is a saying, "That which one can deviate from is not the true Tao."

In other words, in some ways our knowledge is indeed a matter of correcting our inaccurate maps; but also, and at a much deeper level, there is a Tao, a Way, a Current of the Kosmos, from which we have not, and could never, deviate. And part our job is to find this deeper Current, this Tao, and express it, elucidate it, celebrate it.

—Ken Wilber,
A Brief History of Everything

A Note to the Reader

Admittedly, the breadth and beauty of Ken Wilber's writings can never be summarized in a fully adequate or comprehensive fashion. However, I have been in the fortunate position to have personally studied under Ken since 1993, after over ten years of studying on my own. At one point, we felt it might be useful to summarize the chapters of his books; indeed, the original intention was to make these book summaries only a few pages long, a task I found impossible, owing to the incredible wealth of information and novel ideas buried in the man's collected writings. After reading every page of every book and covering them with copious notes, I judiciously picked the parts that caught my attention and which I felt were most important to highlight. Every Wilber student, no doubt, could make their own version given enough time and a great deal of determination. My great advantage was that I could always ask Ken personally for clarification if and when I needed it—and at times I most certainly did—all of which he graciously gave without hesitation. And much of that happened before I even started to compile this book.

Nevertheless, let me be clear, Ken left me alone to do this gargantuan task as I thought best and in no way made suggestions as to how it should go. I have tried to at least give his work a fair representation, one that honors the magnitude of the material yet includes some of the details. Naturally, any errors are mine alone. In the end, it was nothing but my perseverance (and the grace of God) that has resulted in this compilation, the first comprehensive concordance and study guide to Ken Wilber's vast "integral vision" or "theory of everything." This seems justified, for he has become, in many people's opinion, the world's best and most profound living Western philosopher.

Overall, this book is subdivided into the main "five phases" of Wilber's writing career (Phase 1–5 or Wilber I–V) covering over twenty-five years of publica-

NOTE TO THE READER

tion with each phase articulating an even greater embrace of reality or *philosophia,* "the love of wisdom." Each "phase"* or period of his writing identifies and defines the overall "integral vision," each with certain areas of emphasis and concern:

- **Wilber/Phase 1** or "The Spectrum of Consciousness" (1973–1977);

- **Wilber/Phase 2** or "The Evolution Revolution" (1978–1983);

- **Wilber/Phase 3** or "The Integral Vision: Self, Levels, & Lines" (1983–1994);

- **Wilber/Phase 4** or "Four Quadrants & the Postmodern Critique" (1995–2000);

- **Wilber/Phase 5** or "Integral AQAL Approach" (New Millennium).

Nonetheless, as will be demonstrated in the following chapters, there's a strong current of unity and continuity running throughout all of these "phases" of Wilber's collected works and they should always be seen in this integral fashion. Nonetheless, this "phase" approach can be a useful guide in getting to know Wilber's philosophy, simply because no other theorist has compiled a greater collection of integral writings in the history of the world.

Because of the massive amount of material covered in this extensive review volume, the Book Summaries themselves are presented in three basic forms (see the Table of Contents for each book's summary status):

1. a Chapter-by-Chapter summary of an entire Wilber book, usually over ten pages long (there are seven of these);

2. an Expanded Review, which is a reduced chapter-by-chapter overview, generally ten pages or less (there are six of these);

3. a Short Review, which is usually around two pages (there are seven of these).

A couple of important reasons for this type of truncated summary format: first and foremost, to have a handy reading length for the general public was a consideration for a summary-encapsulation book. Therefore, as equitably as possible, much of Wilber's prolific output had to be reduced or edited. Indeed, his lengthy

---

* The phase designations of Wilber's career will be principally presented here as "Wilber/Phase #," although throughout his written work (and those of other scholars) the designators vary from "Wilber #" to "Phase #" to "Wilber-Roman #," all of which are appropriate and shall be used interchangeably.

collected works can easily overwhelm even a condensed review volume, thus I suggest the reader should consult the originals for the most accurate presentation. Second, since certain sections and chapters are only reviewed and not completely summarized, I must mention that I believe they are justifiably condensed and deleted since most of the principle arguments are presented in one of the other books with a complete chapter-by-chapter summary.

Naturally, of course, certain subjects have been missed or omitted since Wilber is extremely detailed in his presentations (especially in his footnotes), yet still, I have given a complete and thorough account of nearly every one of his major arguments, including the standard definitions for most of his principle terms. In fact, learning Wilber's new integral terminology or integral language and the reasons behind them is, I believe, a principal task of the emerging Integral Age, therefore I hope this work assists in that service. As always, the original material contains invaluable information and exquisite writing, thus they should be consulted and enjoyed at any time.

I have redrawn and included many of the principal pictorial graphics (figures, tables, and charts) that are used throughout Wilber's own books. However, in some instances, my versions have been modified slightly in order to better facilitate understanding and clarification where deemed appropriate.

In regard to the editing, I have placed an emphasis on explaining the components and terminology of Wilber's integral system of scientific spirituality (integral psychology), thus somewhat forgoing the more sophisticated philosophical debates that are explained in detail in his more complicated passages (especially in the footnotes). Naturally, the brilliance of Wilber's philosophical views—which give a masterful overview of premodernity, modernity, and postmodernity all set within their historical context, including brilliant synopses of numerous philosophers—cannot be overestimated; they are outstanding and should be pursued on their own. Nonetheless, I stand by the thoroughness of this chapter-by-chapter presentation, for it covers nearly every essential idea presented in Wilber's main texts (sans the voluminous footnotes—and he didn't really use footnotes prior to Phase 4!).

In regard to the various Appendices, the premier publication of *Integral Psychology* (1999, 2000) included comprehensive Correlative Charts (included here as Appendix 1) which were compiled by Wilber himself to cross-reference the evidence collected by hundreds of researchers, including the wealth of data gathered from over three thousand years of humanity's collective wisdom or spiritual traditions. The charts correlate, in great detail, many of these other systems and extensive models of research with Wilber's integral spectrum of consciousness and Kosmos, also known as the Great Holarchy of Being and Knowing (portrayed in the left-hand column of the charts). I believe these graphic presentations make an excellent summary of Wilber's integral model; thus I can only encourage the reader to make good use of them in order to locate many of the specific references and theorists to which his writings often allude. Also in the Appendix, there is a complete Bibliography (Appendix 2) that includes Wilber's many books, major essays, articles, and other writings.

The Introduction, subtitled "Ken Wilber's Personal Odyssey," is a short biography and guided tour through the inception and publication of his principal books, therefore it should help orient the reader to the various phases of his nearly three-decades-long career. This brief biography also attempts to outline, based on the public record, Wilber's personal and spiritual development, and a few of his countless influences, involved in generating his theories and inspired writings. This is relevant because Wilber's theories aren't simply mental constructions but rather they are grounded in vast files of solid research.

This type of knowledge quest is gained from "seeing" and using all "three eyes of knowing," i.e., the physical (sciences), the mental (philosophy, psychology), and the spiritual (transpersonal, meditative) ways of knowing. In the case of the latter more interior realm of the transpersonal, Wilber hasn't only relied upon the collective accounts of the world's wisdom traditions gathered over millennia (the "perennial philosophy") but also upon his own direct personal experience, an approach he heartily recommends to everyone. His story or "personal odyssey," therefore, can be seen as a friendly "map" or guide offering useful "guideposts" for an interior journey that all of us will take sooner or later, one way or another. This is because as personal evolution unfolds, every person, male or female, will have the opportunity to dive deep, deep within only to find the "without" once more, but this time blissfully revealed as God Only (or as nondual Spirit). In other words, the world, the universe, our lives and relationships are *really* the radiant display and divine love of the nameless nondual Spirit.

Ultimately, in its own small way, I hope this effort will further crystallize the universal integral vision, most fully articulated and embraced by Wilber's *philosophia,* and that it will serve the eternal truth spoken about and pointed to within by the world's esoteric spiritual traditions. This great tradition of spiritual understanding—*philosophia perennis* or the "perennial philosophy" of enlightenment—is embodied most personally in the wise teachers and spiritual masters, men and women, throughout the ages and around the globe appearing in every culture, every century, in a wide variety of forms. These are the evolved souls, our "advanced-tip" practitioners, who do the yoga, engage the injunction (as Wilber would say) or actually *practice* what they preach, ultimately transcending self in the divinity of God (whatever that really is in truth).

They have lived, and do live, in order to bring Peace, Love, Justice, Enlightenment, and a higher or deeper understanding of real God to humanity and the global culture. To them, and to you, I bow in gratitude and sing heartfelt praises to the divine Lord of the Kosmos, our bright Buddha-Nature, the One (without second), the Clear Light of Love-Bliss, Who always already is, and Who is nameless, absolutely free, and the real truth of our hearts.

—One Love,
Brad Reynolds
Fall 2003

A Person's Deepest Drive

A person's deepest drive—the major drive of which all others are derivative—is the drive to actualize the entire Great Nest through the vehicle of one's own being, so that one becomes, in full realization, a vehicle of Spirit shining radiantly into the world, as the entire world. We are all the sons and daughters of a Godhead that is the Goal and Ground of every gesture in the Kosmos, and we will not rest until our own Original Face greets us with each dawn.

—Ken Wilber,
Integral Psychology (2000)

EMBRACING
REALITY

Introduction

KEN WILBER'S PERSONAL ODYSSEY

EARLY EDUCATION

Kenneth Earl Wilber II came into this world on January 31, 1949, in Oklahoma City while his traveling parents were moving to another United States Air Force base. Perhaps prophetically, he was nicknamed Ken, a Scottish name meaning "to know; to have perception or understanding." As a child of the baby-boom generation and the son of a decorated air force colonel and his devoted wife, Lucille (or Lucy), the young Ken moved from military base to military base every two or three years during his formative youth. The gifted and straight-A student ended up graduating from Bellevue High School, near Offutt Air Force Base in Nebraska just outside of Omaha, and although he went to a different school each year of high school, he was still at various times "class president, valedictorian, even captain of the football team." By his own admission years later, perhaps it was due to the constant torment of losing friends that he generously overcompensated "with a frantic dance for acceptance, an attempt to have *everybody* love me."[1] Whatever the case, this type of all-embracing, inclusive attitude—one where "everybody is right"[2]— would continue to serve Wilber throughout his life and underpin his theoretical philosophy and comprehensive integral vision.

Since the studious yet athletic and lanky (six feet four inches) Wilber had always shown a "knack and love for science" (as well as for cigarettes, beer, parties, and dating), he had been persuaded to become a medical doctor, and so in the fall of 1967 he entered college at Duke University in Durham, North Carolina.[3] However, the downside of the medical profession and the prospect of being creatively bored soon convinced Wilber to switch majors, from premed to biochemistry. As a result, he transferred to the University of Nebraska, Omaha. In the process, he disappointedly realized, as he explained a decade later, "I had spent my entire life studying science, only to be met with the wretched realization that science was, not wrong, but brutally limited and narrow in scope. . . . I wanted some meaning in the mess of facts I was ingesting."[4] Nonetheless, after almost dropping out of college owing to lack of interest, Wilber went on to graduate with a Master of Science degree and then work on his doctorate at the University of Nebraska in nearby Lincoln. Consequently, the young philosopher ended up living and writing in Lincoln for the better part of the next decade. At the time, since this was the height of the radical '60s and the draft-dodging Vietnam War era, Wilber received a college deferment and went another direction.

By the time Wilber left institutional education for good, he had gained undergraduate degrees in biology and chemistry from UN/Omaha, and if his life hadn't been "interrupted" with his personal odyssey into the world's wisdom traditions, he would have been well on his way to a Ph.D. at UN/Lincoln. Instead, he aborted his doctorate to write his first book, and thus settled for an M.S. in biochemistry in 1972. This means that Wilber has never been professionally trained as a psychotherapist, psychologist, or philosopher, yet his brilliant comprehensive integral synthesis has made an incalculable impact on all of these fields, as well as many others. (Incidentally, as a long-standing policy, Wilber declines all honorary doctorates that are offered to him, which have been numerous.)

By his first year of college, however, Wilber's Western-educated life would radically shift gears as he entered the domain of philosophy or "the love of wisdom" (*philosophia*) and began to freely explore the Eastern metaphysical dimensions of existence. That autumn of 1967, soon after entering Duke as a freshman, Wilber's true life direction and the real doorway to the "secret essences" of the universe were opened up to him when by happenstance he read the first chapter to a little old book called the Tao Te Ching. The classic Tao Te Ching, the world's second-most widely translated book (after the Bible), is a concise spiritual treatise of eighty-one pithy poems composed by the revered Chinese Taoist sage Lao Tzu (c. 600 B.C.E.), whose name literally means "Old Philosopher." When Wilber first absorbed Lao's penetrating wisdom that day, over twenty-five centuries of intervening civilization were erased as the ancient "Old One" appealed directly to the young modern American student by imparting these words:

> *The Way (or Tao) that can be told is not the Eternal Way,*
> *The name that can be named is not the Eternal Name.*

The Nameless is the origin of Heaven and Earth.
The Named is but the mother of ten thousand things.
Truly, only he that rids himself forever of desire can see the Secret Essences;
He that has never rid himself of desire can see only the Outcomes.
These two things issue from the same Source, but nevertheless are different in form.
This Source we can but call the Mystery.
The Doorway whence issues all Secret Essences.[5]

With these powerful yet paradoxical ideas, Wilber clearly realized there would be no turning back now; a revolution in the direction of his guiding spirit (or daemon) had occurred. Over the following decades, all of Wilber's subsequent writings and prodigious output would continue to reflect this primal and mysterious insight first disclosed by the sagacious Lao on that fateful day in '67, only months after the fabled Summer of Love. Indeed, Wilber's life, and the world at large, would never be the same.

THE QUEST FOR KNOWLEDGE

When Wilber awakened to the mysterious "way" of the Tao, his "eye of Spirit" received just enough light, however briefly, to immediately catapult him onto his own personal quest—his "personal odyssey" or "Grail search"—as he would describe it. Nearly a decade later, as he tells us, "the old sage had touched a chord so deep in me that I suddenly awoke to the silent but certain realization that my old life, my old self, my old beliefs could no longer be energized. It was time for a separation."[6]

Once on "the Way," Wilber began the endless task of voraciously consuming much of the world's literature on human knowledge and wisdom, ranging principally from Eastern mysticism (yet including all the world's major religions) to the great expanse of Western psychology, philosophy, sociology, and anthropology. During the late '60s and early '70s, Wilber's formal education at the universities changed into an informal one, where he would "spend every hour out of class pursuing Eastern philosophy and religion, Western psychology and metaphysics." He later acknowledged "intellectually I began an obsessive venture in reading, devouring books on Eastern philosophy at a terrifying rate. I cut chemistry classes to read the Bhagavad Gita; I skipped calculus to study Kabbalah. I was introduced to Huxley and the psychedelics, Watts and beat Zen. . . . I was particularly drawn to Perls, Jung, [Médard] Boss, and the existentialists; Norman O. Brown, Krishnamurti, Zen, Vedanta, and Eckhart; the traditionalists Coomaraswamy, Guénon, and Schuon, but also Freud, Ferenczi, Rank, and Klein—a more motley group you could not imagine."[7]

With the publication of the various translations and sacred texts made available in the modern age, the esoteric or inner core of the world's mystical traditions had come to be called the perennial philosophy (known in Latin as *philosophia perennis*). This was a concept that Aldous Huxley, the esteemed author of *Brave New World* (1932), had popularized with his 1944 book *The Perennial Philosophy*, which was published at the height of World War II in order to offer a possible solution to the world's apparent madness. In this scholarly work, Huxley informs us: "rudiments of the Perennial Philosophy may be found among the traditionary lore of primitive peoples in every region of the world, and in its fully developed forms it has a place in every one of the higher religions." The young Wilber would investigate this expansive wealth of wisdom, both intellectually and experientially, and then made it the basis for the beginning (but not the end) of his understanding concerning the higher transpersonal domains of consciousness.

By commencing his studies with an appeal to the perennial philosophy—or "a much more sophisticated view of the relation of humanity and Divinity, a view held by the great majority of the truly gifted theologians, philosophers, sages, and even scientists of various times"[8]—Wilber was able to help verify and introduce the authenticity of the spiritual (or transpersonal) realms. He was able to use it as a way to substantiate the universality of the "great chain of being" or the nested hierarchy of Spirit. Currently, however, with his integral or "all-quadrant, all-level" AQAL (pronounced "ah-qwal") approach, he continues to reject categorically the way the perennial philosophy has been treated by previous scholars. This is because Wilber's integral vision now tends to emphasize "a more critical, less metaphysical approach, incorporating some of the important insights of post-Kantian and postmodern thought."[9] In other words, he's initiating a further embrace of reality by integrating the premodern heritage of the world's spiritual wisdom traditions with today's modern and especially postmodern sources.

Wilber's gargantuan task of knowledge acquisition has not slackened to this day, although most of the books he currently reads are texts by other theorists in an attempt to stay abreast of the vast proliferation of ideas generated by his contemporaries. Thus he has made it a lifelong habit to readily consume books, often ingesting two to four a day, a practice that started back in college where he spent two years, "almost literally, in solitary reading and research, eight to ten hours a day." It seems he was obsessed by his daemon in trying to see how humanity, in its various guises, understood itself, and especially how it explained its relationship to the mysterious divine spirit, or Tao. Naturally he investigated how all of this related to the existential, psychological condition of the individual, especially himself. Indeed, Wilber soon confessed that this tortured personal odyssey was nothing less than a personal necessity: "the moral resolution of *meaning* and the intellectual resolution of *synthesis,* were necessary for my own personal pilgrimage; they were no mere side issues or intellectual curiosities. . . . The point is that I had to 'read everything' because I was trying mentally and emotionally to put together in a comprehensive framework that which I felt was necessary for my own salvation."[10] In the process, therefore, Wilber covered more books than most people can even dream of reading, absorbing countless volumes in the libraries of scholarly and spiritual treatises, filling endless notebooks with thousands of pages of detailed hand-written notes, even copying many of Alan Watts's books word for word, page by page in order to study his writing style. It also helps to have an IQ of 160 (off the scale, actually).

The number of books Wilber has actually read is practically endless; indeed, he's called it "hilarious." Therefore, one of the great gifts imparted to Wilber's readers is that they may use his excellent synopses from this esteemed list of authors, theorists, philosophers, and religious traditions, and then select the ones they deem the most appealing or relevant to their own interests. Wilber presently accepts shipments of new books every week, which he then processes and places within their proper context, only seriously reading (and rereading) the ones he considers most significant while generally speed-reading the others. In fact, his reading list is a wonderful testimony to the abundance of resources that are now made available to everyone via our modern libraries, bookstores, and the Internet. We all have an unprecedented opportunity to survey and read from the collected storehouse of the world's greatest literature and highest mystical teachings. Indeed, in my opinion, this so-called "divine library" of humankind is a spectacular advantage inherent in the modern age, and one that will favorably support the global expansion of the integral vision.

A short reading list drawn from Wilber's research during the early 1970s shows that he drank deeply from the well of humanity's primary mystical scriptures as well as from the endless stream of modern sources, many of which became the principal sources for his written works. These included such classics as the Jewish Kabbalah, the Hindu Vedas, Upanishads, and Bhagavad Gita, the Chinese Tao Te Ching, the complete Chuang Tzu and other Taoists canons, the numerous Buddhist and Zen sutras, or sacred writings, including many of their greatest philosopher-sages such as Padmasambhava, Nagarjuna, and Hui-Neng, as well as the traditional texts of Sufism, Islam, and Christianity, including their greatest individual mystics such as St. Dionysus, Meister Eckhart, and St. Teresa of Avila. Naturally, then, this also included the twentieth-century's modern translators and scholars such as D. T. Suzuki, Garma C. C. Chang, Edward Conze, Lama Govinda, Charles Luk, and T. R. V. Murti, the traditionalists or the scholars of the perennial philosophy such as Ananda Coomaraswamy, Rene Guénon, and the incomparable Frithjof Schuon, and perhaps, most importantly, a number of living (or recently living) masters from the East such as Chögyam Trungpa, Sri Aurobindo, and Sri Ramana Maharshi. Wilber also made his way through the modern writings of the East-West synthesizers and religious philosophers such as William James, Aldous Huxley, Hubert Benoit, Huston Smith, Joseph Campbell, Eric Fromm, R. D. Laing, Lex Hixon, and Alan Watts. Watts, in turn, led him to the then-living Indian mystic Jiddu Krishnamurti, whereas the eclectic Western philosopher Norman O. Brown pointed Wilber to the real significance of Sigmund Freud. Wilber consequently devoured Freud's entire collected works, mesmerized by his insights into the role of the unconscious and the early stages of development. One of Freud's followers, Ernest Becker, and his Pulitzer Prize–winning "denial of death" synthesis, which had just been released in 1973, had a profound impact on Wilber's developing ideas and understanding of the human condition. But the reading list, of course, far exceeds what I've named here.

In 1971 Wilber met Bob (G. A.) Young, a psychologist who became his primary psychotherapist and mentor, even coauthoring four papers with him. This work sent him into exploring the existential therapies of humanistic psychology (the "third force"[11]), especially Fritz Perl's Gestalt approach, the psychosynthesis work of Robert Assagioli, and Ira Progoff's intensive journal work, and it was doing dream analysis that led Wilber even deeper into the depth psychology and collected works of C. G. Jung and his important followers. Naturally, the founder of transpersonal psychology (the so-called "fourth force"), Abraham Maslow, was another vital influence, as was his cofounder, Stanislav Grof, and his psychedelic research, but perhaps most important was the child development psychologist Jean Piaget and the structuralists.

Thus, we can see, the voracious student was liberally gathering nourishment from the modern fountain of Western psychology, being particularly interested in the newly emerging field of humanistic and transpersonal psychology. Nevertheless, a crucial strategy in his research was that Wilber adhered to no particular philosophy or point of view exclusively but rather was embracing all of reality by seeing each theorist (or theory) as essentially "correct but partial" or "true but partial." Wilber wisely summarized his position: "For my own part, I simply could not imagine that any mind of genius (whether Freud's or Buddha's) could manufacture *only* falsehoods and errors. This was inconceivable to me. Rather, if we must form an early conclusion, the only possible one would be: Freud was correct but partial; Buddha was correct but partial; and so with Perls, Kierkegaard, the existentialists, the behaviorists. And it was on that tentative basis that I preceded."[12]

Simultaneously, of course, Wilber also ranged over the enormous scope of Western philosophy, from the ancient pre-Socratics, Plato, and Plotinus up through the modern Hegel, Heidegger, and Habermas, from Kant and Kierkegaard to Schelling and Schopenhauer to Whitehead and Wittgenstein (plus all the many others), all of whom exerted their own profound influence on his ideas from the onset. Although Wilber always attempted to read the original texts, he found an excellent philosophical companion in the masterful volumes of Frederick Copleston's *The History of Philosophy* (1962). Not to be left out, of course, and of considerable importance, were the brilliant ideas and books of the twentieth-century physical scientists, ranging from Einstein, Schrödinger, Heisenberg, Eddington, and de Broglie, to the many others. In a few words, then, the young philosopher was covering everyone from Shankara to Sartre, Freud to Buddha, Jesus to Jung, Bohr to Aristotle, from East to West (and from North to South)—an integral world philosophy was brewing in the mind of the maturing student.

Incredibly, the college grad actually was reading and digesting all these books, taking copious mounds of notes. No wonder Sam Bercholz, the president of Shambhala Publications, one of the nation's premier metaphysical book publishers that specialize in esoteric spiritual texts, had noticed early on that Wilber bought more books through his mail-order house, covering a wider range of topics, than any other customer. Bercholz rightly anticipated Wilber's publishing potential and became a lifetime friend as his company Shambhala Publications would go on to become Wilber's principle publisher.

1960's EDUCATION: STATES INTO TRAITS

Books, of course, are only part of the picture; actual life experience is what really counts, as Wilber was always quick to point out from the very beginning of his first book and thereafter. Like many of his peers, the young man experimented with the plethora of new ideas and novel techniques emerging from the late 1960s and early 1970s, nonetheless, he generally steered clear of psychedelics even though he was surrounded by the radical cultural movement of those times (he did experiment, however briefly). It was often claimed that, if properly used, certain psychoactive drugs promised a spiritual awakening, a potential "peak experience" (Maslow's well-known psychological term for an ultimate life experience). Wilber, however, quickly realized that although these chemical substances may give a person an experiential "peek" (his humorous modification of Maslow's phrase) into the higher states and stages of consciousness, the real cleansing of perception requires a whole-body and integral lifestyle. This daily approach combines or integrates both personal and transpersonal practice, not just mind-blowing weekend "trips" or esoteric libraries of bound books. In other words, like a few of his contemporaries, the inquisitive grad student found out that a person couldn't just drop acid or read books at lightning speeds, even if he could retain practically all he had read, in order to find the Holy Grail, the fabled elixir of immortality, the ungraspable Secret Essence he so desperately sought during the decade of his late teens and early twenties.

Instead, Wilber wisely surmised that he must actually *practice* the methods and techniques he was intellectually hearing and reading about from the many teachers and spiritual masters who were speaking in unison from across the centuries, from every culture, covering every continent. Years later, he affirmed this pragmatic insight:

> It's a fundamental error to assume that moving into the higher stages of spiritual development is easy—something you can do in a weekend workshop, or by reading a book, or by taking LSD. Only through long-term disciplines can you make these experiences stable, permanent structures of consciousness. It's very hard work. The truth is that transforming oneself is a long, laborious, painful process.[13]

This means that by acting in harmony with the world's wisdom traditions, a person must meditate regularly, understand the separate egoic self or the activity of "I"—or our own suffering contraction away from divinity—and actively do the daily work of consciousness evolution in both heart and mind. This includes meditation and contemplative practices, various sacred rituals, and disciplined restrictions, as well as a fairly strict regime of moral and ethical behavior. Such practice is done in order to cultivate the permanents *traits* of evolved consciousness instead of just the temporary altered *states* (a hallmark principle fully integrated into Wilber's developmental psychology). In other words, the main point of evolution as it continues within consciousness is to unfold the "higher" or more embracing structures of consciousness in order to "transcend-yet-include"[14] the entire spectrum of consciousness and Kosmos.[15] Evolving therefore means not just integrating but transcending the various worldviews of the self, including all possible self-identities or boundaries comprising the spectrum, and ultimately, culminating in Spirit or God-Realization Itself.

Indeed, as the aspiring philosopher had noted, this is what the majority of wisdom traditions have always recommended, in fact, demanded: actual meditation, not drugs; profound discipline, not simple hedonism; awakened awareness, not dull, sluggish unconsciousness. This very point is unflinchingly taught throughout all of Wilber's writings with his reoccurring dictum: "Do the yoga, engage the injunction!" Without illusion, then, he would clearly announce, "The only major purpose of a book on mysticism should be to persuade the reader to engage in mystical practice." Therefore, before he left college, the student of biochemistry eagerly began meditation and contemplative practices, as did many of his fellow "psychonauts" of the '60s, yet, as usual, Wilber engaged them with a commitment and intensity far exceeding most of his peers.

INTEGRAL EDUCATION

Within a short time, Wilber had begun a serious and regular practice of meditation with Zen Buddhism. Nonetheless, as his writings often reveal, he would intently study many esoteric traditions, from Western mysticism to the modern twentieth-century sages of India, particularly Sri Ramana Maharshi and the shabd yoga master Kirpal Singh, since he found their wise teachings were also guiding him on his own spiritual path. Another significant teacher in the mid-1970s exerting a deep influence on Wilber's fundamental understanding was the Western-born adept Adi Da (then known as Franklin Jones and later as Bubba Free John), whose written works, Wilber claimed "are unsurpassed." However, the evolutionary theorist who exerted the most profound influence on Wilber at this time was the great synthesizer of Eastern philosophy and Western science, Sri Aurobindo, especially his incomparable magnum opus *The Life Divine* (1939, 1965).

Throughout most of the 1970s, Wilber's practice was initially a combination of Gestalt psychology and Zen meditation, as he explains: "On the one hand, I had been practicing *zazen* in a serious fashion for a year or two, and I was increasingly drawn to the Mahayana Buddhist viewpoint as a broad context. On the other hand, I was thoroughly attracted to existential therapies (particularly gestalt therapy) both for specific techniques in dealing with my own conflicts and for intellectual clues to the dynamics of the psyche."[16] During most of the 1970s, Wilber studied with several Zen masters, both "in person and by correspondence, Taizan Maezumi Roshi, of the Zen Center of Los Angeles, was one of them," and another was Katagiri Roshi of the San Francisco Zen Center, in addition to Eido Shimano Roshi, Joshu Sasaki Roshi, and Jiyu Kennett Roshi. Once on a spontaneous trip to Mexico, Wilber caught up with the American Zen master Philip Kapleau, renowned author of *The Three Pillars of Zen* (1965), where he convinced Kapleau to do some *zazen* (sitting meditation) together. In addition to meditating about two hours daily, and then once a month or so doing an all-day sitting. The dedicated meditator also attended a number of *sesshin*, or Zen meditation retreats, under the direct guidance of a living Zen master, where they would spend many hours doing *zazen* (meditating).

Importantly, then, Wilber's research project into consciousness was not just an intellectual venture into theories alone but included whole-body, experiential evidence. He was wholeheartedly diving deep into the actual realities behind the words he was reading in order to discover for himself what the transpersonal realm really is. Nonetheless, Wilber was not leaving his body behind, by any means. Over a seven-year period during the '70s, he completed the ten-session rolfing work (a deep muscular-fascial restructuring developed by Ida Rolf) three times; he was taught sensory awareness by one of the main founders of the movement (Charlotte Selver); and he worked with the Alexander technique with his principal therapist, Dr. Bob Young (who was trained by Franz Alexander, one of the primary founders of psychosomatic medicine in America, and was one of Fritz Perls's more influential teachers). Wilber also practiced a lot of hatha yoga, learning from a variety of sources, as well as regularly doing tai chi chuan, the slow and graceful movements taught by the Chinese Taoists to thoroughly exercise the body and its vital energies, or chi.

His close friend and colleague, transpersonal psychiatrist Roger Walsh, explained that Wilber's particular path and method of study has always included a big dose of transpersonal meditation:

> One obvious question is: How does he do it? His own answer is, "I do my homework." He certainly does, devouring books by the hundreds, reading and writing for long stretches each day, and very importantly, being deeply involved in his own meditative practice. He remarks that without this practice his understanding of the contemplative traditions, transpersonal experiences and nonwestern psychologies, both his experiential and intellectual understanding, would be severely limited.[17]

In 1972 Wilber married the beautiful and engaging college student he was tutoring, Amy Wagner, with Bob Young as the best man. They both agreed that Ken should, in fairness, pay half the rent instead of studying all day, and since he wanted to live according to Zen's precepts of honoring menial labor—"chop wood, carry water"—he went out and got a series of "regular" jobs. Therefore during the next seven–plus years that Wilber was "stationed" in Lincoln, Nebraska, he pumped gas, bussed tables, worked at a grocery store, and washed dishes (mostly at the Red Rooster Restaurant) . . . and, oh yes, he also went on to write five internationally acclaimed books.[18] Thus, at times, his wife would simply introduce him as "world famous author and dishwasher."

Wilber found that doing manual labor while still studying, writing, and meditating was an excellent integral program or practice, since, as he says, "this arrangement (work-study-meditation) gave me the balance (body-mind-spirit) to pursue my researches." This "all-level" approach, also pioneered by other spiritually minded people, is now called integral practice or "integral transformative practice"[19] (ITP) because it promotes meditation as well as integral way of life. Contrary to some people's regard for the high-minded intellect, Wilber has always maintained that "I am a staunch supporter of body-oriented therapies and recommend them, along with diet and exercise, as the first step of any overall therapy. We all seem generally out of touch with the body and must begin by rebuilding the base."[20]

Throughout the years, therefore, Wilber has personally maintained a program of living close to a natural environment (yes, with modern conveniences too), maintaining the upkeep on his semirural mountain home, eating a healthy, natural diet (he was vegetarian between the ages of twenty and forty, then shifted to small amounts of meat as he started weight lifting), thus he gets hard physical exercise, mostly from hatha yoga and weight training, engages in psychodynamic and psychotherapeutic work, shares loving relations with a wide circle of family and friends, has an active yet sometimes celibate sexual life, plus he sustains an active correspondence with people from around the world, as well as pursuing numerous creative enterprises and endeavors (sometimes using three computers at once), all while, of course, practicing meditation and spiritual exercises in addition to maintaining his investigative, intellectual research. Recently, by forming the Integral Institute, Wilber has been meeting regularly with people from all walks of life, thus additionally exercising his social and hosting skills, which by all accounts, are most generous and gracious. And of course sometimes he watches TV (news and music videos being some of his favorites), sees practically every movie that's released, enjoys the great outdoors with his dog, and also, I've heard, is a confirmed shower fanatic.

SPIRITUAL EDUCATION

Perhaps the most important factor in Wilber's spiritual development is that over the decades he has availed himself of many of the world's spiritual traditions by studying under and gaining the guidance and instruction of numerous living lamas, gurus, and spiritual masters. Although Wilber has not directly studied under a shaman (though he knows a few), he nonetheless has a deep sympathy with nature mysticism, the shaman's expertise. This direct approach and personal method of studying under, and sitting with, advanced teachers is a highly valued technique in the great wisdom traditions, where it's promoted as being the best way to further one's spiritual growth. This is because, according to these teachings, when a person sits in the presence of more evolutionarily advanced beings, they may receive an actual transmission of consciousness directly from the master, often with purifying or enlightening effects. Based on his own personal experience,

Wilber attests to this little-known fact by explaining that "When a person is fairly enlightened, they can transmit—actually transmit—that enlightened awareness through a touch, a look, a gesture, or even through the written word."[21] Indeed, he has beautifully expounded why he believes the sage or enlightened person has such a deep and powerful attraction for us all:

> I think the sages are the growing tip of the secret impulse of evolution. I think they are the leading edge of the self-transcending drive that always goes beyond what went before. I think they embody the very drive of the Kosmos toward greater depth and expanding consciousness. I think they are riding the edge of a light beam racing toward a rendezvous with God.
>
> And I think they point to the same depth in you, and in me, and in all of us. I think they are plugged into the All, and the Kosmos sings through their voices, and Spirit shines through their eyes. And I think they disclose the face of tomorrow, they open us to the heart of our own destiny, which is also already right now in the timelessness of this very moment, and in that startling recognition the voice of the sage becomes your voice, the eyes of the sage become your eyes, you speak with the tongues of angels and are alight with the fire of a realization that never dawns nor ceases, you recognize your own true Face in the mirror of the Kosmos itself, your identity is indeed the All, and you are no longer part of that stream, you are that stream, with the All unfolding not around you but in you. The stars no longer shine out there, but in here. Supernovas come into being within your heart, and the sun shines inside your awareness. Because you transcend all, you embrace all. There is no final Whole here, only an endless process, and you are the opening or the clearing or the pure Emptiness in which the entire process unfolds—ceaselessly, miraculously, everlastingly, lightly.[22]

These advanced beings are mostly concerned with the enlightenment (or God-Realization) of all sentient beings, based in heartfelt compassion and love combined with penetrating intellectual insight. In Wilber's present lifetime, his awakened guides have included, so far, Zen Buddhist masters Taizan Maezumi Roshi (1931–1995), the Rinzai and Soto Zen master who was the founder of the Zen Center of Los Angeles; also Dainin Katagiri Roshi (d. 1990), the Soto Zen master who helped to establish San Francisco Zen Center and Tassajara Mountain Center. Wilber's Vajrayana Buddhist masters have been: Chögyam Trungpa Rinpoche (1939–1987), one of the first lamas to come to the West as a meditation master of the Kagyu and Nyingma lineages; also the Very Venerable Kalu Rinpoche

(1905–1989), called a modern Milarepa, one of the greatest Tibetan teachers of the twentieth century, who taught Vajrayana Buddhism in a strictly traditional way.

More recently, Wilber has practiced and studied Tibetan Dzogchen (or "Great Perfection"). His teachers include His Holiness Pema Norbu Rinpoche (b. 1932), or Penor for short, an important Nyingma master who left Tibet in 1959 and who, at the time, gave Wilber one of the highest transmissions of Tibetan Buddhism given to the West; also the masterful Tibetan doctor, artist, and Buddhist, Chagdud Tulku Rinpoche (b. 1930), only "one of a handful of Tibetan masters giving the entire Dzogchen teachings, A to Z," as Wilber says. From the West, again, one of the most important has been the unique American-born Siddha-Guru now known as Ruchira Avatara Adi Da Samraj (b. 1939), variously known as Da Free John, Da Love-Ananda, Da Avabhasa. Adi Da is perhaps the most enlightened, yet controversial, of them all since he's an independently styled spiritual master, not subject to the scrutiny of any particular tradition but only to the Great Tradition itself.[23] Nonetheless, at this present time, Wilber informs us, "the type of meditation I do varies, but the basic form is 'the practice of the morning,' or 'ultimate guru yoga,' where the true nature of one's own mind is the ultimate guru."

Over the decades, therefore, Wilber has been initiated into and practiced all three "vehicles" (or *yanas*) of classical Buddhism: Theraveda (Abidhamma) or Hinayana (the "Lesser Vehicle"); Mahayana (the "Great Vehicle"); and Vajrayana (the "Diamond Vehicle"), although currently he is concentrating on Tibetan Dzogchen (including Maha-Ati and Highest Tantra Yoga), studying, as we've seen, under some of the tradition's most esteemed lamas, *tulkus,* and gurus. Nevertheless, Wilber's universal approach to spirituality encourages him to know deeply about all the other contemplative, meditative practices within the great tradition of mystical religions. Thus he's closely studied Christian mysticism, Islamic Sufism, the Jewish Kabbalah, Patanjali's yoga system, Advaita Vedanta (nondual Hinduism), especially appreciating the eighth-century philosopher-sage Sri Shankara, as well as the twentieth-century's yoga-synthesizer and evolutionist Sri Aurobindo, and of course the illustrious Sri Ramana Maharshi, "India's greatest modern sage." In addition, some of Wilber's favorite integral mystic-philosophers include the magnificent Nagarjuna of India (the founder of Mahayana Buddhism), the Neoplatonic genius of Plotinus (the great sage of Alexandria and Rome), and the nineteenth-century evolutionary philosopher Friedrich von Schelling, all of whom became particularly significant since Wilber's Phase 2 writings, although, as he now points out, none of them have adequately covered all four quadrants, which we will explore in chapter 12.

In review, Wilber summarizes: "I had studied Zen with Katagiri and Maezumi; Vajrayana with Kalu and Trungpa; Dzogchen with Pema Norbu and

Chagdud; plus I had studied sometimes briefly, sometimes for extended periods—Vedanta, TM, Kashmir Shaivism, Christian mysticism, Kabbalah, Daism, Sufism . . . well, it's a long list."[24] In this case, although a practicing Buddhist for decades, he's still quick to explain: "I would not especially call myself a Buddhist; I have too many affinities with Vedanta Hinduism and Christian mysticism, among many others. But one has to choose a particular path if one is to actually *practice,* and my path has been Buddhist."[25] In this case, therefore, it was Wilber's commitment to Buddhism that first led him to shave his head (and over the years he began naturally losing his hair anyway so the task has become easier)—though this is only one reason why he's been known to call himself the "egghead theorist."

PHASES OF WILBER'S WRITING AND MEDITATION

To this day, the cornucopia of both ancient mystical and modern philosophical geniuses are the deep well from which Wilber drinks as he passes on their sacred wisdom again and again throughout his voluminous writings. Indeed, he maintains, every living human being should use this fountain since the bodies of spiritual literature and esoteric practices are our common birthright as world citizens transcending the boundaries of our parochial concerns. Indeed, the integral vision of Ken Wilber calls forth descriptive metaphors to explain how we can recognize and "surf" the entire spiraling spectrum of consciousness, thus developing or evolving throughout by riding its various "waves" and developmental "streams," interacting with everything (or every "holon" or "whole/part") that makes up this radiant "Great Nest of Spirit" or "Spirit-in-action." This is the dynamic and divine Kosmic Mandala, which, as Wilber's spectrum pictures, reaches miraculously from the "subconscious to self-conscious to superconscious; from prepersonal to personal to transpersonal; from id to ego to God."[26]

Such multidimensional perspectives and full-spectrum integral living demands the capacity to enjoy diversity, thus Wilber's tastes naturally include art, music, literature, architecture, sports, nature, even high fashion, from the classics to the postmodern forms, from classical music to punk rock, from Andrew Wyeth to Alex Grey, from Giorgio Armani to Thomas Mann; yet, again, he never professes any favorites but enjoys the full palette offered by life's bounty of precious gifts. Thus Wilber's encyclopedic appreciation of earth's rich garden of diversity has allowed him to synthesize a fully integral world philosophy.

Nonetheless, for most of his life, the integral philosopher confesses: "The main work I do in the world is writing. I average six to ten hours a day, seven days a week, 365 days a year. On intense writing days, I go up to 15–18 hours. . . . These are my two main practices: meditating and writing." However, this type of schedule was his practice before he began his extensive work facilitating the newly founded Integral Institute (since 2000), a research foundation set up by Wilber and numerous other people to promote and fund integral projects, which now occupies much of his time. With such impassioned work, by the turn of the new millennium, in less than twenty-five years, Wilber had produced and published eighteen books and over two hundred articles/reviews, with all of the books remaining in print except for some of the edited editions; currently they've been collected together by Shambhala Publications for a ten-volume (and still growing) hardcover set titled *The Collected Works of Ken Wilber.*

Near the end of the 1990s, with over two decades of writing and publishing, Wilber surveyed the entire body of his work and recognized that it contained at least four distinct phases or periods, yet all united in essence and theory. These will be designated as:

1. **Wilber/Phase 1** or "The Spectrum of Consciousness" (1973–1977), which "was Romantic (a 'recaptured-goodness' model), which posited a spectrum of consciousness ranging from subconscious to self-conscious to superconscious (or id to ego to God), with the higher stages viewed as a return to, and recapture of original but lost potentials."

2. **Wilber/Phase 2** or "The Evolution Revolution" (1978–1983) "was more specifically evolutionary or developmental (a 'growth-to-goodness' model), with the spectrum of consciousness unfolding in developmental stages or levels."

3. **Wilber/Phase 3** or "The Integral Vision: Self, Levels, & Lines" (1983–1994), which was "added development lines to those developmental levels, that is, numerous different developmental lines (such as cognitive, conative, affective, moral, psychological, spiritual, etc.) proceeding in a relatively independent manner through the basic levels of the overall spectrum of consciousness."

4. **Wilber/Phase 4** or "Four Quadrants & the Postmodern Critique" (1995–2000), which "added the idea of the four quadrants—the *subjective* (intentional), *objective* (behavioral), *intersubjective* (cultural), and *interobjective* (social) dimensitons—etc.

5. **Wilber/Phase 5** or "Integral AQAL Approach" (New Millennium), a maturation and continuation of the "all-quarants, all-levels" or AQAL approach of Phase 4 but with more emphasis on pragmatic application of integral methodology in various fields, from business to politics, from education to medicine, from science to spirituality.

We will now explore in some detail this unfolding journey of Wilber's writings and the various phases of his career, as well as tracing some of the deeper currents of his spiritual understanding and evolution.

WILBER/PHASE 1. THE SPECTRUM OF CONSCIOUSNESS (1973–1977)

In the winter of 1972, at the age of twenty-three, Wilber's extensive research came to a head when he walked into the kitchen and told his wife, Amy, that he was going to abort his doctorate and write his first book. That book turned out to be *The Spectrum of Consciousness,* a groundbreaking publication that would create an unprecedented synthesis of Eastern and Western psychological systems. Author and noetic researcher John White, with the help of James Fadiman, took on the job of being Wilber's literary agent, which prompted Wilber to dedicate the book to White for his valiant efforts and ensuing friendship. Three years later, after being submitted to nearly three dozen publishing houses, *The Spectrum of Consciousness* was finally published in 1977 by A Quest Book, an imprint of the Theosophical Publishing House in Wheaton, Illinois.

Wilber's major breakthrough was the creative use of the spectrum as a metaphor, consciousness being likened to the electromagnetic spectrum in order to map the various levels, stages, and possibilities of human consciousness, from birth to enlightenment, including physical death and beyond. In doing so, Wilber combined the contributions of both Western scientific psychology and Eastern metaphysical mysticism. This impressive beginning led him to create an integral model that marries the general orientations of all Western sciences with the universal currents running through all authentic mystical paths and practices—"a marriage of Freud and the Buddha," as author Tony Schwartz cleverly termed Wilber's accomplishments in his best-selling book *What Really Matters* (1995).

Wilber's first book therefore elucidated a spectrum psychology that was, as he explained, "not only a synthesis of Eastern and Western approaches to psychology and psychotherapy, *but also a synthesis and integration of the various major Western approaches to psychology and psychotherapy.*"[28] This was quite an achievement, especially for a man so young, since he had brilliantly articulated and updated the notion of a perennial psychology, creating, in effect, a psychological analogue of the *philosophia perennis.* In 1975, in *The Journal of Transpersonal Psychology,* Wilber's second article, which appeared a couple years before *Spectrum* was published, defined this *psychologia perennis* as being "a universal view as to the nature of human consciousness, which expresses the very same insights as the perennial philosophy but in a more decidedly psychological language." Nonetheless, as we'll continue to see, Wilber was already beginning to build upon the premodern traditions of ancient wisdom by integrating and updating their timeless teachings with modern and postmodern sources.

By using the idea of a spectrum, Wilber was following the traditional notion of the Great Chain of Being, yet he extended this powerful analogy to include the scientific research of psychology and all the other sciences, placing them alongside the mystical research (and demonstrable evidence) of humanity's most advanced individuals—that is, the shamans, yogis, saints, sages, and siddhas of human history.

Initially Wilber was influenced by a quote from John White's edited collection titled *The Highest State of Consciousness* (1972): "The final analysis turns out to be an original synthesis, and consciousness becomes the interconnectedness of all creation in a great chain of being." This, in turn, led Wilber to Arthur Lovejoy's classic historical study, *The Great Chain of Being* (1936), in which Lovejoy proved that the perennial idea of a graded hierarchy of existence has, "in one form or another, been the dominant official philosophy of the larger part of civilized humankind through most of its history." Once Wilber took this seed of an idea and combined it with the discoveries of Western science, he "unpacked" it into the immense and fully integral "Great Nest of Spirit." This development in turn ignited a spectrum revolution that's deeply affected many areas of study, but especially, at the time, it rocked the community of transpersonal psychology (or the "fourth force" of psychology). But beyond this revolutionary impact, as we'll see, Wilber began to elucidate an integral approach that speaks about the Great Nest of Spirit more as a *holarchy,* or a "nested hierarchy," a mandala (or "circle") of embracing higher-order unities, instead of the linear rigidity of a ladderlike dominator hierarchy. Indeed, with the publication of *The Spectrum of Consciousness,* as transpersonalist John Rowan pointed out years later, "Something happened to the world of the transpersonal," and that was, a veritable "Wilber revolution" had begun.[29]

Upon the initial publication of *The Spectrum of Consciousness* in 1977, Wilber's professional peers in transpersonal psychology immediately recognized that the twenty-seven-year-old had accomplished something truly significant. He was accorded great accolades, such as when Dr. James Fadiman, former president of the Association of Transpersonal Psychology, suggested that Wilber had written "the most sensible, comprehensive book about consciousness since William James," or when transpersonal psychologist Jean Houston declared that "Wilber might likely do for consciousness what Freud did for psychology," or John White, in *Yoga Journal,* 1986, simply stated: "Ken Wilber: Einstein of consciousness research." White predicted in *Spiritual Frontiers* that "Wilber will soon be recognized as the originator of a new world view affecting our academic, social, medical, religious, and scientific institutions as profoundly as did those of Freud, Marx, and Einstein."

Even the venerable professor of religions, Huston Smith, author of the immensely popular *The World's Religions* (1958), acknowledged, "Though Mr. Wilber is less than half my age, I nevertheless have picked up useful points from his presentation of subtle and important issues I have been working with for thirty years." The journalist and author Claire Myers Owens just bluntly stated: "All I can say is Ken Wilber must be a genius." As flattering as these praises may be, Wilber modestly joked that "Being called the foremost theorist in transpersonal psychology is like being called the tallest building in Kansas City."

By 1978, soon after *The Spectrum of Consciousness* had been published (*No Boundary* had already been written but was not yet published), Wilber at first was enjoying the initial flush of his success while still washing dishes in Lincoln. As author Tony Schwartz tells us, Wilber was "besieged with offers to teach, lecture, give interviews, and appear at conferences. After accepting several speaking dates, he quickly pulled back." Wilber himself in the 1995 winter volume of *The Quest,* reflected on these earlier times: "I could continue this public path and get virtually no new work done, or I could close down the public route and return to the more solitary, and lonely, pursuit of the writer." In a journal entry Wilber further clarified his intentions: "I decided I could either teach what I had written yesterday, or write something new. . . . For the next twenty years, I stuck to that plan with virtually no exception." Although very sociable by nature, Wilber therefore would retreat in order to write, to continue his massive research and studies, and to increase his meditation and contemplation.

The now-famous author was in a position to continue his job washing dishes, reading tons of books, and meditating for two or more hours a day. Indeed, as he would soon admit, "By the time I had finished writing *No Boundary* [1978], my meditation practice, while not exactly advanced . . . was no longer in the beginner's phase." Therefore, the last few years of the '70s would yield some important breakthroughs as Wilber began to reap the fruits gained from years of spiritual cultivation and education. He would directly discover the deeper meaning of the interior realms that were being intellectually imparted to him by the esoteric literature he was voraciously reading and through the contemplative practices he was persistently undertaking several hours a day. Most importantly, as for any of us, after years of dedicated work and spiritual practice, Wilber would begin to awaken to the ultimate realization of the very Divine itself, the Radiant Emptiness that is our ever-present condition and source—the inexplicable Godhead (or Dharmakaya in Buddhism) or Tao (in Chinese)—the real truth of all existence. In fact, he was finding his way through the doors of perception to the very reality or "secret essences" that the ancient Lao had pointed him to all those years ago.

The Complex of Mind (Apollo) and Soul (Vishnu)

As we've just seen, one of the most important factors of Wilber's philosophy is that it is based upon actual transpersonal practice set within the context of integral exercises or what is now known as integral transformative practice. Indeed, this approach gives integral *philosophia* some of its unique strength and capacity. In other words, Wilber's theories are actually grounded in lived and verifiable experiences, not just the realm of intellectual pondering. Nonetheless, even with his intense dedication to meditation practice and the integral lifestyle, he confesses that several years went by before he got his first real "rush" from his higher, transpersonal training. Nonetheless, in time he was graced to gain at least some experience with many of the higher spiritual levels of consciousness, those he now calls the psychic, subtle, causal, and nondual realms. As his meditation practice grew and deepened under masterful guidance, he first had to face what he would later term the Apollo complex (named after the rational-thinking Greek god). In this challenging transition from the life of the mind to that of the soul, or the subtle dimensions of the human psyche, Wilber plainly revealed that "The struggle with my own obsessive/compulsive thinking . . . was as arduous a task as I would ever handle."[30]

However, with persistent contemplative practice, "the fluctuations of mental contractions" were somewhat relaxed; therefore Wilber began to see beyond the ordinary rational mind as he was initiated into "a 'tour' of the subtle realm," or the more ephemeral sphere of astral projections, psychic perceptions, and archetypal awarenesses. Fortunately for him, the brilliant written works of the modern Sufi mystic-yogi, Kirpal Singh, "the unsurpassed master of the subtle realms," served as a guide in the young student's journeys into these rarefied dimensions. It was thus that Wilber received, as he explains, "an introduction to *archetypes,* to *deity,* to *yidam* (the Buddhist term), and *ishtadeva* (the Hindu term). These were, without doubt, the most profound experiences I had ever encountered . . . it was my first direct and unequivocal experience of the actual sacredness of the world."

And it was here too, in the psychic-subtle realm of existence, that Wilber began to encounter the Vishnu complex (named after the Hindu god), a condition that is usually only experienced by advanced meditators. This particular complex, however, wasn't a mental fixation like the Apollo complex but a "subtle-level fixation" that reflected the difficulty in transforming from the subtle soul to the "causal spirit" of formlessness. However, by continuing to transcend these extremely blissful experiences of "archetypal glory and immortal release" Wilber started to see them as inherent limitations of the subtle sheath (or *kosha*) of existence. Even these most profound, subtle, divine experiences must be finally surrendered into the realization of true nondual enlightenment, or the divine realm. Wilber began to realize, as his teachers had warned, "The ultimate state was *not an experience*. . . . It was not a particular experience among other experiences, but the very nature and ground of all experiences, high or low."[31] By seeing through the limitation of any type of experience, gross or subtle, benign or horrific, the experienced meditator would realize that "all experiences, high or low, fall short of nondual consciousness as such, and thus must be penetrated."[32] The intellectual American Zen student was unfolding the foundation for a divine awakening.

Ken's Kensho: *Awakening Beyond the Limits of Experience*

In early 1978, at an intensive Zen meditation retreat (or *sesshin*) with Wilber's primary Zen master, Katagiri Roshi, on a ranch in Nebraska sited on sacred Pawnee ground, this realization or divine awakening first dawned. By this time in his life, Wilber's form of meditation was centered on an inquiry into the nature of the self, or finding the witness, the causal consciousness behind all experiences. The mystics consider this to be the very core or most subtle root point of existence (thus the causal realm) for it's the last stance in the so-called duality between subject and object, seer and seen, experiencer and experienced. Yet, as Wilber already "knew" intellectually through his intensive studies, "The real awakening is the dissolution of the witness itself, and not a change of state in that which is witnessed."[33] Twenty years later he would explain again in *The Eye of Spirit*,

> So "soul" is both the highest level of individual growth we can achieve, but also the final barrier, the final knot, to complete enlightenment or supreme identity, simply because as transcendental witness it stands back from everything it witnesses. Once we push through the witness position, then the soul or witness itself dissolves and there is only the play of nondual awareness, awareness that does not look at objects but is completely one with all objects (Zen says, "It is like tasting the sky"). The gap between subject and object collapses, the soul is transcended or dissolved, and pure spiritual or nondual awareness—which is very simple, very obvious, very clear—arises. You realize that your being is of all space, vast and open, and everything arising anywhere is arising in you, as spirit, spontaneously.[34]

On this clear day, in '78, when the Zen Roshi said: "The witness is the last stand of the ego," the young man's separate, egoic self spontaneously dissolved or died—an experience traditionally known as the "death of the ego" or the "great death" in Zen—and there only remained, in silence, the "radiant, all-pervading, unobstructed, and prior consciousness, which is neither subjective nor objective but merely whole. . . . At that point, the whole stance of the witness absolutely disappeared." Wilbur goes on to try to describe the indescribable realization he had that beautiful day:

> There was no subject anywhere in the universe; there was no object anywhere in the universe; there was only the universe. Everything was arising moment to moment, and it was arising in me and as me; yet there was no me. It is very important to realize that this state was not a loss of faculties but a peak enhancement of them; it was no blank trance but perfect clarity; not depersonalized but transpersonalized. No personal faculties—language, logic, concepts, motor skills—were lost or impaired. Rather, they all functioned, for the first time it seemed to me, in radical openness, free of the defenses thrown up by a separate self sense. This radically open, undefended, and perfectly nondual state was both incredible and profoundly ordinary, so extraordinarily ordinary that it did not even register. There was nobody there to comprehend it, until I fell *out* of it. (I guess about three hours later.)
>
> In other words, while in that state, which was no experience whatsoever, there was *only* that state, which was the totality of everything arising moment to moment. I did not watch or experience all that, I simply *was* all that. I could not see it because it was everything seen; I could not hear it because it was everything heard; I could not know it because it was everything known. That is why it is both the great mystery and the perfectly obvious.[35]

Wilber tacitly understood in those "extraordinarily ordinary" moments that the marvelous yet unspeakable mystery of life is identical to the essence of his own consciousness. He would go on to more fully incorporate this enlightened realization into his writings.[36] For example, in his first book *The Spectrum of Consciousness* (1977) Wilber had already explained that "whether called Enlightenment, awakening, *wu, satori,* or whatever, we recognize it as the emergence of . . . *prajna,* passive and nondual awareness." Since this nondual awareness is eternal and infinite (thus perennial and ever-present), then it's no surprise that two decades later in *The Eye of Spirit* (1997) Wilber continues to tell us: "This 'subject permanence' is a constant state of witnessing carried unbroken through waking, dream, and deep sleep states, a constancy which, I entirely agree, is prerequisite and mandatory to full realization of nondual Suchness (and a constancy which, if you have experienced it, is unmistakable, self-referential, postrepresentational, nondual, self-validating, self-existing, and self-liberating)." When the witness of the self finally dissolves there's a complete liberation from the primary dualism that creates and binds the subject/object, seer/seen, knower/known, thus unveiling an indescribable condition of paradox that's unique to nondual enlightenment, yet our "original conditon" is "always already the case."[37]

As the "I" dissolved in Wilber's case, his most natural and innate condition was revealed to him as the Godhead, the ever-present Dharmakaya, the real Tao, and thus this authentic primal awareness gave the young American his first taste of what Zen Buddhism calls *kensho*[38] or satori. A *kensho,* technically, is equivalent to a small satori, often being a first enlightenment experience. *Satori* is a Zen term derived from *satoru,* which means "to know," yet, of course, it's much more than ordinary knowledge for there's no distinction made between the knower and the known, the subject and all objects. In essence, this is exactly what Gautama—the Buddha—experienced under the Bodhi tree—the true realization of Buddha-mind itself. Hence, this "experience" is the goal of Buddhism. Spiritually, this profound experience is known as enlightenment, this "experience" is a sudden divine awakening to the ever-present clear light of reality. As the supremely enlightened Zen sage Bodhidharma, for example, would often say, it's about "directly seeing into one's spiritual nature," thus he called it "a special transmission outside the scriptures." Indeed, as Wilber explains in his second book, *No Boundary,* written shortly thereafter: "This is the message . . . of the saints, sages, and mystics, whether Amerindian, Taoist, Hindu, Islamic, Buddhist, or Christian. At the bottom of your soul is the soul of humanity itself, but a divine, transcendent soul, leading from bondage to liberation, from enchantment to awakening, from time to eternity, from death to immortality." Nearly twenty years later, this message of the mystics still rings true for Wilber: "When I am not an object, I am God. (And every I in the entire Kosmos can say that truthfully.)" In other words, Wilber's philosophy and psychology reflects the central, esoteric message of all religions: we all are God and it's possible to know just this. As he stated a couple years later in *Up from Eden:*

> For if the Ultimate is indeed a real integral Wholeness, if it is equally part and parcel of all that is, then it is also completely present in men and women. And, unlike rocks, plants, or animals, human beings—because they are *conscious*— can potentially discover this Wholeness. They can, as it were, awaken to the Ultimate. Not believe in it, but discover. . . . This is the aim of Buddhist meditation, of Hindu yoga, and of Christian mystical contemplation. That is very straightforward; there is nothing spooky, occult, or strange in any of this.

This ultimate state of consciousness, as we can see, is a paradoxical condition, for it is "always already" the truth of reality yet generally unrecognized. Thus, as

Wilber would soon pen: "the Condition of all conditions and the Nature of all natures, is always ever-present, and therefore could no more be reached or attained than we could attain our feet." Indeed, he would proclaim: "For it is finally, ultimately, profoundly, God alone who looks through your eyes, listens with your ears, and speaks with your tongue." Yet, obviously, most people do not realize this innate and divine condition of consciousness:

> At the very base of men and women's consciousness, then, lies the ultimate Wholeness. But—and here is the rub—it is *not,* in the vast majority, consciously realized. Thus, the ultimate whole is, for most souls, an *Other* . . . a psychological Other—it is ever-present, but unrealized; it is given, but rarely discovered; it is the Nature of human beings, but lies, as it were, asleep in the depths of the soul.

This mystical fact, this "notorious paradox," reflects the transcendent-immanent nature of Spirit, which is persistently acknowledged throughout all of Wilber's writings. Indeed, it is its theoretical (and mystical) foundation and support. In fact, he would soon predict: "If spirit is completely transcendent, it is also completely immanent. I am firmly convinced that if a new and comprehensive paradigm is ever to emerge, that paradox will be its heart." It most certainly is the heart of Wilber's integral vision.

Such claims of innate divinity (indeed, in the West, many people have been burned at the stake for such "blasphemous" utterings) can only be verified by spiritual masters or gurus, men and women who themselves are already awake to this pinnacle of consciousness. These yogically cultivated human beings follow the wisdom traditions and their own enlightened masters from whatever tradition. Thus they're uniquely qualified to confirm the authenticity of these revelatory insights. Katagiri Roshi did just this for Wilber, although years later they both laughed and said it was just a "real little one [satori]."[39] In Wilber's case, his life has exemplified this important qualification, one which is constantly addressed throughout his written works, i.e., authentic verification of higher transpersonal experience needs to be affirmed by a master or adept in a community of spiritually oriented practitioners. In other words, in colloquial terms, it simply takes one to know one.

Washing Dishes: Brilliant Clarity, Ordinary Life

With his earlier minor *kensho* experiences, and now with this blessing of satori, to be followed over the years by other such moments, Wilber now intimately knew, without doubt, that the ineffable divine condition of the universe was "both a great mystery and the perfectly obvious." In this case, as a paradox, he clearly saw there was in truth "no experience whatsoever, there was only that state, which was the totality of everything arising moment to moment." Nonetheless, as we have pointed out, satori proper is only a temporary enlightenment, whereas the real practice of spirituality allows "the brilliant clarity of ever-present awareness" to become the permanent ground for the moment-to-moment, twenty-four-hours-a-day whole-body enlightenment, such as with Zen's *honsho-myoshu*. This deeper understanding, therefore, would later help Wilber articulate the difference between temporary *states* and permanent *structures* (or *traits*) of consciousness, a common confusion among many transpersonal practitioners, especially those drawn to altered states. As he explains, "a 'peak experience' is one thing; a stable adaptation, quite another." Therefore the process of transforming "states into traits" remains a common thread running throughout all of Wilber's collected works.

From 1978 onward, Wilber would become, as he explained, "profoundly suspicious of any transpersonalist who spoke of the highest states as 'experiential realities,' even as I had tended to do in *Spectrum*. I also saw the perfect inadequacy of the otherwise extremely useful paradigm of 'altered states' to deal with the ultimate spiritual realm." He would become a great defender of nondual mysticism, welding his pen and IBM Thinkpad like a modern-day Manjushri, the Buddhist deity of wisdom, whose sword of enlightenment cuts through unillumined misconceptions.

The pinnacle chapter of *No Boundary*, his second book, written in 1978, shortly after Wilber's satori and appropriately titled "The Ultimate State of Consciousness," is unmistakably a direct first-person description of ever-present awareness; whereas his already-published article of the same title (which became *Eye to Eye*'s last chapter) gives a more academic and sympathetic account of nondual consciousness, often quoting famous sages from the world's wisdom traditions. Here, however, he would simply state: "Everything we do becomes our practice, our prayer—not just zazen, chanting, the sacraments, mantra meditation, sutra recitation or bible readings—but everything, from washing dishes to doing income taxes. And not in the sense that we wash dishes and think of original enlightenment, but because washing dishes is itself original enlightenment." As we've seen, Wilber had already been motivated to balance his study and meditation with daily work at regular jobs, and so, since "meditation exercised the spirit and writing-thinking exercised the mind," then working "as a gas station attendant, a dish washer, a grocery clerk" would exercise his body and social skills. Indeed, such menial tasks would become "an extraordinary education," for as he explains in *Personal Odyssey*:

It was an education first and foremost in humility. Forget the degrees, forget the books and articles, forget the titles, forget everything, really, and wash dishes for two years. It was also an education in *grounding,* in engaging the world in an immediate, concrete, tangible fashion, not through words or concepts or books or courses. . . . I came away from that with a sense of common and shared humanity, or sister-brotherhood, something no book and no university had given me.

Thus Wilber's *philosophia* not only depends intellectually on the evidence gathered from both ancient and modern literary sources but he also uses life's full range of experiences, in addition to his own spiritual exploration. By 1980, and with the premiere of his next series of books, *No Boundary* (1979), *The Atman Project* (1980), and *Up From Eden* (1981), Wilber would clearly illuminate and differentiate the different types or levels of esoteric mysticism, placing them alongside the stages or structures of human development as discovered by Western psychology. Now he was poised to much better color in the rainbow of consciousness, giving his readers an even more detailed account of the spectrum's various hues and shades shimmering as the prepersonal, personal, and transpersonal bands of existence.

Self-Boundaries in No-Boundary Territory

Wilber's follow-up to *Spectrum* was a much less dense book, for it was intended as a simpler, more popular version that would review some of the principal themes introduced in his groundbreaking first book. This second book was titled as *No Boundary: Eastern and Western Approaches to Personal Growth* (Center Publications, 1979; Shambhala Publications, 1981). Wilber used his spectrum map as a background in introducing and explaining these various therapies or therapeutic methods and disciplines to the reader by offering a simple yet comprehensive guide to both Eastern and Western psychologies and therapies—from psychoanalysis to Zen, Gestalt to TM, existentialism to Tantra.

Each chapter in *No Boundary* gives specific exercises to help the reader grasp the nature and practice of each therapy, culminating in Wilber's marvelous "pointing-out instructions" to help see or recognize the ever-present witness consciousness or the transpersonal self within everyone. Years later, he reflected on what he had attempted to express within these chapters: "*No Boundary* captured that essential 'always already' insight, I believe, which is probably why it is still one of the most popular of my books." Indeed, his Zen Roshi, Taizan Maezumi, after reading the last "ultimate state of consciousness" chapter, recognized it as an expression of nondual consciousness, which had reminded him of Dogen's famous saying: "The wind is all-pervading and there is no place it does not reach."[40] Because of

Maezumi's important influence on Wilber's spiritual development at this time, he donated the first publication of the book (and half of its royalties) to Maezumi's Center Publications.

In what would later become known as Wilber's Romantic period, or Wilber/Phase 1, his first two books suggested that the various "bands" in the spectrum of consciousness are essentially different levels of identity, therefore, "each successive level of the spectrum represents a type of narrowing or restricting of what the individual feels to be his 'self,' his true identity." Psychologically speaking, each level of self-identity or boundary is generated by a primary repression/projection, but fundamentally, all of them are based on what Wilber called the primary dualism of subject/object, knower/known, inside/outside, etc. In addition, by relying upon the evidence of Western psychology, he also noted that there arise a number of related dualisms that run through the human psyche, splitting it into the various levels of awareness, such as the persona/shadow, ego/body, or organism/environment. Wilber therefore proposed that human consciousness evolution is a developmental process of moving through these various boundaries or levels of self-identity until a person finally awakens to ultimate unity consciousness or consciously knowing our supreme identity with the nondual divine, a heart-awakened no-boundary awareness.

Since Wilber himself had personally experienced this nondual state of consciousness, which really isn't a state at all, he knew, without doubt, that it can never be adequately described, only directly realized. Wilber's early spectrum psychology, however, attempted to map out and fully embrace as many different maps or models of human psychology as possible, which were all attempting to describe, with partial pictures and dualistic understanding, the various aspects of the real (nondual) territory of consciousness and existence.

After Wilber's satori earlier in the year of 1978, and the subsequent writing of *No Boundary*, he was now in a much better position to accurately align his research with his own experiential spiritual experiences—"however partial, initial, and incomplete they may have been." Now he could compare the literature of the transpersonal and spiritual traditions, having a "fairly solid, firsthand introduction to the various higher spheres of consciousness." This prompted him into "subdividing the transpersonal sphere into four broad levels: the psychic (realms of *siddhi*, psi, and so on), the subtle (home of archetypes and personal deity), the causal (the unmanifest Void), and the ultimate (spirit, *turiya*, Svabhavikakaya). . . . [Thus Wilber had developed a] more complete spectrum of consciousness or Great Chain of Being: matter-pleroma, reptile-uroboros, mammal-body, persona, ego, centaur, psychic, subtle, causal, ultimate. Or, in the shorthand of Western theology: matter to body to mind to soul to spirit."[41] Further refinements of the spectrum model would naturally emerge over the years, but in the meantime, Wilber felt he had arrived at a "more-or-less complete cartography of consciousness, one that, while far from perfect and occasionally somewhat sloppy, had at least the merit of comprehensiveness."

Wilber/Phase 2 Transition: An Evolutionary Romantic Discovers the Pre/Trans Fallacy

By 1978, as Wilber was continuing to deepen his understanding about the evolution of the spectrum or nested order of consciousness, or the Great Chain of Being, and while taking meditation retreats, he was philosophically floundering in an intense intellectual quagmire, one he would later call "the most turbulent theoretic times of my life." Shortly after completing *No Boundary,* he realized to his own dismay that he had so expertly presented the Romantic position in his earlier books and articles that he couldn't crack his own arguments. This thorny philosophical problem resulted from the fact that Wilber's first two books, *Spectrum* and *No Boundary,* had basically adapted to and presented a Romantic or retro-Romantic position, a view that elevates the past or ancient wisdom to a superior status because it's basically a "recaptured goodness" model of development.

Initially, as Wilber later explained, he began "writing both *The Atman Project* and *Up From Eden* in an attempt to validate that [Romantic] view ontogenetically (*Atman Project*) and phylogenetically (*Eden*)." However, before he could complete *The Atman Project,* which focused on individual development (known as ontogeny) as seen from the transpersonal perspective, he had to work out his fourth book, another developmental volume titled *Up From Eden* since it examined the collective evolution of humanity (known as phylogeny) by using the transpersonal paradigm. The timing of this transition to a more evolutionary point of view could not have come at a better time because, as mentioned, Wilber had been struggling with the thorniest theoretical problem he had ever encountered.

The first chapters of *The Atman Project* had already appeared in the newly established journal *ReVision,* where Wilber was a coeditor, when the young author began to realize something was profoundly wrong with this "recaptured goodness" position. Wilber had no choice, therefore, but to retrace his steps and reanalyze in fine detail the available evidence gathered from a wide variety of disciplines, branching off into anthropology and the collective history of humanity. Indeed, in something like an existential crisis, this effort was not just an intellectual exercise for Wilber but one in which he "physically ached with the effort to straighten things out." In anguish, he complained, "the more I tried to make this Romantic model work—and believe me, I tried, very, very hard—the more I realized its central inadequacies and confusions." The problem, he discovered, "the big difference—

the crucial difference—is that Romantic/Wilber-I *must* see the infantile pre-egoic structure as being, in some sense, a primal Ground, a perfect wholeness, a direct God-union, a complete immersion in Self, a oneness with the whole world."[42] Therefore, as he admits, when he wrote the seminal essay, "The Pre/Trans Fallacy," he was "in effect cataloging all the errors that I myself had made in this regard."

Wilber's Romantic direction, therefore, radically shifted when he broke through to formulate the "pre/trans fallacy." The culmination of years of research, the pre/trans fallacy is perhaps one of Wilber's most novel theories clarified through the lens of transpersonal psychology (although, as we'll see, Wilber would soon break with this "fourth force" in 1983). This articulation of a clear and well-defined difference in the prepersonal and transpersonal realms of human conscious-nesss evolution is exactly what precipitated a drastic shift in Wilber's earlier theo-retical course, the largest such change, or refinement, in any of his philosophical positions.

Consequently, Wilber sharply abandoned the Romantic position and would instead champion the "growth-to-goodness" model of evolutionary development, a view also endorsed by the modern sciences (especially developmental psychology and anthropology). He was attempting to take into account the significant differ-ences between 1) the *prepersonal* (or pre-egoic and prerational) and 2) the *personal* (or egoic and rational) and then 3) the *transpersonal* (transegoic and transrational) stages of growth (especially as seen in the unfolding of developmental lines). Ad-mittedly, this was a very difficult distinction to make because the *pre-* and the *trans-* do appear similar in many ways, which is precisely why they're so slippery and hard to differentiate. Nevertheless, as Wilber continues to explain, the pre/trans fallacy results when "pre-ego is confused with trans-ego simply because both are non-ego."[43] This crucial and fundamental distinction between these developmental real-ities is still a dominant principle running throughout Wilber's various "phases" and is still with his integral vision in the twenty-first century.

By pointing out these pre/trans distinctions, Wilber would reverse, yet still in-clude, the standard psychological model of what's known as "regression in service of ego." Instead, he would emphasize the progression of development toward the highest or ultimate state of God-Realization or divine enlightenment. This devel-opmental spectrum model, then, could include the psychology of mysticism and spirituality by postulating their development as the higher stages in the evolution of consciousness. In other words, Wilber's psychology model posits that true spir-ituality is not found in the "depths" of the prepersonal (although, as he explicitly maintains, nondual Spirit is "always already" present on every level), but within the "higher" bands of the transpersonal culminating with the "height" of Atman (the Hindu term for the highest Self or the bright divine within). As Aurobindo and Teilhard de Chardin had understood earlier in the century and proclaimed: "the future of humankind is God-consciousness," thus Wilber too realized that this divine unity, or the ground and condition of existence, is only discovered, ultimately, with the pinnacle of consciousness evolution, not at the beginning of human infancy, or even in the infant's bliss at the mother's breast.

By 1979, with the pre/trans resolution in his command and with the awareness of his recent satori, Wilber was able to declare a much stronger developmental position bolstered by not only a correct reading of developmental psychology but also by his own direct insight of illumined understanding: "To Return to the Divine, one doesn't regress to infancy. Mysticism is not regression in service of the ego, but evolution in transcendence of the ego." In every phase of his writing, from this point forward, Wilber would forcefully state the same thing over and over: "the transpersonal Self—and true mystic union—lies *in precisely* the opposite direction" of retro-Romantic or lower-level regression or even the notion of "infantile cosmic consciousness." And yet, due to his transpersonal spiritual practice, Wilber came to realize the profound paradox that "not only is Spirit itself the ultimate stage of evolution, it is the ever-present ground of evolution as well."

The distinction of prepersonal versus transpersonal became especially evident to Wilber, as he later explained, when he was reading Piaget about the earliest period of infancy where, in the child's developmental psychology, "the self is here *material,* so to speak." And thus an epiphany occurred since he then tells us "Instantly the entire scheme became clear . . . [for it was] brought home to me in a very forceful way . . . primitive material fusion simply cannot be equated with the Self or with Self-identity." The resulting differentiation between the prepersonal (or preegoic) and transpersonal (or transegoic) structures of consciousness and their corresponding worldviews has become known throughout Wilber's writings as the *pre/trans fallacy* because "both pre-rational states and trans-rational states are, in their own ways, non-rational, then they appear similar or even identical to the untutored eye."[44] Since both the prepersonal and the transpersonal are often erroneously confused and equated, there's a tendency among theorists, as Wilber explains, to either reduce the transpersonal to the prepersonal or to elevate the prepersonal to transpersonal status.

Wilber was able to go on and demonstrate that "We can set history in a context that is at once scientific and spiritual, immanent and transcendent, empirical and meaningful." For example, he would point out in the last chapters of *Up From Eden* that the transpersonal view could clearly differentiate between two very different "Falls": 1) the "theological fall" (or that of *involution*) which is when, *spiritually* speaking, "humankind (and all things) did fall from real Heaven" (or the Divine Realm), yet in actuality this "Fall from Grace" occurs not in the past but is "re-created *now,* moment to moment to moment, as a psychological state of igno-rance."[45] The process of involution helps create the notion that we need to *regress* (or go back) to discover the transpersonal (or spiritual) domain. On the other hand, Wilber continues, there's also 2) the "scientific fall" (or that of evolution) which points to the developmental process whereby, historically speaking, "hu-mankind came up (but not from) the apes." This complex process of evolution seems to create the impression that we need to evolve or progress forward through the higher stages to discovery of the transpersonal or ultimate reality, while tran-scending yet including the lower domains in the process.

Wilber's transpersonal view could also integrate both involution and evolu-tion, for from his "correct but partial" or integral perspective, he could reasonably conclude: "Those are perfectly compatible views, and both are correct. The union of science and religion is the union of evolution and involution." Today such an inte-gral statement may seem somewhat obvious, or at least plausible, but at the time it was a radical breakthrough in understanding the evolution of consciousness, for it seamlessly combined the ancient premodern view with the modern scientific one, yet it also clearly differentiated them. Wilber's writings, once more, attempt to ar-ticulate this paradox as "Spirit-in-action," and in doing so, he gives meaning to that "which we call history: its movement is divine and its meaning transcendent."[46]

By the 1980s, Wilber had introduced these insights into the canon of mod-ern psychology and philosophy with a series of well-written and well-researched publications. The pre/trans fallacy and its implications may be Wilber's most pro-found, novel, and yet probably most misunderstood idea. After establishing the pre/trans differentiation as a fundamental tenet of a true integral vision, Wilber has become intent on both promoting its insight and critiquing the fallacy, wher-ever it may appear. This is partly because, as he later explained, "You are never so vi-cious toward a theory as toward one that you yourself recently embraced."

By the end of the twentieth century, with the emergence of Wilber/Phase 4 or the integral AQAL "all-quadrant, all-level" approach, Wilber has developed the full-spectrum model to such a degree of sophistication that it's now seen as some-thing like a "vast morphogenetic field or developmental space" creating "kosmic patterns" or "evolutionary grooves" (or "kosmic karma") that reflect a grand com-plex multileveled interaction of levels (or waves), lines (or streams), horizontal types, and states of consciousness (and more). Thus it pictures the self as spiraling up, sometimes down, the various developmental lines, "translating" horizontally within the various stages and the potentially "transforming" vertically to other higher stages. When considering the entire display, as Wilber continues to argue, overall development is principally a phenomenon of progression and evolution. He optimistically concludes: "This view tells us that history is indeed going somewhere—it is going, not toward a final judgment, but toward that ultimate Wholeness [or toward God, Brahman, the Divine]." Indeed, in harmony with other evolutionary philosophers teaching in the past hundred years or so, he also insists that the evidence clearly suggests this grand journey and developmental process is driven by telos, the force or end purpose of evolution, which itself is ultimately generated by Eros or divine love. By 1980, twenty years before the new millennium, Wilber's evolution revolution had clearly dawned.

WILBER/PHASE 2. THE EVOLUTION REVOLUTION (1978–1983)

The elucidation of the pre/trans fallacy, and the strong shift to an evolutionary or developmental perspective, brought to an end this important transitional period that culminated in 1979, truly an annus mirabilis, or "year of wonders," as Wilber's literary agent, John White, termed it. This was because the thirty-year-old philosopher would go on to produce a prolific output of writings, from books to articles, that brilliantly reflected his account of the spectrum of consciousness. This year marked the shift into a new period, now called Wilber/Phase 2.

The emerging integral vision would continue to picture a holistic spectrum of consciousness in which each level has its own unique characteristics, its own particular needs, its own structural potentials, even its own diseases and pathologies, as well as their corresponding treatment modalities. Yet there was a further codification, as he later explained: "I began drawing together the personal and transpersonal realms in a developmental and dynamic fashion and not just in a structural fashion as I had done in *Spectrum*." Indeed, he was profoundly influenced by many sources, from Aurobindo in the East to Hegel in the West, being especially encouraged by "Hegel's critique of Kant: the structures of consciousness are not just given at the start; they can only be conceived as ones that have developed."

In 1978, after his experience of satori during a Zen sesshin, and after finishing *No Boundary*, but prior to resolving the pre/trans fallacy, Wilber had already begun his third book, the psychologically oriented *The Atman Project*. However, he would soon have to set it aside until he fully understood this pre/trans differentiation, meanwhile turning his attention to the anthropologically based *Up From Eden*, which itself had sprouted from the *Atman Project*'s opening chapter. By doing so, the perplexed theorist attempted to resolve his problem with the retro-Romantic position by focusing on the historical research gathered from modern anthropology, sociology, and comparative mythology, therefore moving beyond the fields of psychology and mysticism yet including them as well.

It was only after Wilber, as a transformed Romantic, had resolved the pre/trans fallacy that he was finally able to finish *Atman* and *Eden*. Once that happened in

1979, the two books began to write themselves, so to speak, being published in succeeding years, *The Atman Project* in 1980 and *Up From Eden* in 1981. In addition, Wilber published a number of important articles that also clearly reflected the Phase 2 evolutionary position grounded in a nondual perspective. The first summary of Wilber/Phase 2, however, initially appeared in 1979 as "A Developmental View of Consciousness," in *The Journal of Transpersonal Psychology.*

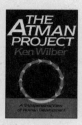

The Atman Project: A Transpersonal View of Human Development (Quest Books, 1983) covers both the outward and inward arcs of individual human development, or ontogeny, as the movement in the general life cycle from birth to enlightenment, from "the womb to God." It emphasizes the fact that "the psyche—like the cosmos at large—is many-layered ('pluridimensional'), composed of successively higher-order wholes and unities and integrations," therefore, "at each point in evolution, what is the *whole* of one level becomes merely a *part* of the higher-order whole of the next level." Or more simply: "development is evolution; evolution is transcendence," and with this transpersonal understanding of evolution, Wilber concluded:

> The form of each growth is essentially the same, and it is the form of transcendence, the form of development: it traces a gentle curve from subconsciousness through self-consciousness to superconsciousness, remembering more and more, transcending more and more, integrating more and more, unifying more and more, until there is only that Unity which was always already the case from the start, and which remained both the alpha and omega of the soul's journey through time.

In other words, not only does Wilber offer a step-by-step delineation of the various levels of mind (or the egoic self), including five different types of the unconscious in the terms of Western psychology, but unlike most modern psychologists, he gives a masterful overview of the transpersonal stages, gleaned from a thorough study of the Eastern mystical traditions and grounded in his own spiritual practice. *Atman Project*'s fairly concise chapters thus outline the general features and characteristics of this evolutionary journey through the prepersonal, personal, and transpersonal stages in a manner that Wilber retains more or less to this day (although, technically, he now sees them all operating within the context of all four quadrants).

The Atman Project brilliantly outlines the dynamics involved in the development of consciousness, moving stage by stage, from infancy to adulthood to higher-order evolution (including the *bardo* stages of preconception, prenatal, and postlife states). It is capped with a profound chapter on involution or "a movement from the higher to the lower," which he explained in terms of the wisdom found in *The Tibetan Book of the Dead* (or *Bardo Thotrol*). Wilber defined *involution* as "the movement whereby Brahman [or God] throws itself outward to create the manifest worlds," thus being a "descent" of Spirit. Only then does *evolution* begin as "a movement from the lower to the higher." In other words, "Development or evolution is simply the unfolding of these enfolded structures, beginning with the lowest and proceeding to the highest: body to mind to subtle [soul] to causal [spirit]."

One of the book's principal themes, then, is that all the stages and drives of this evolving self are actually nothing more than the endless attempts "to regain Atman consciousness in ways or under conditions that prevent it and force symbolic substitutes," the working definition of the Atman project. (*Atman* is the Hindu term for "the divine within" or the "true self.") According to Wilber, "Psychological development in humans has the same goal as natural evolution: the production of ever-higher unities. And since the ultimate Unity is Buddha, God, or Atman (to use those terms in their broadest sense as 'ultimate reality'), it follows that psychological growth aims at Atman." In this case, he reasoned, "Each individual wants only Atman, but wants it under conditions which prevent it," thus he concluded, "The Atman project is a substitute for Atman, but it also contains a drive to recapture Atman." Indeed, he explained, this is "the dynamic, the goal, of evolution and development" simply because the "Atman-project continues until there is only Atman."

Importantly, *The Atman Project* also included several dozen reference tables compiled from numerous theorists, both ancient and modern, all of whom were correlated to Wilber's seventeen-stage master template of consciousness.

Overturning the Myth of Eden

Also culminating in the annus mirabilis of 1979 was the bulk of Wilber's historical and anthropological research that would compose *Up From Eden: A Transpersonal View of Human Evolution* (Anchor/Doubleday, 1981)—*Up From Eden* presented an unprecedented examination of human history from a transpersonal understanding, based on an interpretative reading of the deep developmental structures in the spectrum of consciousness. Yet, importantly, this archeological and anthropological evidence helped Wilber break his difficult impasse and untangle his thorny theoretical quandary. However, *Up From Eden* is perhaps Wilber's most controversial book to date, since it may, at times, seem to overgeneralize certain aspects of human history, but, as a sound defense, it was only intended to be a brief outline. Nonetheless, to this day, many people consider it one of their favorite, and the most intriguing, of Wilber's books.

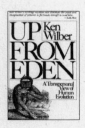

To briefly summarize Wilber's intellectual progress in solving the retro-

Romantic fallacy, he first noted that world mythology seems to universally confirm and demonstrate the Romantic notion that there was somewhere in the dim past a type of Golden Age, a Garden of Eden, an earthly paradise, whether in the collective experience of early humankind or in the infancy of a newborn child. This Eden was supposedly where all things and beings were one with nature, living in a state of bliss. This "Fall of Man" was usually caused, as the Romantic story goes, by increasing knowledge, separation, and consequent egoic alienation, symbolized by Adam and Eve eating from the tree of knowledge and being expelled from the Garden of Eden.

However, the more the integral scholar studied the available scientific and mythic evidence, the more he saw "that was exactly the clue I had been looking for: the Eden myths confused prepersonal ignorance with transpersonal bliss, so that when men and women finally evolved up and out of Eden, it was mistaken for a Fall down from heaven." In other words, according to the historical record and the paleoanthropological evidence based upon fossils and archaeological artifacts, the Eden of the early hominids (or protohumans) was actually "the bliss of ignorance, not transcendence" since it was "the peace of prepersonal ignorance, not transpersonal wisdom." For Wilber, the empirical evidence of Darwin's evolution revolution could not be philosophically (or practically) ignored.

Human evolution, and individual development, at least according to the recent scientific and empirical evidence, was actually a story that recounted or reconstructed the historical move *up from* Eden, not the fall *down from* it. After applying this type of reconstructive science, Wilber realized, by thoroughly reviewing anthropology and its associated evidence, he must include this irrefutable fact:

> Eden was simply the period of the subconscious, prepersonal, pre-egoic, and subhuman stages of evolution, up to and including that of early or protohumans (*Australopithecus, Homo habilis,* and so on). It was paradisical in a crude sense because protohumans [hominids], being pre-egoic, had no capacity for self-reflexive thought, and thus no capacity for real anxiety, doubt, or despair.[47]

In this case, as Wilber would go on to demonstrate, that each stage of collective human development, including the move beyond the biological into the cultural, added its own novel emergents (or higher-order unities) as humankind evolved through the millennia. But, as Wilber noted, because of this increased complexity, so too there's the increased potential for corruption or pathology, thus the "progress" of evolution is not in any way an easy or sweet affair; it's extremely complicated and difficult, in fact quite harrowing at times. Wilber clearly admitted as much in his opening page to *Eden:* "There is a price to be paid for every increase in consciousness, and only that perspective, I believe, can place mankind's evolutionary history in the proper context." Thus he began his book by agreeing with the second-century mystic-philosopher Plotinus, who observed: "Mankind is poised midway between the gods and the beasts," to which Wilber responded:

> For if men and women have come up from the beasts, then they will likely end up with the gods. The distance between man and the gods is not all that much greater than the distance between beasts and man. We have already closed the latter gap, and there is no reason to suppose that we shall not eventually close the former. . . . But if men and women are up from the beasts and on their way to the gods, they are in the meantime rather tragic figures. Poised between the two extremes, they are subjected to the most violent of conflicts. No longer beasts, not yet god—or worse, half beast, half god: there is the soul of mankind. Put another way, humankind is an essentially tragic figure with a beautifully optimistic future—if they can survive the transition.

Wilber, too, basically agreed with Hegel's notion of the dialectic of progress since evolution is obviously shaped by both positive (Eros) and negative (Thanatos) energies. Nonetheless, history is still progress, for it's the novel addition of new emergents that unfold toward greater consciousness, wider embrace, deeper understanding and wisdom. As an attempt to integrate all this available evidence, Wilber knew he had to include the scientific facts buried in the historical record and not simply romanticize human history or project desires or hopes onto the distant past, whether on ancient civilizations or primitive tribes. Only with this perspective could he affirm: "We had to evolve past the ape of subconsciousness in order to rediscover superconsciousness. This being so, then we may all take heart, for it now appears certain that you and I came up from Eden so that we may all return to Heaven." Yet now, Wilber suggested, this tale of evolutionary development had to begin with the scientific evidence that had only comparatively recently discovered "what preceded people was not transpersonal souls but prepersonal apes." Then with the further evolution of human beings came the advent of the "nature of culture and the denial of death." But ultimately when "a person rediscovers that his deepest Nature is one with the All, he is relieved of the burdens of time, of anxiety, of worry; he is released from the chains of alienation and separate-self existence. . . . [Therefore] the rediscovery of this infinite and eternal Wholeness is man's single greatest need and want." The pre/trans distinction, therefore, became one of the primary themes in *Up From Eden* as it traced, in broad outlines, the long evolutionary arc of human history from the deep past to the present day, even speculating about the near future.

In the 350 pages of *Eden,* Wilber's view on the evolution of consciousness, which integrated recent discoveries of science, showed in an unparalleled fashion how the grand drama of collective human history can be correlated, in general terms, with individual human development, expressed as onto-phylo parallels, not strict recapitulations. By doing so, the innovative theorist went on to briefly outline the numerous prepersonal, personal, and transpersonal phases and subphases in world history, including both the "average-mode" and "advanced-tip" modes of consciousness (itself a novel discovery). With this type of understanding, by the end of the volume he also presented the sociocultural "levels of exchange" that are generated among the interacting and evolving bands or structures comprising the entire spectrum of consciousness, both collectively and individually.

In a very real sense, therefore, Wilber was already anticipating the "four-quadrant" and "all-level" or AQAL approach of Wilber/Phase 4 by seeing the importance of the sociocultural dimensions in human evolution. In any case, *Eden*'s transpersonal account of human history would, right on the opening page, declares his general agreement with the theological assertion made by the wisdom traditions that "history [i]s the sport and play (*lila*) of Brahman [the Hindu word for the ultimate God]." Years later, he still asserts that "Spirit is not by any means a deterministic machine, but rather an organically playful Spirit, whose own sport and play (*lila*) includes the wonderful game of 'surprise' at every possible turn, undermining determinism as all creativity does." Thus, Wilber's writings continue to re-create this grand evolutionary story of universal and world history, including the evolution of cultures and human individuals, captured in the phrases "Spirit-in-action" and "God-in-the-making" in order to express our shared journey "up from" prehistoric Eden.

A Time of Revision

A few years after this turbulent transitional period, Wilber reflected on his intense journey of the late 1970s in the biographical essay "Personal Odyssey: A Personal Inquiry into Humanistic and Transpersonal Psychology."[48] However, even by then, with Wilber/Phase 2 culminating in the evolutionary paradigm published in *The Atman Project* and *Up From Eden,* Wilber/Phase 3 was already under way during the first years of the 1980s. On a personal level, the transition completed itself around the time Wilber finally moved from Lincoln, Nebraska, where he had been living for the past decade with his wife, Amy. Incredibly, during the past two years from 1978 to 1980 the young married man, who just turned thirty in 1979, continued to wash dishes, meditate under the guidance of Zen masters, and pursue his intellectual investigations all while simultaneously producing three major books, numerous professional journal articles, and writing many of the essays that would appear in *Eye to Eye*. Yet when Wilber was invited to move to the East Coast, he and Amy found they were essentially moving in "different directions," therefore they decided to divorce after spending "ten almost-always happy years" together (and they still remain "friends to this day").

Shortly before this, Jack Crittenden, a young political science professor and new friend of Wilber's, collaborated with Wilber to found the integral journal *Re-Vision: A Journal of Consciousness and Change*.[49] Wilber began to work as coeditor while still living in Lincoln, but by the fall of 1981, he had packed his bags and moved to Cambridge, Massachusetts. Here he would help get *ReVision* off the ground and propel it to a high level of esteem among his professional peers. Shortly after his arrival, however, Crittenden would kindly but cleverly "trick" Wilber into being the sole editor in chief, which by then he did with enthusiasm. The primary task for the pioneering journal was to promote the integral message around the world by offering a diverse range of ideas from a plethora of theorists discussing the growing trends of consciousness studies. However, before the turn of the century, after being sold to a different group of editors (and investors), *ReVision* had been criticized by its two original founders as displaying a Romantic or "regressive bias," although Wilber, as always, wishes the journal and its editors well.

1983: Transcending, Yet Including, Tradition

Nineteen eighty-three was another watershed year for Wilber. After being on the East Coast working on *ReVision* for only a year, he would move back across country to Tiburon near San Francisco. It was there, in August, that he would meet his second wife, Treya (Terry Killam), who would draw him into the embrace of love and her five-year battle with cancer, later documented in the very moving and popular book *Grace and Grit*. This year would also mark the point when Wilber would clearly establish his own unique integral direction separate from the "fourth force" of transpersonal psychology, the field with which he was most closely associated. This happened in spite of the fact that his monumental first book, *The Spectrum of Consciousness*, had become one of the seminal texts of this recently emerging discipline of psychological study and research. In addition, not only did he break with transpersonal psychology but he also distanced himself from the conventional interpretations surrounding the perennial philosophy itself. By doing so, he was venturing out on his own in order to stabilize the integral approach as its own discipline, grounded in spectrum psychology and the integration of East and West but also reaching out and embracing a wider range of disciplines such as sociology, anthropology, and the larger sociocultural matrix. In essence, then, although not specifically using these terms yet, Wilber was anticipating the importance of including all four quadrants (or the integral AQAL approach) in making detailed studies or critical analyses.

Importantly, 1983 also saw the publication of a number of important books and essays that helped establish his new direction by further advancing his shift into Wilber/Phase 3 and his work with the AQAL model of Wilber/Phase 4, which clearly distinguishes between basic structures and developmental lines. This was the year he introduced his groundbreaking critique of the perennial philosophy titled "The Neo-Perennial Philosophy," first published in the bastion of traditional spiritual studies, *The American Theosophist,* in their special fall issue. By doing so, Wilber began to initiate his fully postmodern—actually post-postmodern worldview—now better known as integral studies, which itself is a phrase borrowed from Sri Aurobindo, yet wasn't used extensively until Wilber/Phase 4. It refers to an integrative approach set across a wide spectrum of disciplines and research studies. Yet the mold was set, as he later explains: "Integral studies must fight on two fronts, as it were: against a modernity that is slow to recognize the full spectrum of consciousness and against a traditionalism that refuses to recognize any substantial advances made by modernity itself." In other words, as a "correct but partial" proposition, Wilber's integral vision continued to embrace the premodern, modern, and postmodern worldviews and their corresponding insights, yet by holding no exclusive allegiance to either of them.

Postmodernism, Wilber explains in Phase 4, states that interpretation is an inherent part of the Kosmos: "The world is in part a construction and interpretation; all meaning is context-bound; contexts are endlessly holonic."[50] Nonetheless, even with such a broad embrace, Wilber has always made an appeal to "the esoteric or inner core of the wisdom religions," or what's generally been known as the perennial philosophy. He still finds it's an easy way to explain the wisdom of the spiritual traditions, thus he continues to summarize its importance in his later works, such as in *One Taste:*

> So what are the details of this perennial philosophy? Very simple: *The Great Nest of Being, culminating in One Taste*—there, in a nutshell, is the perennial philosophy. This is not to say that everything about the perennial philosophy is set in concrete or etched in gold. I actually wrote a paper called "the Neo-Perennial Philosophy," pointing out that much of it needed to be updated and modernized. Nonetheless, the core of the world's great wisdom traditions is a framework we ought to consult seriously and reverentially in our own attempts to understand the Kosmos.

Wilber's current position, which was already becoming established by 1983, is that even though this great philosophy can appear "perennial," in actuality there's nothing perennial about any of these forms of spirituality because they are *evolving*. His main point is that the only thing that's truly timeless is the unmanifest formless (or the causal and nondual) realm itself, the divine Godhead (Brahman, Tao, *sunyata*, etc.). Although, as he always admits, "That One, or the timeless and absolute Spirit" is ever-present throughout all time, Wilber's "neo-perennial philosophy" includes evolution; in other words, he sees it as Spirit-in-action, a phrase he first introduced in this 1983 paper. Years later he continues to maintain: "Manifestation is not 'apart from' Spirit but an activity of Spirit: the evolving Kosmos is Spirit-in-action." Thus, he professed that the entire universe "is evolving toward Spirit; God does not lie in our collective past, God lies in our collective future; the Garden of Eden is tomorrow, not yesterday; the Golden Age lies down the road, not up it."

By defining his notion of a neo-perennial philosophy, Wilber stated in this pivotal essay: "The point is that the evolution of the forms of Truth clearly show a succession of increasingly adequate and more comprehensive structures for truth's expression and representation. . . . [Thus] the past had the Great Religions. The future will have the Greater Religions." In other words, the world's religions have continued, and will continue, to evolve or refine their understanding and particularly their expression throughout the centuries and millennia, often being renewed or revitalized by increasingly sophisticated religious geniuses (as evidenced, for example, by the development of Advaita Vedanta Hinduism and Vajrayana Buddhism throughout the centuries). Nonetheless, Wilber concedes: "At the core of the neo-perennial philosophy is the same Radical and Formless Truth glimpsed by the wisdom cultures of the past," yet he also warns, "Our loyalty to the past is just this misplaced intuition of absolute Spirit, diverted from the present Realization onto a past idolization by the inability to fall now into timeless transcendence." This is clear evidence that the integral philosopher had turned a corner at this time in his appreciation of the perennial philosophy. From now on he would courageously level a strong critique at the tendency of scholars, in their assessment of ancient religious traditions, to downplay the important evidence being accumulated by modern and postmodern sources and approaches.

In a similar vein, Wilber also wrote an obscure article titled "In Praise of Ego: An Uncommon Buddhist Sermon," appearing in the British Buddhist journal *The Middle Way*, vol. 58, where, although he stated that he was "a fan of the journal," he still lamented "the abyss of misunderstanding that has arisen between many Buddhists and psychologists." Since spectrum psychology understands why "the average psychologist is dumbfounded to find us Buddhists recommending, indeed actively encouraging, 'no-ego' states," Wilber goes on to point out that each discipline is generally phase-specific to their particular level of development. Indeed, he explains, "The whole point of the ego is to create a self strong enough to die in nirvanic release," a point summarized six years later by Jack Engler's famous phrase: "You have to be somebody before you can be nobody." Based on the insights of spectrum psychology, Wilber concludes, "By and large, Western psychology is a pre-ego-to-ego psychology, and Buddhism is an ego-to-transego psychology." Once again, an integral embrace or "marriage" of East and West is recommended: "The West has much to learn from Buddhism; but Buddhism has just as much to learn from the West." Both Buddha (or mysticism) and Freud (or psychology) could now see "eye to eye," since with Wilber's philosophy they were both seen as simply "correct but partial" or "true but partial."

Seeing Eye to Eye: The Integral Books of 1983

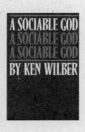

In the spring of 1983, after *The Atman Project* and *Up From Eden* had been published and were making their influence felt, Wilber presented all of these essential themes in a dense and much smaller book titled *A Sociable God: A Brief Introduction to a Transcendental Sociology* (McGraw-Hill, 1983). This short book was essentially written "in one fevered weekend" during the summer of 1982, and is a strong summary of Wilber/Phase 2, which had become dynamic, evolutionary, and developmental, and was by now clearly liberated from the Romantic pre/trans fallacy. Since its initial inspiration came somewhat in response to the mass-suicide tragedy at Jonestown in 1978,[51] in addition to being a major contribution to a seminar led by sociologist Dick Anthony, this review systematically extends Wilber's work in spectrum psychology and anthropology to include the sociocultural context sought by the sociology of religion. By doing so, *A Sociable God* includes an integral look at the so-called new religions appearing in the modern world. This treatise was part of Wilber's attempt to help society discriminate and differentiate between dangerous (generally prepersonal) cults and the more beneficial spiritual (or transpersonal) enterprises (such as Buddhist *sanghas,* or communities), thus serving to discriminate authentic spirituality from inauthentic religious involvement. A few years later, he would further reinforce this important distinction with a written contribution and being a co-editor to *Spiritual Choices* (1987).

With *A Sociable God,* published in 1983, Wilber confirmed his unofficial break from transpersonal psychology, for he now wanted to embrace an even more integral, full-spectrum model. Such an approach would not only include psychology (emphasizing the inner worlds), but also sociocultural analyses (emphasizing the outer world) and their multidimensional relationships or "relational exchanges." While Wilber still incorporated the important research of transpersonal psychology, and certainly affirmed the transpersonal realm itself, he wanted to distance himself from many of its theoretical premises and assumptions, especially its tendency to be Romantic or regressive in its outlook.

Another one of Wilber's more important books, *Eye to Eye: The Quest for the New Paradigm* (Shambhala Publications, 1983), was also published during that important transitional year of 1983. This collection of mostly Wilber/Phase 2 writings, with some initial Wilber/Phase 3 offerings, was gathered together from essays written in the late '70s and early '80s. It tended to emphasize the philosophical implications generated from an evolutionary yet transpersonal perspective on human nature via the spectrum model, or "a mandalic map of consciousness." It was here, in a book dedicated to finding "the new paradigm," that Wilber introduced the Christian mystic's metaphor of the "three eyes of knowing," i.e., the eye of flesh, the eye of reason, and the eye of contemplation, or the sensory, mental, and spiritual realms, currently referred to as epistemological pluralism. This idea, a simple reduction of the multilayered spectrum of consciousness to three eyes or levels, had first appeared in 1979 with an earlier version published in *ReVision*. Wilber used these three eyes of knowledge as an epistemological tool to integrate the entire spectrum of body, mind, and spirit. He found this approach effectively offered not only a strong critique of scientific materialism but it could also shine an illuminating light to guide the New Age out of its dark cave of mythic thinking and its tendency to use regressive, or prerational, approaches to spirituality.

Eye to Eye contained numerous important essays, such as "The Problem of Proof," "A Mandalic Map of Consciousness," "Structure, Stage, and Self" (an early Wilber/Phase 3 presentation), and "The Ultimate State of Consciousness" (a slight revision of Wilber's second published article, different from the personal confession of *No Boundary*'s last chapter with the same name). Perhaps most important was "The Pre/Trans Fallacy," which first appeared in *ReVision* in 1980, for it defined in detail the crucial concept that, a few years back, had overturned the Romantic fallacy adopted by Wilber's earlier writings. As he explained years later, "When I wrote 'the Pre/Trans Fallacy,' I was in effect cataloguing all of the errors that I myself had made in this regard, which is why I seemed to understand them with an all too-alarming familiarity." His critique of pre-transphenomena is now widely accepted and acknowledged as being valid and extremely useful.

Amazingly, this prolific period of 1983 also saw the completion of the main essays used in *Transformations of Consciousness* (not published until 1986), about a month before Treya and Ken were married. In general, *Transformations of Consciousness* is more psychological in orientation, whereas *Eye to Eye* (1983) is more philosophical in nature. Also in the spring of '83, Wilber published an article called "Kierkegaard's Passion" where he recalled, from the point of view of a transpersonal outlook, the motivations behind the philosophy penned by the passionate, existential philosopher. In fact, that essay, appearing in *ReVision,* was claimed to come from another recently composed book titled *The History of Western Psychology* (still unpublished), a work that attempted to write a scholarly history "from a perspective that acknowledges the transcendental dimensions of most of the great influences of modern psychology because he believes "someone has got to tell."[52]

In addition to this prodigious output, although it was not published at the time, Wilber also produced an excellent summary essay, or short book, reviewing his work up until that time. Now titled *Sociocultural Evolution* (appearing in *CW4*), it clearly shows his response to the then "surging currents of extreme postmodernism, anti-evolutionism, contextualism, and relativism," or what he would later term "the first of my many defenses of dynamic dialecticism against dynamic relativism." Written in the same short, direct style as *A Sociable God,* it was originally named "Reply to Critics," for it was a refutation to a privately circulated paper by Dick Anthony, who had gathered together some recent criticism and added some of his own. This summary of Wilber's emerging Phase 3 orientation, where he emphasized the necessity to differentiate clearly the basic and transitional structures, presented a gallant defense of evolutionary theory, especially within the human sociocultural realm, in addition to reviewing the work or positions of many prominent scholars and theorists in various fields.

However, in the significance of meeting Treya that August, and the whirlwind of events surrounding her cancer diagnosis three months later, Wilber actually forgot he had written this book until he found it in the mid-1990s while looking over his earlier writings for *The Collected Works of Ken Wilber* (1999, 2000). With the fortuitous meeting of his soul mate, Treya, who would pass away five years later from cancer, 1983 also marked the beginning of a profound transformation in the character and soul of Ken Wilber. It was a transformation that would change his life forever, and would professionally culminate over ten years later with the publication of his magnum opus, the first eight-hundred-page volume in *The Kosmos Trilogy,* now known as *Sex, Ecology, Spirituality* (1995), which itself would herald Wilber's Phase 4 or the AQAL "all-quadrant, all-level" approach to integral studies.

By the end of 1983, during which he spent his honeymoon and Christmas with his new wife in the hospital, where she was being treated for cancer, it was becoming obvious with the steady stream of Wilber's published record that Phase 3 was already emerging only a year after Phase 2's publications of *Atman* and *Eden.* Beginning with his first books that had originally established his spectrum psychology within the "fourth force" of transpersonal psychology, he now had broken away to allow his philosophy and psychology to transform into a more all-embracing integral approach, reaching out to include all dimensions and quadrants of reality in an attempt to construct new models of human psychology, philosophy, and Kosmic reality.

WILBER/PHASE 3. THE INTEGRAL VISION:
SELF, LEVELS, & LINES (1983–1994)

In 1981, after *The Atman Project* and *Up From Eden* had been published, Wilber/Phase 3 began with an article in *The Journal of Transpersonal Psychology* called "Ontogenetic Development: Two Fundamental Patterns" (it would later become *Eye to Eye*'s chapter titled "Structure, Stage, and Self"). The two fundamental patterns in the original title, Wilber explained, "referred to the difference between the enduring *basic structures* (the major levels or waves in the spectrum of consciousness) and the *transitional lines* or streams that make their way through the basic levels." Explicitly, he continues, this Wilber/Phase 3 period "distinguishes *the different developmental lines that unfold . . . in a quasi-independent fashion through the general levels of basic structures of consciousness.* There is no single, monolithic line that governs all of these developments." Developmental lines of consciousness plus the basic structures or levels of consciousness—this is precisely what defines the Phase 3 period, yet it's a point overlooked by many critics of the stage-oriented model, even twenty years later.

The essential Wilber/Phase 3 book coauthored with some Harvard professors was *Transformations of Consciousness: Conventional and Contemplative Perspectives on Development* (Shambhala Publications, 1986) by Ken Wilber, Jack Engler, and Daniel P. Brown, with important contributions by Mark Epstein, Jonathan Lieff, and John Chirban. Written in 1983, this expression of Phase 3 contained a few complex, detailed essays, such as "The Developmental Spectrum and Psychopathology, Part 1: Stages and Types of Pathology," and "Part 2: Treatment Modalities," both of which had initially appeared in *The Journal of Transpersonal Psychology* in 1984. They demonstrated how to differentiate, correlate, and integrate not only the spectrum of development but also the spectrums of psychopathology and their corresponding spectrums of treatment modalities. This monumental achievement caused *The New York Times* to identify the book as "the most important and sophisticated synthesis of psychologies East and West to emerge yet."

The authors themselves concluded that a comprehensive integral psychology must at least include these three primary components: 1) the basic structures or the enduring levels (or waves) of consciousness evolution, so called because once they emerge they tend to remain in existence; 2) the transition structures, which include the many developmental lines (or streams); and 3) the overall self or self-system: the main locus of identification, volition, defenses, etc., which is the self—the "I"—or the separate-self sense who navigates and negotiates these various dynamic structural developments. In conclusion, the book shows that when these scholars compared and contrasted numerous developmental maps or models from around the world, including Christian, Buddhist, Hindu, Western psychology, and more, it resulted in a master template that outlined these varied facets of consciousness. In other words, by pulling together all of these different strands of development—conventional and contemplative, orthodox and meditative, Western and Eastern—they suggested that there is indeed a universal spectrum of consciousness through which every individual in their lifetime develops or evolves at their own pace and in their own unique way.

It should also be noted that throughout *Transformations of Consciousness,* Wilber often referred to an even more detailed presentation of these Wilber/Phase 3 refinements by pointing to a book he had tentatively titled *System, Self, and Structure* (later retitled *Patterns and Process in Consciousness,* and then *The 1-2-3 of Consciousness Studies*). This detailed work was originally intended to be Wilber's promised "textbook on transpersonal psychology" outlining his integral psychology, spirituality, and consciousness studies. However, interestingly, the author has always maintained: "I deeply do not want to do this book, and wish somebody else would take the outline and run with it," therefore he admits it's a piece he's "been working on (and mostly not working on) for fifteen years." Currently, this as-yet-unpublished two-volume set has appeared as another more condensed version under the title of *Integral Psychology* (2000).

Ten years after the essay "Two Fundamental Patterns" appeared in 1981, thereby initiating Wilber/Phase 3, another article in the fall of 1991, published in the *Journal of Humanistic Psychology* and titled "Two Patterns of Transcendence: A Reply to Washburn," fully reflected the mature Wilber/Phase 3 position. (It now appears as "A Unified Theory of Development" in *CW4*). This essay is, Wilber later explained, "my clearest statement . . . of my 'Phase 3' model of development and evolution (which, in the context of the four quadrants, is the model I still hold)." This integral view clearly embraces all the various components of consciousness development, as mentioned: the basic structures or levels (or waves), the developmental lines (or the various streams), a self-system that develops through these waves while navigating and juggling the streams, as well as the states of consciousness (waking, dreaming, deep sleep, altered, etc.)—indeed, this well-delineated view is the sophisticated reading of Wilber's Phase 3 work, since at least 1981.

In other words, with the resolution of the pre/trans dilemma of Wilber/Phase 2 in the late 1970s, itself following only a couple of years after Wilber's first book, he had already "abandoned the strictly linear or 'ladder-like' view of development."

Yet this is the position, even today, that's usually cited by many of Wilber's critics, who often concentrate only on the *structures* of consciousness as fully representing his integral vision. Thus they egregiously misrepresent his true views, though they do so inadvertently. Nonetheless, it needs to be fairly recognized that for the entire length of Wilber's career his theories have been constantly upgraded and modified, although most of the basic premises still remain valid throughout, as we've seen. Wilber's critics would be well served by being as current as possible with his integral views, rather than aim critiques that distort his current work.

The Quest for the New Paradigm

During the period of maintaining both the journal *ReVision* (1979–1983) and his own writings, Wilber somehow found time to edit several books. The first was *The Holographic Paradigm and Other Paradoxes* (Shambhala Publications, 1982), which originated from several *ReVision* articles authored by various theorists who were discussing the new holographic paradigm, which had created quite a stir in transpersonal circles. The main premise of the holographic paradigm was based on the intriguing theories of physicist-philosopher David Bohm and neuroscientist Karl Pribram, who were attempting to construct an interface between science and religion. Wilber, however, concluded that this subject is actually an extraordinarily complex affair that resists popular generalizations and which certainly cannot be reduced to a two-level scheme such as Bohm's implicate and explicate order. Therefore, as editor, Wilber was in the awkward position of being virtually the only contributor who, as he tells us, did "not believe the holographic paradigm was based on good science nor adequate mysticism." Nonetheless, as he wryly noted, it became an international bestseller.

In another edited collection, *Quantum Questions: Mystical Writings of the World's Great Physicists* (Shambhala Publications, 1984), Wilber gathered together some selections of what he considered to be the mystically oriented writings of the twentieth century's greatest physicists. This was an attempt to answer the "quantum questions" that were being raised by the so-called new physics, popularized with such books as *The Tao of Physics* (1975) by Fritjof Capra and *The Dancing Wu Li Masters* (1979) by Gary Zukav. Therefore *Quantum Questions* offered another of Wilber's strong critiques to the popular New Age interpretation of modern physics as a justification or proof for mysticism and a spiritual worldview. By including the actual writings culled from the founders of modern physics (Heisenberg, Schrödinger, de Broglie, Jeans, Planck, Pauli, Eddington, and Einstein), all of whom were deeply concerned about these matters, Wilber unequivocally showed, according to these esteemed physicists themselves, that "modern physics neither

proves nor disproves, neither supports nor refutes, a mystical-spiritual worldview." One of the main problems, Wilber emphasized, is that "If today's physics supports mysticism, what happens when tomorrow's physics replaces it? Does mysticism then fall also?" The selections from *Quantum Questions* highlight this relatively unknown and fascinating fact: all these twentieth-century physicists moved beyond the limited "shadow symbols" of mathematics and turned to mysticism to find true knowledge about the real world, and, in doing so, they became modern mystics in the process.

A few years later, in 1987, Wilber collaborated further with Dick Anthony, a sociologist who specializes in the study of new religious movements. As an outcome of this friendship, Wilber contributed a chapter selected from *Eye to Eye* called "Legitimacy, Authenticity, and Authority in the New Religions," which was retitled "The Spectrum Model," to be featured in the book *Spiritual Choices: The Problems of Recognizing Authentic Paths to Inner Transformation* (1987, Paragon House) edited by Dick Anthony, Bruce Ecker, and Ken Wilber. With notable contributions from numerous transpersonal psychologists and spiritual teachers— including Frances Vaughan, John Welwood, Jacob Needleman, Claudio Naranjo, Ram Das, Werner Erhard, Meher Baba, and others—it aimed at answering the spiritual seeker's dilemma of how to distinguish or "better discriminate between safe, genuine spiritual authority and dangerous imitators." With the all-important pre/trans distinction, Wilber's spectrum model was recognized by other researchers as being an excellent tool for helping to solve "the problem of recognizing authentic paths to inner transformation."

Spiritual Choices extended many of the sociological issues raised in Wilber's *A Sociable God,* especially since the authors relied heavily upon Anthony's year-long research project studying "spiritual tyranny versus legitimate spiritual authority." Overall, this timely text presented a very valid method and critique, since understanding the spectrum model and the pre/trans fallacy helps a person or society better ascertain "valid approaches to inner spiritual development" amongst the many being offered in the diverse marketplace of modern spirituality. With this guidance, the authors proposed, people could possibly steer away from the more mythic and cultic (i.e., prepersonal) options in the search for "spiritual choices," usually in a real effort to find true spirituality

The Integral Embrace

With each publication that appeared during the 1980s, Wilber was going even further beyond the basic paradigm of transpersonal psychology, especially since now he had distanced himself from some of the field's more popular views. After the introduction and success of Wilber's first books, many other psychologists, especially transpersonal ones, had begun to integrate the spectrum approach into their professional practices. This branch of psychological inquiry and research was being called, since Wilber's first book, *spectrum psychology*, even though today, as we'll see, it's more accurately known as *integral psychology*. This integral approach presents an even broader discipline than transpersonal psychology, simply because integral psychology recognizes *all* the possibilities of human development, from the prepersonal to the personal to the transpersonal, and not just the possibility for having peak or nonegoic experiences. New studies and surveys were being undertaken by other researchers that verified Wilber's basic propositions, which suggested that the same cross-cultural developmental structures (or universal features) of consciousness tend to show up, in some variation, throughout the evidence gathered from around the world.

Indeed, because of the excitement and enthusiasm that Wilber's work generated, some of his professional colleagues had become good friends, including Jack Crittenden, Michael Murphy (the founder of Esalen), and John Welwood (a transpersonal psychologist and relationship counselor), as well as Roger Walsh and his wife, Frances Vaughan, both transpersonal psychologists and excellent authors, to name a few. Many others corresponded from a distance, sometimes dropping by for an occasional visit. By the mid-'80s, with seven books published in less than ten years, most of his peers were amazed at the prodigious wealth of information synthesized by Wilber's integral vision, even his most vocal critics, such as Michael Washburn and Stanislav Grof.

By the time Wilber entered his second decade of publishing, many people were discovering that his comprehensive paradigm could resolve some of the divisive factionalism that sprang from the modern dilemma of diversity. In other words, in today's modern world there was a plethora of maps and models all attempting to describe the same territory, yet each one tended to be partial or biased toward its own set of evidence. Nevertheless, it seemed that by acknowledging the full spectrum, including the prepersonal, personal, and transpersonal realms of evolution, someone had ingeniously brought a semblance of order to the diverse mountains of data and competing theories that had been accumulating in the modern world. And perhaps, most importantly, there finally seemed to be a map of reality that legitimately resolved much of the conflict between modern science and ancient wisdom or religion in general, and yet, in a thoroughly modern vein.

When *Transformations of Consciousness* was published in 1986, it clearly defined the theoretical parameters of Wilber/Phase 3. However, it would actually be Wilber's last theoretical book for almost ten years (until *Sex, Ecology, Spirituality* was published in 1995). Within a year of arriving in Cambridge, Massachusetts, to be editor in chief at *ReVision* in 1981, Wilber found that the East Coast's intellectual atmosphere didn't really appeal to him, thus he made plans to move to the San Francisco Bay Area. In late 1982 he stayed in Roger Walsh's and Frances Vaughan's beautiful hillside home in Tiburon, California, a small, well-to-do enclave in Marin County just north of the Golden Gate Bridge. Here he would finish assembling the complicated essays comprising 1983's *Eye to Eye,* unaware that his work would soon be interrupted with a nearly ten-year hiatus. Soon thereafter, at his housemates' urging, Wilber would meet his future wife, leading to a period during which he acknowledged "Although [there] was an absence of writing, [there] was an abundance of blessings. And anguish."[53]

Grace and Grit: Love of the Two-Armed Forms

On August 3, 1983, Wilber's life took a major turn when he was graced to met Terry "Treya" Killam. At this time, as he tells us, "I was in effect a Zen monk. When I met Treya I owned one desk chair, a typewriter, and four thousand books."[54] With the beautiful and keenly intelligent Treya, however, it was, as they liked to say, "love at first touch." Two weeks after meeting Treya, Ken proposed to her in front of her favorite mountain range in Boulder, Colorado. They were married within four months on November 26, 1983. Nonetheless, Ken's good friend and publisher Sam Bercholz, after meeting Treya, was worried about her "getting shortchanged."

Yet, tragically, ten days after their blissful wedding, Treya was diagnosed with breast cancer. She passed away a little more than five years later in January of 1989. During that short time, she and her husband went through an incredible ordeal, a heartbreaking story of courage and love.

During those extraordinary five years their spiritual practice and love for each other were severely tested, yet grew in unimaginable ways. They moved from Muir Beach, California to Incline Village at Lake Tahoe, Nevada, where Ken displayed symptoms of chronic fatigue syndrome; then back down again to Muir Beach, finally settling in Boulder, Colorado, during the summer of 1987, where Ken still lives today in the hillside mountain home he partially designed. Over the years, they pursued all types of medical treatments for cancer, from Western allopathic medicine to traditional, natural, and nonconventional techniques, but mostly they deepened their spiritual understanding as being the best way to deal with life's wonderful and tragic realities.

The Wilbers were both dedicated practicing Buddhists (with one of Treya's main teachers being Goenka, a vipassana, or insight meditation master), yet they always availed themselves of many wise teachers and teachings, a number of whom are wonderfully portrayed in the book *Grace and Grit* (1991). At one point, during the summer of 1986, Ken and Treya attended a very powerful and divine *darshan* occasion with Adi Da (then known as Da Love-Ananda) in northern California. That fall for four days in Boulder, Colorado, they both went to a very rare Vajrayana Buddhist ceremony, or Kalachakra empowerment, given by Kalu Rinpoche. There they realized, as Ken explains, "after taking one look at Kalu . . . we had found our teacher." Shortly afterward, they attended "a ten-day transmission of wisdom given by Kalu at Big Bear, outside Los Angeles," where the Rinpoche initiated Ken and Treya into *tonglen,* or "healing compassion" meditation, deity yoga, and other profound Tibetan tantras. When Terry turned forty on November 25, 1986, she changed her first name to Treya, inspired in part by the awesome Kalachakra empowerment where Kalu himself had named her Dakini Wind, which means "the wind of enlightenment."

Because Ken was diligently serving as Treya's primary support person during her intense bout with cancer and diabetes, he stopped writing for the time being, although he did help edit several books. Nonetheless, in the summer of 1987, during a brief remission of Treya's cancer, Wilber wrote an eight-hundred-page tome titled *The Great Chain of Being: A Modern Introduction to the Perennial Philosophy and the World's Great Mystical Traditions* (still unpublished), which, unfortunately, he's decided to shelve indefinitely, although some chapters have appeared as articles in various magazines.

In the couple of years following Treya's death, Ken compiled and wrote the highly successful personal testament titled *Grace and Grit: Spirituality and Healing in the Life and Death of Treya Killam Wilber* (Shambhala Publications, 1991). The phrase *Grace and Grit* was taken from her very last journal entry written just twenty-four hours before she passed away: "It takes grace—yes!—and grit." Although the book was credited solely to Ken, with Treya's blessings, it actually contains writings by both Ken and Treya, since she permitted him to use her journals to describe how they spent "five years fighting a losing battle with the disease [cancer], though in the process we both won our souls."

Interspersed with their intense personal story, there are also interviews and brief descriptions of Wilber's spectrum model, comments on the perennial philosophy, plus a few other topics that had appeared in his previous writings. *Grace and Grit* also provided valuable considerations centered on issues of health, including the popular essays "What Kind of Help Really Helps?" "Do We Make Ourselves Sick?" and "On Being a Support Person," all vital issues for the terminally ill. The overwhelming success of the book wonderfully attests to the fact that Treya's life story actually points to the Unborn and Undying Spirit. In her illness she learned to transcend death in the true Self, thus allowing countless others to gain strength and inspiration from her life of "passionate equanimity."

Despite the pain and loss of this period, Wilber came to find that his life experience with the "wound of love"[55] was indispensable for his further growth. Within a few years of Treya's death in 1989 and the subsequent publication of their popular coauthored memoir in 1991, the brilliant, more mature theorist was ready to explode back onto the scene, once again rocking the world of integral studies.

Jnana Yoga: "I'm a Pandit, Not a Guru!"

Wilber is especially lucid when it comes to reflecting spiritual or transpersonal matters, although regardless of his growing acclaim, he does not regard himself as a guru or spiritual teacher but rather as an intellectual practicing what's known in Hinduism as jnana yoga. In the spiritual tradition of India, intellectual wisdom or jnana yoga is often contrasted with devotional or bhakti yoga, although a truly integral spiritual practice would use both the mind (*jnana* or "wisdom") and the heart (*bhakti* or "devotion") in order to generate an enlightened disposition. As Wilber explained, "the way of jnana yoga is both a path to enlightenment and an expression of an already accomplished awakening."

In this case, Wilber's extraordinary insight and deep understanding of spirituality have led Huston Smith, the respected scholar of world religions, to qualify the American transpersonal pundit as a jnana yogi. Jnana yoga itself, Dr. Smith tells us, is a form of yoga that's "intended for spiritual aspirants who have a strong reflective bent, [it] is the path to oneness with the Godhead through knowledge."[56] Wilber explains further: "In the genuine path of the Jnana yogi, the intellect is servant, not master, and just there resides the strangest secret to the successful path of Jnana Yoga."[57] Wilber again clarified his intentions in *The Eye of Spirit,* recognizing the strengths and limitations of his powerful intellectual *philosophia:*

> When philosophy, or intellectual awareness in general, is highly focused on its own source (i.e., witnessing subjectivity, the pure self), then such philosophy can indeed begin to shade into jnana yoga, the yoga of using the mind to transcend the mind. By deeply, profoundly, uninterruptedly inquiring into the Witness of all knowledge, this specific type of philosophical inquiry opens onto contemplative awareness: the mind itself subsides in the vast expanse of primordial awareness, and *philosophia* gives way to *contemplatio.* Rare is the philosopher who uses the mind to transcend the mind.

Nonetheless, Wilber has no exaggerated illusions about his own abilities and gifts:

> I must say that I do not particularly think of myself as exclusively a jnana yogi. I've spent too many years—two decades actually—sitting in a meditation hall to think of myself as an intellectual yogi. But it has been my good fortune to find that when the intellect is polished until it becomes radiant and shining, it is a staunch defender of a Truth and Beauty that reaches quite far beyond its own capacities, and in that reach it serves its master [the Divine Spirit] more than faithfully.[58]

In this time-honored spiritual tradition, therefore, Wilber may perhaps be best described as a *pandit,* a Sanskrit word from which the English word *pundit*—defined as "a learned person"—derives its roots. In India, then, a *pandit* is more accurately seen as an intellectual scholar who's also a spiritual practitioner, only they have a special talent for the academic or intellectual paths, and so they exercise it. Wilber plainly states: "I am a pandit, not a guru, and I have made that clear from day one."

WILBER/PHASE 4. FOUR QUADRANTS & THE POSTMODERN CRITIQUE (1995–2000)

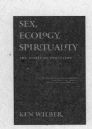

Wilber/Phase 4 emerged in full force in the mid-1990s with the publication of Wilber's magnum opus, *Sex, Ecology, Spirituality: The Spirit of Evolution* (Shambhala Publications, 1995), often shortened for convenience to *SES*. Michael Murphy, the founder of the Esalen Institute, claimed that "Along with Aurobindo's *Life Divine,* Heidegger's *Being and Time,* and Whitehead's *Process and Reality,* Wilber's *Sex, Ecology, Spirituality* is one of the four great books of the twentieth century." Benefiting from his personal growth since meeting and then losing Treya, and after three years of relentless research and tireless study, Wilber began publishing again in earnest, embarking upon his most prolific series of works since he had begun writing.

Wilber's reemergence began in the summer of 1991, after finishing the heart-wrenching *Grace and Grit,* with a series of pieces that appeared in the magazine *The Quest* in response to an interview Wilber gave titled "Sex, Gender, and Transcendence." This candid conversation generated a number of letters, especially from women, which Wilber answered in the following issues. Provoked by these exchanges and following upon his tribute to Treya, Wilber's daemon had returned at last and he was inspired to write. Initially, the integral theorist attempted to finish *System, Self, and Structure,* his oft-aborted textbook, but after writing a couple paragraphs he found it was full of currently unpopular terms such as "development, hierarchy, transcendental, universal." Therefore, once more, he set aside that perpetually stalled project and turned his attention to the sad state of academia that had arisen since his hiatus from publishing, especially the politically correctness of pluralistic relativism. This attempt to address the situation led Wilber to something like a traditional three-year silent retreat, a practice used in Buddhism as training to become a lama or spiritual adept. During this time he essentially lived a hermit's life, seeing only four people the whole time, one being his colleague Roger Walsh, who periodically stopped by to see if he was well.

One of the primary results of all this intensive research was Wilber's development of what's now known as the *four quadrants* although he admits, "There is nothing magical about the number four." These domains of existence or "quadrants" include the *inside* and *outside* of both *individual* and *collective* holons (defined as whole/parts). Technically these four are:

1. **Upper-Left:** individual subjective (intentional) interiors (first-person "I");

2. **Upper-Right:** individual objective (behavioral) exteriors (third-person "it");

3. **Lower-Left:** collective intersubjective (cultural) interiors (second-person "we");

4. **Lower-Right:** collective interobjective (social) exteriors (third-person "its").

This groundbreaking idea came to Wilber after making detailed comparisons of various hierarchical maps he had gathered together from many fields of study, everything from "conventional and new age, Eastern and Western, premodern and modern and postmodern . . . from systems theory to the Great Chain of Being, from the Buddhist vijnanas to Piaget, Marx, Kohlberg, the Vedantic koshas, Loevinger, Maslow, Lenski, Kabbalah, and so on."[59] At one time, he explains, "I had over two hundred hierarchies written out on legal pads lying all over the floor, trying to figure out how to fit them together." Suddenly, after intensely pondering the situation for months, he realized that instead of each map being a different version of the same hierarchy, they were actually *different* territories based on four different types of holistic sequences. In other words, "the various hierarchies fall into four major classes . . . [where] some of the hierarchies are referring to individuals, some to collectives; some are about exterior realities, some are about interior ones, but they all fit together seamlessly."[60] Once this breakthrough insight dawned on Wilber, then, as he says, "much of *Sex, Ecology, Spirituality* began to write itself," so that he produced over 2,500 pages within a three-month period.

Within a matter of months, the originally titled *The Spirit of Evolution: Cosmos, Bios, Psyche, Theos* had grown into three massive volumes with each one consisting of two complete books. These three huge tomes, each being more than eight hundred pages long, are tentatively titled *Kosmos,* or *The Kosmos Trilogy,* and are supported by a vast body of evidence covering thousands of books and hundreds of theorists (the footnotes alone would extend to two hundred pages per volume). Planning to release one volume a decade, Volume Two was originally titled *Sex, God, Gender: The Ecology of Men and Women* while Volume Three was to be called *The Spirit of Post/Modernity.* At the turn of the twenty-first century, at least, Wilber claimed they were both "on hold," although this schedule has recently been modified since Volume Three will now be published before Volume Two (see below).

When the first volume of this vast integral vision was published by Shambhala Publications in 1995, titled *Sex, Ecology, Spirituality: The Spirit of Evolution,* it quickly became the best-selling academic book in any category of that year. Indeed, Wilber's emergence from his ten-year hiatus created quite a stir. Wilber has found that this book has had a liberating effect on many people and on their view of the world, or Kosmos. He's grateful, but isn't surprised by this response because "*SES* is, after all, a story of the feats of your very own Self, and many readers rejoiced at that remembrance. . . . Apart from *Grace and Grit,* I have never received such heartfelt and deeply moving letters as I received from *SES,* letters that made those difficult three years seem more than worth it."[61]

Without any difficulty, each one of the two books in *SES* can stand on its own. Book One was initially titled *Spirit-In-Action,* for it's mostly about evolutionary development, and in it Wilber introduced and defined many of his important Phase 4 notions, such as the four quadrants, holons (or wholes that are parts of other wholes), holarchy (or nested hierarchies), the twenty tenets of evolution (or the patterns that connect), as well as reintroducing the original Greek spelling of Kosmos to indicate "the patterned nature or process of all domains of existence, i.e., from matter to mind to God, and not merely the physical universe [or 'cosmos' with a 'c']." Indeed, Wilber's entire integral system of Phase 4, blossoming fully into Phase 5's AQAL and postmetaphysical approach, has its epistemological roots in this giant philosophic masterpiece.

Book Two, on the other hand, was called *Flatland* because it is a strong polemic and philosophical critique of modern reductionism and scientific materialism, and, in particular, a stinging attack on "extreme postmodernism and pluralistic relativism."[62] In making his case, Wilber presents an in-depth philosophical critique of modernity and postmodernity, including a review of the "fractured footnotes to Plato," or the history of Western philosophy. It also introduces the differentiated "Big Three" of modernity (art, morals, and science;

or self, culture, and nature), as a way of defining and critiquing the competing paradigms of the Ego (atomistic) and the Eco (holistic) camps of modern thought. In place of a reductionistic flatland or "disqualified universe," Wilber offers his readers a "universal integralism," an integral vision that holistically honors all the levels, lines, states, and types, etc., within the great spectrum of consciousness, in both its inner/outer, singular/collective aspects. Yet, as always, by thoroughly acknowledging the ever-present nondual ground and condition of both consciousness and Kosmos, he gives us a model for an interacting, dynamic, evolving Great Nest of Spirit.

Wilber/Phase 4, therefore, brings forward all the principal themes of his previous phases: the evolutionary spectrum of consciousness model from the earlier Phase 1 and Phase 2, plus the integration of the basic levels (waves), developmental lines (streams), and self (from Phase 3). Now, however, in the twenty-first century, his work was more fully situated in the context of all four quadrants, which comprise the many faces or facets of the full-spectrum Kosmos. This AQAL approach of all-quadrants, all-levels, all-lines is Wilber's systematic attempt to include all the correlations between the "within" (or holonic interiors) and the "without" (or holonic exteriors) arising in a developmental or evolutionary dynamic. It is crucial, he insists, at least to include all of these elements and dynamics (or holons) in any comprehensive or integral synthesis of scientific and spiritual studies. And it's just this delineation that's having such a profound effect on many diverse fields ranging from politics to medicine, from business to education, from ecology to minorities outreach, and so on. Indeed, many of Wilber's most enthusiastic supporters are coming from some of the brightest minds and leaders in each field, many of whom are now associated with the Integral Institute, founded by Wilber to facilitate cross-fertilization among various integral pioneers and visionaries.

In the Wake of SES

Once Wilber returned to the scene of publishing in 1995 with *Sex, Ecology, Spirituality,* the prolific philosopher published at least one new book every year during the closing years of the twentieth century. He was now actively promoting integral studies or the AQAL approach commonly known as Wilber's "Integral Vision." His first book published in the wake of *SES,* released the next year in paperback only, was *A Brief History of Everything* (Shambhala Publications, 1996)—titled in a facetious nod to Stephen Hawking's immensely popular book *A Brief History of Time* (1988). This was Wilber's concerted attempt to offer a comprehensive yet shorter version of the lengthy and difficult *Sex, Ecology, Spirituality,* a tome that many people found quite daunting. Set in an interview format, the manuscript was initially compiled as a massive study guide to *SES,* but was subsequently reduced in scope; nonetheless, it still introduced a few unique ideas not found in its larger predecessor.

Philosophically, *Brief History* is especially critical of today's current academic cultural studies, strongly critiquing schools of thought from the positivistic rationalists to the many New Age ecophilosophers. Therefore, the book, as Wilber admits, makes a polemical attack on regressive flatland philosophies, including New Age holistic theories, that reduce (either grossly or subtly) the pluridimensional, multileveled Kosmos into a realm of material particles or "it-exteriors" scattering about by chance, even if they're holistically perceived as being an interacting "web of life." Nonetheless, Wilber's overall tone emphasizes a compassionate embrace coupled with a wise transcendence, all in order to present a genuine integral approach to, well, everything.

Beginning in January, a public conference called "Ken Wilber and the Future of Transpersonal Inquiry: A Conversation" was sponsored by and held at the California Institute of Integral Studies (CIIS) in San Francisco. Participants gathered from around the world to meet with the conference leaders, who were the editors and authors of a three-issue series of *ReVision* articles that had appeared in 1996 critiquing Wilber's recent work and impact on transpersonal psychology. The general response from the people attending was very positive yet they were somewhat surprised by the critical tone of the conference leaders. Unfortunately, much of the panel's criticism was based on a misunderstanding of Wilber's broad scope of work, often concentrating on the more linear Wilber/Phase 2 models (*The Atman Project* and *Up From Eden*). Thus, overall, the critics failed to fully grasp and appreciate the full integral vision revealed not only with *SES* but also with each succeeding book.

The critical reviews of *ReVision* also resulted in the book *Ken Wilber in Dialogue: Conversations with Leading Transpersonal Thinkers* (1998, Quest Books), edited by Donald Rothberg and Sean Kelly, including essays written by some of Wilber's critics, as well as his own responses. Although Wilber was grateful that "*ReVision* went out of its way to make ample room for my response," he nevertheless was truly disappointed in this presentation since, as he explains, "quite a few of them distorted my work in significant and extensive ways." Dr. Donald Beck of Spiral Dynamics, after doing a detailed analysis noting the critics' distortions of Wilber's actual views, stated that *Ken Wilber in Dialogue* "is a model of how to treat a scholar unfairly."[63]

Around the same time as the CIIS conference, Shambhala published *The Eye of Spirit: An Integral Vision for a World Gone Slightly Mad* (Shambhala Publications, 1997) because it presented some of Wilber's specific answers to his critics, often focusing on the misrepresentations made in the 1996 *ReVision* articles. By even further delineating the integral vision (including an insightful foreword by Jack Crittenden titled "What Is the Meaning of 'Integral'?"), Wilber set out to appraise "today's world of modernity gone slightly mad: myth for the peasants, flatland naturalism for the intelligentsia," as stated in one of *SES*'s last lines. Interestingly, *The Eye of Spirit* also provides an overview of Wilber's own work by introducing the so-called four phases of his career, or Phases 1–4. Nevertheless, as he carefully explains, "the works of these phases form a fairly coherent whole. It is not so much that one period was rejected and replaced by its successor, but that the works of each period remain, in my opinion, largely valid, and the succeeding works simply add new material, not erase old."

The essays of *The Eye of Spirit* include an in-depth scholarly treatment of the AQAL approach to integral studies that Wilber was fashioning at the time, while also providing a profound critical theory for integral analysis. The book again placed a heavy emphasis on the transitional *developmental lines* (or streams) that develop or co-evolve through the *basic structures* (or waves) of the Kosmos, all being navigated by *the self* (or self-system), the separative sense of "I," or the ego. Because many of his critics seem to bypass the ten-year Wilber/Phase 3 period of levels and lines, he continued with these masterful essays to strongly refute the linear criticism that often stems from those critics who focus on the earlier Phase 2 writings, especially *Atman* and *Eden* (which, as we've seen, placed more of an emphasis on the structures of consciousness). *The Eye of Spirit,* then, besides offering Wilber's precise and beautiful prose, is basically a theoretical review of his earlier phases with a Phase 4 update of his psychological spectrum model and his previous concerns; thus he tell us, "In some ways this is one of my favorite books."

One Taste of Sense and Soul

Within the first months of 1997, Wilber also traveled to New York City, a rare event for the reclusive philosopher, in order to seek out another publisher (with Shambhala's blessings) for a concise book he had written during the last months of 1996. Originally titled *The Marriage of Science and Religion: The Union of Ancient Wisdom and Modern Knowledge,* he was encouraged by Random House to rename it based on the epigram he had used from Oscar Wilde: "There is nothing that will cure the senses but the soul, and nothing that will cure the soul but the senses." This book, consequently retitled *The Marriage of Sense and Soul: Integrating Science and Religion* (Random House, 1998), was released the following spring as a terse philosophical argument that attempted to bridge the gap between modern science and premodern religion. Importantly, it was intended to reach a larger audience of orthodox and mainstream religious and scientific communities, not just the New Age, new-paradigm crowd. Apparently *The Marriage of Sense and Soul* was a success, for it was reviewed widely by the mainstream press and its readership extended to the highest political offices of the United States, being read by then-president Bill Clinton and Vice President Al Gore, who enthusiastically announced as much to the press. Indeed, Wilber's work has become involved in a bold attempt to help articulate a "Third Way" politics that "unites the best of liberal and conservative" approaches by transcending yet including the traditional battlelines.

In the mid-1990s Wilber's original publisher, Quest Books in Wheaton, Illinois, reissued new versions of his earlier trilogy, i.e., a twentieth-anniversary edition of *The Spectrum of Consciousness* (released in 1993), plus reprint editions with new photographic covers of *The Atman Project* and *Up From Eden* (both released in 1996). In conjunction with these rereleases, Shambhala also put out a new paperback version of *Eye to Eye* (1997). Each book contained a new and insightful introduction by Wilber reflecting back on his earlier works and their current viability, all of which are now included in the *Collected Works*.

The following spring, *One Taste: The Journals of Ken Wilber* (Shambhala Publications, 1999), subtitled *Daily Reflections on Integral Spirituality* (appearing on the paperback version), allowed the fifty-year-old philosopher to present his own personal insights on how the integral perspective is actually *lived,* at least in the context of one year in his own life. Wilber's primary reason for doing so, he explains in the book, was because "As one who has written extensively about the interior life, it seemed appropriate, at some point, to share mine." In addition, the longtime meditator wanted to focus on "a detailed journal of my own meditation and spiritual practices; and a type of philosophical journal, or a chronicle of some of the ideas that I felt were most appropriate as they unfolded in my own case," thus demonstrating, again, "the importance of meditation as part of an integral practice." As a result, Wilber reports that numerous people have written him saying that *One Taste* inspired them either to take up meditation or to further deepen their practice, which, according to him, is probably the highest compliment he can receive.

"One Taste" is itself a Tantric Buddhist phrase, as Wilber explains, which points to the unified awareness of nondual mysticism, since it refers to "the experience of One Taste, where every single thing and event in the Kosmos, high or low, sacred and profane, has the same taste, the same flavor, and the flavor is Divine." During the three-year writing retreat that would lead to *Sex, Ecology, Spirituality* (and *The Kosmos Trilogy*), especially during an eleven-day period in 1994, Wilber experienced this "One Taste awareness" most profoundly and lucidly. He describes this spiritual transformation in *One Taste:*

march 23

> . . . during a very intense 11-day period—in which the separate-self seemed to radically, deeply, thoroughly die—it all seemed to come to fruition. I slept not at all during those 11 days; or rather, I was conscious for 11 days and nights, even as the body and mind went through waking, dreaming, and sleeping: I was unmoved in the midst of changes; there was no I to be moved; there was only unwavering empty consciousness, the luminous mirror-mind, the witness that was one with everything witnessed. I simply reverted to what I am, and it has been so, more or less, ever since. . . .
>
> Once you find your formless identity as Buddha-mind, as Atman, as pure Spirit or Godhead, you will take that constant, nondual, ever-present consciousness and re-enter the lesser states, subtle mind and gross body, and re-animate them with radiance. You will not remain merely Formless and Empty. You will Empty yourself of Emptiness: you will pour yourself out into the mind and world, and create them in the process, and enter them all equally, but especially and particularly that specific mind and body that is called you (that is called, in my case, Ken Wilber); this lesser self will become the vehicle of the Spirit that you are.

This divine One Taste of nondual reality allowed the integral philosopher to explain: "From One Taste all things issue, to One Taste all things return—and in between, which is the story of this moment, there is only the dream, and sometimes the nightmare, from which we would do well to awaken."

The Essential Works of Ken Wilber

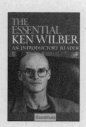

In the fall of 1998, Wilber's longtime editor at Shambhala Publications, Kendra Crossen Burroughs, with a short and concise book titled *The Essential Ken Wilber* (Shambhala Publications, 1998), offered a selection of "nontechnical passages that impart the essence and flavor of Wilber's writings and that touch on his major concerns." This less than two-hundred-page compilation is an excellent introductory volume, offering Wilber's poetic and mystical musings, which evidence not only an integral vision of the Kosmos but an enlightened disposition toward its spiritual transcendence.

A year later, after a period of meticulous preparation also led by Crossen Burroughs, Shambhala Publications proudly presented *The Collected Works of Ken Wilber, Volumes One–Eight* (Shambhala Publications, 1999, 2000)—often called simply *CW*—in order to satisfy the demand for Wilber's books and writings, which has always been steady. In the autumn of 1999 the first four volumes, ranging from *The Spectrum of Consciousness* through *Transformations of Consciousness,*

were published in beautifully crafted brown hardcover books. The following spring, in the new millennium of 2000, the next four volumes were released, including *Grace and Grit* and new revised editions of *Sex, Ecology, Spirituality, A Brief History of Everything,* and *The Eye of Spirit,* plus other late-1990s Wilber/Phase 4 publications, including important journal articles and published interviews. This magnificent hardbound set, containing all of his primary books, many of his published articles, essays, interviews, and book forewords, gave Wilber the rare honor of being one of the only psychologists or philosophers to have their collected works published while still alive, let alone by the time one is fifty!

Importantly, Volume Four of the *Collected Works,* which contains many selected essays and book forewords, also includes two unpublished books (with one, *Integral Psychology,* published as a paperback the following year). The first unpublished gem was another concise book written in 1983, around the same time and in the same direct style as *A Sociable God.* Originally tagged *Reply to Critics,* since it was a response to a private paper being circulated by Dick Anthony, it was later renamed *Sociocultural Evolution* for inclusion in this volume.

The other crucial book embedded in the treasure chest of Volume Four was the premiere of one of Wilber's most important books yet to be published, for it clearly summarizes most of his principal theories and definitions of his psychology and philosophy in approximately two hundred brilliant pages. *Integral Psychology: Consciousness, Spirit, Psychology, Therapy* (1999, 2000) was feverishly written in just over a month during the spring of 1999. It was another updated version of the still-as-yet unpublished textbook *System, Self, and Structure,* frequently mentioned in *Transformations of Consciousness,* as we've noted. After first debuting a half year earlier in Volume Four of *The Collected Works of Ken Wilber, Integral Psychology* was released as a single-volume paperback in the spring of 2000. This lucid treatise is, as Wilber explains, "at this time the definitive statement of my general psychological model, and my other writings in the field should be coordinated with its views."

With this extremely well crafted book, Wilber has succinctly summarized not only his psychological theories but also his philosophical positions regarding premodernity, modernity, and the great quest or bright promise of postmodernity, which is to recover from the flatland disaster of modernity (including scientific materialism) and postmodernity's regressive slide into deconstructive nihilism. In response, Wilber's position offers a post-postmodern philosophy, or at least a "constructive postmodernity"—actually, an integral vision—which generously embraces "all-quadrants, all-levels, all-lines, all-states, all-types" or an AQAL approach that may be adequately applied to literally everything, from consciousness studies to marketplace business, from international politics to science (and system sciences), from ecophilosophy to gender studies, from mythic religion to authentic spirituality. In fact, this is exactly why *Integral Psychology* was quickly followed by an even more concise book, *A Theory of Everything,* addressing these same issues.

Another one of *Integral Psychology*'s outstanding features, other than being a work of highly developed Wilber/Phase 4 writing (even essentially, some students have noticed, the first Wilber/Phase 5 book) that presents a fully developed AQAL approach, was that it contains numerous detailed correlative charts (see Appendix 1). These eleven charts were compiled by Wilber himself as he cross-referenced more than a hundred other developmental theorists, all of whom, to varying degrees, recognized the same basic developmental structures or waves in the Great Nest of Being. These clearly correlated charts are a wonderful way to get a good reading of Wilber's full-spectrum, all-quadrant integral model. Therefore, again, we see that Wilber's integral studies and integral vision attempt to honor and embrace every legitimate aspect and enterprise of human consciousness in all four quadrants, thus helping to give humanity a truly comprehensive map of the human mind (epistemology) and of the divine Kosmos (ontology) expressed here as the Great Nest of Being and Knowing. Or as he so eloquently and matter-of-factly suggests: "An integral approach—a sane approach—attempts to honor, acknowledge, and incorporate the enduring truths into the ongoing sweep of consciousness evolution, for they are the truths of our very own Self, even here and now."[64]

The end of 2000 saw the release of another short overview book titled *A Theory of Everything: An Integral Vision for Business, Politics, Science, and Spirituality* (Shambhala Publications, 2000), often abbreviated as *TOE.* This book further extends Wilber's involvement with "Spiral Dynamics," a pragmatic method of social transformation based on the work of Clare Graves, Don Beck, and Christopher Cowan, which is also in general alignment with Wilber's spectrum theories, at least up to the transpersonal stages. Yet, in addition, this accessible book explains why Wilber's integral vision is having such a broad appeal to, and is influencing, many of today's more interesting advances in mind/body medicine, cognitive science, Third Way politics, organization theory, and a host of other fields. In this book Wilber explains how his groundbreaking AQAL approach can be applied in a number of vital domains, including addressing some of today's hot-button issues: Boomeritis: The Promise and Problems of the Me Generation; Can Science and Religion Get Along?; Third Way Politics: Moving Beyond the Left and Right; Postmodern Hypocrisy; Health Care for the Whole Person; The Human Consciousness Project.[65]

Once more we see Wilber promoting his ambitious project—the integral embrace—to bring together science, morals, and aesthetics, Eastern in addition to Western, premodern, modern, and postmodern, as well as including the enlightened wisdom of the world's great contemplative traditions. Drawing inspiration from the attempt by contemporary physics to unite all the physical laws of the universe into a single unified model—or a T.O.E. (a theory of everything)—and the growing field of evolutionary psychology, of which Wilber is a pioneer, he offers his own daring attempt by defining and declaring that an integral vision, or a genuine Theory of Everything, "attempts to include matter, body, mind, soul, and spirit as they appear in self, culture, and nature. A vision that attempts to be comprehensive, balanced, inclusive." In other words, as the integral philosopher contends, "a little bit of wholeness is better than none. An integral vision invites us to be a little more whole, a little less fragmented in our work, our lives, our destiny."

TOE was originally intended as a companion to *Boomeritis,* since it presents his strong critique of scientific materialism and "boomeritis," or the "mean green meme," whose worldview has dominated academia during the past couple of decades. As an alternative, an integral approach offers "a four-quadrant epistemology [that] steers between mere objectivism and mere subjectivism by finding room for an inherent balance of those partial truths." Therefore, in the end, Wilber's principle motivation is perhaps best summarized thus:

> The Greeks had a beautiful word, *Kosmos,* which means the patterned Whole of all existence, including the physical, emotional, mental, and spiritual realms. Ultimate reality was not merely the cosmos, or the physical dimension, but the Kosmos, or the physical and emotional and mental and spiritual dimensions altogether. Not just matter, lifeless and insentient, but the living Totality of matter, body, mind, soul, and spirit. The Kosmos!—now there is a real theory of everything!

Another volume conceived around the turn of the twenty-first century, and one that's currently on hold mostly due to coordinating the overwhelmingly large number of contributions, is *Kindred Visions: Ken Wilber and Other Leading Integral Thinkers,* which is being edited by Jack Crittenden. This collection of appreciative essays, written by other transpersonal/integral theorists reviewing Wilber's work and influence,[66] contains thousands of pages penned by many notable contributors, even by some of his more vocal critics. Yet they're all united in one voice to praise the independent theorist who's so dramatically affected the field of transpersonal and integral studies while blazing a new trail of universal integralism in the process.

The Integral Institute

In the summer of 2000, Wilber, who was already extremely busy, with some financial backing contributed by numerous supporters embarked on the founding of the Integral Institute or I-I.[67] I-I is a nonprofit organization designed to help finance and support the growing network of numerous integral theorists now working in various fields and who are having an important impact on their professions. The main emphasis, therefore, is in *application* of the integral vision, based upon an integral operating system (IOS), thus demonstrating in practice the veracity of its comprehensive, intellectual theories. Wilber specifically defines the Integral Institute as being "dedicated to the integration of body, mind, soul, and spirit in self, culture, and nature," therefore it intends "to honor and integrate the largest amount of research from the greatest number of disciplines." It will act as a networking center, an information clearing house, even a grant foundation for the growing number of integral researchers and theorists from around the world.

The Integral Institute has numerous branches specializing in the various fields of human knowledge, such as the Institute of Integral Psychology, the Institute of Integral Politics, the Institute of Integral Business, the Institute of Integral Medicine, and so on. Wilber likes to picture them as spokes on a wheel with the center hub, the Integral Institute, acting as a multidimensional feedback dynamism so that each of the branches are giving and receiving research from all of the others. One of the projects that members of I-I are working on, for example, is an *Encyclopedia of Human Transformation,* in which they're literally reviewing all of the methods of transformation available for human beings, thus imparting effective techniques for positive human change and growth. With a board of directors, over four hundred founding members in the various branches, and affiliates composed of friends and associates, the Integral Institute is a growing gathering of those people who want to apply the AQAL, or all-quadrant, all-level, all-line, approach to their particular field of research and study.

Intended to act as a vehicle of integral influence on the major institutions of politics, business, science, medicine, and higher education, I-I and its sister project, Integral University (IU), will make a strong case, initially through a series of well-defined academic textbooks and multimedia presentations, to help our society embrace a more integral AQAL approach. Thus I-I will be a vanguard organization representing a fully developed second-tier or integral position in the global culture. Indeed, Wilber maintains, it should be one of the primary tasks of second-tier people to get together and translate their integral awareness into institutional forms. In this way, I-I will be, ideally, only one among many integral lights shining in a world fraught with regressive premodern Romanticism, materialistic modern madness, and dreary postmodern darkness, thus leading us to a more embracing present and brighter future.

Boomeritis: Baby-Boomer Narcissism and the Perfect Postmodern Novel

As a unique event in Wilber's twenty-five-year writing career, in the summer of 2002 he published his first novel, a fictionalized critique of postmodernism titled *Boomeritis: A Novel That Will Set You Free* (Shambhala Publications, 2002). As a psychological term coined by Wilber's integral psychology, *boomeritis* is defined as a dysfunctional narcissism rampant in the "green meme" or the "sensitive self," and it is epitomized by a large section of the Baby Boomer generation although anyone can suffer from it, including Wilber himself. The novel is an attempt to summarize his Wilber/Phase 4 views on postmodernism, both its positive and negative or extreme aspects, as well as encapsulating his evolutionary model cast in the terminology of Spiral Dynamics, which uses color memes to represent the various worldviews of development. The manuscript began as a critique of extreme postmodernism, backed with volumes of meticulous research, but its critical tone soon convinced Wilber to change it into a more engaging narrative. Although the 450-page novel is cloaked in his Wilber/Phase 2, or "growth-to-goodness," model of evolutionary development in order to more easily appeal to a general audience, he has subsequently supported it with 150 pages of academic endnotes and over 400 pages of sidebars and postscripts posted on www.wilber.shamabhala.com. He has done this in an attempt to further document his current AQAL approach to human knowledge, as opposed to just the stage-level model of Wilber/Phase 2.

Since the novel is set amidst a series of lectures conducted in the Integral Center located at Harvard, as well as being intertwined with a kaleidoscopic series of fantasy vignettes, Wilber is able to cleverly and clearly present the different memes (or worldviews) of the spectrum of consciousness while simultaneously aiming a powerful critique at the culture of narcissism thriving among his own generation. Naturally, the author expects to provoke strong reactions from all quarters.

By citing the recent work of numerous researchers in human development and the social sciences, the novel unfolds as an outrageous narrative centered around Gen-Xers and Millennials, which is filled with lively and obnoxious characters, from silly students to sophisticated professors, from sexual fantasies to cosmic experiences, from rock stars to boomer parents. Yet, within its pages Wilber also summarizes his integral theories and especially his critique of postmodern thought, which he's presented in the various Wilber/Phase 4 books since 1995, including *Sex, Ecology, Spirituality* (especially Book Two), *The Eye of Spirit, The Marriage of*

Sense and Soul, and particularly *Integral Psychology* and *A Theory of Everything* (itself a tongue-in-cheek boomeritis title).

Integral or AQAL philosophy strongly critiques the pluralistic relativism and subjective narcissism that's running rampant throughout academia and New Age theories. These theories, even if ostensibly holistic, are often filled with reductionistic tendencies in order to assuage the modern ego, thus they're most aggressively and emotionally supported by aging baby boomers, who can be characterized as the "green meme" or "sensitive self," in the terminology of Spiral Dynamics. By honoring the "many gifts of green," such as its multiculturalism and pluralistic sensitivity, Wilber identifies what it will take to overcome boomeritis, or the extreme forms of the mean green meme. As he explains, only the integral approach can achieve a true embrace of mutual recognition and respect among *all* the world's people, from tribes to nations to international corporations to free "worldcentric" individuals. Thus, one of Wilber's main tasks in writing a postmodern novel that appeals to the larger society is to help push these well-intended yet misguided "greens" toward the next level of "yellow and turquoise," or what's now known as second-tier thinking, or integral consciousness. Indeed, in an introduction to his recently released *Collected Works,* Volume Seven, he explained his intentions explicitly:

> [This is] exactly what I believe is the central issue for spiritual and integral studies at the millennium: we will remain stuck in the green meme—with both its wonderful contributions (e.g., pluralistic sensitivity) and its pathologies (e.g., boomeritis). Or we will make the leap to the hyperspace of second-tier consciousness, and thus stand open to even further evolution into the transpersonal waves of Spirit's own Self-realization.

Since many of the people reading *Boomeritis* will already be green-oriented thinkers, Wilber found it useful to loosely construct the narrative like a therapy session, in an attempt to encourage the reader to look at his or her own identification with the unhealthy green meme. However, instead of playing out the postmodern ploy of endless deconstruction, Wilber is offering a constructive postmodernism that integrates its positive aspects while criticizing "the extreme and deconstructive postmodernism that, bereft of second-tier integral consciousness, lets pluralism run riot as the mean green meme." This approach, therefore, should help boomers (and any others) to release green's negative aspects and move beyond the flatland pluralism and endless irony of postmodernism and into the integralism of the more evolved second-tier consciousness—and eventually into the authentic spirituality of third-tier or transpersonal awareness. In the end, we discover, the third tier is seen as an Omega Point for further evolution, both collectively and individually. Nonetheless, as in all of Wilber's books, he still maintains the paradoxical notion that the clarity of timeless and ever-present awareness can never be reached through any sort of development or evolution in the world of time. In other words, while Wilber's diagnosis of the current malaise is boomeritis, his prognosis is a more integral future. He continues to claim that beyond today's ailing world, and the illusions of the separate self, there "always already" exists the liberating freedom of the radiant Divine itself.

WILBER/PHASE 5. INTEGRAL AQAL APPROACH (NEW MILLENNIUM)

With the appearance of *Integral Psychology* and *A Theory of Everything* at the turn of the new millennium as well as *Boomeritis,* Wilber is extending his integral model and theory of everything even further into the realm pragmatic applications, moving from intellectual theories based on empirical evidence into the world of real economics, education, medicine, business, academia, international corporations, and even realpolitik. And he's doing this with the helping hand of other integral thinkers, visionaries, students, and associates.

Significantly, by founding the Integral Institute and its corollary, Integral University (IU), Wilber's work has blossomed into a creative collaboration with renowned individuals, many of whom are leaders or significant contributors in their respective fields. This includes a plethora of researchers, authors, artists, professors, psychologists, business people, political parties, and others, all of whom have been motivated by Wilber's integral vision to such a degree that they're directly applying his theories in their own work. Hence, during the opening years of the new millennium, Wilber has hosted numerous meetings, usually at his Boulder house, to discuss, finance, and plan the best way to implement the integral vision into the world at large. The initial task through IU is to target higher education, thus providing integral textbooks for universities and students. These meetings with some of the brightest minds in the business have inspired Wilber to further reformulate his integral vision into an even clearer postmetaphysical statement that fully utilizes the AQAL approach to integral studies in general.

The full-spectrum model of consciousness development (Upper-Left quadrant) that debuted with *The Spectrum of Consciousness* (1977), was more fully developed in the four-quadrant emphasis of Wilber/Phase 4, introduced nearly twenty years later with *Sex, Ecology, Spirituality* (1995) and articulated in detail with the next six books. Now, moving into the twenty-first century, Wilber has produced and is actively utilizing an "integral methodological pluralism," which allows an approach that integrates both the developmental "insides" and "outsides" of the Kosmos and their correlative interaction with both individuals and the collective. For example, in his twentieth-century Phase 4 writings Wilber introduced the notion of a Human Consciousness Project that intends to produce "a cross-cultural mapping of all of the states, structures, memes, types, levels, stages, and waves of human consciousness. This overall map . . . then becomes the psychological component of a possible Theory of Everything, where it will be supplemented with findings from the physical, biological, cultural, and spiritual dimensions."[68] Therefore, within the first few years of the twenty-first century, Wilber appears to have entered an even more mature phase based upon his unique articulation and presentation of an integral postmetaphysics and its corollary of integral methodological pluralism. Indeed, after some initial resistance to labeling it Phase 5 in response to the suggestion of some of his students, the integral philosopher has conceded that his work has entered another stage labeled (only as a convention) Phase 5 or Wilber/Phase 5. It exceeds the capacity of this review book, which is necessarily limited to covering only his first twenty-five years, right up to the beginning of the new millennium.

Currently, this type of massive project is under way with the cross-pollination of numerous pragmatic ideas gathered from the four hundred-some members of the Integral Institute. In this case, Wilber continues to upgrade his AQAL model by giving people in different fields of study a "holonic indexing system," based on a cross-level analysis, which in turn can run a critical analysis using an integral critical theory derived from a full-spectrum, all-quadrant perspective. Implementing this type of integral operating system (IOS), Wilber then proposes that researchers within their respective fields focus their attention by specializing in a quadrant-specific inquiry, yet they're still operating within the overall paradigm. This approach avoids either the repression or dominance of any one level or meme (or color) over any of the others in the spectral rainbow of existence.

As we've already seen in the twentieth century's Phase 4, this approach allows easy recognition of the four basic dimensions or quadrants of "I, We, It, and Its." These all exist within the AQAL matrix of all-levels, all-lines, all-states, or, as we've seen, within the Great Nest of Spirit. As Wilber points out, these four dimensions are universally found in all human languages as first-person ("I"), second-person ("we"), and third-person ("it") pronouns, thus this differentiation permits a more integral accounting of all the various subjective, intersubjective, and interobjective aspects of life and existence. Again, one of the main features emphasized by Wilber's integral stance, as we saw, is to not marginalize or repress, or absolutize and unduly privilege any level or quadrant—a common theme running throughout his collected oeuvre. This position is just another translation, independently derived, of Spiral Dynamics, which proposes: "The health of the entire spiral is the prime directive, not preferential treatment for any one level."

In Wilber's integral model, the wave of consciousness that expresses this type of tolerant moral position is generated from and associated with postconventional "vision-logic" or the "integral-centaur" stage of development. The centaur,[69] as Wilber explains, generally corresponds with Spiral Dynamics' second-tier thinking, which is also the yellow and turquoise memes of development. In fact, as just one other example, Wilber's profound and far-reaching influence has even inspired one of Spiral Dynamics' principle pioneers, Dr. Donald Beck, to evolve and expand his original model, based on the work of Clare Graves, to more accurately embrace the four-quadrant approach. In a perceptive move, Beck has suggested a 4Q/8L (or four-quadrant, eight-level) model which he now calls Spiral Dynamics integral or SD*i*.

Another vital theme that Wilber continues to emphasize in this twenty-first century AQAL phase is the full integration of the great premodern wisdom traditions, including religion in general, with the reality of modernity, or the "naturalistic [scientific] turn of the modern traditions," all embraced within an appreciative understanding of postmodernity or the "linguistic turn of the postmodern traditions." Such a theory of everything is precisely Wilber's stated integral mission: "For a genuine T.O.E., I believe we need a judicious blend of the best of premodern, modern, and postmodern, which is the explicit task of *SES* and all post-*SES* books." This bold integral task, as always, is an attempt to respect and acknowledge and embrace all the traditions of world history by finding a way to rightly honor each, yet without favoring any of them or elevating any one to superior status. Therefore, as the integral vision unfolds in the new millennium, it comprehensively integrates all the schools of philosophy, East and West, ancient and modern, by offering a post-postmodern *philosophia,* or a full-spectrum, all-quadrant integral approach to research and knowledge, yet also, one that's grounded in authentic mystical insight and wisdom.

The AQAL model and its pragmatic applications are therefore attempting to heal the split between premodern metaphysics and the modern deconstruction of metaphysical truths, as well as addressing postmodernity's nihilistic slide into relative pluralism and egoic narcissism (or boomeritis). Instead of positing *a priori* "realities" that must be discovered and regarded as ontologically real, Wilber's post-postmodernism, or integral pluralism, includes the critical postmodern insight that clearly recognizes the vital role played by the subjective interpretation of objective realities and histories. This type of constructive postmodernism, countering extreme forms of deconstructionism, permits Wilber to predict: "We are truly entering a post-postmodern, post-pluralistic world—by any other name, integral. . . .

With every passing year, a universal integralism becomes more and more welcome." In this way, integral philosophy becomes a light shining a way out of the confusion of the modern mind, and yet, ultimately, it also beams the illumination of liberation directly from the Clear Light Void or the heart of God itself.

In his own way, then, by trying to embrace and include as much human knowledge collected from as many different eras of history as possible, Wilber's post-Kantian, postmetaphysical philosophy acknowledges the necessity to integrate epistemology with ontology. These are sometimes described as the Great Nest of Being and Knowing. Wilber fully recognizes their interdependent unity, yet he also incorporates the differentiation of these aspects of reality. Yet, in the end, both existence and consciousness are best understood as the "One Taste" of divine Spirit. Today, by thoroughly understanding and mastering the ideas of the great philosophers who came before him, perhaps more broadly than any other individual, Wilber is involved in a sustained attempt to establish such a post-Kantian integral philosophy. Whether such a noble enterprise succeeds or not remains to be seen.

The twenty-first-century AQAL metatheory, therefore, presents a sophisticated method of differentiating yet integrating all the various levels and lines, states and quadrants of the entire spectrum of consciousness, exhibiting both interior (subjective) and exterior (objective) correlates intertwined with the intersubjective and interobjective dimensions of the Kosmos. Also termed the holonic approach, the AQAL system holds that all holons (or whole/parts) arising within the four quadrants interact or evolve in a spiraling, complex, dynamic process of developmental evolution. Yet it's also a holistic system of Spirit-in-action introducing novelty and miraculous creativity set within a "morphogenetic field or developmental space"[70] of evolving Kosmic habits[71] or the deep patterns manifesting as the AQAL matrix. Or from an even more enlightened perspective, it's nothing more than the divinely radiant Nest of Spirit, the transcendent Kosmic Mandala.

All of these ideas, and many more, are being expounded in detail and depth in Wilber's recent writings. They're not only influencing the members of the Integral Institute as they prepare to move out into the larger sociopolitical sphere with a global outreach program but the books also touch and move countless readers around the world, having been translated into over thirty languages.

Even as this review book goes into production, Wilber has already completed other new books, which are being prepared for future publication. With the appearance of the novel *Boomeritis* in the summer of 2002, the integral philosopher completed Volume Three of *The Kosmos Trilogy* before Volume Two, thus reversing their scheduled order. The current Volume Two is now tentatively titled *Kosmic Karma and Creativity*, although he doubts that this title will be used (excerpts have already been posted on the Shambhala Web site). This huge volume, weighing in at around a thousand pages, is a sustained defense of Wilber's AQAL position high-lighting his strong critique of extreme postmodernism and the "mean green meme." Thus, since Wilber felt he needed to further document his exhaustive research regarding premodernity, modernity, and postmodernity, the "second" volume of *The Kosmos Trilogy* began to write itself—a sure sign that a book needs to be born. In it he intends to further elaborate an integral postmetaphysics and its corollary, an integral methodological pluralism.

This type of development is only natural, for Wilber's philosophy will always continue to evolve and expand, being a dynamic living process itself. This is especially true as he continues to coordinate his worldwide interaction with other researchers and their important work, absorbing their comments and critiques, extending himself to accommodate their interpretations and to further clarify his intentions.

No doubt given such a prolific output generated during nearly three decades of writing, Wilber is sure to publish even more books and papers. Ideally, they'll stretch far into the new millennium, possibly even dwarfing what has already appeared. We can only hope so, for thus far Wilber's philosophical system has proven to be of inestimable value. Wilber's writings can be seen as the work of Spirit-in-action thus inspiring us all to keep evolving, to keep on moving, keep on compassionately and lovingly embracing reality yet transcending it all in Spirit. Mostly, therefore, Wilber's integral vision reminds us to free ourselves from the strictures of chronological time, to undo the chains of history by embracing yet transcending the wheel of evolution in the radiant emptiness of the infinite and eternal divine—your "always already" Original Face—which itself, as Spirit, is dynamically alive as this amazing display of the holy Kosmic Mandala or Great Nest of Spirit.

The Mystical Cookbook

The only good function of a book on Zen should be to persuade the reader to engage in zazen (meditative practice).

In the same way, the only major purpose of a book on mysticism should be to persuade the reader to engage in mystical practice.

It is precisely like a cookbook: You give recipes and invite the reader to go out and perform the recipe, actually do it, and then taste the results. You are not supposed merely to learn the recipes, memorize the recipes, and then claim you're a cook.

—Ken Wilber, *Eye to Eye*

Teach like a cook, gives recipes stated, and invite the reader to go out & perform the recipe, actually do and the task the results.

THE SPECTRUM OF
CONSCIOUSNESS
(1973–1977)

The Spectrum of Consciousness

BY KEN WILBER

(Wheaton, Ill.: Quest Books, 1977);

reprint 20th Anniversary Edition edition (Quest Books, 1993);

The Collected Works of Ken Wilber, Vol. 1 (CW1) (Boston: Shambhala Publications, 1999)

Preface

The Spectrum of Consciousness (1977) is a "Romantic" Wilber/Phase 1 work emphasizing the integration of Western psychology with Eastern mysticism, focusing primarily on individual interior consciousness (Upper-Left quadrant), yet without a complete pre/trans developmental understanding.

Wilber first wrote the book "in [his] head" during the winter of 1972 while still a biochemistry graduate student at the University of Nebraska in Lincoln, Nebraska; the following winter of 1973, it was hand-written in about three months, yet it took nine months to complete one typing by the fall of 1974. The manuscript was then solicited to author and noetic researcher John White who, with strong support from psychotherapist Jim Fadiman (president of the Transpersonal Psychology Association), submitted it to nearly three dozen publishing houses over the next three years before it was finally accepted and published by Quest Books. It was published in 1977 (A Quest Book, an imprint of The Theosophical Publishing House); in 1993 Quest Books produced a twentieth-anniversary edition with a new Preface by Wilber and Foreword by John White; it is now part of *The Collected Works of Ken Wilber, Volume One* (CW1) (Shambhala Publications, 1999).

The **PREFACE** begins with a quote from the venerable philosopher Frithjof Schuon explaining the book's primary theme: *"There is no science of the soul without a metaphysical basis to it and without spiritual remedies at its disposal."* Thus Ken Wilber tells us that this insight will be the aim of this volume, as well as being a summary "statement that the siddhas, sages and masters of everywhere and everywhen have eloquently embodied."

In the opening paragraph, therefore, Wilber placed his work within the context of the *"perennial philosophy"* (in Latin, *philosophia perennis*) and the wisdom of the enlightenment traditions and the enlightened sages who are their source. As he does so, he combats the reductionism of science and the modern world. Nonetheless, he also vows not to eliminate science but to expand its horizons. The best way out of the modern world's dualistic dilemma, Wilber maintains, is to realize that *"consciousness is pluridimensional,* or apparently composed of many levels; that each major school of psychology, psychotherapy, and religion is addressing a different level; that these different schools are therefore not contradictory but complementary, each approach being more-or-less correct and valid when addressing its own level." This spectrum approach, in essence, is Wilber's unprecedented achievement.

This integral or "*spectrum psychology*" approach begins by agreeing with the world's wisdom traditions (and with Schuon's assessment) that "the *roots* of psychology [lie] in the fertile soil of metaphysic," yet it also finds "room for the *ego,* the *super-ego,* and the *id,* but also for the *total organism,* and for the *transpersonal self,* and finally for *cosmic consciousness*—source and support of them all." Nevertheless, even from the opening pages, Wilber also realizes that "Any book that purports to be a 'synthesis of psychotherapies East and West' must fail miserably in living up to the claim. I can only say what follows is but the *briefest outline,* the barest skeleton, of this incredible spectrum we call consciousness."

Part I. Evolution

CHAPTER 1. "PROLOGUE" begins with William James's famous quote, which claims "Our normal waking consciousness is but one special type of consciousness, while all about it parted by the filmiest of screens there lie potential forms of consciousness entirely different. . . . No account of the universe in its totality can be final which leaves these other forms of consciousness quite disregarded." Thus Wilber's thesis is that "This volume is an attempt to provide a framework for just such an account of the universe." Admittedly, by being "deliberately simplistic," Wilber introduces a comprehensive integral synthesis that uses the metaphor of a *Spectrum of Consciousness,* which is roughly based upon the electromagnetic spectrum, borrowed from modern physics. Nonetheless, as a theorist, Wilber clearly understands that "Consciousness is not, properly speaking, a spectrum—but it is useful, for purposes of communication and investigation, to treat it as one."

From this beginning, Wilber unveils a universal spectrum psychology that is able to integrate both Western psychology and its diverse schools with Eastern mysticism and its diverse religions. This integration can also be properly seen a "psychological interpretation of the *philosophia perennis* [or the perennial philosophy]," an idea that Wilber presents as *psychologia perennis,* or the "perennial psychology." In summary, the central thesis of the spectrum paradigm is that "The major fields of Eastern and Western psychotherapy are each concerned with a different level of the Spectrum," in which case, each level simply has its own "information from and about the different vibratory levels or bands of consciousness." With this breakthrough insight, Wilber will continue to argue: "If there be any truth at all to the Spectrum of Consciousness and to the great metaphysical traditions that subscribe to its major theme, then it immediately becomes obvious that *each of the differing schools of psychotherapy—East and West—are primarily addressing different levels of the spectrum.*"

In other words, in an unprecedented manner, Wilber has set out to demonstrate that both the Eastern and Western psychologies are just different bands of one spectrum harmoniously "integrated and synthesized into one spectrum, one rainbow." By applying this comprehensive study of the Spectrum of Consciousness, Wilber's model "is not only a synthesis of Eastern and Western approaches to psychology and psychotherapy, but *also a synthesis and integration of the various Western approaches to psychology and psychotherapy.*" This becomes especially important since Western psychology tends to concentrate on the "problem" of the ego, whereas mystical awareness answers the self's psychological quandary by positing ego transcendence and liberation.

From the very beginning of his work and publishing career, Wilber emphasizes that these Eastern ideas "are not theories, philosophies, psychologies, or religions," but rather they're "*a set of experiments* in the strictly scientific sense of that term" since they mostly "comprise a *series of rules* or *injunctions.*" By appealing to the essence of mysticism, which realizes "the illusory nature of the self and the absolute and only Reality of Mind [or Consciousness]," Wilber too recognizes that his spectrum model will always be "made prey to . . . paradoxes, logical contradictions, and baffling assertions" since nondual consciousness "is ultimately not an idea but an intensely intimate experience." With this depth of understanding, the young theorist proves he's ultimately concerned with reality itself, not just rational theories describing it.

As a bold attempt, the theory of a Spectrum of Consciousness sets out "to discover a semblance of order, an inner logic, a thread of continuity in this vast complexity of different and frequently contradictory psychological systems." In only this way, Wilber maintains, can we possibly "integrate, in a fairly comprehensive fashion, not only the major schools of Western psychotherapy, but also what are generally called 'Eastern' and 'Western' approaches to consciousness." This psychological model shows how "the major fields of Eastern and Western psychotherapy are each concerned with a different level of the Spectrum . . . [therefore] each is more-or-less correct when addressing its own level." By taking this "correct but partial" approach, Wilber's worldcentric integral vision suggests "even if Eastern disciplines can awaken us from this dream [of the dualistic ego], Western ones can, in the meantime, prevent it from becoming a nightmare. Let us avail ourselves of both."

CHAPTER 2. "TWO MODES OF KNOWING" starts off by recognizing that "with the awakening of symbolic knowledge there *seems* to arise a split in the universe between the knower and the known, the thinker and thought, *the subject and the object.*" Wilber then tells us this *dualistic knowledge* or symbolic representational knowledge is what "today forms an important part of the methodology of science."

He therefore gives a perceptive review of modern science and its "new idea of measurement, of quantity." Yet, still, with the twentieth-century discoveries in quantum physics, culminating with the Heisenberg uncertainty principle, it was finally understood that "symbolic knowledge is dualistic knowledge." In other words, since in reality the map is not the territory, then so too "our scientific and philosophical ideas about reality are not reality itself."

As an alternative, in harmony with the perennial philosophy, Wilber's spectrum model maintains that only the *nondual mode of knowing* is capable of finding that "deeper reality behind" the "shadowy symbols" of representational knowledge, even as the greatest physicists themselves discovered. Nonetheless, Wilber too readily admits that these various *symbolic maps* "are of immense practical value and are quite indispensable to a civilized society." In summary, then, people have essentially *two basic modes of knowing:*

1. "Symbolic, or map, or inferential, or *dualistic knowledge;*"

2. "Intimate, or direct, or *nondual knowledge.*" Since "these two modes of knowing are universal," Wilber gives several examples from such diverse fields of human knowledge as Taoism, Hinduism, Christian theology, and Buddhism, plus a few modern Western philosophical thinkers, such as Alfred North Whitehead and William James. Then he proposes that all these views essentially converge because in essence they all understand that "our only hope of contacting Reality—if indeed there be such—will necessarily lie in the utter abandonment of the dualistic mode of knowing . . . [for] *if we are to know Reality, it is to the second mode of knowing [the nondual] that we must eventually turn.*"

CHAPTER 3. "REALITY AS CONSCIOUSNESS" emphasizes the fact that the "nondual mode alone is capable of giving . . . 'knowledge of Reality.'" Thus Wilber begins by explaining that according to the perennial philosophy, or "a single philosophical consensus of universal extent" (from Alan Watts), men and women are only able to know "this one reality by temporarily abandoning symbolic-map knowledge and by directly experiencing this underlying reality, the single territory upon which all of our maps are based."

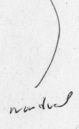

nondual

This leads Wilber to point out that there are traditionally three basic ways to "point to" Reality:

1. **analogical** or positive assertions as to *"what it is like";*

2. **negative ways** (*via negativa*), which simply maintain the Absolute is "not this, not that" (*neti, neti*);

3. **injunctive** or "a set of *experimental rules,* to discover Reality for oneself." The third way of *injunction* or *experiential practice* and *direct experience* forms the basis of all authentic spirituality since, according to Wilber and the perennial philosophy: *"Reality is what is revealed from the nondual level of consciousness."* This enlightening discovery compels the mystics to universally proclaim, as Wilber summarizes: "this one reality is actually Mind-Only (*cittamatra*), or One Mind (*ekacitta*), or various similar terms," such as "Absolute Being, or Absolute Way, or the Void or Abyss, or—in more familiar terms—God, the Godhead, or the one Spirit."

Once more, Wilber takes his stand in "the Truth, insofar as it can be stated in words, must always be a *set of instructions* on how to awaken to the nondual mode of knowing, therein to experience Reality directly." Only then will Reality be truly seen and really understood as nondual. Such profound nondual awareness is affirmed with numerous examples gathered from the world's mystical traditions, from the enlightened sages of Mahayana Buddhism, Vedanta, Taoism, and Zen, yet Wilber also amply draws from the writings of many of the modern "physicists [who] frequently refer to Reality as Mind or Consciousness."

Since reality as "suchness" or "thusness" (*tathata*) or "Void" (*sunyata*) is not "the 'object' of thought but the 'object' of *Prajna,* nondual awareness," then Wilber concludes: "What we ordinarily call 'distinct things' must, in some sense, actually be identical to all other 'distinct things.'" This leads him to introduce the Mahayana Buddhist "doctrine of Dharmadhatu or the Realm of Reality" (from the Hua-Yen school). He agrees that reality can be more accurately seen as a universal field or universal system since it's something like a "realm of *mutual interpenetration.*" Metaphorically, as the Buddhists say, "the universe is likened to a net of glittering gems" when it's seen holistically as "one in all, all in one," thus modeling a universe of "unity in diversity, diversity in unity." Although Wilber too realizes that this holistic position is actually nothing more than "a different approach to the Void," he still concludes: "the doctrine of *mutual interpenetration* and *mutual identification* of the Dharmadhatu represents man's highest attempt to put into words that nondual experience of Reality which itself remains wordless, ineffable, unspeakable, that nameless nothingness."

Once more, since Wilber is emphasizing that "Reality cannot be verbally communicated" but can only be discovered or realized by following the "injunctive approach," he's passing along "an invitation, in the form of a set of experimental rules, to discover Reality for oneself." This is an important principle because only then will people be able to "see through the illusions that dualistic-symbolic knowledge has given us, and thus awaken to the real world," where we'll discover "to know Reality is to *be* Reality."

In this case, as Wilber explains, "the real world is also called Brahman-only, Christ-only, Suchness-only, Tao-only, Consciousness-only, itself only, one without second, the universe *not* separate from *nor* false to itself." Yet, paradoxically, he also confesses that "whether Reality is called Brahman, God, Tao, Dharmakaya, Void, or whatever is of no great concern, for all alike point to that state of non-dual Mind [consciousness] wherein the universe is not split into seer and seen." Happily, as he tells us, this nondual awareness "is not a difficult one to discover, nor is it buried deep within your psyche. Rather, it is very close, very near, and ever-present."

CHAPTER 4. "TIME/ETERNITY, SPACE/INFINITY" is based upon a thorough reading and presentation of the perennial philosophy, therefore Wilber begins by explaining that "Absolute Reality is Absolute Subjectivity." In this case he ultimately concludes: "Absolute Subjectivity is nondual consciousness," which simply means that God is both "within" as well as "without," a precept in deep harmony with the wisdom traditions of the world. Therefore, like them, Wilber too maintains that human beings are in essence "Godhead, Brahman, Dharmadhatu, Universal man of no rank, Mind [Consciousness], Reality itself."

Next, he gives an extremely insightful and in-depth consideration on eternity, which he defines as being "timeless (or *beyond time*)" and not a phenomenon of duration or "everlasting time," therefore, "absolutely all time is NOW." Likewise, Infinity is "spaceless (or *beyond space*)," sizeless, and dimensionless, and is not an object of endless extension, therefore, "every single point of space is absolutely HERE." Wilber also adeptly discusses memory, the past, and the future, yet he also explains that "nature does not proceed in a line—it happens simultaneously—everywhere-at-once."

Therefore, the spectrum psychologist reasons that if there is an ever-present nondual awareness, then "it alone is always the case, for, whether we realize it or not, the subject is never actually split from the object." It is this type of radical understanding that allows Wilber to claim "Our problem is not to engineer this Reality in some future [time] but to understand it as a present fact." In other words, in order to heal "the dualism that obscures our Supreme Identity," we must "take a profound journey, not backwards into time, but deeply into *the present*, to re-call, re-collect, re-cognize, and re-member who and what we really are."

CHAPTER 5. "EVOLUTION OF THE SPECTRUM" follows the "generation of the Spectrum of Consciousness from its eternal ground," and, when this is done, as

evolution movement
of the Moment now

Wilber points out, "the entire spectrum of consciousness *evolves.*" Yet, also, because "this evolution is actually of the Moment, not of the past," then, he explains, it is "through the process of *maya,* of dualistic thought, we introduce illusory dualities or divisions." This psychological process, unfortunately, creates a sense of *self-identification* and *self-limitation,* which is why "most of us are so lost in maps that the territory remains buried." As a consequence, Wilber continues to argue that *"With each new level of the spectrum, this identification becomes more narrowed and exclusive."* Most people therefore end up fragmenting consciousness into various forms of subject-object duality, often feeling they're an "I" trapped in a body.

In fact, this *subject/object split* takes on a number of *dualisms* (each with a "major Dualism-Repression-Projection") including:

1. the **primary dualism** of organism vs. environment or self vs. other;

2. the **secondary dualism** of life vs. death and being vs. non-being;

3. the **tertiary dualism** is that of psyche vs. soma or mind vs. body, which is principally generated "under the anxiety of fleeing death."

In this presentation, as a reminder to the reader, it should be noted that Wilber is still in his earlier "Romantic" or "recaptured goodness" model (Wilber/Phase 1) exhibiting examples of the *"pre/trans fallacy"* or the tendency to confuse *prepersonal* and *transpersonal* phenomena because they're both *nonpersonal.* Thus, for example, he erroneously claimed that "pure organismic consciousness participates fully in the nondual awareness called *Absolute Subjectivity.*" However, once this important differentiation is later clarified in subsequent writings with the "growth-to-goodness" or evolutionary model (of Wilber/Phases 2, 3, 4), the names and terms in this particular Spectrum of Consciousness model are superceded and further refined. (See Introduction to this book: "Ken Wilber's Personal Odyssey.")

Next, Wilber presents a graphic diagram of the Spectrum of Consciousness, using the terms of this book, which shows a diagonal line representing the split of consciousness into the various dualisms, primarily associated with the apparent inside (interior) and outside (exterior) aspects of awareness. (See Figure 1: "The Spectrum of Consciousness.")

Wilber also uses psychoanalytic insights to discuss the *Ascending Spiral* or the apparent fragmentation *within* the self by presenting a series of repressions, projections, and dualistic illusions (or maya). This psychological process includes the unconscious, the ego, the persona, and the shadow, all of which are outlined and discussed in detail, drawing from both Eastern and Western sources. In summary, Wilber states: "the process of the Self's involution and evolution is viewed as a universal drama of the eternal play (*lila, krida, dolce, gioco*) of hide-and-seek, of cre-

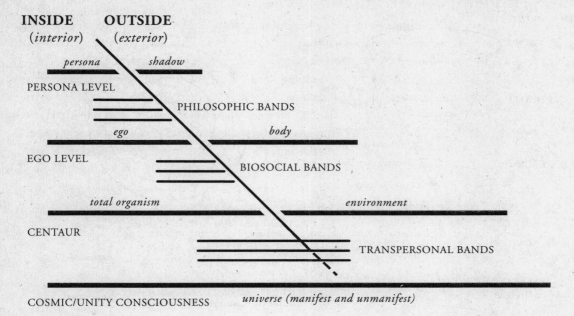

persona   *shadow*

PERSONA LEVEL

PHILOSOPHIC BANDS

ego   *body*

EGO LEVEL

BIOSOCIAL BANDS

total organism   *environment*

CENTAUR

TRANSPERSONAL BANDS

COSMIC/UNITY CONSCIOUSNESS   *universe (manifest and unmanifest)*

The Spectrum of
Consciousness
FIGURE I

ation and redemption, of manifestation and dissolution, of anabolism and catab-
olism, but the sole actor in this drama is the one and only Self, playing an infinite
number of roles (such as you and me) without ceasing in the least to completely
remain itself, spaceless and timeless, whole and undivided."

CHAPTER 6. "SURVEYING THE TRADITIONS" compares the Spectrum of Consciousness "with those [descriptions] given by the great metaphysical traditions,
including Zen, Yogachara Buddhism, Vedanta Hinduism, and Tibetan Vajrayana,
as well as those set forth by individual [Western] explorers such as Hubert Benoit."
He first introduces the notion of Vedanta's "sheaths" (*koshas*), then the "eight *vijnanas* of Mahayana psychology," as well as their various "pathological states." (See
Figure 2: "Levels and Sheaths of the Spectrum.")

Wilber then suggests that "the Spectrum of Consciousness, in fact, is a modern-
day presentation of this perennial psychology [*psychologia perennis*], but drawing
equally upon Western as well as Eastern insights." In synch with this perennial understanding, he also concludes: "the spectrum of consciousness represents identifications of the Absolute Knower with certain known objects." Once again, Wilber
encourages us to discover and "know that Reality lies upstream of all conceptual-
ization at the very Source of my Energy, at Absolute Subjectivity itself—surely this
points out the door, the opening in the cave of shadows, through which we all must

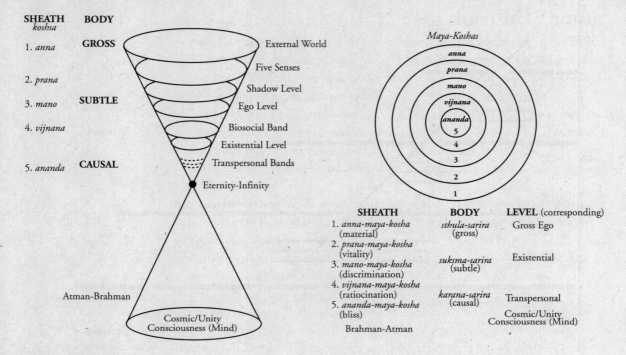

SHEATH *koshsa* | **BODY**
1. *anna* — **GROSS** — External World
— Five Senses
2. *prana* — Shadow Level
3. *mano* — **SUBTLE** — Ego Level
4. *vijnana* — Biosocial Band
— Existential Level
5. *ananda* — **CAUSAL** — Transpersonal Bands
— Eternity-Infinity

Atman-Brahman

Cosmic/Unity Consciousness (Mind)

Maya-Koshas
anna
prana
mano
vijnana
ananda
5
4
3
2
1

SHEATH	**BODY**	**LEVEL** (corresponding)
1. *anna-maya-kosha* (material)	*sthula-sarira* (gross)	Gross Ego
2. *prana-maya-kosha* (vitality)		
3. *mano-maya-kosha* (discrimination)	*suksma-sarira* (subtle)	Existential
4. *vijnana-maya-kosha* (ratiocination)		
5. *ananda-maya-kosha* (bliss)	*karana-sarira* (causal)	Transpersonal
Brahman-Atman		Cosmic/Unity Consciousness (Mind)

"Levels" and "Sheaths"
of the Spectrum

FIGURE 2

pass if we are to catch a glimpse of the Light of the Universe, of that within which is beyond."

Part II. Involution

CHAPTER 7. "INTEGRATING THE SHADOW" begins with Freud's important insight that "Humans don't know what they want; their real desires are unconscious and therefore never adequately satisfied." Wilber goes on to explain that this stark realization was made into the psychoanalytic systems of Freud and his followers from Adler to Jung to Gestalt to Maslow. Further, he contends: "If there is any truth at all to the Spectrum of Consciousness and to the great metaphysical traditions that unanimously subscribe to its basic theme, then it immediately becomes obvious that *each of the major but differing schools of 'psychotherapy' is simply addressing a different level of the Spectrum.*" In other words, it follows that *"The various schools of psychotherapy, East and West, fall naturally into an order that spans the entire Spectrum of Consciousness."*

Next, Wilber gives a thorough review of contemporary psychological evidence in order to describe the various psychopathologies (or "dys-eases") as well as their corresponding therapies. These both occur at each major level of consciousness, but especially with the ego level and its shadow, which generate at least four major classes of projection. Another critical conclusion he draws is that "Therapy on the Ego Level therefore entails a re-membering and re-owning of our forgotten tendencies, a re-identifying with our projected facets, a re-uniting with our shadows." In other words, by following the discoveries of modern psychology, Wilber demonstrates that "In all areas of psychic life . . . we must confront our opposites and re-own them—and that doesn't necessarily mean to act on them, just be aware of them."

CHAPTER 8. "THE GREAT FILTER" examines the psychological pathologies and therapies that address social conditioning or the "Biosocial Band of the spectrum of consciousness." And as Wilber points out, since a person is heavily influenced by "the maps that he is given by society to translate and transform reality," then "the way in which an individual experiences reality and subsequently *himself* is profoundly influenced by sociological factors," or the "conventionalization of reality." Importantly, by blindly or unconsciously accepting "the social description of the world as reality itself," then our dualistic social maps create a "major filter" (after Erich Fromm) from really experiencing the real world in all its depth and ultimate potential.

This view is especially true from the point of view of reality or nondual territory, for as Wilber reminds us, there's really "no Problem of Life because there is fundamentally nothing wrong." Therefore, he suggests, since "a dualistic map of a nondual territory just has to be booby-trapped," then it's only by using therapy and mystical insight that people can make their "unconscious maps conscious, so that even if they continue to obscure reality, we at least realize that reality *is* being obscured—and here is the beginning of insight." In other words, the spectrum psychologist observes: "in seeing our maps as maps, we are finally in a position to go beyond them to the [nondual] territory itself, to relinquish the hold these social dreams exercise over us . . . for as a person divides Reality, he so acts."

CHAPTER 9. "CENTAUR" examines in depth the "Tertiary Dualism of *psyche vs. soma* or *mind vs. body.*" By reviewing the recent evidence of psychology, Wilber explains that this dualism is only resolved (in part) with the integrated level of consciousness known as the Existential Level or the *centaur,* which is defined as the total organism. Thus he suggests that for a person to become "the centaur is simply to contact the body itself, to give some awareness, to explore its feelings, urges, tinglings, responses, and vibrations." He points out that once the "problems" or "knots" of the bodymind are relaxed and released, then we may more fully live as

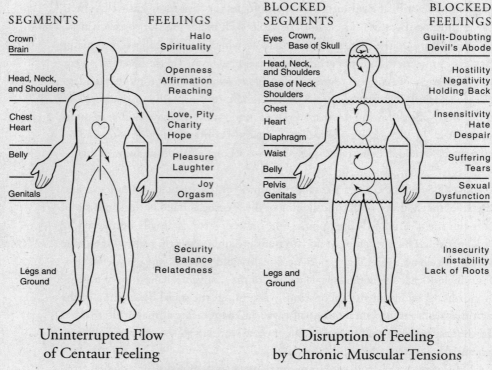

SEGMENTS	FEELINGS	BLOCKED SEGMENTS	BLOCKED FEELINGS
Crown Brain	Halo Spirituality	Eyes Crown, Base of Skull	Guilt-Doubting Devil's Abode
Head, Neck, and Shoulders	Openness Affirmation Reaching	Head, Neck, and Shoulders Base of Neck Shoulders	Hostility Negativity Holding Back
Chest Heart	Love, Pity Charity Hope	Chest Heart Diaphragm	Insensitivity Hate Despair
Belly	Pleasure Laughter	Waist Belly	Suffering Tears
Genitals	Joy Orgasm	Pelvis Genitals	Sexual Dysfunction
Legs and Ground	Security Balance Relatedness	Legs and Ground	Insecurity Instability Lack of Roots

Uninterrupted Flow of Centaur Feeling

Disruption of Feeling by Chronic Muscular Tensions

Illustrations adapted from Alexander Lowen, *Depression and the Body*
(New York: Coward, McCann & Geoghegan, 1972)

Flow and Disruption of Centaur Feeling
FIGURE 3

centaur or the "Existential Level, our 'centered self,' our 'total being,' the 'unity of which' the psyche and soma represent a fragmentation." (See Figure 3: "Flow and Disruption of Centaur Feeling," adapted from the work of Alexander Lowen.)

This is followed by a fairly extensive review of *somatic* (body-oriented) and *existential therapies,* ranging from Sartre, Rolf, Perls, Reich, Rogers to hatha yoga, all of which permits Wilber to summarize "Our main point: the *progressive dissolution of the tertiary dualism,* of the split between ego and body, is a progressive expansion of identity, and therefore responsibility, to one's entire organism, to '*all organic activities.*'" In other words, the various existential therapies, from the somatic-existential approach to the "uninterrupted flow of existential feeling," all enrich the centaur level once it has been reached beyond ego development.

This in turn leads into a sophisticated discussion on the exoteric versus esoteric aspects of the world's religions (following Huston Smith and Fritjof Schuon). Here Wilber clarifies that "in terms of the spectrum of consciousness, *this dividing line between esotericism and exotericism is the primary dualism.*" He also thoroughly

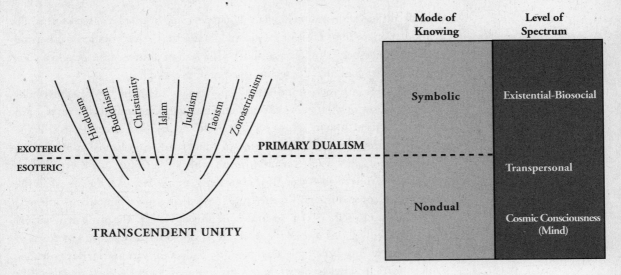

The Esoteric Unity
of Religions

FIGURE 4

agrees that the "transcendent unity of religions" (after Schuon) itself supports the argument that "existence is graded, and with it, cognition" (after Smith). (See Figure 4: "The Esoteric Unity of Religions.")

In summary, Wilber suggests "This is precisely the crux of the Spectrum of Consciousness—that existence is graded into several levels, and that each level has its own peculiar mode of knowing, modes that grade, shade, and range from pure nondual awareness (Mind) to pure symbolic representation (Ego)." With this type of multilayered understanding, spectrum psychology acknowledges "'healing' or 'whole-ing' a level [in the spectrum of consciousness] makes it easier to leave or transcend, for then our energies are not preoccupied and bound up with problems of that level." And at the deeper (or transpersonal) levels, if a person (or a *jivat-man*) is finally "ready to know God instead of worship him, to be the world instead of encountering it, to accept death instead of fearing it tomorrow . . . then [he or she] is ready to begin the *Nivritti Marga,* the Path of Return, the Religion of Eternity, the Descent to Mind."

CHAPTER 10. "A NO-MAN'S-LAND" discusses one of the more "mysterious, unexplored, misunderstood, fear-inducing, and generally puzzling portion of the spectrum—the Transpersonal Bands." These bands or levels in the spectrum of consciousness include the psychic or the paranormal and the subtle or astral phenomena. Nevertheless, Wilber affirms that generally these levels must be quickly passed through in order to find the real nondual Godhead. This leads to an insightful consideration on the Jungian archetypes (*bijas* or *vasanas* or seed-forms). In contradiction to Jung's position, Wilber maintains that "'true' mysticism is beyond even the archetypes," simply because at the highest or ultimate transpersonal stage "one no longer contemplates reality, one becomes reality!"

This brings up the "supra-individual Witness: that which is capable of observing the flow of what is—without interfering with it, commenting on it, or in any way manipulating it." However, this profound mystical awareness is still distinguished from the nondual awareness of enlightenment because "in one [structure], a person may witness reality; in the other he is reality." And yet, Wilber realizes that "'out of this Absolute Subjectivity, *in this moment,* there evolves the spectrum of consciousness." In this case, the evolving spectrum of consciousness creates a "pseudo-self" or the "separate and subjective 'self,' the 'little man within' that supposedly looks out at the universe of objects," and whose spectrum of worldviews, or "my case of mistaken identity," reflect the various "levels of pseudo-subjectivity." In order to illustrate this principle, Wilber presents a detailed psychological review of various therapies, including numerous tables, each of which "consists, on each level, in bringing this particular pseudo-subject fully into consciousness." He presents an expanded version of the Spectrum of Consciousness graphic to represent pictorially the three areas of conscious and unconscious awareness (See Figure 5: "The Spectrum of Unconscious.")

Once this entire topography of consciousness is seen in its totality, Wilber suggests: "Any slight appreciation of our pluridimensional awareness, of the spectrum-like nature of consciousness, forces these considerations upon us—and they are extremely important considerations at that." Next, and perhaps most critical of humanistic psychology, Wilber presents a serious consideration of transpersonal meditation, in which he maintains that although any "upper level therapy can be beneficial," ultimately, only meditation will allow a person to "follow the mystics . . . the venture of all ventures, the quest for the Holy Grail, the search for the Philosopher's Stone, the Elixir of Immortality, the Master Game itself. It is not without risks, but no voyage is."

CHAPTER 11. "THAT WHICH IS ALWAYS ALREADY" concludes Wilber's first book with numerous selections from the world's greatest mystics who universally claim that "Ultimate Nondual Consciousness" is "always already the case" or "everywhere and everywhen." This is based upon the clear understanding that Absolute Reality or "Brahman is not a particular experience, level of consciousness or state of soul—rather it is precisely whatever level you happen to have now, and realizing this confers upon one a profound center of peace that underlies and persists throughout the worst depressions, anxieties, and fears." This seemingly paradoxi-

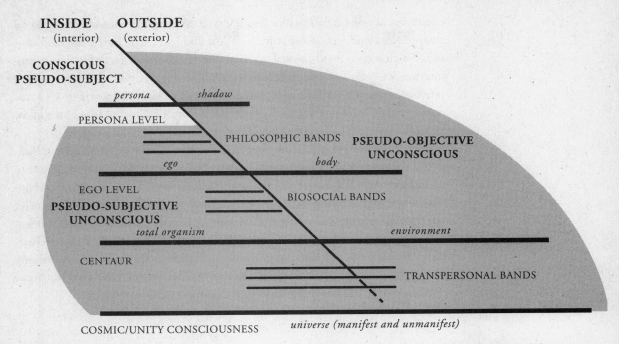

INSIDE **OUTSIDE**
(interior) (exterior)

CONSCIOUS
PSEUDO-SUBJECT

persona *shadow*

PERSONA LEVEL

PHILOSOPHIC BANDS **PSEUDO-OBJECTIVE**
UNCONSCIOUS

ego *body*

EGO LEVEL
PSEUDO-SUBJECTIVE BIOSOCIAL BANDS
UNCONSCIOUS

total organism *environment*

CENTAUR

TRANSPERSONAL BANDS

COSMIC/UNITY CONSCIOUSNESS *universe (manifest and unmanifest)*

The Spectrum of
Unconscious
FIGURE 5

cal position is explained since Wilber realizes "That in you right now which knows, which sees, which reads this page—that is the Godhead, Mind, Brahman, and it cannot be seen or known as an object, just as an eye cannot see itself."

By giving numerous examples from the mystics' wisdom traditions, Wilber summarizes his main thesis: since our search to overcome the "gap between subject and object, this primary dualism, is the initiator of the spectrum of consciousness, and continues to operate throughout all levels," then our search is actually fruitless because always already, "We are It, we can never attain It, get It, reach It, grab It, or find It, any more than we can run after our own feet." Therefore, "It" or nondual awareness can always already be *directly experienced* whether it's "called enlightenment, awakening, *wu, satori,* or whatever, we recognize it as the emergence of . . . *prajna,* passive and non-dual awareness." In all cases, then, our ultimate "release [or liberation] is not a future hope but a present fact. All dualisms being illusory, there is nothing that really binds us, no chains to break, no freedom to attain."

In other words, as Wilber explains in depth by citing the authors of the perennial philosophy, whenever "one's sense of identity explodes into *everything* that is experienced—then there is no separate experiencer nor separate objects experienced, but just one encompassing and nondual experience." Thus by "letting mind and speech alone," we will naturally follow and live what the Taoists call "*wu-wei,* which means no volitional activity, no intentional or forced activity, non-interference—w*u-wei* thus represents the art of letting the mind alone, of letting it move as it will, of not forcing it or restraining it, of *totally authorizing all of the mind's tendencies in a moment of perfect impartiality,* of allowing thoughts to flow just as we let the clouds drift through the sky."

In conclusion, the spectrum psychology of Ken Wilber suggests that by "heal-ing the primary dualism, we assume responsibility for *everything* that happens to us, because now what happened to us is our own doing." This is exactly what hap-pens when "one's sense of identity explodes into *everything* that is experienced— but then there is no separate experiencer nor separate objects experienced, but just one encompassing and nondual *experiencing . . .* thus is healed the Primary Dual-ism." Therefore Wilber concludes by telling us that by "always already suffering death Now, we are always already living eternally. The search is always already over."

CHAPTER 2

No Boundary

Eastern and Western Approaches to Personal Growth

BY KEN WILBER

(Boulder: Shambhala Publications, 1979, 1981);

The Collected Works of Ken Wilber, Vol. 1 (CW1) (Boston: Shambhala, 1999);

paperback reprint edition (Boston: Shambhala, 2001)

Preface

No Boundary: Eastern and Western Approaches to Personal Growth is a "Romantic" Wilber/Phase 1 work emphasizing the integration of Western psychology with Eastern mysticism, therefore mostly focusing on individual interior consciousness (Upper-Left quadrant), yet still without a complete pre/trans developmental understanding.

No Boundary was finished in about a month in 1978, shortly after Wilber's first satori on a Zen retreat, therefore it is an unmistakably personal account of ever-present awareness culminating in the enlightening last chapter "The Ultimate State of Consciousness" (which is different from his previous article of the same title published in 1975).

No Boundary: Eastern and Western Approaches to Personal Growth was published in 1979 (Center Publications) by the Zen Center of Los Angeles (where Wilber was studying under the tutelage of Maezumi Roshi) before it was released in 1981 by Wilber's primary publisher (Shambhala Publications); it is now part of *The Collected Works of Ken Wilber, Volume One (CW1),* (Shambhala Publications, 1999); reprint paperback edition (Shambhala Publications, 2001).

The **PREFACE** begins by stating that this introductory "book examines how we create a persistent alienation from ourselves, from others, and from the world by fracturing our present experience into different parts, separated by boundaries." Ken Wilber therefore presents his central thesis which uses the Western psychological sciences (including orthodox, humanistic, and transpersonal psychologies) in conjunction with the mystical traditions in general (epitomized by the Eastern spiritual psychologies). Wilber draws from numerous sources—texts and enlightened sages—since he suggests that "by using these readily accessible masters of the different layers of the soul, the overall nature of the spectrum of consciousness will itself be more easily grasped."

CHAPTER 1. "INTRODUCTION: WHO AM I?" ultimately answers this question with the universal assertions claimed by the perennial philosophy, or the "transcendent unity of religions," which, in essence, emphatically states that our **Supreme Identity** is a unity consciousness or cosmic consciousness or no-boundary awareness. From there Wilber proceeds to explain that consciousness is fractured into various boundaries of "inside vs. outside" (or dualisms) creating a spectrum of consciousness. Consequently, as he explains, "the major schools of psychology,

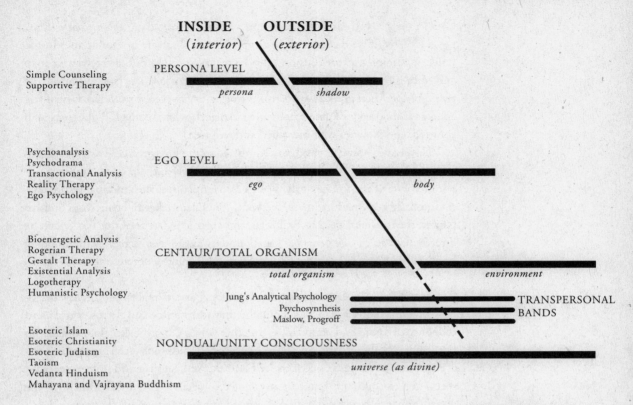

INSIDE **OUTSIDE**
(interior) *(exterior)*

PERSONA LEVEL

Simple Counseling
Supportive Therapy

persona *shadow*

Psychoanalysis
Psychodrama
Transactional Analysis   EGO LEVEL
Reality Therapy
Ego Psychology

ego *body*

Bioenergetic Analysis
Rogerian Therapy
Gestalt Therapy   CENTAUR/TOTAL ORGANISM
Existential Analysis
Logotherapy
Humanistic Psychology

total organism *environment*

Jung's Analytical Psychology
Psychosynthesis   TRANSPERSONAL
Maslow, Progroff   BANDS

Esoteric Islam
Esoteric Christianity
Esoteric Judaism   NONDUAL/UNITY CONSCIOUSNESS
Taoism
Vedanta Hinduism
Mahayana and Vajrayana Buddhism

universe (as divine)

Therapies and the
Levels of the Spectrum
FIGURE I

psychotherapy, and religion are simply addressing the different major levels of the spectrum." The purpose of growth or development, therefore, is "an enlarging and *expanding* of one's horizons, *a growth of one's boundaries,* outwardly in perspective and inwardly in depth." (See Figure 1: "Therapies and the Levels of the Spectrum.")

CHAPTER 2. "HALF OF IT" begins by discussing how human life is divided into apparent dualisms that people create by drawing boundaries, and in doing so, they set themselves up for a world of conflict because, "in short, to draw boundaries is to manufacture opposites." However, in accord with the perennial philosophy, Wilber explains there is an "inner unity of opposites" or a *"coincidentia oppositorium,"* since both the opposites in a dualism are actually "two aspects of one reality." Therefore, the integral psychologist suggests that by the "surrendering of all boundaries" it's possible "to unify and harmonize the opposites, both positive and negative, by discovering a ground [nondual territory] which transcends and encompasses them both."

CHAPTER 3. "NO-BOUNDARY TERRITORY" reveals that "the *ultimate meta-physical secret,* if we dare state it so simply, is that there are no boundaries in the universe. Boundaries are illusions, products not of reality but of the way we map and edit reality. And while it is fine to map out the territory, it is fatal to confuse the two." Wilber then gives a wonderful introductory overview to the history of science, as embodied by Adam who named, Aristotle who classified, Pythagoras who counted, and Newton who measured and weighed.

Nowadays, however, modern-day physicists see Energy as a "Universal Realm or Field of Reality," similar to the Buddhist's *Dharmadhatu* or as a radiant no-boundary territory. Importantly, Wilber also emphasizes this nondual territory—traditionally known as suchness, the Void, "the Dharmakaya, the mystical body of Christ, the universal field of Brahman, the organic patterns of the Tao"—can be directly *realized* or *experienced* as "no-boundary awareness," which is traditionally been called "nirvana, moksha, release, liberation, enlightenment, satori."

CHAPTER 4. "NO-BOUNDARY AWARENESS" asserts that no-boundary awareness or unity consciousness is actually "beyond names and forms, words and thoughts, divisions and boundaries." In other words, "to say reality is non-dual is to say reality is no-boundary." In this case, Wilber establishes that the primary boundary for human beings is between "self and not self, subject and object, seer and seen." Yet, to counter this apparently subject/object split, Wilber shows how "the mystic universally answers" this primary dilemma of human life by saying: "Look inside. Deep inside . . . [until] you realize that the inside and the outside, the subject and the object, the seer and the seen are one, and thus you spontaneously fall into your natural state." This, too, is the essence of Wilber's spectrum psychology and mysticism: "Reality, by all accounts, is no-boundary awareness—that just that is one's Real Self."

CHAPTER 5. "THE NO-BOUNDARY MOMENT" eloquently explains that the world's mystics, both East and West, have unanimously encouraged us to directly "contact the eternal" because "until we thoroughly grasp the nature of eternity, the sense of the Real will elude us." Wilber thus leads the reader into an insightful presentation on Eternity as being "timeless . . . not everlasting time"; therefore Eternity exists only in the present or the now, not the past or future, which is precisely when and where no-boundary (or nondual) awareness is realized.

CHAPTER 6. "THE GROWTH OF BOUNDARIES" discusses how "every level of the spectrum can be understood as a progressive *bounding,* or limiting, or constricting of one's real self, of unity consciousness and no-boundary awareness."

Most important, Wilber emphasizes, it is "through [these] successive boundaries, the spectrum of consciousness evolves." This developmental evolution creates the "dance of opposites," which is only resolved in the timeless present (or eternity), itself "a *coincidence of opposites,* a unity of birth and death, being and nonbeing, living and dying." Since the play of opposites (dualisms) often creates a "primal mood of fear," mostly based around the concern with death, Wilber explains this reaction manufactures an ego with a persona or self-image, a shadow or "unacceptable aspects of the ego," and unconscious projections. In this case, the transpersonal therapist recommends: "Let us lift the boundaries so that we can once again touch our shadows, our bodies, and our world, knowing too that all we touch is at heart the original face of our own true self."

CHAPTER 7. "THE PERSONA LEVEL: THE START OF DISCOVERY" acknowledges that there is an important discovery to be gained when "a person who is beginning to sense the suffering of life is, at the same time, beginning to *awaken* to deeper realities, truer realities." Wilber then gives a review of the various psychotherapies, which themselves are divergent in nature because "they are approaching *different levels* of human awareness from different angles." In this event, he provides "a map which might help guide [us] through the amazement of [our] boundaries." Then he leads the reader through an excellent description of the tumultuous sufferings of the ego level, especially the shadow projections or "your unconscious opposites." Overall, Wilber explains that "translation is the key to therapy" because it allows us to reown or reclaim the darker and often hidden aspects (or shadows) of our self (the persona), thus giving us a more accurate and healthy self-image.

CHAPTER 8. "THE CENTAUR LEVEL" demonstrates how we need to reown the body in order to "expand our identity from an impoverished persona to a healthy ego." Wilber clarifies that this level of the centaur is about integrating body and mind—the total organism, especially since this "integration of the body and the ego is indeed a deeper reality than either alone." Wilber then offers some practical ways to move beyond our "blocks (mini-boundaries)," such as with breathing exercises, so we may grow to consciously rediscover our authentic, existential self, or what humanistic psychology calls self-actualization.

CHAPTER 9. "THE SELF IN TRANSCENDENCE" introduces "the vast and subtle world of the Transpersonal," which is defined as "an awareness that transcends the individual and discloses to a person something which passes far behind himself." In order to guide the reader, Wilber provides some "pointing-out instructions" that will help lift the self into the collective world of archetypes. This will ultimately lead into direct contact with our "transcendent self," the "unmoved witness," which can only be found "by dis-identifying with *all* particular objects, mental, emotional, or physical, thereby transcending them." In perhaps one of his most refined achievements, Wilber explains the very subtlest developments of mysticism by pointing out that "one must first discover that transpersonal witness, which then acts as an easier 'jumping-off point' for unity consciousness."

CHAPTER 10. "THE ULTIMATE STATE OF CONSCIOUSNESS" makes abundantly clear, in paradoxical fashion that "there is no way to *arrive* at that which already *is*." Wilber clarifies that *unity consciousness* or the ultimate state is a great paradox since, as "the true sages proclaim, there is no path to the Absolute, no way to *gain* unity consciousness." This radical understanding leads to enlightened practice or *honsho-myoshu* (after Zen) which literally means "original enlightenment is wondrous practice." Wilber explains that the most effective method to actually realize this nondual awareness is to practice transpersonal and contemplative disciplines by using special conditions, such as "*zazen,* or deep contemplation, or devotion to God or guru."

Wilber's integral model, therefore, takes the approach that we are constantly resisting unity consciousness with our present activity of self-contraction or the feeling of resistance (indeed, the primal resistance) until, finally, "there spontaneously comes a deep and total surrender of resistance." Then it's possible to fully realize "there is only Consciousness as Such in all directions, absolute and all-pervading, radiant through and as all conditions, the source and suchness of everything that arises moment to moment, utterly prior to this world but not other than this world. All things are just a ripple in this pond; all arising is a gesture of this one." And with this gesture, Wilber's last sentence in the book ends with a blessing: "May you be graced to find a spiritual master in this life and enlightenment in the moment."

 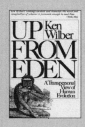  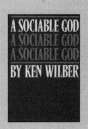

THE EVOLUTION
REVOLUTION
(1978–1983)

The Atman Project

A Transpersonal View
of Human Development

BY KEN WILBER

(Wheaton, Ill.: Quest Books, 1980);

reprint edition (Quest Books 1996);

The Collected Works of Ken Wilber, Vol. 2 (CW2) (Boston: Shambhala
Publications, 1999)

Preface

The Atman Project: A Transpersonal View of Human Development is a principal Wilber/Phase 2 work that emphasizes developmental psychology or the evolution of the spectrum of consciousness, therefore focusing mostly on the involution and evolution of individual interior consciousness (Upper-Left quadrant) in the Great Nest of Spirit and Kosmos.

The Atman Project (1980) was written in 1979 in about three weeks, after over a year of going through "an inordinately difficult intellectual passage" in order to uncover the critical pre/trans fallacy. The book dramatically shifed Wilber's work into Phase 2, which focused on the developmental evolution of the spectrum of consciousness. Written simultaneously with its "sister" volume, *Up From Eden* (1981), earlier versions of *The Atman Project* still reflected Wilber's "Romantic" period (Wilber/Phase 1) and were published in 1978 as issues in the newly founded journal *ReVision* (financed and coedited with Jack Crittenden).

The Atman Project: A Transpersonal View of Human Development was published in 1980 (A Quest Book); paperback reprint in 1996 (Quest Books); it is now part of *The Collected Works of Ken Wilber, Volume Two (CW2)*, (Shambhala Publications, 1999).

The **PREFACE** begins with Ken Wilber simply stating a cardinal tenet of integral philosophy: "Development is evolution; evolution is transcendence." This sets the tone and primary theme throughout Wilber's entire oeuvre, as well as this, his third book. And even more specifically he continues to explain what development or evolution or transcendence is all about: "Transcendence has as its final goal Atman, or ultimate Unity Consciousness in only God. All drives are a subset of that Drive, all wants a subset of that Want, all pushes a subset of that Pull—and that whole movement is what we call the Atman-Project: the drive of God towards God, Buddha towards Buddha, Brahman towards Brahman, but carried out initially through the intermediary of the human psyche, with results that range from ecstatic to catastrophic."

Nonetheless, as Wilber will demonstrate (especially in *Up From Eden,* his next book and the companion to this volume), "If men and women have ultimately come up from amoebas, then they are ultimately on their way towards God, but in the meantime they are under sway of the incredible half-way house known as the Atman-Project." In the process of coming to terms with this evidence of development and evolutionary transcendence, Wilber gained a "new understanding of a different context for that data (*pre* and *trans*)." In other words, in this book the transpersonal theorist introduced his important and innovative ideas on what's now known as the pre/trans fallacy. Nonetheless, from the enlightened position of unity consciousness or having "always already" realized Atman, Wilber understands that, in the end, this grand "story of the Atman-project . . . is finally a lie in the face of that Mystery which only alone is." Wilber's project, therefore, is *not* to search but to understand.

CHAPTER 1. "PROLOGUE" introduces the reader to the concept of *holism* (after Jan Smuts), which suggests that "everywhere we look in nature, we see nothing but *wholes*. And not just simple wholes, but hierarchical ones: each whole is a part of a larger whole which is itself a part of a larger whole. Fields within fields, stretching through the cosmos, interlacing each and every thing with each and every other." Further, Wilber tells us, "This overall cosmic process, as it unfolds in time, is nothing other than evolution," thus it's very "energetically dynamic and even creative." Wilber therefore acknowledges ("as a general approximation") that in this "drive to ever-higher unities . . . we may conclude that the psyche—like the cosmos at large—is many-layered (*'pluridimensional'*), composed of successively *higher-order wholes* and unities and integrations."

This "holistic evolution of nature" appears in human beings as development or growth, thus Wilber concludes: "The same force that produced humans from amoebas produces adults from infants. That is, a person's growth, from infancy to adulthood, is simply a miniature version of cosmic evolution." After maintaining that modern developmental psychology examines the lower stages, the integral theorist suggests (along with such illuminati as Bergson, Toynbee, Tolstoy, James, Schopenhauer, Nietzsche, and Maslow) that "The world's great mystics and sages represent some of the very highest, if not the highest, of all stages of human development." By combining the two positions of psychology and mysticism, Wilber arrives at a "fairly well-balanced and comprehensive model of the Spectrum of Consciousness."

This natural overall life cycle of individual human beings, Wilber continues, manifests as the "life cycle [that] moves from subconsciousness (*instinctual, impulsive, id-ish*) to self-consciousness (*egoic, conceptual, syntaxical*) to superconsciousness (*transcendent, transpersonal, transtemporal*)." Therefore, Wilber subdivides the overall life cycle of the human being into the *Outward Arc* and *Inward Arc*. (See Figure 1: "The General Life Cycle.")

The Outward Arc is "the story of the ego, for the Ego *is* the Hero," which itself developmentally moves from the subconscious or prepersonal (*pleroma, uroboros, Typhon*) stages to the self-conscious or personal (*egoic-mental, centaur*) ones.

The Inward Arc, on the other hand, is the "Path of Return," which moves

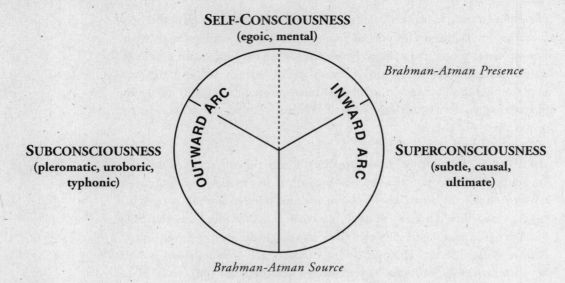

The General Life Cycle
FIGURE I

from the self-conscious (*egoic*) to superconscious or transpersonal (*subtle, causal, ultimate*) stages of life. (See Figure 2: "The Complete Life Cycle.")

In other words, Wilber outlines the grand journey from infancy to adulthood that is "the whole process of *ontogeny.*" He explains that the early stages are broadly covered by developmental psychology, yet after becoming an adult the process moves into the inner dimensions of transpersonal consciousness evolution which are generally covered by "the mystical schools East and West."

As an important aside, in relation to Wilber's later phases of his integral model (Wilber/Phase 3) where he emphasizes developmental lines (instead of concentrating mostly on the structures or levels), he does clearly acknowledge, at this time, in one sentence on the opening pages of *The Atman Project* that he "will absolutely not distinguish the different lines of development, such as cognition, moral, affective, conative, motivational, emotional, and intellectual, since . . . I wish from the start to avoid such intricate debate."

CHAPTER 2. "THE PRIMITIVE ROOTS OF AWARENESS" begins at the birth of the human being with the *pleromatic self,* which is the undifferentiated awareness of the fetus and early infant, who has not yet developed a sense of selfhood, since at this stage there is still very little subject/object, inside/outside, body/environment separation. But soon this stage leads into the *"alimentary uroboros,"* which is the beginning of the separation of the self from its environment, although initially it is

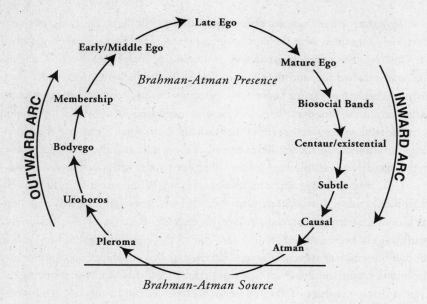

Brahman-Atman Presence

OUTWARD ARC

INWARD ARC

Late Ego

Early/Middle Ego

Mature Ego

Membership

Biosocial Bands

Bodyego

Centaur/existential

Uroboros

Subtle

Pleroma

Causal

Atman

Brahman-Atman Source

The Complete Life Cycle
FIGURE 2

"collective, archaic, still mostly oceanic." Thus the corresponding worldview of the uroboros is dominated by "unconscious nature, by physiology, by instincts, by reptilian perception, and the most rudimentary emotional discharges."

However, in exposing the orthodox pre/trans fallacy (often buried in most psychological theories), Wilber maintains that although this early stage of life may appear as a paradisiacal state of "blissful ignorance and pre-Fall awareness," it's really an error of understanding to associate this period with "the supreme bliss of no longer being an ego: the bliss of transcendence." Indeed, the transpersonal theorist carefully clarifies, this uroboric stage is actually "the roots of a primordial fear . . . [or as] the Upanishads put it, 'Wherever there is other, there is fear.'" In the various phases of cognitive development this stage corresponds to "the earliest stages of the sensorimotor realm . . . although it is gradually transcended in favor of an increasingly personal and individual awareness."

CHAPTER 3. "THE TYPHONIC SELF" covers the stage of early growth when the infant develops into the *bodyego self* or the *axial-body.* This is the period when the first stable images appear and thus the physical body begins to feel itself as being distinct or differentiated from the surrounding physical environment. This separation process creates an emerging emotional component or *proto-emotions,* which, Wilber points out, involves two broad motivational aspects: immediate survival, and the pleasure-unpleasure principle.

With the further emergence of extensive imagery or the image-body, this stage is strongly identified with the significant concrete image of the mothering one or the Great Mother, which naturally has corresponding images of self-worth, such as the good-me, bad-me, and the not-me. This is all coupled with an extended present or the expansion of time beyond the mere moment-to-moment experience of the earlier uroboros. Wilber explains that this new experience of self is still involved in the prelogical *primary process* (after Freud) which occurs when the young child "confuses the subject and the predicate as well as the whole and the part." Therefore, in this stage there's a " 'blurring' of the subjective psyche with the material world."

This "magical" stage of the undeveloped mind, Wilber explains, is known "almost totally through *bodily categories* and schemes," therefore this self-sense constitutes what's known as the *bodyego* or *bodyself.* Because of this fusion (or confusing) of body and self, Wilber uses the mythological symbol of the Typhon (or half human, half serpent) to represent the fact that "the reptilian complex and the limbic system dominate" during this period of self-development. Nonetheless, even at this lower stage of development, Wilber points out, this is still a higher-order unity that is actually "the first expression of individuality."

CHAPTER 4. "THE MEMBERSHIP SELF" explains how and why language (and thus social membership) is so crucially important in the further development of a self-sense. Indeed, Wilber realizes that it's probably "the single most significant process on the Outward Arc of the individual's life cycle." This *"membership self,"* as Wilber calls it, includes higher cognitive styles, an extended notion of time, a vastly expanded emotional life, and the elementary forms of reflexive self-control. These characteristics end up constructing a "descriptive reality" of the world, so much so that "the structure of one's language is the structure of one's self." Wilber interestingly points out that this structure conforms to the "membership" sense of self shown by Carlos Castenada's Yaqui shaman don Juan, who revealed that "through language, grammar, and syntax, [a person] learns a particular description of the world which [they] will be taught to call reality."

Further, the membership mind is a form of "paleological thinking" or the beginning of abstractions, proto-concepts, and thinking proper, all of which has a mythical atmosphere to it since this stage of mental activity is "more refined than magic [the preceding Typhon], but not quite capable of logical clarity [the succeeding mental-egoic]." Nonetheless, the membership self is a significant growth in consciousness, yet Wilber is careful to maintain that this stage too is accompanied by its own set of "difficulties and potential conflicts." With a clearer awareness of both past and future, this developing "mental or verbal or syntaxical being" is better able to delay impulsive and instinctual responses (the uroboric and Typhon levels), and thus exert some degree of self-control, including the "roots of proto-volition and will power."

With the emergence of language this *lower verbal mind* becomes a *mythic self*, which further differentiates from the body as it emerges as a higher mental or *verbal self*. Wilber goes on to explain that this lower mental self creates a "world of vast temporal extension" which in turn ends up generating an even more "tensed self-sense." Wilber elaborates on a general rule of evolutionary development (also demonstrated in *Up from Eden*) holding that "There is a price to be paid for every increase in consciousness." Therefore at this particular stage "The price one pays for this growth in consciousness is an increased recognition of one's own separateness and thus one's own vulnerability." Nevertheless, he argues that this is indeed "a monumental advance along the evolutionary curve of consciousness," for it's a way of transcending the world. Psychologically, this occurs mostly because "Through language one can anticipate the future, plan for it, and gear one's present activities in accordance with tomorrow." Wilber also notes this is also "the beginning of the sublimation of the body's emotional-sexual energies into more subtle, complex, and evolved activities."

CHAPTER 5. "MENTAL-EGOIC REALMS" begins with Wilber defining the ego as "a thought-self, a self-concept . . . or constellation of self-concepts, along with the images, phantasies, identifications, memories, sub-personalities, motivations, ideas and information related or bound to the separate self-concept." This *ego-concept stage* also includes the *superego* or the *"intra-egoic thought structures,"* as well as *script programming,* which develops when "the previous *inter*-personal relationships became *intra*-psychic structures," i.e., they're generated by the various dynamics in parent-child relations. Wilber draws on the evidence garnered from developmental psychology and psychoanalysis to show that the total ego is composed of various components: personae or the social masks or the fraudulent self, and shadows, or the suppressed aspects.

Therefore, he gives a very simple and useful formula: persona + shadow = ego.

In following the development of this overall ego realm, Wilber summarizes its emergence with three major chronological stages:

1. the **early ego,** age four to seven;

2. the **middle ego,** age seven to twelve;

3. the **late ego,** age twelve to the beginning of the Inward Arc.

The integral psychologist continues by explaining this developing ego is a "newly emergent higher-order structure." As with all developmental structures, this stage generates "the triadic form of *differentiation, transcendence,* and *operation*," which essentially means "that the higher structures can both *operate* upon and *integrate* the lower structures":

1. **early mental-egoic self** or rep-mind emerges between the ages of four and seven, and it "therefore can to a certain degree operate upon the biological world (and the earlier physical world) using the tools of simple *representational* thinking [hence the rep-mind]."

2. **middle ego/persona stage** or con-op usually emerges around age seven, and it consolidates around *concrete operational* (con-op) thinking (after Piaget), therefore, this stage of the mental-self "can *operate* on the concrete world and the body using concepts."

3. **late ego/persona stage** or form-op emerges by the time of adolescence, also known as *formal operational* thinking, therefore, when "the self simply starts to differentiate from the concrete thought process . . . it can to a certain degree *transcend* that thought process and therefore *operate* upon it."

Wilber concludes by correlating this verbal ego-mind with some of the great wisdom traditions: the Manovijnana (of Mahayana Buddhism); the Manomaya-kosha (in Hinduism)—(with *mano* meaning "mind" in Sanskrit); the fourth and fifth *skandhas* (of Hinayana Buddhism); the fifth and lower aspects of the sixth *chakra* (of yoga); the Tiphareth ("egoic self"), Hod ("intellect"), and Netzach ("desire") (of Kabbalah); and Maslow's self-esteem needs.

CHAPTER 6. "SYMBOLS OF TRANSFORMATION" discusses the "transformation-upward or Ascent of Consciousness." In this case, Wilber emphasizes that "each emergent level is thus not so much a total negation of the previous level, nor does it come from the previous level, but rather is a transformation (and transcendence) of [the previous level]"; thus he explains:

- a **transformation** involves the *vertical* transition (differentiation, transcendence, operation) or the move from one *deep structure,* the "defining form of a level," to another;

- a **translation** involves a *horizontal* movement of *surface structures,* which are those forms "constrained by the form of deep structures."

With these clear differentiations, Wilber is thus able to delineate an important operating principle of development: *"Whenever translation fails, transformation ensues—and it can be regressive transformation or progressive transformation."*

In an insightful review, Wilber suggests that psychopathology results when "a particular type of transformation sets the stage for a particular type of dis-ease, while translation itself governs the nature of the specific symptoms which eventually surface." Nonetheless, the transpersonal theorist fully acknowledges that the development of *vertical transformation* is actually "the most important symptom of all: those which are symbols of *higher levels* trying to emerge in consciousness, symptoms which point not to the id but to God."

CHAPTER 7. "CENTAURIC REALMS" goes into detail about the particular level of consciousness development that integrates, for the first time, the "ego-mind with all the lower levels." Thus there emerges an integrated self wherein mind and body are harmoniously one." Wilber named this stage for the centaur, "the great mythological being with animal body and human-mind existing in a perfect state of at-one-ment." This total bodymind or centaur gives the evolving, more highly integrated self a new and greater sense of "autonomy, self-actualization, and intentionality."

This leads into Wilber's first sustained and in-depth presentation of what's now known as the pre/trans fallacy, or the understanding that acknowledges that "although there are naturally superficial similarities between pre- and trans-structures, the two simply cannot be equated." This detailed differentiation brings forward the interesting and insightful observation that "many structures on the Outward Arc that are 'pre-' appear on the Inward Arc as 'trans-':

- pre-verbal deep structures give way to verbal structures, which give way to trans-verbal structures;

- pre-personal gives way to personal, which gives way to trans-personal;

- pre-egoic, moves to egoic, which moves to trans-egoic;

- pre-mental goes to mental, which goes to trans-mental—and so on."

Wilber presents a diagram depicting this sequence and summarizing few of these major differences. (See Figure 3: "Pre/Trans Highlights in the Life Cycle.")

Next, in a detailed example drawn from human developmental, Wilber discusses the identifiable differences between the "pre-verbal primary process" (or the prepersonal) and what's also known as "vision-image" and "high-phantasy" (or the transpersonal). Wilber explains that vision-image is "not a lower but a higher mode

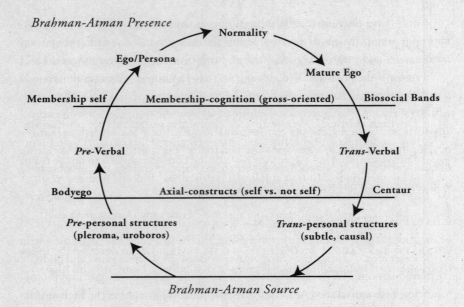

Brahman-Atman Presence

Normality

Ego/Persona

Mature Ego

Membership self   Membership-cognition (gross-oriented)   Biosocial Bands

Pre-Verbal   *Trans*-Verbal

Bodyego   Axial-constructs (self vs. not self)   Centaur

Pre-personal structures   *Trans*-personal structures
(pleroma, uroboros)   (subtle, causal)

Brahman-Atman Source

**Pre/Trans Highlights
in the Life Cycle**
FIGURE 3

of cognition," in other words, it's really trans-verbal. When this type of pre/trans distinction is clearly made, it's possible to better realize that "the infant bodyego has a *pre-verbal, pre-control, pre-inhibition spontaneity,* whereas the mature centaur evidences a *trans-verbal, trans-control, trans-inhibition freedom.*"

In conclusion, Wilber explains, the existential-centaur is part of the ever-increasing and embracing process of higher-order integration, one that transcends the verbal mind and body while integrating them. In this event, this centauric transformation and integration is also, he claims, "the major transition towards the higher subtle and transpersonal realms of being."

CHAPTER 8. "SUBTLE REALMS" introduces some of the higher transpersonal realms, using Buddhist terms to help identify and define them and outline their characteristics. Wilber passes over the previous and lower *"gross realm,"* or the Nirmanakaya, where "almost all of the data generated by orthodox Western psychology pertains." Instead, he turns to the mystic-sages of the world's spiritual traditions, East and West, in order to glimpse the contours of the higher and inner *subtle* dimensions of existence, or the Sambhogakaya (which itself is divided into low and high, or early and late):

• The **low subtle,** or the astral-psychic, includes most paranormal experiences, such as astral travel, out-of-body-experiences, occult knowledge, auras, true magic, psi phenomena, ESP, precognition, and so on. Wilber states that in this realm, "consciousness . . . is able in some ways to *transcend* the normal capacities of the gross bodymind and therefore *operate* upon the world and the organism in ways that appear . . . [to be] a natural extension of the transcendent function of consciousness."

- The **high subtle** or "extraordinarily high-order transcendence, differentiation, and integration," is the experience of higher archetypal forms and symbolic visions that have been "universally and consistently said to be the realm of high religious intuition and literal inspiration." Indeed, Wilber reveals, at its peak or most evolved potential, the high subtle culminates with the realization of "God as an Archetypal summit of one's own Consciousness."

CHAPTER 9. "CAUSAL AND ULTIMATE REALMS" tries to describe the indescribable causal or the Dharmakaya realm, also subdivided into low and high:

- The **low-causal** structure completes the process initiated in the high-subtle, i.e., the self's identification with final-God or the "ground or essence of all the archetypal and lesser-god manifestations." This obtains when "one's own Self is here shown to *be* that final-God, and consciousness itself thus transforms upwards into a higher-order identity with that Radiance."

- In the **high-causal,** beyond even the One God, there's complete realization of the "*Formless Consciousness, Boundless Radiance* . . . [where] all manifest forms are so radically transcended that they no longer need even appear or arise in Consciousness."

This, in turn, leads to the final transformation of the **ultimate realm** or the Svabhavikakaya:

- "Consciousness totally awakens as its *Original Condition* and *Suchness* (*tathata*), which is, at the same time, the condition and suchness of all that is, gross, subtle, or causal." This is the "ultimate state of consciousness" where the "entire World Process then arises, moment to moment, as one's own Being." This ultimate unity, Wilber clarifies, is paradoxically a "Perfect Transcendence, which is not a transcendence from the world but a final transcendence as the World."

Wilber goes on to emphasize that these trans-personal conditions are entirely different from, although often similar in appearance (or description) to, the prepersonal realms. Therefore, with great detail and clarity, this important pre/trans differentiation is explained in the chapter's conclusion. In summary, Wilber attempts to answer the perennial psychological quandary of "Eternity: God or Id?" by emphatically differentiating that "the id *is* timeless—but it is pre-temporal. God *is* timeless—but it is trans-temporal."

CHAPTER 10. "THE FORM OF DEVELOPMENT" is the most important chapter in the book because it outlines the primary theme behind the *Form of Development*—or the *Form of Transformation*—which is constant on all levels throughout the spectrum of consciousness, or, as Wilber simply says, "from the womb to God."

The Form of Development is when each emerging higher-order structure of the self

1. first identifies with that structure;

2. then differentiates from it;

3. therefore effectively transcends it.

The succeeding higher structure is then able to operate on those previous lower levels simply because the higher level embraces or subsumes them. Throughout this process of growth or development, Wilber emphasizes, "As each higher-order structure emerges, the self eventually identifies with that structure—which is normal, natural, appropriate."

This tripartite process in the Form of Development is precisely the "transcend-and-include" aspect of evolution. Wilber's main point, then, is that "At each point in evolution, what is the *whole* of one level becomes merely a *part* of the higher-order whole of the next level." In this case, with the transformation of each level, "Each growth is essentially the same, and it is the form of transcendence, the form of development." Therefore, the entire process of development or the complete evolution of consciousness "traces a gentle curve from *subconsciousness* through *self-consciousness* to *superconsciousness,* remembering more and more, transcending more and more, integrating more and more, unifying more and more, until there is only that Unity which was always already the case from the start, and which remained both the alpha and omega of the soul's journey through time."

CHAPTER 11. "TYPES OF THE UNCONSCIOUS" outlines five distinguishable features of the unconscious, all of which can be clearly differentiated when applied to an integral and dynamic or developmental viewpoint:

1: the **ground-unconscious** is most fundamental since it is "all the deep structures existing as potentials ready to emerge, via remembrance, at some future point";

2. the **archaic-unconscious** is "simply the most primitive and least developed structures of the ground unconscious";

3. the **submergent-unconscious** includes what "was once conscious, in the lifetime of the individual but is now screened out of awareness";

4. the **embedded-unconscious** is similar to Freud's idea of the unconscious, or those aspects of the self that are "embedded *as* the self, [thus] the self cannot totally or accurately see it. It is unconscious, but *not* repressed";

5. the **emergent-unconscious** contains all "those deep structures which have not yet emerged from the ground unconscious."

Basically, Wilber's spectrum psychology maintains that these various types of the unconscious are not differentiated enough in orthodox psychology, therefore, they're often confused by psychoanalysis and traditional psychological theories, a point integral psychology can clearly address.

Indeed, Wilber points out that this confusion is so profound that some even go so far as to "trace samadhi back to infantile breast-union; they reduce transpersonal unity to prepersonal fusion in the pleroma; God is reduced to a teething nipple and all congratulate themselves in explaining the Mystery."

CHAPTER 12. "MEDITATION AND THE UNCONSCIOUS" reviews the process of meditation, which Wilber defines as "a sustained instrumental path of transcendence," thus, from the developmental point of view, "Meditation is evolution; it is transformation." Wilber argues that meditation supports sustained development or growth because it will tend to "frustrate the present translation and encourage the new transformation" into higher transpersonal realms (beyond the translations of the egoic and lower levels). This transformational process is usually accomplished by a series of special conditions often practices given by a spiritual master, guru, roshi, etc., all of whom are here discussed by Wilber with a sympathetic understanding based on actual practice and insight. In essence, he asserts, when the ego is frustrated by authentic spiritual practices, this means "growth occurs by adopting higher translations [the particular form of practice] until one can actually transform to that higher realm itself." In other words, by using the spectrum of consciousness framework, Wilber maintains "orthodox therapy can certainly complement meditation," thus he's postulating a new form of genuine integral psychology.

In conclusion, Wilber outlines the various levels of transpersonal growth. By doing so, he maintains that meditation is "simply higher development, which is simply higher evolution—a transformation from unity to unity until there is simple Unity, whereupon Brahman, in an unnoticed shock of recognition and final remembrance, grins silently to itself, closes its eyes, breathes deeply, and throws itself outward for the millionth time, losing itself in its manifestations for the sport and play of it all. Evolution then proceeds again, transformation by transformation, remembering more and more, until each and every soul remembers Buddha, as Buddha, in Buddha—whereupon there is then no Buddha, and no soul. And that is the final transformation."

CHAPTER 13. "THE ATMAN PROJECT" points out that mankind "wants only Atman [or the ultimate unity consciousness, Buddha, Godhead], but wants it under conditions which prevent it." Wilber demonstrates that we constantly condemn ourselves to "allow only compromises: substitute unities and substitute gratifications." This becomes the working definition of the so-called Atman-Project. Wilber summarizes in this chapter the breadth of philosophical and spiritual history by revealing many of the various strands of this psychological project, including Atman-telos, Atman-denial, and the endless variety of substitute unities and substitute gratifications.

Wilber then brings forward the two major drives of the Atman-Project where each have both positive and negative qualities (named after Freud's primary drives):

- **Eros** or the "perpetuation of its [the self's] own existence";

- **Thanatos** or the "avoidance of all that threatens its [the self's] dissolution"

Next, Wilber goes on to speak about humankind's fundamental dilemma, i.e., the basic anxiety or primal fear which is mostly generated from "an awareness of death and the terror of death." And, he continues, since "this Death Terror is inherent in the separate-self sense . . . [then] men and women have two choices in the face of death and Thanatos: they can deny and repress it, or they can transcend it in the superconscious All." Wilber's integral vision, based in the perennial philosophy of the world's wisdom traditions, here recommends this "arch battle" or this "primal mood of fear [can be] removed only by true transcendence into Wholeness [or Atman Itself]." In the end, he concludes: "Evolution proceeds by a series of . . . abortive attempts to reach Atman-consciousness—proceeds, that is, via the Atman-project, with each step, as it were, getting a bit closer . . . until *all substitutes for Unity are tried and found wanting, and only Unity itself remains.*" Only then does a person finally realize "there is only the Real and the soul grounds itself in that superconscious All which was the first and last of its only desire."

CHAPTER 14. "EVOLUTION THROUGH THE LOWER LEVELS" deals with a century's worth of research gathered by modern psychology, which has theorized and studied in great detail the lower realms or early stages of human development. Traditional psychology is therefore often epitomized by the recognition of various forms of incest (desire or Eros) and castration (painful disruption or Thanatos).

- First, by tracing the ascent up the spectrum of consciousness and reviewing each level's accompanying Atman-project, Wilber guides us through the meaning of uroboric incest, or the "tendency to seek out that lowest-level unity of all—simple material embeddedness, wherein all conscious forms melt back into the utter darkness of the prima material"; and then he addresses uroboric castration or the tendency to resist the "death" or transcendence of this primal level.

- Next, he reviews the succeeding level of typhonic incest, which involves oral eroticism or the "desire to find some sort of unity through merging with the Great Mother by incorporating or swallowing the Great Mother"; and then typhonic castration (or death) which is only accepted when the self "can differentiate itself from the Mother and thus transcend that primitive maternal embeddedness."

- Then the membership phase (or the emergence of the verbal self) goes through an anal stage when "the body becomes the focus of life and death," which is because "the self now experiences separation anxiety with regard to the physical body or its appendages or its representatives (such as feces)."

In particular, this terror of bodily vulnerability and possible death or pain is correlated with a similar lesson in one of the Buddha's three marks of existence, i.e., *anicca,* or the "suffering of impermanence." The point, Wilber maintains, "is simply that the child is seeking some sort of Unity—union with the Mother, trying to be *both* Self and Other—through the symbolic manipulation of the body. The search itself, and the context of the search, is simply for that Unity which is the ground of all grounds. Consciously or unconsciously all beings gravitate towards that Estate."

CHAPTER 15. "EVOLUTION THROUGH THE EGOIC LEVELS" continues the discussion of psychological incest and castration, this time centering around the emerging psychosexual phase of early childhood development, famously known as the Oedipal/Electra complex. It is here that Wilber explains that "precisely what lies behind the Oedipal complex" is "the project of becoming God—or rather, *the project of moving toward God-consciousness,* unity consciousness, Atman-consciousness." The Oedipal/Electra complex, in other words, means that basically the child "imagines he can bodily unite with the Great Mother and thereby gain a type of prior unity." However, the self finally realizes it "has to die to the desire to reunite the bodyego with the world in an exclusively sexual fashion."

This type of intense and difficult *separation process* brings up the necessity to clearly distinguish between psychological *differentiation,* which is a healthy advance over previous-level fusion, and *dissociation,* which is differentiation taken to the extreme, and thus, it turns into a pathological form of awareness.

In other words, the healthy and natural emergence of the mental-egoic levels definitely involves a shift or "movement from 'maternal incest' to 'paternal incest,'" which means that the overall transformation to the egoic level is basically one of moving from the "body/maternal to egoic/paternal," a notion that's associated with the "whole realm of superego psychology." These Atman-project substitutes also appear as the ego-ideal (or the Eros "positive" side) and conscience (or the Thanatos "negative" side), which, once again, has to be surrendered (or castrated) in order for evolution to proceed into the higher trans-egoic realms.

CHAPTER 16. "HIGHER-ORDER EVOLUTION" begins by explaining that based on the insights of existentialism and humanistic psychology, in order for the centaur level to emerge, or for the self to enter into the realm of an integrated bodymind, then "one must accept the death of the ego." Today, Wilber explains, this transformation is especially difficult since the "average mode of the self-sense in society at large seems to be early, middle, or late egoic . . . thus, individuals who grow *beyond* the egoic stages have to do so either on their own exceptional talents or through special professional assistance."

- Specifically, Wilber mentions, this assistance includes the "existential-humanistic therapist (and beyond that, the spiritual Masters)." Again, special conditions act as symbols of transformation, which help to establish a strong autonomy, based on intentionality, or finding an authentic meaning in life, also seen as the "drive to self-actualization, consciously engaged." This process of self-actualization, Wilber defines as a form of centaur-incest because "Here we are faced for the first time, with the life and death [castration] of the total bodymind." Nonetheless, he emphasizes, this existential stage (centaur) is also "the first self-sense strong enough to openly face and confront death." Indeed, at this stage, in order to gain the furthest reaches of human nature, the self must finally surrender or "die to centauric incest," which actually means the self must even "go beyond self-actualization."

- The same incest-castration process (as in all consciousness evolution) also continues into the subtle realms, once again, "through special conditions imposed by the Guru or Master." Thus subtle incest can involve subtle visions, sounds, ecstatic releases, and so on, whereas subtle castration is a "relentless fear of losing Light" or worse, "the actual obliteration of the self by Light."

• When the self finally surrenders its subtle incest and separation anxiety, it thereby transcends itself emerging into the next stage, the formless causal realm, or the "fall into Formlessness." Here causal incest becomes "an extremely subtle tension (if that's the right word) between the Manifest and Unmanifest." In other words, Wilber recognizes that the "Manifest castrates Formless Radiance . . . the last knot to uncoil from around the Heart."

• After this causal castration occurs there only remains the ultimate state, the "Great Mystery" or the "unqualified Consciousness" which is "always already the case." Seeing and knowing this state "where Form and Formless are each other" is traditionally known as enlightenment, which itself "appears to be the end limit of evolution, but is actually the prior reality of every stage of evolution, first to last, endlessly."

In concluding the process of higher-order evolution, Wilber poetically and mystically champions this ultimate boundless vision of enlightened wisdom: "As infinite, all-pervading and all-embracing Consciousness, it is both One and Many, Only and All, Source and Suchness, Cause and Condition, such that all things are only a gesture of this One, and all forms a play upon it. As Infinity, it demands wonder; as God it demands worship; as Truth, it demands wisdom; and as one's true Self, it demands identity. In its being, it has no obstructions, and this no trace continues forever. Bliss beyond bliss beyond bliss, it cannot be felt. Light beyond light beyond light, it cannot be detected. Only obvious, it is not even suspected. Only present, it shines even now."

CHAPTER 17. "SCHIZOPHRENIA AND MYSTICISM" offers a classic example of the pre/trans fallacy, explaining that modern psychology's conflation of schizophrenia and mysticism is rooted in their failure to distinguish between prepersonal and transpersonal phenomena. Orthodox psychiatry, in other words, often erroneously claims: "If the mystic-sages aren't purely pathological, then they are at least halfway there." Instead, Wilber first clarifies that schizophrenia is usually due to some sort of failure of egoic translation where "the self is drawn into pre-egoic realms, it is open to invasion (castration) from the trans-egoic realms." However, Wilber does concede that this process may be, only at times, a true type of regression in service of the ego, which is an attempt at rebuilding a healthier ego. On the other hand, when the schizophrenic self returns to a state of normalcy, in most cases, this new self does not exhibit stable adaptation to those higher transpersonal realms, therefore Wilber maintains it's best seen as a prepersonal regression.

With mysticism, however, Wilber counters that "the satori-mystical state is a different type of unity." Instead, he clarifies, unlike the schizophrenic the "mystic seeks progressive evolution. He trains for it. It takes most of a lifetime—with luck—to reach permanent, mature, transcendent and unity structures. . . . He is not contacting past and infantile experiences, but present and prior depths of reality." Therefore, with Wilber's spectrum model "the all-important distinction between pre and trans" is fully made, in which case it's consciously modeled that in order "to Return to the Divine one doesn't regress to infancy. *Mysticism is not regression in service of the ego, but evolution in transcendence of the ego.*"

CHAPTER 18. "INVOLUTION" concludes the book with a discussion on how and why involution occurs, which is defined as "the enfolding of the higher in the lower . . . the pre-condition of evolution." Wilber discusses *The Tibetan Book of the Dead* (or *Bardo Thodol*) (*bardo* means "gap," "transition state," "intermediate state," or as the integral philosopher prefers, the "in between").

Wilber then traces this reported forty-nine-day journey "in between" death and (re)birth as being simply "what happened to you before you were born." This ancient sacred Tibetan text refers to three major stages that occur after death:

1. Stage One: the ultimate-causal realm or the Clear Light of Reality (the Chikhai), which is "the state of the immaculate and luminous Dharmakaya, the ultimate consciousness, the Brahman-Atman." This momentary regaining of ultimate Atman Unity is lost again by desire (or Eros-seeking) and in a contracting from the radiant intensity of the Divine. Therefore Wilber continues to outline the traditional descriptions of the self as it moves through the various *bardo* stages down from the Clear Light, which is also a description of the self proceeding through involution.

2. Stage Two: "the subtle realm or the Sambhogakaya" (the Chonyid), which involves "the appearance of peaceful and wrathful deities," as well as displaying blissful visions and divine sounds. Wilber continues: "According to the Thotrol, most individuals simply recoil in the face of these divine illuminations—they contract into less intense and more manageable forms of experience . . . they are attracted to the lower realms, drawn to them, and find satisfaction in them [as substitute gratifications]." Wilber draws interesting relationships between Agape (Atman-telos) and Contraction (Atman-

restraint) as constituting vertical transformation; and between Eros (evolution) and Thanatos (involution) as constituting horizontal translation.

3. Stage Three: "the gross-reflecting mind [the Sidpa], the realm where the mind starts to turn towards the gross, physical world in search of substitutes." At this stage of the involutionary process, the soul is "tending towards body-bound modes, typhonic and uroboric, and its substitute gratifications are reduced to simple hedonistic pleasure and sexual release." (See Figure 4: "Evolution and Involution," and Figure 5: "The Bardo Passage.")

This process of involution is a form of "amnesia and the in between," thus Wilber explains it's actually a reversal of the Atman-project which is when *"looking for Wholeness in ways that prevent it, the individual is driven to create tighter and narrower and more restricted modes of identity."* These "step downs" where the self is lost in "a swoon of forgetfulness" mean that from the beginning "all of the higher levels are present, but they are simply forgotten." This then becomes the ground-unconscious where "all the higher stages of being . . . exist there as undifferentiated potential. Development or evolution is simply the unfolding of these enfolded structures, beginning with the lowest and proceeding to the highest: body to mind to subtle to causal."

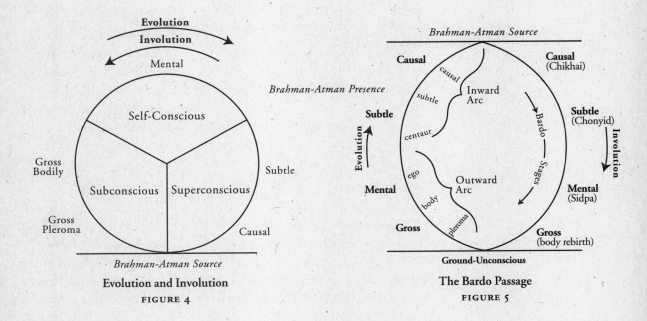

Evolution and Involution

FIGURE 4

The Bardo Passage

FIGURE 5

Wilber has presented a summary of his model's essential thesis of involutionary/evolutionary process: beginning with the newborn baby "All the deep structures of the various levels—gross, mental, subtle, causal—*already* exist as potentials in the ground unconscious, they do not have to be created, just remembered . . . and they simply crystallize out and differentiate from the lower modes as evolution proceeds. . . . Evolution, then, is a remembrance of involution—a rediscovery of the higher modes which were enwrapped in the lower ones during the soul's flight from God. . . . Evolution is holistic because it is nature's remembrance of God."

Yet Wilber does not limit this process solely to history or reflecting an individual's past ontogeny because, right now, "what happens In Between the beginning and ending of *this* moment is identical to what happened In Between death and rebirth as described by the Thotrol." This present involutionary process is also known as *microgeny* or the "moment-to-moment . . . micro-genetic involution of the spectrum of consciousness."

In the end, Wilber can only reflect on the perennial wisdom expressed by the world's religious traditions: "The soul's duty in this life is to remember. The Buddhist *smriti* and *sati-patthana,* the Hindu *smara,* the Sufi *zikr,* Plato's recollection, Christ's *anamnesis:* all those terms are precisely translated as remembrance." In other words, when evolution ends with the "final remembrance, the impact of only God in absolute Mystery and radical Unknowing dismantles once and for all the Atman-project." Thus, while fully awake, any person may consciously yet paradoxically realize, as does Wilber, "because there is always only Atman, the Atman-project never occurred."

CHAPTER 4

Up From Eden

A Transpersonal View of Human Evolution

BY KEN WILBER

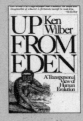

(Garden City, N.Y.: Anchor Press/Doubleday, 1981);

reprint edition (Wheaton, Ill.: Quest Books, 1996);

The Collected Works of Ken Wilber, Vol. 2 (CW2) (Boston: Shambhala Publications, 1999)

Preface
Introduction

Up From Eden: A Transpersonal View of Human Evolution is a major Wilber/Phase 2 work emphasizing human developmental evolution, anthropology, and collective human history, therefore focusing on the relational exchanges or the interaction between individual interior consciousness (Upper-Left quadrant), interior cultural worldviews (Lower-Left quadrant), and exterior social techno-economic systems (Lower-Right quadrant) in the Great Nest of Spirit, or Kosmos.

Up From Eden was written in about two months in late 1979, after it had started as the opening chapter to *The Atman Project* (1980), yet both books were forestalled until Wilber resolved the pre/trans fallacy, a period he described as "the most turbulent theoretic times of my life." Consequently, he reexamined his earlier "Romantic" position of a "recaptured-goodness" model (Wilber/Phase 1), and turned to anthropological and historical evidence to supplement the psychological orientation of his spectrum of consciousness theories. After a substantial amount of research he realized he needed to abandon certain aspects of his earlier views as presented in his first two books and shift the spectrum's emphasis toward developmental evolution or a "growth-to-goodness" model (Wilber/Phase 2). Once Wilber's pre/trans dilemma was resolved, he was able to complete both *The Atman Project* (focusing on individual human development, or ontogeny) and *Up From Eden* (focusing on collective human evolution, or phylogeny).

Up From Eden: A Transpersonal View of Human Evolution was published in 1981 (Anchor Press/Doubleday); reprint paperback edition (Quest Books, 1996); it is now part of *The Collected Works of Ken Wilber, Volume Two (CW2)*, (Shambhala Publications, 1999).

The **PREFACE** begins with a quote from the second-century Neoplatonic philosopher Plotinus, who asserted: "Humankind is poised midway between the gods and the beasts." Wilber makes it his task in this book "to trace the curve of history and prehistory that brought humankind to that delicate position." This evolutionary story, according to Wilber, not only embraces the prehistorical past but the present as well as "our possible future evolution." By doing so, this "transpersonal view of human evolution," based upon a wide spectrum of evidence, argues that "The future of humankind is God-consciousness, and [therefore] we will want to examine this future in the entire context of human history."

Nonetheless, even with such grand potentials, Wilber argues that "If men and women are up from the beasts and their way to the gods, they are in the meantime rather tragic figures. Poised between the two extremes, they are subjected to the most violent of conflicts. No longer beast, not yet god—or worse, half beast, half god: there is the soul of humankind. Put another way, humankind is an essentially tragic figure—with a beautifully optimistic future—if they can survive the transition."

In short, Wilber emphasizes that with human evolution "*There is a price to be paid for every increase in consciousness,* and only that perspective, I believe, can place humankind's evolutionary history in the proper context." Neither an idealistic nor pessimistic view, Wilber's overall big picture of the "historical development and evolution of consciousness" holds that, "in the main, both views are correct. Each step in the evolutionary process was an advance, a growth experience, but it was bought at a high price—it demanded new responsibilities, and responsibilities that humankind did not always live up to, with such tragic results." Thus Wilber's theoretical platform is based on the perennial philosophy, a developmental logic, and a sociological theory that will be discussed throughout the volume (and in principle, by incorporating the sociocultural dimensions in the evolution of consciousness, he's anticipating his future integral Wilber/Phase 4 or AQAL "all-quadrants, all-levels" approach).

The **Introduction** presents important terms and concepts needed to navigate the wealth of information presented herein, drawing on numerous disciplines ranging from psychology, anthropology, sociology, the history of religions, and mysticism (especially as affirmed by the perennial philosophy). Wilber declares on the opening page that it's best to view history "not as a chronicle of individual or national feats, but as a movement of human consciousness . . . the story of men and women's love affair with the Divine," even mystically invoking "history as the sport and play of Brahman." Yet Wilber also wants to include the evidence of scientific evolution as well, even though we cannot determine the meaning of history solely on the basis of scientific evidence. For that we need a transpersonal view, which helps give insight into "the *meaning* of that going-somewhere, which we call history: its movement is divine and its meaning transcendent."

However, to make this point Wilber won't use the Judaeo-Christian understanding of the Divine or God as a "great Other" but rather will rely on the wisdom of the perennial philosophy (in Latin *philosophia perennis,* a name credited to Leibniz and popularized by Huxley), and which, in summary, "forms the esoteric core of Hinduism, Buddhism, Taoism, Sufism, and Christian mysticism, as well as being embraced, in whole or part, by individual intellects ranging from Spinoza to Albert Einstein, Schopenhauer to Jung, William James to Plato." For example, as Wilber explains, "As a first approximation, the perennial philosophy describes the Ultimate as a seamless whole, an integral Oneness, that underlie but includes all multiplicity. The ultimate is prior to this world, but not other to this world, as the ocean is prior to its waves but not set apart from them." Since this is "a view held by the great majority of the truly gifted theologians, philosophers, sages, and even scientists of various times," Wilber maintains that "In its purest form it is not at all anti-science but, in a special sense, trans-science or even ante-science, so that it can happily coexist with, and certainly complement, the hard data of the pure sciences."

Giving a masterful overview of the world's mystical wisdom in just a few pages, Wilber states that "The essence of the perennial philosophy can be put simply: it is true that there is some sort of Infinite, some type of Godhead, but it cannot properly be conceived as a colossal Being, a great Daddy, or a big Creator set apart from its creations, from things and events and human beings themselves. Rather, it is best conceived (metaphorically) as the ground or suchness or condition of all things and events. . . . the Nature of all natures, the Condition of all conditions. . . . But notice, in this regard, Nature is not other than all life forms: Nature is not something set apart from mountains, eagles, rivers, and people, but something that, as it were runs through the fibers of each and all. . . . The Absolute is not Other . . . the Absolute is One, Whole, and Undivided . . . [thus] the perennial philosophy defines God not as a Big Person but as the Nature of all that is . . . whether we say all things are forms of Nature, forms of Energy, or forms of God."

Being quite different from a petitionary religion or one of salvation, the "religion" of the perennial philosophy also posits this integral Wholeness (the Absolute) as being "always already" present in men and women. "Unlike rocks, plants, or animals, human beings—because they are conscious—can potentially discover this Wholeness. They can, as it were, awaken to the Ultimate. Not believe in it, but discover it." Indeed, this discovery of Wholeness, as the transpersonal philosopher clarifies, is "the phenomenon of transcendence—or enlightenment, or liberation, or *moksha,* or *wu,* or *satori* . . . finding the Light of Being. . . . This is the aim of Buddhist meditation, of Hindu yoga, and of Christian mystical contemplation. That is very straightforward; there is nothing spooky, occult, or strange in any of this—and that is the perennial philosophy."

In order to help model this path of transcendence, Wilber introduces the *Great Chain of Being,* a concept used extensively in the perennial philosophy, and which is a movement, "to use Western terms, from matter to body to mind to soul to spirit." In this event, "History, from this viewpoint, is basically *the unfolding of those successively higher-order structures,* starting with the *lowest* (matter and body) and ending with the *highest* (spirit and ultimate wholeness)." When seen this way, Wilber will convincingly demonstrate that "Just as ontogeny recapitulates phylogeny, man's evo-

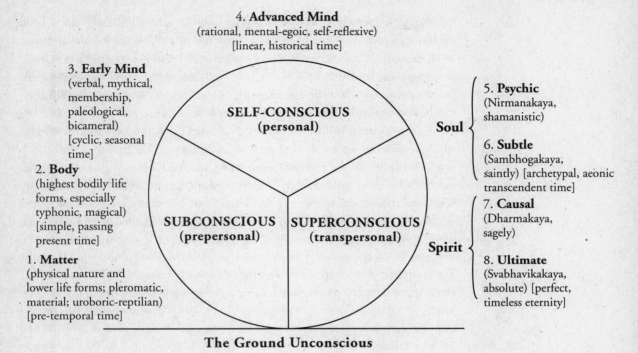

4. Advanced Mind
(rational, mental-egoic, self-reflexive)
[linear, historical time]

3. Early Mind
(verbal, mythical,
membership,
paleological,
bicameral)
[cyclic, seasonal
time]

2. Body
(highest bodily life
forms, especially
typhonic, magical)
[simple, passing
present time]

1. Matter
(physical nature and
lower life forms; pleromatic,
material; uroboric-reptilian)
[pre-temporal time]

SELF-CONSCIOUS
(personal)

SUBCONSCIOUS
(prepersonal)

SUPERCONSCIOUS
(transpersonal)

Soul

5. Psychic
(Nirmanakaya,
shamanistic)

6. Subtle
(Sambhogakaya,
saintly) [archetypal, aeonic
transcendent time]

7. Causal
(Dharmakaya,
sagely)

Spirit

8. Ultimate
(Svabhavikakaya,
absolute) [perfect,
timeless eternity]

The Ground Unconscious

The Great Nest of Being
FIGURE I

lutionary history began at the lower rungs of the Great Chain of Being, and it did so *because* it had to recapitulate, in human form, all the earlier and prehuman stages of evolution." Indeed, this view explains why human beings are seen as "something of a *halfway mark* on the path of transcendence. . . . That is, *self-consciousness* is halfway between the *subconsciousness* of nature and the *superconsciousness* of spirit. The subconsciousness of matter and body gives way to the self-consciousness of mind and ego, which in turn gives way to the superconsciousness of soul and spirit—such is the 'big picture' of evolution and history, and such is the context of humankind's history as well." (See Figure 1: "The Great Nest of Being.")

Wilber's transpersonal approach to history also introduces one of his more unique yet clarifying concepts, which comes from thoroughly understanding the evolutionary development of the spectrum of consciousness, and which is that throughout history there are actually two parallel strands of evolution: 1) the average human consciousness, which is "an evolution of average experience and awareness," and 2) the most advanced level of consciousness, which is embodied in "the prophets, the saints, the sages, the shamans, the souls who . . . discovered the higher levels of being through an expansion and precocious evolution of their own consciousness."

Yet, as Wilber is constantly aware, "Not only is Spirit itself the *ultimate stage* of evolution, it is the *ever-present ground* of evolution as well," or the ground and goal of all existence. He explains that "For the perennial philosophy, the Great Other is not an outside God but the Nature and Suchness of one's own being, and thus history points to, and is the unfolding of, one's own true Nature. . . . And history can be consummated because that All can be fully *rediscovered*."

In this context, Wilber introduces the Atman Project, which uses the Hindu idea of Atman to represent "ever-present and ultimate Wholeness," and the fact that, "According to the perennial philosophy, the rediscovery of this infinite and eternal Wholeness is man's single greatest need and want." Yet, still, "Because man wants real transcendence above all else, but because he will not accept the necessary death of his separate-self sense, he goes about seeking transcendence in ways that *actually prevent* it and force symbolic substitutes. And these substitutes come in all varieties: sex, food, money, fame, knowledge, power—all are ultimately substitute gratifications, simple substitutes for true release in Wholeness." Thus, as a definition: "this attempt to regain Atman consciousness in ways that prevent it and force symbolic substitutes—this I call the Atman project." In other words, he continues, "the Atman project is a substitute for Atman, but it also contains a drive to re-capture Atman."

With this comprehensive yet transpersonal perspective on the human drama, Wilber goes on to introduce the nature of culture and the denial of death since, with human beings, "the world of objective substitute gratifications is nothing other than the world of culture." This is especially true since, in essence, "Culture is the major outward antidote to the terror generated in the face of death; the promise, the wish, the fervent hope that the skull will not in fact grin in at the banquet." Wilber concludes: "History is the saga of men and women working out their Atman projects on one another, in both negative (Thanatos) and positive (Eros) ways, creating thereby kings and gods and heroes on the one hand, and strewing recklessly the corpses of Auschwitz and Gulag and Wounded Knee on the other." In this case, with both extremes in mind, Wilber still optimistically affirms: "history does indeed have meaning . . . [yet] it will probably be thousands, maybe millions, of years before humankind as a whole evolves into superconsciousness. Except for those few . . . who individually choose the path of transcendence. . . ."

Part I. Tales of Dim Eden

CHAPTER I. "THE MYSTERIOUS SERPENT" begins by observing that ever since "the so-called Big Bang [approximately 15 billion years ago], Evolution had succeeded in moving, *in hierarchic order,* from simple insentient and lifeless atoms to vegetal life, and beyond vegetation to simple animal forms (protozoan, amphibian, reptilian), and then to higher animal forms (mammalian, with simple mental images and paleosymbols) . . . [thus] each stage of evolution *goes beyond* its predecessors but must nevertheless *include and integrate* them into its own higher order." In this context, Wilber presents a basic tenet running throughout all his writings: "Each stage of evolution *transcends but includes* its predecessors." Significantly, this means that "By implication, humans include but transcend *all* prior evolutionary stages."

Wilber then goes on to point out since "earliest *human ontogeny* was a recapitulation of *cosmic phylogeny,*" then the "Dawn Human . . . began its career *immersed* in the subconscious realms of nature and body, of vegetable and animal, and initially 'experienced' itself as indistinguishable from the world that had already evolved to that point." By the time of the earliest hominids or the protohumans (such as *Australopithecus afarensis* to, perhaps, Homo habilis), Wilber carefully notes that although "the first protohumans had already moved *beyond* those lowest of stages [of the Great Chain, therefore] they were initially *dominated* by them." In this case, it's only natural that these primal creatures, although the crown of creation, would still seem to dwell in a type of pre-personal Eden or *primal atmosphere* of *primitive awareness* since they were "embedded in physical nature (pleroma) and dominated by animal-reptilian impulses (uroboros)."

Therefore, Wilber designates this stage of "primal naturic unity" metaphorically as the *pleroma-uroboros* since the *uroboros* is the circular symbol of the mythic snake eating its own tail, thus representing "the serpent of nature, the home of Dawn Man."

Evidence is then presented from numerous scholars (such as Cassirer, Neumann, and others), but in particular, the Swiss cultural historian Jean Gebser, who labels this period the archaic structure, and according to Wilber, it "corresponds closely with our 'pleromatic-uroboric (level 1).'" They both claim that although these evolving apelike hominids are an extraordinary advance, they actually lived in a subconscious world where "the Dawn State of Humans was one of dreamy immersion in and oneness with the material and natural world." In this case, in accord with Wilber's important pre/trans distinction and differentiation (of Wilber/ Phase 2), Wilber insists that although their Eden-like existence may "appear angelic in many ways, it is the bliss of ignorance, not of transcendence."

From this point on, Wilber radically applies this type of critical distinction called the pre/trans fallacy, which is defined as making a clear differentiation "between *pre-personal* and *trans-personal,* pre-mental and trans-mental, pre-egoic and trans-egoic." Wilber argues that "The actual state of the Garden of Eden universally described by mythology . . . was *pre-personal,* not trans-personal, and sub-conscious, not superconscious." Nonetheless, with the perspective of the full spectrum of consciousness, he still maintains that philosophically "We cannot let the account rest there . . . for the essence of a being is determined not by the lowest to which it can sink—animal, id, ape—but the highest to which it can aspire—Brahman, Buddha, God."

Wilber introduces the notion of the ground unconscious, which is "similar to, but not quite the same as, the Ultimate Atman," and this is because it represents the "enfolded potentials" which "unfold as actualities." Therefore the spectrum model makes a clear differentiation between deep structures, which are the fundamental patterns of the "structural potentials," and surface structures, which "are molded and conditioned by the force of cultural and historical contingencies."

In addition, this sophisticated type of transpersonal understanding allows Wilber to bring to light the fact that the uroboros can be associated with "a potential known in general terms as 'kundalini energy' . . . [thus] we can bring our entire historical account of the evolution of consciousness into full accord with kundalini theory, a fact of no little significance."

Part II. Times of the Typhon

CHAPTER 2. "THE ANCIENT MAGICIANS" describes the next major stage, which probably emerged with our archaic hominid ancestors known as Homo erectus (these delineations are admittedly approximations), but even more so, with anatomically modern human beings currently labeled archaic Homo sapiens and Homo sapiens sapiens (including the Neanderthals and Cro-Magnon). Importantly, in complete agreement with Gebser, Wilber suggests that "The first men and women to appear on the earth during these times (about 200,000 years ago) were not just simple hunters and gatherers—they were magicians." As ancient hominids emerged from the realms of the archaic and subconscious uroboros, the sense of being a definite separate self unfolds with greater intensity, thus there develops a magical worldview since, in summary, "although the self is distinguished from the naturic environment, it remains *magically intermingled* with it."

Wilber symbolizes this era with the Typhon—the mythological half-human, half-serpent—in order to symbolize the fact that our early human ancestors lived during this ancient "stage of development wherein self and body are not yet clearly differentiated." He points out that although this was a "new and higher self being constructed by the centering and focusing of awareness," it's still primarily a type of dream world similar to Freud's primary process. The world of the *magical-Typhon* is perfectly exemplified by the *totem,* whereby humans are "still structurally linked to animal ancestors," as can be seen in paleolithic cave paintings, which are believed to be a type of sympathetic primitive magic.

However, unlike most scholars, Wilber is careful to distinguish "magic [as] a more or less correct perception of a primitive and lower level of reality" from psychic ability, which was only a trait of "the most advanced individuals of this period." Therefore, in acknowledgment of our ancient ancestors' roots, Wilber proposes that "as men and women emerged from their uroboric slumber in Eden, they emerged as magical-Typhons. . . . They emerged as magicians."

CHAPTER 3. "THE TWILIGHT OF DEATH" discusses the important psychological fact that not only did early humanity, or the magical-Typhon, live in a "dream-like world of animistic connections—interfused with body, cosmos and nature," they also experienced a world of nightmares. This was because as early humans were beginning to realize their own separateness from nature, they also discovered their own imminent mortality, which was generated by "a basic, unavoidable, inescapable terror inherent in the separate self-sense."

In this case, Wilber establishes the "defining formula for this period: when the Typhon emerged from the uroboros, he emerged with the imprint of death." In other words, "The more death threatens, the more extended a time series is needed to deny it," in which case, this denial of death (following Becker) effects all the levels of self-identity expressed by the polar symbols of Eros or the life-affirming positive side: "all sorts of substitute gratifications that *pretend* to fulfill its desires for Unity, for infinity and eternity and cosmocentricity," and Thanatos or the life-threatening negative side: "it screens out or represses anything that threatens death, dissolution, transcendence, extinction."

Wilber generally subdivides this new form of the Atman project and period of human prehistory known as the "Magical-Typhonic Period" into (all dates are approximations):

1. **Low-Typhonic Period:** c. 200,000–50/40,000 B.P.; or when "low-typhonic man was almost entirely preverbal, possessing only images (primary process) and the crudest of paleosymbols"; (including archaic Homo sapiens, Homo neanderthalensis (Neanderthals), probably Homo erectus);

2. **High-Typhonic Period:** c. 50/40,000–10,000 B.P.; or when "high-typhonic man was still largely preverbal, but in addition to images he probably possessed more complex paleosymbols, modifiers, commands, and some nouns"; (including Cro-Magnon and other anatomically modern Homo sapiens sapiens).

In reviewing the lifestyle of these protohumans and early Homo sapiens, the evidence tends to indicate a temporal mode revolving around the "passing present." Nonetheless, although these typhonic humans were still largely preverbal, Wilber suggests this was probably the first real sense of time for any type of human creature. He also points out that there were other forms of death denial that were evolving simultaneously, such as the "prop of Culture," whose basic aim has been "to serve the two arms of the Atman project: the manufacture of more Mana (Eros) and less Taboo (Thanatos)." During typhonic times this included the magic of the hunt (or the day-to-day spilling of blood), as well as the earliest practice of rituals and the reality of blood sacrifices. Indeed, as Wilber concludes, the Magical-Typhonic Period was collectively involved in "a cultural activity of magical compensations—a magical Atman project writ large."

Wilber therefore summarizes another important tenet in human evolution (and the Atman project): "the new time, self, and culture were all simultaneously the products of a higher and expanding consciousness, a system of elaborate substitute gratifications, an expression of higher life, and a fetishistic denial of higher death." In other words, as evolution proceeds it doesn't necessarily get better or easier, because "The more men and women emerged on that *necessary* climb from the subconscious, the more *difficult* their substitute gratifications became to achieve and sustain, so that they were soon forced into playing out their Atman projects on their fellow human beings. And as people became substitute objects, those people became *victims* of one sort of cruelty or another."

In regard to today, as evolution continues, Wilber suggests that it may be possible "to arrange individual Atman projects so that they overlap in mutually supportive ways [synergy]." Thus the integral theorist concludes: "There is only one solution to this tangled mess of inter-clobbering Atman projects, and that is to open the soul to that which it ultimately desires—Atman consciousness itself."

CHAPTER 4. "VOYAGE INTO THE SUPERCONSCIOUS" more closely examines those few extraordinarily advanced-tip or leading-edge individuals who lived during the Magical-Typhonic Period: the tribal shamans. Wilber makes a strong case that "the shaman—the true shaman—was the first great voyager into the realms of the superconscious." As many other scholars have noted (such as Eliade and Campbell), the shaman's perceptions were usually revealed in "trances of ecstasy," a form of self-transcendence that "lifts the shaman out of the ordinary and marks him or her as extraordinary."

In order to better explain this phenomenon, Wilber reviews the "difference between translation and transformation" where "once an individual *transforms* to a particular level of consciousness, then he continues to *translate* both his self and his world according to the basic structures of that level," thus transformation is a change in deep structures or "a type of *vertical* shift or even mutation in consciousness structures," while translation is a change in surface structures or "a simple *horizontal* movement within a given structure."

In other words, "Evolution is a successive shift and unfolding, *via transformation,* of higher-order *deep structures,* within which operate, *via translation,* higher-order *surface structures."* This reduces to an important but simple formula: "When translation fails, transformation ensues, and the transformation can—depending on numerous variables—be toward higher structures or lower structures, *progressive* or *regressive."* Thus he concludes, "What we are actually following in our survey of human evolution is the successive failures of certain modes of *translation,* followed by a *transformation* to new modes of translation."

In relation to shamanic consciousness or voyage, "The true shamanistic experience was nothing less than the death and transcendence of the separate self," yet, nevertheless, "True shamanistic religion is extremely crude, very unrefined, and not highly evolved." This is because "Since consciousness *on the whole* had advanced no further than the typhonic level, then when the typical shaman 'jumped' into the superconscious realms, the *farthest* he got was into the Nirmanakaya class—the class of ecstatic body trance, of actual psychic capacity, of ajna chakra opening, and so on." Nonetheless, they were the "true Heroes of the typhonic times . . . and their individual and daring explorations in transcendence could only have had a truly evolutionary impact in consciousness at large."

Once more, in order to really bring about the end of the Atman project, instead of just bringing "little offerings of barter sacrifices, wherein ritual, whether of the hunt or of the modern office, remains," Wilber insists on emphasizing that "Men and women cannot be whole until they rediscover that ultimate Whole—until death-and-transcendence is accepted, until total sacrificial surrender of the separate self." This brings up a detailed classification of the successive hierarchic structures of superconsciousness or "the evolution of spiritual experience" [also called "the hierarchic evolution of religious experience" in earlier editions] which are based upon "three broad but rather different classes [from Buddhism] each with its own techniques, its own path, and its own characteristic visions and experiences":

1. **Nirmanakaya** (or the *psychic*) is associated with kundalini yoga and bodily-sexual energies;

2. **Sambhogakaya** (or the *subtle*) is centered around "the subtle realm of light and audible illuminations and subtle sounds";

3. **Dharmakaya** (or the *causal/ultimate*) "follows consciousness to its ultimate root, where man and God are transformed into each other, where the subject/object dualism is permanently dismantled, where ultimate Atman is resurrected . . . by uprooting the separate-self sense altogether."

Since, as Wilber explains, "These three classes are not three different yet equal 'experiences' of the Ultimate Source, but rather successively closer approximations of that Source (or Atman-Spirit)," then he concludes, perhaps controversially, that the shaman "was not the first great mystic-sage; he did not even understand the saintly realms; he was simply the *first master of kundalini/hatha yoga* (and only then in a rudimentary form)." Now, however, as our human evolutionary story rushes "out of the Paleolithic and towards the Mesolithic, humankind was poised for the second major step."

Part III. Mythic-Membership

CHAPTER 5. "**FUTURE SHOCK**" deals with the difficult transformation brought about with the emergence of a full-fledged language (a fairly recent event, according to the evidence gathered here) as well as by "a new and heightened death seizure." This new emergent sets the stage for simple agriculture, which arose sometime around the tenth millennium B.C.E., and was simply "one of the single greatest transformations in the history of our species." Therefore, arising with language, the mesolithic and neolithic epochs of the agricultural revolution, according to Wilber's analysis, were "the most obvious effect, or perhaps vehicle, of a deeper transformation in structures of consciousness." Since "the world of farming is the world of extended time, of making present preparations for a future harvest, of being able to gear the actions of the present toward significant future goals, aims, and rewards," then this "basic and profound expansion of consciousness allowed man to picture the future more clearly, and thus plan and farm for it." Consequently, as one example, since ceremonial graves were now becoming common practice, as Wilber points out, "commonplace graves meant commonplace death seizure. The skull, indeed, was grinning in at the banquet—and humankind knew it."

Wilber subdivides this Mythic-Membership Period, where "For the first time in humankind's two- or three-million-year history, a large number of people were asked to live together in permanent villages," into

1. **Low-Membership Period:** c. 9500–4500 B.C.E.; or when "by 7000 B.C.E. innumerable farming settlements existed throughout the Near East, and by 5000 B.C.E. agricultural colonization had spread throughout the Tigris-

Euphrates and Nile valleys, swelling the population of some cities to 10,000 inhabitants";

2. **High-Membership Period:** c. 4500–1500 B.C.E.; or "the period dominated by the great classical civilizations of the hieratic city-states, theocracies, and dynasties."

Since the evidence shows that "farming consciousness was *membership* consciousness—that is, community consciousness or comm-*unity* consciousness," then Wilber defines this new membership self as a verbal self where "the key feature of the membership structure is language itself." This is a uniquely *human* accomplishment never before known in the realm of nature, therefore, following other scholars (such as Julian Jaynes), Wilber too is convinced that "the Mesolithic and Neolithic farming consciousness could *only* have been supported by a *linguistically tensed consciousness* . . . [thus] language became the *predominant vehicle of the separate self* (and thus of culture at large)."

And, as he continues, because "language transcends the present, the new self could transcend the body," therefore it creates a "*verbal* manifestation of the magical primary process," or what's also known as paleologic thinking (after Silvano Arieti). Paleologic involves a "mythical cognition" which is a "'mixture' of magic and logic" since it's still fusing whole/part, subject/predicate, therefore "the first language, the first mind, is a mind of mythic or paleological form." Consequently, it's from this Mythic-Membership structure of consciousness that there arose "the world's greatest and most enduring classical mythologies and classical civilizations: of Egypt and Babylon and Sumer, of Aztec-Mayan Mexico, and Shang China, and Indus Valley India, of Mycenaean Crete and earliest Greece."

With the symbolizing mind of mythic-membership cognition and the expansion into farming and the "symbolate world," there also come new forms of social control based on the growing surplus production of mythic culture, including increasing social power, more money, extra goods, and the greatly increased growth of tribes and villages into "cities approaching 50,000 people." Thus, as Wilber summarizes: "With the mythic-membership structure of consciousness: it is the very nature of this structure that it supports a very basic type of membership cognition and therefore membership culture." Also, the increase in population concentrated first in villages and then in cities gave rise to specialized classes that "freed certain individuals (freed consciousness itself) for other and more specialized tasks," including some "time for mental contemplation."

Nevertheless, as Wilber outlines when he examines "the Atman project in farming consciousness," these cultural projects are nothing more than the sophisticated substitute gratifications and immortality symbols of the new verbal membership self, especially since "every stage of evolution is not only moving toward God, it is also fighting God." Yet, nevertheless, this also means for Wilber (in disagreement with Ernest Becker on this point) that "Humans desire God because their highest potential is real God and they won't rest until they actualize it." In place of Atman/God, humanity settles for misplaced substitutes such as seeking for "immortality through future time, excess farmed goods, money, and gold." Consequently this creates the need for some "type of social organization and social control which is more complex than that of simple hunting bands of the magical-typhonic era." And this is exactly what the shared mythic-membership structure of consciousness provides. In other words, this stage of collective human consciousness evolution is "precisely the psychological structure that supported the early farming communities of the low-membership stage as well as the first great civilizations of the high-membership stage." In conclusion, Wilber offers a review of, and comparison with, the recently acclaimed work of Julian Jayne's theory of the bicameral mind.

CHAPTER 6: "THE GREAT MOTHER" first announces, once more, that "the Ego is perched midway between total slumber in the subconscious and total enlightenment in the superconscious, and for this reason alone is the most distressful period of all." In this case, as "evolution became conscious of itself" (after Huxley and Teilhard de Chardin), and "as each new structure of consciousness is laid upon the previous ones, the task becomes one of integrating and conciliating these different structures," especially since, as always, "the growing complexities of consciousness bring not only new opportunities but also dreadful responsibilities."

Wilber continues to gather together reams of anthropological and archeological evidence, drawn from the work of some of the world's greatest scholars of consciousness evolution (from Joseph Campbell, Pierre Teilhard de Chardin, Jean Gebser, Erich Neumann, Sri Aurobindo, and others), in order to explain why with the new mythic-membership consciousness we find that "suddenly, very suddenly, civilization had begun." As only one example Wilber reviews "the grandeur that was Egypt," as well as the expressions of "Egyptian madness." Yet with this development of consciousness there was of course the accompanying Atman project (including its associated symbolic substitutes and death denials, all arising from an increased separate self-sense, etc.).

Importantly, in conjunction with this emergent structure, around 4500–2000 B.C.E., there's "the appearance of an unprecedented constellation of sacra—sacred arts and sacred things"; yet they're also accompanied by "new terrors and new horrors." Specifically, Wilber makes clear that "In the central rite of the great religions of the mythic-membership cultures, we find the secret key not only to the ultimate states of transcendence but also to the terrifying depths of human cruelty," and that is bloody sacrifice, where "initially, it was almost universally human beings, but later animals (the goat, bull, boar, horse, lamb) were substituted." This is an important point often overlooked by theorists involved in romantic yearnings for the resurrection of past eras (or golden ages).

In a comprehensive review of sacrifice as the core of membership mythology, Wilber first points out that during the mythic stages of neolithic villages and growing civilizations, the "dominant Figure running throughout the religions of the mythic-membership cultures, is mostly without doubt that of the Great Mother." Yet, according to paleologic thinking (i.e., confused magic and mythic cognition), people believed, based on menstrual and natural cycles, that "the Great Mother *needs blood* in order to bring forth new life." Therefore "The first great ritual was a ritual of blood sacrifice, offered to the Great Mother—to Mother Nature—in a bartered attempt to quench her desire for blood, blood that, for various reasons, was (not altogether incorrectly) equated with life itself." However, Wilber makes an astute differentiation between the Mother image when she's seen in her "natural/biological aspects" as the Great Mother, as distinct from her "transcendent/mystical aspects" when's she recognized as the Great Goddess.

The Great Mother is the symbol of nurturing, of biology, nature, and cyclic renewal, representing "bodily existence itself, matter and nature, water and earth, and life and death in that naturic realm." Thus the Great Mother would either take the form of "the Great Nourisher, the Great Protectress, and the Great Destroyer, the Great Devourer—what Sullivan would call the Good Mother and the Bad Mother. But by all accounts, this is an intense relationship, basic, awe-inspiring, fundamental, and consequence-laden." This innate belief goes back as far as the Paleolithic caves of typhonic times where Venus figurines are often found in abundance, especially since "we see the Great Mother arise as a correlate of bodily existence itself." But by the time of the Mythic-Membership Period, where the Great Mother was often symbolized by the serpent uroboros, the separate self-sense was becoming more structured and so Her demand was greater: "And what she demanded was sacrifice—human sacrifice."

In fact, as Wilber claims, when this is understood in the context of the Atman project and the evolution of consciousness, it's possible to know why "what we call civilization, and what we call human sacrifice, came into being together." Human sacrifice (and sacrifice in general) was a form of symbolic substitute generated in the frightening face of death and its denial, especially since it apparently gave the emerging separate self (or ego) a greater sense of cosmocentricity. Nonetheless, this bloody substitute also burdened humanity with a false projection of immortality (the Atman project in action). As Wilber explains, "The sacrificial ritual was carried out to appease and expiate death guilt," therefore "the ritual served as a magical substitute for transcendence and immortality."

Wilber then proceeds to review in detail the psychological reasons behind the mythic phenomena of the Great Mother and her consort, including the monthly lunar and menstrual cycle as being a periodic journey into the underworld, epitomized with the myth of the "three-day-dead-and-resurrected god." He also emphasizes that the Great Mother was the Chthonic Mother or "the Earth Mother, which pulled the newly crystallizing mind back into the body, back into mother nature, back into instincts and will-less subservience to the typhon and the uroboros." In other words, as he underscores, "The self at this stage of evolution was not yet strong enough to detach itself from the Great Mother, from mother nature, from the body, the emotions, and the flood of the unconscious."

However, Wilber also recognizes that "The essence of the Great Mother is that she demanded the dissolution, the sacrifice, of the separate self. Let us note that: the Great Mother demands the dissolution of the self."

CHAPTER 7. "THE GREAT GODDESS" balances the preceding chapter on the natural/biological Great Mother with the transcendent/mystical aspects of nature, better known as the "Great Goddess—a subtle Oneness of actual Transcendence, representative of true Divinity." This differentiation, usually never brought forward in historical or mythological surveys, clarifies that the true sacrifice being asked for by the One Goddess is a self-sacrifice on a deeper esoteric (or inner) level, not just on the surface exoteric (or outer) level of blood sacrifice. Again, another advantage of spectrum psychology is that it distinguishes the esoteric practices of the few "advanced-tip" individuals, who use symbols in the process of vertical transformation, from the exoteric rituals of the "average-mode" masses, who use signs to initiate horizontal translations, although "the very same outward symbols, rituals, and ceremonies can be and often were used for both."

Therefore, Wilber's analysis contends that "Most modern anthropologists fail to ask this question because they fail to distinguish between sign and symbol, exoteric and esoteric, translation and transformation."

In contrast to the Great Mother's demand for blood sacrifice as a symbolic substitute of the Atman project, Wilber clarifies that with the Great Goddess of Divine Oneness what's really being called for is a symbolic self-sacrifice, not a literal blood sacrifice. In other words, what the Great Goddess really wants is self-sacrifice, thus Wilber summarizes: "The Great Mother demands blood; the Great Goddess demands consciousness." By referring to the "supreme Western example" of Christ's sacrifice in Christianity, Wilber explains how "Those same sacraments, without murder, and carried out in a self-sacrificial frames, are perfectly legitimate symbols of transformation and *aids* to transcendence. . . . In that capacity, they are outward and visible forms of inward and spiritual truths." In other words, by making a clear distinction between the exoteric sacrificial rites "for the masses of membership individuals," and the esoteric "sacrificial ceremony" used by the advanced few to achieve "the essence of transpersonal liberation via self-transcendence," it's then possible to see that the "most highly evolved souls of this period saw into the realm of Sambhogakaya, or the subtle realm of the superconsciousness."

In a discussion of the "Sambhogakaya Vision: Subtle Oneness," Wilber points out that this "beginning insight into subtle and archetypal oneness leads to the conceptions of a One God or One Goddess which underlies and gives birth to all manifest worlds and all lesser god or nature-spirit figures." In other words, technically, "The first widespread glimpses into subtle oneness occurred under the auspices of the Great Goddess, so that even to this day, modern saints and sages continue to refer to this initial realization as belonging to the Mother Goddess (as even the most cursory study of Hindu and Vajrayana texts will disclose)." Nevertheless, although this "core of esoteric religions" fully realizes that "the sacrifice of self discloses the Eternal," Wilber's main point is that "This esoteric understanding was possessed by few, and the masses themselves turned to a fury of sacrifice for other and decidedly less noble reasons, and in literal renditions that could not conceal the underlying barbarism of the great and Devouring Mother."

This transpersonal perspective, therefore, contends that it's absolutely necessary to take into account the "two strands of evolution," which Wilber again reviews in depth: "Where average (or overall) evolution was producing successively advanced exoteric civilizations and world cultures, the further reaches (or most advanced tip) of consciousness evolution were disclosing successively higher levels of the superconsciousness sphere," therefore he formulates:

- "Average-Mode = Mythic-Membership (level 3) = farming consciousness = biological Earth Mother or Great Mother = magical sacrifices for fertility and expiation = substitute sacrifices (the Atman project);

- Most Advanced Mode = beginning of Subtle Level (level 6) = insight into one archetypal deity or god/dess = Great Goddess = self-sacrifice in awareness = realization or communion with archetypal oneness = true sacrifice (toward Atman)."

In this case, Wilber contends that "It is obvious that the *average mode* and the *most advanced mode* often interact in their symbolism and tangentially support each other to some degree." Yet it's also possible to better understand why historically the average masses were engaging in blood sacrifices, or a substitute sacrifice, while a few advanced-tip individuals, who knew "it was necessary to die to the separate-self sense," were the individuals who were really sacrificing the self, that is, engaging in real self-transcendence. These esoteric few were some of humanity's first true priests and religious saints since they were "perfectly aware of psychic and subtle realities, of kundalini or serpent-power transformations, and, likewise, of the Great Goddess of the subtle realm." Nonetheless, Wilber also reminds us that "Every great world religion, in fact, has *both* exoteric and esoteric aspects, and those aspects usually coexist perfectly with one another, the *exoteric* rituals serving the masses, the *esoteric* serving the advanced." Therefore, he concludes: "There is not just a variety of religious experience, but *a true evolution of religious experience,* hierarchic in nature, developmental in structure."

Further, as this evidence suggests, Wilber emphasizes that the advanced-tip individuals, on the leading edge of evolution are also examples of humanity's most highly evolved people in a spiritual sense, thus he states another important evolutionary principle: "This overall evolution of religious experience, culminating in radical Atman consciousness, is simply a prefiguration of the future course of the evolution of average consciousness (or consciousness on the whole)." In other words, these evolved few individuals, both men and women, are beacons to our own evolutionary future, yet, in continuing our current human evolutionary story, Wilber points out it's "only in the next stage of growth, that of the mental-egoic, would consciousness break free from the seduction of the Dark and announce in its myths the coming of the Sun-Light."

CHAPTER 8. "THE MYTHOLOGY OF MURDER" begins by emphasizing that "*The ultimate psychology is a psychology of ultimate Wholeness,* or the superconsciousness All [i.e., the 'one ultimate Whole (Atman)' or *sunyata*]." This approach explains how the Atman project continuously erects "a self-boundary or barrier" that "requires a constant expenditure of energy, a perpetual contracting or restricting activity," and which, ultimately, "obscures the prior Wholeness itself." Elsewhere (as in *The Spectrum of Consciousness*), Wilber has identified this activity of the separate-identity feeling as being the primal repression which, as already noted, has "two major dynamic factors: Eros and Thanatos":

Eros "ultimately is the desire to recapture that prior Wholeness which was 'lost' when the boundary between self and other was constructed. . . . Eros, then, is the undying power of seeking, grasping, wishing, desiring, perpetuating, loving, living, willing, and so on. And it is *never* satisfied because it finds only substitutes. Eros is ontological hunger."

Thanatos is "the simple force of reality, the 'pull' of the ultimate Whole, [which] acts moment to moment to tear down that boundary [between self/other, subject/object] . . . as the individual, moment to moment, re-creates his illusory boundaries, so reality, moment to moment, conspires to tear them down. . . . Thanatos is not a force trying to reduce life to inorganic matter. . . . Thanatos is the power of sunyata, the power and push to transcend illusory boundaries . . . [thus] its real meaning is *transcendence*" instead of just "death."

In Wilber's penetrating analysis of the human race's penchant for "murderous hostility" appearing en masse with the mythic-membership level, he emphasizes that since "the pseudo-self is becoming more complicated, more articulate, and more structured in the world of form," then "whatever natural aggression may be innately present in humans . . . is amplified through conceptual domains, and part of the amplification includes the heightened apprehension of death, which, when turned outward, explodes into really vicious aggression and hostility, and in proportions not given instinctually. And that murderous hostility is pre-eminently the substitute sacrifice, *a killing of others to magically buy off the death of the self.*"

This violent struggle of life and death (between self and others) gets dramatically played out in the mythology of murder, for on its deepest level, according to this transpersonal view, "Murder is a form of substitute sacrifice or substitute transcendence." Collectively, then, on the level of large city-states and growing civilizations, with populations of thousands upon thousands of people, this translates into the killing war machine or "sacrifice run riot." This is especially true since, dreadfully, "when people become objects of the negative Atman project, they become victims, substitute sacrifices, scapegoats—and War, the mass potlatch of death-dealing for immortality, is merely wholesale victimage in outright form." And, as Wilber rightly observes, "The history of mankind, beginning precisely at the membership stage, is the history of the wholesale substitutes sacrifices and murderous wastages that have specifically marked the animal called *Homo sapiens.*"

Historically, therefore, as Wilber continues, "around the third millennium B.C.E., especially in Sumer those early city-states of Ur, Uruk, Kish, Lagash, and all— modern, massive warfare of one state against another was born." And, grimly but soberly, he acknowledges: "One fact stands alone: War has been popular. It has thus served a necessary function, and served it well. And it served the cultural Atman project, the attempts to make egos into gods, power-soaked and blood immune." Thus, Wilber starkly concludes: "Money and War were the cultural forms of the Atman project that were most accessible to vast numbers of the common folk. . . . For not only could you traffic for immortality in the marketplace, you could traffic for it on the battlefield. And historically, *both* have been the necessary glues for complex societies—one positive, one negative, covering both sides of the Atman project." Yet Wilber affirms the true remedy: "*Transcendence,* true transcendence, is the only cure for the homicidal animal."

CHAPTER 9. "POLIS AND PRAXIS" accounts for how, with the rise of mythic-membership societies, there is a concurrent rise in human cultural activity—or "what the Greeks would eulogize as *polis*"—and which, as Wilber explains, was "the first arena of truly human relationship, the relationship found nowhere else in nature, the relationship that *specifically* defined the new species of *Homo sapiens*"; therefore he defines his integral use of these ancient Greek terms: Polis is "*shared human community,* and a community based on unrestricted communication (via language). In the best sense, polis is simply the arena of membership, a higher form of unity based on transcendent symbol exchange"; praxis is the "*activity in polis,*" or more fully (following Aristotle), the "purposive, enlightened, moral behavior pursued in the company of polis. It is meaningful and concernful activity, not based on subhuman wants and desires, but based upon mutual human recognition and unrestrained communication."

In conjunction, Wilber goes on to explain that "Polis-consciousness, or membership-consciousness, *transcends* (but includes) the needs and characteristics of the subhuman stages which preceded it in evolution. With polis-praxis, consciousness takes on its *first truly human characteristics.*" Extending beyond the capabilities of the lower plant and animal world (or of the uroboros and Typhon), language and communication was the primary level of exchange for this "arena of the membership-self," where "humankind, in developing a true (if initial) mentality, came into possession of *history, intention, culture, discourse,* and *ethics.* Came, that is, into possession of *polis-praxis.*"

To help outline the various levels or the hierarchical structures of the compound individual (a human compounded of the spectrum of consciousness), Wilber introduces the "various systems of exchanges," or the levels of exchange, with which each level has its own paradigm, sphere of influence, and "archetypal champions" (see complete list in Chapter 19). In other words, he explains, "*Each successive level of exchange* represents a higher evolutionary growth and therefore expresses a higher-order attempt at unity (or a higher-order Atman project)." Since the spectrum model is defining the human being as "a compound individual of all lower levels of reality, capped by its own particular and defining level," then they too "can—like any other compound—not only function but *malfunction,* not only grow but degenerate, not only serve but oppress." And, he continues, "Society, or polis, is simply a *compound* of these compound individuals. Likewise, praxis is the activity of compound individuals in that compound society." As only one example, in the sphere of polis-praxis this means the power of "the state—as Marx, Freud, Socrates, and Christ discovered in their own spheres—can be brutally oppressive of everything from religion to ideas to sex to labor."

In order to promote these generalized observations, Wilber goes on to thoroughly review the fact that the growing civilized community (or membership) of human beings, due to their increasing size and population, evolved a new social order, that of "kingship—as opposed to simple tribal chieftainship." This political arrangement, based on emerging surplus, "began sometime in the low-membership period," but "kingship itself truly blossomed during the high-membership period." Importantly, as Wilber fully acknowledges: "The invention of kingship is a phenomenon of unequaled impact. Politically, it was probably the single greatest change in humankind's consciousness that had ever appeared; its repercussions were awesome—and its effect are still with us today."

Since kingship was based in the mythic-membership structure of consciousness, then "the first kings were gods," therefore they were literally sacrificed in ritual regicide being "ritually immolated" in honor of the Great Mother/Goddess Herself as *sacrificial symbolic substitutes* for the positive benefit (Mana/Eros) of the society as a whole. However, as power and wealth continued to grow and a "massive surplus" was accumulated, and when "the temples, in their exoteric function, soon gave way to banks," it became useful for other substitute victims to be put to death in place of the king. Indeed, as Wilber sardonically points out, "The *first* thing that had to change in order for politicos to step into the office of 'divine' kingship, was to get rid of that nasty sacrifice business."

In further examining "the psychological function of the king," Wilber maintains that they became a psychological necessity for the emerging mental-egoic structure of consciousness since "the king served as the original bearer of *individualized* or egoic consciousness." Therefore, simply, the "king was rightly viewed as a Hero." This psychological transference allowed the powerful elites to be seen as divine kings or as the god-king since, according to the Atman project: "Men and women *need* visible Atman figures because they have forgotten that they themselves are Atman. And until that recollection is made, men and women will always be slaves to heroes. Psychologically, and therefore politically."

Part IV. The Solar Ego

CHAPTER 10. "SOMETHING UNHEARD OF" introduces the next major turning point in human history when "Sometime during the second and first millennia B.C.E., the exclusively Egoic Structure of Consciousness began to emerge from the ground unconscious (Ursprung) and crystallize out in awareness." In fact, because this is the "last major stage—to date—in the collective historical evolution of the spectrum of consciousness (individuals can carry it further, in their own case, by meditation into superconsciousness)," then it is indeed the "first glimmerings of the modern era."

To begin with, for convenience, Wilber subdivides the Mental-Egoic Period of development, or at least for the West (Europe and Near East), into three general periods:

1. **Low Mental-Egoic Period:** c. 2500–500 B.C.E.; or "a time of transition; the breakdown of the membership structure, the emergence of the [early] egoic structure; the resulting rearrangement of society, philosophy, religion, and politics";

2. **Middle Mental-Egoic Period:** c. 500 B.C.E.–1500 C.E.; or beginning "[for Gebser] with the appearance of the *Iliad,* Jaynes with the *Odyssey,* others might like to mark Solon of Greece as most outstanding (sixth-century B.C.E. Greece: Solon, Anaximander, Thales, Pythagoras—people we of today can understand with little difficulty) . . . from the sixth-century B.C.E., the world was never the same—this middle egoic period lasted until around 1500 C.E., with the Renaissance";

3. **High Mental-Egoic Period:** c. 1500 C.E.–present; or "with the Renaissance, and shortly after, Galileo and Kepler, and then Newton, and . . . suddenly we arrive at the present, still in the High Egoic Period."

This new Mental-Egoic Structure is presented as a great advancement in consciousness and since "it was a tremendous growth experience—it marked a transcendence over the dimly conscious, still somewhat pre-personal, mythic and diffuse structure of the membership stage. It opened up the possibility of *truly rational and logical thought.*" Yet, most significantly, Wilber recognizes that it also "marked the final emergence from the subconscious realm, which meant that the self could now return to the superconscious in ways and to a degree never before quite possible." At least this was on the positive side (of Eros), for among other things, it "brought introspection and self-analysis, penetrating science and philosophy." However, on the negative side (of Thanatos), the egoic mentality also "rose up arrogant and aggressive, and—blown sky high by its Atman project—began to sever its own roots in a fantasy attempt to prove its absolute independence." In this case, again, Wilber acknowledges that "The ego—lying precisely halfway between the subconscious and the superconscious—was in a position to deny its dependence on both."

Wilber too, following the lead of other scholars (such as Neumann, Gebser, Campbell, etc.), concedes that during "the beginning of the egoic period, what we discover is unequivocally clear: *an entirely different form of myth begins to emerge,* a myth never before seen to any great extent. . . . In the new myths, we find an extraordinary occurrence: the individual triumphs over the Great Mother—breaks free from her, transforms her, defeats her, or transcends her. And this is the 'Hero Myth,' the myth that *is* this period of history." In other words, as Wilber defers to Gebser: "the *naturic-mythic circle* . . . was blasted apart by the emergence of the *heroic ego.*" With a few mythic examples of this evolutionary drama, Wilber points to the great Hero vanquishing the typhonic realms of the serpent (the uroboros), such as with the victory of Zeus, the Greek god, over the Typhon, or, in ancient India, the successful triumph of "Indra, king of the Vedic pantheon, over the cosmic serpent Vritra."

Wilber also continues to highlight that this great struggle to release the ego from the magic/mythic realms of the subconscious has had drastic, deadly, and far-reaching consequences, especially "once the Great Mother myths were transcended by the Hero myths, the Great Mother was not integrated into subsequent mythology." With penetrating insight into this complex matter, Wilber maintains that in the West instead of integrating "the old Great Mother image into a new and higher corpus of Great Goddess mythology," the Western mind pathologically dissociated the feminine force as a powerful mythological archetype, until she was thoroughly expunged or eliminated (e.g., by the Protestants). The East, however, such as with the great goddess Kali, more properly integrated the Great Mother, even her more deadly and threatening aspects, until she becomes "the prefect Great Goddess: she preserves but transcends the Great Mother, and thereby integrates the lower with the higher."

In this case, by following the principles of spectrum psychology which carefully distinguishes between differentiation (a healthy integration) and dissociation (a pathology) of any given level, Wilber diagnosis for the Western world is a mythic dissociation since "the themes, moods, and structures of the Great Mother corpus were simply *left out* of subsequent mythology." In other words, with the suppression of the feminine (or the Great Mother/Great Goddess), the West "went too far, as it were, and turned transcendence and differentiation into repression and dissociation: the dissociation and alienation of the Great Mother." Indeed, this is the great tragedy that humanity still suffers from, especially in the modern West (which is now global), because, as Wilber rightfully laments, "when the Great Mother [or the prepersonal realm] is repressed, the Great Goddess [or the transpersonal realm] is concealed."

CHAPTER 11. "THE SLAYING OF THE TYPHON" primarily uses the remarkable work of L. L. Whyte, especially as presented in *The Next Development in Man* (1948), to further examine the process that occurred historically "with the emergence of the ego level," or when "the ego arose in the 'breakdown' of the membership mind" and "humans became self-conscious." In basic agreement with Whyte's general assessment, Wilber maintains that "there was not just a *differentiation* of mind and body—which was a necessary and positive step in evolution—but a *dissociation* of the mind from the body." As Whyte sees it, this was brought about by a "dual specialization" since the human "organism can, on one hand, act spontaneously in the present, but on the other, it can preserve records of past actions." Whyte terms this the "European Dissociation," which is defined a primary "dissociation between the mind and body—once again, not just a differentiation, but a dissociation." Indeed, his historical calculations correlate closely with Wilber's Mental-Egoic Period (low, middle, high). In fact, this split between mind and body is such a pathological condition, Whyte identifies it as the true Fall of Man.

Wilber adeptly discusses how this psychological process was carried to extremes because "The alienation of the self from nature (and the Great Mother) is the alienation of the self from the body." Yet he again emphasizes that it's not "the existence of the ego per se that is regrettable, but the inability to *integrate* the newly emergent ego with the prior typhonic realms, the realms of instinct, emotion, feeling, and body-self activities." In accord with Whyte's studies (and others), this happens in a large part because the ego is a "memory-self," yet, as these scholars attest, it was "through the use of memory that humankind was able to pull itself out of its slumber in the subconscious." To be clear, Wilber succinctly lists that "there are only two basic problems with the ego:

1. after the ego is formed, it is *very, very difficult to transcend* . . . the ego has to be very badly bounced around by life before it will open itself to transcendence . . . [and];

2. the very characteristics of the ego (its *memory components*) tend toward several complications, foremost among which is the European dissociation."

In conclusion, these scholars suggest that the ego, with its memory, is the major contributor to humanity's current pathologically dissociated condition because "the self-sense, in flight from death, abandoned the body, the all too mortal body, and took substitute refuge in the world of thought. We are still, as it were, hiding there today." In wrapping up, Wilber suggests a vision for the future evolution of collective consciousness: "Having used thought to transcend the body, we have not yet learned to use awareness to transcend thought. That, I believe, will be the next development in men and women."

CHAPTER 12: "A NEW TIME, A NEW BODY" brings to light the fact that the emergent mental-ego mode of consciousness—with "so many changes, so many potentials, and so many disasters"—also brought about "a new mode of time and a new mode of body," one where "the time was historical, linear, conceptual; the body, devitalized and deformed." Using the work of numerous scholars and psychologists (from Campbell, Jaynes, Whyte, Becker, and Norman O. Brown, among others), Wilber reviews history in order to examine this decisive shift from mythic cyclic time or the "natural mode of seasonal time," to a mental conception of "linear and historical time." Yet, for the heroic ego, lost in the throes of the Atman project and more interested in substitute "power drives seeking unlimited addition," history became "first and foremost, a chronicle of the ego's accomplishments and heroic feats," and not, as Wilber critically notes, "a chronicle of the evolutionary steps toward Atman—[with] one of those steps being, of course, the death and transcendence of the ego itself." As a possible remedy, he informs us: "In my opinion, the sooner the mental-ego realizes that history is a tale of its own demise, the sooner it will cease misinterpreting that tale as an exclusive chronicle of its own feats."

Wilber therefore emphasizes that this type of extended, calculated awareness (linear history) had dangerous repercussions since this "stretching out beyond seasonal circles—played directly into the often power-crazed appetites of the heroic ego." Importantly, this includes the dissociation and repression of the lower realms, shown with the Western example of sending the "devil" (or the Typhon) down to "hell." And, sadly, all of this dangerous drama ended up being projected as shadows and "immortality projects" onto other people and the world at large, thus often creating havoc. As another example, Wilber gives a concise consideration of the devil, or devil worship, such as with the persecution of witches.

As an evolutionary principle, Wilber points to one of the tendencies of successive consciousness evolution: "The god(s) or sacred images of one stage of development become the demons, devils, demiurges, or disparaged gods of the *next* stage of evolution." In the case of the newly emerging mental-ego, it was the older magical-typhonic structure that became the alienated force of consciousness, therefore, as Wilber observes in a detailed discussion, the "excessive zeal to embrace the mental realms and deny the animal aspects of the human compound individual was precisely what led to the alienation of the typhonic realms."

Often citing numerous sources (especially Brown and Becker), Wilber argues that when the ego tends "to avoid death, it has to dilute life," therefore, this dissociation leads to "the divorce between the 'permanent' ego and the mortal fleshy body." As a consequence, "The mythology of sex and murder, which began in the mythic-membership period, is now *retained, intensified, and compounded* due to its repression—[thus] it explodes with a compulsive vengeance in (dissociated) egoic times." In conclusion, the integral theorist claims the mental-self (and collective humanity) often falls into pathological dissociation (not just differentiation), especially when it's understood that "humankind had simply progressed to the point where the rapid growth of consciousness allowed it to reach far beyond the physical bounds of the body. . . . The body became a mechanism."

CHAPTER 13. "SOLARIZATION" is a dense pivotal chapter presenting a discussion on sexism, feminism, and natural male/female tendencies, for it reveals the process, by following ontogenetic clues, in which the emergent mental-ego unfolded. Wilber explains that this period of development involves the extremely difficult "transition or transformation from body to mind," which is associated with the great transition from Earth/Body to Heaven/Mind, from darkness to light, and significantly, from "matriarchy (and the Great Mother) to patriarchy (and the Sun Gods)." After giving a review of childhood development based on the findings of modern developmental psychology, he gives a detailed explanation about why *both* sexes were involved in the rise of the patriarchy, although, admittedly, "natural tendencies might have disposed the heroic mentality to be initially masculine." However, Wilber maintains that such an important transition cannot be solely reduced to a conspiracy of sexism (although this element was to some extent involved), for the patriarchy was undoubtedly the outcome of a natural and necessary growth in consciousness, except, of course, in its extreme dissociated forms.

The answer is first sought in the development of the individual human being. Indeed, the infant's transition to verbal mentality sets the stage for the all-important "drama of the 'separation of the parents'—the classic Oedipus and Electra complexes." By encapsulating the scope of modern depth psychology, particularly Freudianism (including a rousing critique found in the subsection "Oedipus"), Wilber clearly explains that in order for psychological development to create a new mentality—or a "truly mental self, a strong ego, and a superego"—the self-system must separate from (or transcend) the lower chthonic realms of the Great Mother (of earth, body, food, emotional-sexuality) and then move from *body union* to *mental union* (or identity)."

Therefore, Wilber concludes: "The transformation to the new mentality— the Heroic Ego—was an appropriate move away from the chthonic, the Earth Mother, the subhuman body." Yet he also accounts for the fact that "while the body *tends* to be dominated by the Great Mother, the mind is definitely structured by *both* the mental-mother and the mental-father, or mental-feminine and mental-masculine (or again, Solar-Femininity and Solar-Masculinity)." He maintains that this new mentality should also be more fully represented with a "mental-femininity," but he admits that too often the "feminine principle was denied access to the newly emergent mind," with tragic consequences. In other words, to summarize: "The

Earth is ruled fundamentally and most significantly by the Great Mother, but Heaven is potentially ruled by *both* the mental-feminine and the mental-masculine."

These novel insights based upon developmental and spectrum psychology help Wilber explain why patriarchy became a new symbol or "a new twist on the Atman project" for both men and women. He also explains that when the patriarchy gained increased access to substitute gratifications such as property, gold, and inheritances, then the people looked to "the life of their kings," who had the most property, most power, privileged progeny, etc., for their projected egoic ideals of what constituted the "new forms of cosmocentricity and immortality symbols." This was particularly significant during the Middle-Egoic Period (500 B.C.E.–1500 C.E.) when the emerging middle class began to pursue and imitate the life of kings: for instance, "every man's home was his castle," and the woman was relegated to being his "subject." In fact, as Wilber points out, this fallout from the Atman project has directly contributed to "the masculine terror of 'feminine power,'" which still runs rampant today.

Wilber then explains that this natural "emergence of free mind [mental-ego]—was everywhere represented in mythology with the coming of Heaven and the Hero-gods of Heaven," or the "Sun Gods" (*sol invictus* or "victorious sun"). This, however, is "the *light of reason* . . . Apollonian rationality," which Wilber here terms solarization, regarding it as a very necessary transformation and growth in consciousness. By drawing on mythology, he observes that, "The mind was Heaven, the body was Earth, and the transcendence of the latter by the former was everywhere celebrated in the Hero Myths of this period. The Hero, then, was Ego-Mind-Heaven." This reduces to the simple formula: "Hero = Ego = Mind = Heaven = Light = Sun." He clarifies, "The light was not physical light, and not the Ultimate Light, but the light of mental clarity, which was dramatically symbolized by the blaze of the Sun shining in the mental heaven."

Nevertheless, Wilber points out that the "*suppression* of those [old chthonic and telluric] mythologies (and the realms they represented) was a catastrophe that still affects us all." Collective humanity, therefore, is similar to the individual child breaking free of the Oedipal/Electra complex, which "means he/she is unconsciously seeking union (seeking Atman release) via body, via sex, via emotional discharge, and, rebelling against the demands of a higher solar mentality." Wilber concludes that everyone must therefore consciously strengthen (and transcend) the ego by integrating the lower realms before truly embarking on the journey of the higher transpersonal stages of development.

CHAPTER 14. "I AND THE FATHER ARE ONE" asserts that there are recognizable differences between the higher levels of the transpersonal realms of con-

sciousness (and their respective religions). Wilber maintains that these characteristics are most readily demonstrated by the advanced-tip individuals (men or women)
who embodied "the most advanced mode of consciousness." In the Mental-Egoic
Period sages were "the most highly evolved souls of this period . . . such sages
as Buddha, Christ, and Lao Tzu . . . [who] penetrated the realm of the Dharmakaya . . . the realm beyond even the personal God or Goddess, the realm of the
unmanifest Void." Wilber explains that during the very beginning of the Middle
Egoic Period, also known as the Axial Age (so named by Karl Jaspers to denote the
worldwide critical turning point of the sixth century B.C.E.), there appeared "the
first great 'axial sages,'" since "these types of highly advanced sages, the growing
tip of consciousness moved from Sambhogakaya religion . . . to Dharmakaya religion . . ." Wilber further delineates their subtle differences:

- **Sambhogakaya** (or the Subtle Realm of One God) is when "a transcendent
  oneness—one God, One Goddess—makes itself evident to the soul, and the
  soul communes, in sacrificial awareness, with that archetypal oneness."

- **Dharmakaya** (or the Causal Realm of the radiant Void) is when "the path
  of transcendence goes even further, for the soul no longer communes with
  that oneness or worships that oneness—it *becomes* that oneness. . . . They
  are both, God and soul, dissolved in and returned to the radiant ground of
  the prior Void, or unobstructed and all-pervading Consciousness as Such."

This means, as the great mystics have always realized, that "to reach Godhead,
one must go beyond God altogether." Wilber thus presents these subtle differentiations and disclosures with a consideration on the "Mosaic and Christic Revelation": Moses revealed the Sambhogakaya One God, which is voiced as "our Father
who art in Heaven"; whereas, Christ revealed the Dharmakaya Void, which is
voiced as "I and the Father are One."

Wilber highlights that the important evolutionary advance of the Dharmakaya sages is similar to the well-known message of the Hindu Upanishads: *"Tat
tvam asi,"* in other words: *"'Thou art That,'* you and God are ultimately one." This
divine revelation is known in the West as gnosis, which refers to "a reception of
transcendent knowledge," and with "the same root: *gno = jna.*" In the East it's known
as *"jnana* (or *prajna*)."* Wilber explains this is "exactly what gave Buddha his enlightenment . . . [and] disclosed Brahman-Atman to Shankara, and so on." He reminds us that historically "the flowering of the Dharmakaya was left by and large,
to the East, to Hinduism, to Buddhism, to Taoism, to Neo-Confucianism." Wilber
demonstrates this fact with examples from the teachings of Gautama Buddha,
Bodhidharma, Nagarjuna, Padmasambhava, and Lao Tzu. In the West, however,

many of the Dharmakaya sages (such as Jesus and other Christian saints), unfortunately, "were savagely opposed and eventually uprooted, often by execution." Thus, "In the orthodox religions of the West, the spheres of the Divine and the Human never evolved to the natural point where they become one."

As presented earlier in Chapter 4, Wilber more fully outlines the hierarchic evolution of spiritual experience ["hierarchic evolution of *religious* experience" in earlier editions]. Although relying heavily on the terminology of Mahayana Buddhism, these stages are intended to reflect the universal character and disclosures reflected with a perennial-philosophical interpretation as they reach from the successive unfolding of "Goddess to God the Father to Godhead":

- **Nirmanakaya** or the Psychic Level (level 5): "shamanistic trance, shakti, psychic capacities, siddhi, kriyas, elemental forces (nature gods and goddesses), emotional-sexual transmutation, body ecstasy, kundalini, and hatha yoga";

- **Sambhogakaya** or the Subtle Realms (level 6): "angelic and archetypal visions; One God/dess, the Creator of all lower realms, the demiurge or Archetypal Lord; saintly religion of halos of subtle light and sound (nada, mantra); nada and shabd yoga, savikalpa samadhi, saguna Brahman";

- **Dharmakaya** or the Causal Realm (level 7): "unmanifest Void, Empty Ground, the Godhead; unity of soul and God, transcendence of subject-object duality, coalescence of human and divine; the Depth, the Abyss, the Ground of God and soul; I and the Father are One; jnana yoga, nirvikalpa samadhi, nirguna Brahman";

- **Svabhavikakaya** or the Nondual (level 8): "culmination of Dharmakaya religion; identity of manifest and unmanifest, or identity of the entire World Process and the Void; perfect and radical transcendence into and as ultimate Consciousness as Such, or absolute Brahman-Atman; sahaja yoga, bhava samadhi."

Wilber clarifies: "I am not saying religion necessarily evolves from Goddess to God the Father to Godhead; I am saying it evolves from Nirmanakaya to Sambhogakaya to Dharmakaya to Svabhavikakaya, but that historically the Goddess, God the Father, and the Godhead have typically aligned themselves with that hierarchic evolution." In an excellent schematic interpretation of this unfolding hierarchy, Wilber summarizes that "*Historically*, the Great Goddess begins in the Nirmanakaya and disappears into the Sambhogakaya; God the Father begins in the Sambhogakaya and disappears into the Dharmakaya; the Void/Godhead begins in the Dharmakaya and disappears into the Svabhavikakaya (and the Svab-

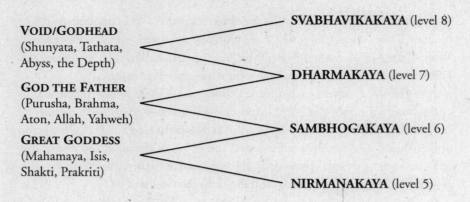

VOID/GODHEAD
(Shunyata, Tathata,
Abyss, the Depth)

GOD THE FATHER
(Purusha, Brahma,
Aton, Allah, Yahweh)

GREAT GODDESS
(Mahamaya, Isis,
Shakti, Prakriti)

SVABHAVIKAKAYA (level 8)

DHARMAKAYA (level 7)

SAMBHOGAKAYA (level 6)

NIRMANAKAYA (level 5)

The Evolution of
Spiritual Experience
FIGURE 2

havikakaya is the Ground and Condition of them all)." (See Figure 2: "The Evolution of Spiritual Experience.")

Wilber then explains that the evidence for this sequential development of the hierarchical religious (or spiritual) experience comes directly from our past transcendent heroes, as well as from present-day meditators, who show the way to our collective future evolution. Indeed, as this volume has demonstrated, these levels of consciousness have also been reflected historically in certain mythos figures as they unfold in the Great Nest of Being or the spectrum of consciousness. (See Figure 3: "Mythos Figures on the Great Nest of Being.")

In a review of paternal images, Wilber sees that with the father image there needs to be a clear distinction made between the "paternal image of Cultural Authority (in the egoic patriarchy) and the Progenitor Source (whether God the Father or the Godhead itself)." Since, as he explains, "Individuals, both male and female, depended upon the fathers for the transmission of mental culture and mental security," and since the basic "Father Image itself arose as a simple correlate to mental existence," then for the average-mode masses it's generally become "a simple projection of the paternal superego." But for the most advanced few, this image was metaphorically used as a transcendent symbol to represent the "higher realms as 'God the Father' or 'the Godhead.'" In other words, Wilber continues, "The obvious conclusion is that there is a radical difference between the mental father figure (level 4) and the Transcendent God or Godhead (level 6 or 7), and the two can be confused only by ignoring the incredibly complex subtleties involved."

In conclusion, the integral theorist maintains that everyone must ultimately integrate and transcend our paternal images of the Great Mother and God the Father as they are generated from the lower (and especially mythic) levels (1–5) in order to continue our individual and collective evolution into a well-developed ego

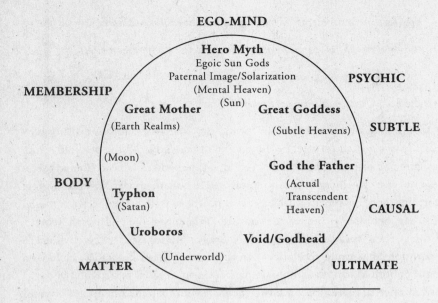

EGO-MIND

Hero Myth
Egoic Sun Gods
Paternal Image/Solarization
(Mental Heaven)
(Sun)

PSYCHIC

MEMBERSHIP

Great Mother
(Earth Realms)

Great Goddess
(Subtle Heavens)

SUBTLE

(Moon)

God the Father
(Actual
Transcendent
Heaven)

BODY

Typhon
(Satan)

Uroboros
(Underworld)

Void/Godhead

CAUSAL

MATTER

ULTIMATE

Mythos Figures on the
Great Nest of Being
FIGURE 3

and the transpersonal realms (levels 6–8). Thus, Wilber predicts our future: "We of today face a new dragon fight, and we need a new Hero Myth. . . . The new Hero will be Centauric (which means mind and body united and not dissociated), whole-bodied, mentally androgynous, psychic, intuitive *and* rational, male *and* female—and the lead in this new development most easily can come from the female, since our society is *already* masculine-adapted."

CHAPTER 15. "ON BECOMING A PERSON" concentrates on a comprehensive sociopolitical view informed by a thorough understanding of the developmental patterns found in the evolution of consciousness. In presenting universal principles gleaned from some reconstructions based on the spectrum model, Wilber first reviews the fact that people are actually a compound individual, "composed of matter, prana, verbal-membership, ego, soul, and spirit." In other words, "The human compound individual begins its growth and development by adjusting to the physical world, then to the emotional world, then the verbal, then the self-reflexive, and so on (until growth stops in its case)." Therefore, compound individuals are interactively involved with corresponding "Levels of Exchange" (including pathological "exchange distortions") where:

- "the Material Body is exercised in *labor;*

- the Pranic Body is exercised in *breath, sex,* and *feeling;*

- the Verbal-Membership Mind is exercised in *communication;*

- the Ego, in *mutual personal recognition* and the exchange of *esteem;*

- the Soul, in *psychic* and *subtle transcendence;*

- the Spirit, in *absolute absorption* in Atman."

Continuing with the story of the mental-ego, Wilber specifically explains how the newly emergent structure, because it's compounded of all the previous structures, contains a far greater possibility for "emergent contamination," so that therefore "once the ego emerges, it can repress and distort the lower levels, and these distortions then 'boomerang' back to the ego." Indeed, since the spectrum model holds that "because the higher does transcend the lower, the higher can 'repress' the lower," then "the internalization of society's oppression leads the individual to [a condition of] surplus repression." In this case, Wilber's discussion includes a critique of both Marx (who emphasized external oppression) and Freud (who emphasized internal repression), the two theorists who each made a precise analysis of the "exchange distortions" of their particular level of focus (Marx on material exchange and economic exploitation; Freud on emotional-sexual exchange and the distortions of sexuality). Nonetheless, Wilber reminds us, the various types of exchange distortion "can occur on every level of the compound individual [except the ultimate] by virtue of its living in a compound society: self-repression, external oppression, and internalized surplus repression."

Based on an extended review of the Habermas/Hegelian position, Wilber argues that the new level of exchange of the mental-egoic structure is "the level of egoic esteem and exchange of mutual self-recognition based upon communication free of domination and distortion." In other words, he acknowledges, for the first time in history there was a "legal or institutional/conventional recognition of, and respect for, egoic personhood" or the rights of a "legal person." In other words, a "real person" was defined as a "legally recognized self-consciousness or ego" who could own personal property, which was then mutually recognized and protected (however, of course, initially only for the male/father). Thus, in short, "*each 'I' had its own 'me' and 'mine.'*" Nevertheless, Wilber is also quick to point out that "What was deplorable, but perhaps initially unavoidable, was not that egoic 'I-me-mine' became legally recognized, respected, and protected, but that this right was not extended to more people." The real tragedy is that "For many individuals—both then and now—the ego and its possessions (I, me, and mine) served not just a temporary moment in the Atman project, but rather the *sole* form of the Atman project." Thus, "'to be a real person' . . . means 'to avoid superconsciousness.'"

As another principle in the evolution of consciousness, Wilber points out that although there are expanded potentials brought about by a true evolution of consciousness with the mental-egoic structure, there are also inevitably new terrors. This included an expanded sense of time coupled with a deepened feeling of guilt ("of being a separate self") all aggravated by a dreadful apprehension of death or the "death impact." This increase in guilt, time, and aggression—or the "three sides of one existential terror"—also turned "death terror *outward* into death dealing, into the really overblown potlatch of murderous hostility which so often has characterized mankind."

All of this existential drama generated by an expanded sense of being a separate person, is "amplified through [mental] conceptual domains" which then converts natural aggression into excessive aggression. In other words, this new selfhood, as Wilber explains, brutally played out its "new egoic Atman project" of "massive substitute sacrifices" on other people with even more oppression and terrifying "mass homicide, in the form of war." Pathologically, it was with the rise of the egoic period that "the war machine in many ways is totally out of control" in its ill-fated attempt "on the one side, to gain cosmic self-esteem and, on the other, to replenish or avenge the shortages in its immortality account—by whatever means available." Wilber concludes: "The primary and immediate aim of any sane and humane social theory would be the relaxation and relief of *oppression* and *repression,* at every level of exchange in the compound individual." To this he adds: "And humankind will never, but never, give up this type of murderous aggression, war, oppression and repression, attachment and exploitation, until men and women give up that *property called personality.* Until, that is, they awaken to the trans-personal."

CHAPTER 16. "THE DAWN OF MISERY" concludes the review of the Mental-Egoic Structure by stating again: "It is not the existence of the egoic structure itself that constitutes our cage, but only the *exclusive identification* of our awareness with that structure." Wilber therefore reviews this exclusive identification, which has created the "dismal state of affairs" of our present age, especially since "we have burdened the ego with the Atman project and corrupted the ego's productions with demands that they could not fulfill."

Beginning in the second and first millennia B.C.E., this greatly increased sense of being a separate self becomes most evident when the written "records exploded in grief, doubt, sorrow." This is the period when "the moral problem of suffering moved to the center stage," and because, as Wilber explains, since "the ego lies at the extreme point of vulnerability, halfway between the Eden of the subconscious and the true heaven of the superconscious," then there was a universal "yearning for release." This climatic point of human history—"halfway along the path of evolution"—is called the time of the Great Reversal (after Campbell) or what theologians have often referred to as the Fall of Man. Wilber, too, sees this "fall" historically as being "primarily the awakening of self-conscious knowledge that correctly disclosed, among many other things, that men and women were *already* and *priorly* alienated from true Spirit and real Atman."

In a concise summary of this "dawn of misery," the transpersonal theorist still contends that although "the ego *does* serve its necessary and appropriate phase of evolution," it does so while losing the membership self's reliance on earlier infantile mythic protectors or the mythic-parental images. As a consequence, people (as egos) were further alienated and "opened to natural guilt and existential dread," "a nightmare of terror," and a "horrifying moral atmosphere" that was either unconsciously repressed or was "forcefully closing its eyes to, not only the lower realms of consciousness, from which it had finally emerged, but also the higher realms, which should have been its destiny."

This collective existential tragedy, in metaphorical terms, created a "denial of necessary Earth and a refusal of actual Heaven," and therefore "this doubly defended consciousness (repressing the Below and denying the Above), the new ego, with its visions of cosmocentricity, proceeded to remake the Western world." Consequently, because "real Heaven could not yet be reached, and yet men and women are aware of its existence," then "the necessary ascent or solarization itself brings self-conscious panic, fear, and guilt." And yet all of this drama is only relieved or released when "the story concludes with the shattering fate of all egos." It is here, Wilber assesses, that "the Western world still waits."

Part V. The Context

CHAPTER 17. "**ORIGINAL SIN**" summarizes many of the major themes in *Up From Eden* by claiming that, in the author's opinion, "There is one and only one way in which a scientific evolutionary theory can join hands with a truly religious or spiritual view, and that is by seeing that there was not one major Fall of Man— there were *two*," known as "the *scientific fall* out of Eden, out of the uroboric and typhonic times; and the prior but paradoxically present *theological fall* out of superconscious Heaven."

The *scientific fall* (evolution) is the move *up from* Eden whereby "humankind did not historically fall *down* from Heaven; it fell *up* and out of the uroboros and the subconscious, and *into* self-consciousness and the pain and guilt involved therein"; this view is derived from scientific evolutionary theory. The *theological fall* (involution) is the move *down from* Spirit whereby "Spirit playfully loses and forgets itself in successively lower levels," thus "each level is created by a forgetting of its senior level, so that ultimately all levels are created by a forgetting of Spirit"; this view is derived from "the insights of esoteric religion."

Wilber reminds us that this volume has actually been tracing "a series of mini-Falls" wherein "humankind had finally emerged from its slumber in subconsciousness and awakened as a self-reflexive and isolated awareness." From this transpersonal and evolutionary point of view, Wilber then addresses the theological concern of original sin, which he proposes is actually more like the "original apprehension of original sin" because human beings were "awakening to a world already mortal and finite." In other words, the entire scope of prehistory and history "was not a Fall from a transpersonal Heaven but a Fall out of the pre-personal realm, the realm of earth, nature, instinct, emotion, and unselfconsciousness." Consequently, Wilber maintains, "by eating from the Tree of Knowledge . . . men and women . . . did not get thrown out of the Garden of Eden; they grew up and walked out."

However, from the scientific position, "Men and women awoke as self-conscious egos and thus fell out of their slumber in subconscious nature, magic, and myth . . . [for] the scientific record of evolution to date, on the whole, shows us that historical Eden was definitely a *pre-personal* immersion in nature." Therefore, as Carl Sagan has already said, and Wilber agrees, "The Fall occurred more or less when man went from *subconscious* (or semi-conscious) ape to *self-aware* human, who could then reflect on his fate and worry about it—hence, the Fall." In fact, as we've seen, the "Fall of Man" can actually be historically more or less dated because it was "crystallized in egoic times (about 4,000 years ago) . . . [thus] the scientific fall, the Great Reversal, the emergence of the ego, occurred around the second millennium B.C.E."

Wilber therefore begins to examine in depth both involution and evolution, which, as he points out, follow the hierarchical levels of the Great Chain of Being. He suggests that involution involves the theological fall, which is understood through "the insight of esoteric religion," and that evolution involves, as mentioned, the "scientific record of evolution to date":

Involution (theological fall) is the "whole 'downward' movement, whereby Spirit playfully loses and forgets itself in successively lower levels," therefore it's the "*enfolding* or in-turning of the higher structures into successively lower ones," which in turn creates the ground unconscious where each descending level is rendered unconscious; this has been traditionally described as a "great sport and play [*lila*]" since "each level is an illusory separation from Spirit because each level is really a separation of Spirit by Spirit through Spirit. The *reality* of each level is only Spirit; the *agony* of each level is that it *appears* or *seems* to be separated from Spirit"; in other words, "humankind (and all things) did fall from real Heaven."

Evolution (scientific fall) is "the reversal of involution," or the "subsequent *unfolding* into actuality of this *enfolded potential*," therefore it's the "successive unfolding of these structures in the reverse order that they were enfolded"; this has been described as holistic growth (after Jan Smuts) because "Everywhere we look in evolution," said Smuts, "we find *a succession of higher-order wholes:* each whole becomes part of a higher-level whole, and so on throughout the evolutionary process"; in other words, "humankind came up (but not from) the apes."

In conclusion, Wilber contends that both theology/involution and science/evolution "are perfectly compatible views, and both are correct," thus, "the union of science and religion is the union of evolution and involution." (See Figure 4: "Involution and Evolution.")

From this perspective, then, as Wilber explains, "once involution is complete, evolution can begin. As involution was the enfolding of the higher in the lower, evolution is the unfolding of the higher from the lower . . . when the higher emerges it does indeed pass *through* the lower." In other words, "in our view, the Big Bang is simply the *explosive limit of involution,* at which point matter was flung into existence out of its senior dimensions, or, ultimately, out of Spirit." In giving an excellent synopsis reviewing "the order of the evolutionary tree," from the Big Bang to human beings, from the physical universe to simple life forms to "the laborings of the prana-life level," Wilber sees the human and its advanced mind, or "the first mind truly free of body," as standing and existing "midway between matter and God."

Therefore, in contradiction to the orthodox scientific theory of natural selection, which Wilber argues "seems correct on the *what* of evolution, but is profoundly reductionistic and/or contradictory on the *how* (and why) of evolution," he instead suggests that a much more integral view would be "the 'force' of evolution" as "Atman Telos." Such a sophisticated model or transpersonal perspective, as he points out, is in harmony with "everybody from Aristotle, to Hegel, to Aurobindo," and they conclude: "evolution is not a statistical accident—it is laboring toward Spirit, driven, not by happy-go-lucky chance, however comforting that notion is to those who deny reality to any level higher than insentient matter, but by Spirit itself." Consequently, Wilber summarizes: "The essential point is that evolution on the whole appears in humans as psychological *development* and *growth*—the same 'force' [telos] that produced *humans* from *amoebas* produces *adults* from *infants* and *civilization* from *barbarism.*"

In summary, after integrating both views of involution and evolution, Wilber recapitulates the entire evolutionary story of increasing embrace, moving from "translations" (*within* a level) to "transformations" (to a *different* level) so that as "Thanatos outweighs Eros; *translation* winds down and *transformation* to the next higher-level structure begins." Yet, as Wilber reminds us, in the evolutionary "Re-

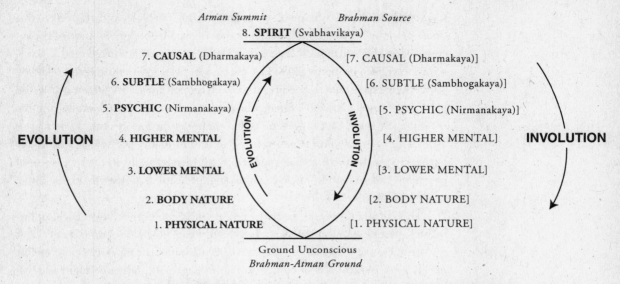

Right side: **INVOLUTION** "being rendered unconscious" and enfolded
Left side: **EVOLUTION** unfolding in reverse order the enfolded structures of involution

Involution and Evolution
FIGURE 4

turn to Source it is not necessary to destroy and annihilate the lower levels. It is necessary only to transcend them, to cease identifying *exclusively* with them. . . . In true and unobstructed evolution, we take all the lower levels with us, out of love and compassion, so that *all levels* eventually are reconnected to Source. To negate everything is to preserve everything; to transcend all is to include all. We must go whole-bodily to God; failing that, we fall into dissociation, repression, inner fragmentation. Ultimate transcendence is thus *not* ultimate annihilation of the levels of creation, but rather their ultimate inclusion in Spirit. *The final transcendence is the final embrace.*" In other words, "At Ultimate Enlightenment or return to Spirit, the created world can still exist; it just no longer obscures Spirit, but serves it. All the levels remain as *expressions* of Atman, not substitutes for Atman."

To further support this view proclaiming the spiritualization of evolution, Wilber encapsulates some of the great evolutionary philosophers of our time from both East and West, such as Sri Aurobindo, Father Teilhard de Chardin, Friedrich von Schelling, the incomparable "towering genius of Georg Wilhelm Friedrich Hegel," and Nicolas Berdyaev, "that towering Russian Christian mystic." In the end, Wilber offers an uplifting and optimistic conclusion: "We had to evolve past the ape of subconsciousness in order to rediscover superconsciousness. This being so, then we may all take heart, for it now appears certain that you and I came up from Eden so that we may all return to Heaven."

CHAPTER 18. "IN PROSPECTUS: THE FUTURE" reminds us that, prior to this book, never before had both "parallel strands of evolution: the evolution of the average mode of consciousness and the evolution of the most advanced mode of consciousness" been explicitly pursued. One reason this is so interesting and relevant, Wilber suggests, is that "these advanced levels remain still as the *present and higher potential* of every man and woman who cares to evolve and transform beyond the mental-egoic stage. Our suggestion is that the *deep structures* of all the higher levels exist in the *ground unconscious,* waiting to unfold in any individual who today bothers to pursue them, just as they unfolded, hierarchically, in the succession of past transcendent heroes," including the range of history's greatest shamans, saints, sages, and siddhas.

This is truly significant because the authentic contemplative practices of humanity's past sages and spiritual masters, such as true meditation, can actually "halt the mental-egoic *translation* so that *transformation* into the superconscious realms may begin." In fact, Wilber contends that if we, as both individuals and as a collective species, "are to further the evolution of humankind, and not just reap the benefit of past humanity's struggles, if we are to contribute to evolution and not merely siphon it off, if we are to help the overcoming of our self-alienation from Spirit and not merely perpetuate it, then meditation—or a similar and truly contemplative practice—becomes an absolute ethical imperative, a new categorical imperative." In other words, with most people of today "self-consciousness faces transition to superconsciousness. The average individual at large can *start* to become a transcendent hero."

Wilber summarizes that "All sorts of evidence, from historical growing-tip evolution to specific present-day meditation studies, points to the fact that the stage *beyond egoic science* (but still including it) is that of *psychic intuition* (level 5), followed by *subtle awareness* (level 6), then *causal insight* (level 7), then *ultimate identity.*" However, without differentiating average-mode and advanced-tip consciousness (based on correcting the pre/trans fallacy), then all too often scientific anthropologists (or reductionists) confuse "*magic* (level 2) with *psychic* (level 5) and *myth* (level 3) with *subtle* archetype (level 6), and thus whenever true psychic and subtle features emerge, they naively claim regression to magic and myth." Yet, as this transpersonal history has demonstrated, "in fact, we have evolved past magic, *not* psychic, and past myth, *not* subtle archetype."

Likewise, the "same criticism applies to the romantic transcendentalists" (or elevationists) who make the inverse fallacy when they "claim that past epochs were some sort of Golden Age which we have subsequently destroyed." As Wilber clearly points out, many scholars have failed to "distinguish between the truly *advanced, transcendental heroes* of yesterday and the *average mode* of unmistakable primitive and *unevolved superstition* which totally dominated archaic history." In other words, "if one does not take care to differentiate psychic from magic, subtle from mythic, transpersonal from prepersonal, then naturally all transpersonal sages appear to be prepersonally regressing," and, as demonstrated, this is a fallacy of profound proportions.

Wilber predicts that if humanity is to really evolve to a new age of consciousness, then we must first continue to become stably adapted to the rational-egoic level because, as already established, "one does not and cannot reach the transpersonal without first establishing the personal." In fact, due to the stress created by modern "civilizations' failures to support truly rational and egoic structures," Wilber observes that many "individuals are actually *regressing* to prepersonal, cultic, narcissistic pursuits." Therefore he contends that it's imperative to engage in the actual practice of contemplative and meditative disciplines. Only this type of authentic transformative practice will become the real basis for any genuine wisdom culture, or what Wilber calls the "Nirmanakaya Age [which] will mean a society of men and women who, by virtue of an initial glimpse into transcendence, will start to understand vividly their common humanity and brother/sisterhood . . ." Only then, he claims, when an individual "ceases mental translations, and starts subtle transformations" will people begin to reach the next "level of psychic intuition, the beginning of transcendent openness and clarity."

In answer to both New Age and orthodox critics, Wilber concludes that humanity at large still has to face "the entire second half of evolution." However, this will be no simple task, thus he soberly appraises today's situation: "At this point in history, the most radical, pervasive, and earth-shaking transformation would occur simply if everybody truly evolved to a mature, rational, and responsible ego, capable of freely participating in the open exchange of mutual self-esteem."

CHAPTER 19. "REPUBLICANS, DEMOCRATS, AND MYSTICS" ends the book with Wilber again suggesting that "a detailed, multi-disciplinary analysis of the developmental-logic and hierarchic levels of exchange that constitute the human compound individual" are needed to construct "the eventual core of a truly unified critical sociological theory." This unified social theory would include, at a minimum, the various levels of exchange as reviewed throughout this book:

1. "the Physical-Uroboric level of **Material Exchange,** whose paradigm is *food consumption* and *food extraction* from the natural environment; whose sphere is that of *manual labor* (or *technological labor*); and whose archetypal analyst is Marx";

2. "the Emotional-Typhonic level of **Pranic Exchange,** whose paradigm is *breath* and *sex;* whose sphere is that of *emotional intercourse,* from feeling to *sex* to *power;* and whose archetypal analyst is Freud";

3. "the Verbal-Membership level of **Symbolic Exchange,** whose paradigm is *discourse* (*language*); whose sphere is that of *communication* (and the beginning of *praxis*); and whose archetypal analyst is Socrates";

4. "the Mental-Egoic level of the **Mutual Exchange** of self-recognition, whose paradigm is *self-consciousness* or *self-reflection;* whose sphere is that of *mutual personal recognition* and *esteem* (the culmination of *praxis*); and whose archetypal analyst is Hegel (in his writings on master/slave relationship)";

5. "the Psychic level of **Intuitive Exchange,** whose paradigm is *siddhi* (or psychic intuition in its broadest sense); whose sphere is *shamanistic kundalini;* and whose archetypal analyst is Patanjali";

6. "the Subtle level of **God-Light Exchange,** whose paradigm is *saintly transcendence* and *revelation* (nada); whose sphere is *subtle Heaven* (Brahma-Loka); and whose archetypal analyst is Kirpal Singh";

7. "the Causal level of **Ultimate Exchange,** whose paradigm is *radical absorption* in and as the Uncreate (*samadhi*); whose sphere is the *Void-Godhead;* and whose archetypal analyst is Buddha/Krishna/Christ."

Wilber explains that these central themes can be simplified into the three categories in which consciousness can exist: the subjective, the objective, and the nondual (or Atman).

Therefore Wilber's integral model of analysis directly addresses the "central problem which has always faced critical social and political theorists [which] is just this: *why are men and women unfree?*" Based upon the above three categories, Wilber goes on to suggest that:

1. Liberal political views can be called the *subjective* Democrat or the *progressive* Humanist-Marxist approach, exemplified by the view that "men and women are born essentially free" but then "something in the *objective,* outer world imposes unfreedom on its subjects," therefore the solution to this oppressive situation, liberals claim, is that "The objective world must be significantly altered."

2. Conservatism can be called the *objective* Republican or the *traditional* Freudian-Conservative approach, for conservatives do *not* want to change traditional society at all, thus they "do not approve of progressive liberal

reshuffling of social institutions since odds are high that things will only get worse." This approach concludes that "inequality and social injustice are absolutely inevitable, for positive reasons," therefore conservatives claim that "the 'true' self must be repressed and oppressed" in order to control possible "madness and anarchy."

Various types of modern social theories have arisen within these two basic categories of liberal and conservative, yet from the vantage point of a full-spectrum view of consciousness, the transpersonal theorist presents the third alternative:

3. Nondual Mystics are those sages who universally claim "that men and women are unfree because there exists a belief in the existence of a 'true' self in the first place," therefore these highly evolved souls claim that "we are not to repress or unrepress the self, but rather undermine it; transcend it; see through it." The aim of the mystics is "the discovery of the ultimate Whole is the only cure for unfreedom, and it is the only prescription offered by the mystics . . . the ultimate solution to unfreedom, then, is neither Humanistic-Marxist nor Freudian-Conservative, but Buddhistic: *satori, moksha, wu,* release, awakening, *metanoia.*"

In review of the contentious Atman project, where "once a boundary is constructed between subject and object, self and other, organism and environment," then psychologically the "self-sense" feels "inherently unfree and [is therefore] inherently capable of total viciousness to itself and to others out of sheer reactive panic to its own mortality and vulnerability." Throughout human history, then, "The objective cost of the Atman project can be appalling, because when people become objects of the negative Atman project, those people become victims." Yet, with a greater embrace of reality based on a transpersonal and mystical understanding, Wilber concludes that "Men and women are not inherently or instinctually evil, but merely substitutively evil," therefore it's best to "offer actual transcendence" since "both subjective unfreedom and objective exploitation are fallouts from the Atman project." Short of complete enlightenment for all people, which "would be a utopian society or sangha," Wilber suggests that the best approach is "to arrange for individual Atman projects to overlap each other in something of a mutually supportive way." This would be somewhat like synergistic societies (after Ruth Benedict) where "the satisfaction of the individual Atman project tends also to benefit the community at large."

Up From Eden then closes by restating that the evolutionary "move from *sub-consciousness* to *self-consciousness* is to make *death conscious;* to move from *self-consciousness* to *superconsciousness* is to make *death obsolete.*" In other words, it's only through "*prajna,* or transcendent insight into *sunyata,* the seamless coat of the Universe, which is nothing other than Atman, one's own true Self, the Dharmakaya" that people finally realize "the self-sense is ultimately illusory, it is a simple product of boundary, and thus ultimately death is likewise a complex illusion (the point the existentialists miss)." In this grand process, however, it is "the violent friction of these overlapping Atman projects [that] sparks that nightmare called history." Thus, in a sober summary Wilber concludes, "Men and women want the world because they are in truth the world, and they want immortality because they are in fact immortal. But instead of transcending their boundaries in truth, they merely attempt to break and refashion them at will, and caught in this Atman project of trying to make their earth into a substitute heaven, not only do they destroy the only earth they have, they forfeit the only heaven they might otherwise embrace."

CHAPTER

The Holographic Paradigm and Other Paradoxes

Exploring the Leading Edge of Science

EDITED BY KEN WILBER

(Boulder: Shambhala Publications, 1982);

The Collected Works of Ken Wilber, Vol. 4 (CW4) (Boston: Shambhala, 1999)

Introduction by Ken Wilber

The Holographic Paradigm and Other Paradoxes: Exploring the Leading Edge of Science (1982) was edited during Wilber's Phase 2 period emphasizing the holographic paradigm, therefore focusing on the Right-Hand exterior quadrants of individual holons (Upper-Right quadrant) and their holonic systems (Lower-Right quadrant), although Wilber himself critiques this form of subtle reductionism (flatland holism).

    The Holographic Paradigm is an edited collection of articles and interviews that had first appeared in the journal *ReVision* during the time Wilber was its coeditor with Jack Crittenden. It includes contributions by Marilyn Ferguson, Karl Pribram, David Bohm, Renée Weber, Fritjof Capra, Stanley Krippner, John Welwood, and William Irwin Thompson, among others.

    The Holographic Paradigm: Exploring the Leading Edge of Science was published in 1982 (Shambhala Publications); Wilber's essay and interview also appeared a year later in *Eye to Eye* (Shambhala Publications, 1983); his contributions to the book are now part of *The Collected Works of Ken Wilber, Volume Three (CW3) and Volume Four (CW4),* (Shambhala Publications, 1999).

The holographic paradigm is largely based on the intriguing theories of neuroscientist Karl Pribram and physicist-philosopher David Bohm, whose work is highlighted throughout, as the various authors/theorists examine a possible interface between science and religion. However, Wilber's conclusion was that this subject is actually an extraordinarily complex affair that resists popular generalizations, let alone being reducible to only a two-level scheme (Bohm's "implicate" and "explicate" order). Wilber insists that the discoveries of modern physics only apply to the level of nonsentient mass/energy, and that this understanding cannot be equated to the pluridimensional interpretations of mystics. Wilber, as editor, was therefore in the awkward position of being virtually the only contributor who did not believe that the holographic paradigm was based on good science or adequate mysticism. Nevertheless, as he has ironically pointed out, it became an international best-seller.

CHAPTER 6

A Sociable God

Toward a New Understanding of Religion

BY KEN WILBER

(New York: New Press/McGraw-Hill, 1983);

paperback edition (New York: Random House, 1984);

The Collected Works of Ken Wilber, Vol. 3 (CW3) (Boston: Shambhala Publications, 1999)

Foreword by Roger Walsh
Prologue

A Sociable God: Toward a New Understanding of Religion (1983) is a principal Wilber/Phase 2 treatise emphasizing human developmental evolution and sociology, and focusing on the relational exchanges or the interaction between individual interior consciousness (Upper-Left quadrant), interior cultural worldviews (Lower-Left quadrant), and exterior social techno-economic systems (Lower-Right quadrant) in the Great Nest of Spirit and Kosmos.

A Sociable God was written quickly over a three-day weekend in the summer of 1982, partly in response to the mass suicide of Jonestown in 1978, but primarily to offer the field of sociology a master template based on current consciousness research in transpersonal theory and spectrum psychology. It was originally subtitled *A Brief Introduction to a Transpersonal Sociology* (*transpersonal* being used in the subtitles of both *Atman* and *Eden*), but before it was published Wilber renamed it *A Brief Introduction to a Transcendental Sociology* in order to unofficially break with the popular orientation of transpersonal psychology (thereby embracing their partial truths while being critical of their limitations). In the paperback reprint published in 1984, the subtitle was changed to *Toward a New Understanding of Religion.*

A Sociable God: Toward a New Understanding of Religion was published in 1983 (New Press/McGraw-Hill); paperback edition (Random House, 1984); it is now part of *The Collected Works of Ken Wilber, Volume Three (CW3),* (Shambhala Publications, 1999).

The **PROLOGUE** introduces the idea that "modern sociological theory might benefit from a dialogue with the perennial philosophy (*philosophia perennis*)—that is, from transcendental or transpersonal perspectives," therefore Wilber attempts to "provide the briefest possible statement of, and introduction to, a general transcendental sociology." He directs our attention to the fact that "the modern psychology of religion ought to have something to offer the modern sociology of religion."

CHAPTER I. "THE BACKGROUND PROBLEM VIS-À-VIS RELIGION" begins by reviewing some of the "major sociological (and orthodox psychological) responses" to the varied topics of religions and the "cognitive value of religious knowledge," as well as how "transpersonal psychology might eventually contribute." These theories see religion as: *primitivization theory* or "the product of lower or primitive stages of human development or evolution"; *functionalism,* or "serving some type of potentially useful or necessary function"; *phenomenological-hermeneutics,* or a science of interpretation including the *hermeneutic circle,* thus imparting a type of "empathetic interpretation" to religions; *developmental structuralism* or the notion that "psychological structures develop in a hierarchic fashion." As an integralist, Wilber acknowledges some empathy with each approach; however, his deepest sympathy lies with the overall hierarchization of developmental structuralism, which seems, along with a hierarchy of authentic religious development, to offer the best opportunity for an overarching critical sociological theory.

CHAPTER 2. "THE NESTED HIERARCHY OF STRUCTURAL ORGANIZATION" briefly outlines the orthodox and transpersonal version of "the hierarchical levels of structural organization." Wilber establishes that emergent evolution, or milestone development, is available in both *"phylogenetic/ontogenetic parallels,"* nonetheless, each stage also overlaps. Thus "each line is evolution; each gap, revolution." (See Figure 1: "The Emerging Spectrum of Consciousness.")

Wilber also outlines and reviews the various levels in "the developmental and structural spectrum of consciousness," highlighting the three major domains of development:

1. "*prepersonal* or subconscious components;

2. *personal* or self-conscious components; and

3. *transpersonal* or superconscious components."

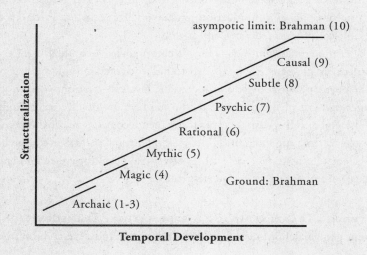

The Emerging Spectrum
of Consciousness

FIGURE I

(See Figure 2: "Three Domains of Human Development.")

Wilber's model subdivides the transpersonal (superconsciousness) into a hierarchy of religious experience:

- **psychic** or "The Way of Yogis";

- **subtle** or "The Way of Saints";

- **causal** or "The Way of Sages";

- **causal/Ultimate** or "The Way of Siddhas."

Wilber's point is that "not only is there a variety of religious experience, there is a *hierarchy* of religious experience with each successive stage—*psychic, subtle, causal*—being higher (by developmental, structural, and integrative standards) than its predecessor, and each correlative practice—*yogic, saintly,* and *sagely*—being likewise more ultimately revelatory."

CHAPTER 3. "THE COMPOUND INDIVIDUAL AS A LINK BETWEEN PSYCHOLOGY AND SOCIOLOGY" defines the human being as a compound individual who embodies "all the past levels of development and [is] capped by the present level itself," yet "each level of the compound human individual is exercised in *a complex system of ideally unobstructed relationships* with the corresponding levels of structural organization in the world process at large." Therefore, as the process of self development unfolds in a manner that transcends but includes, the self is involved in a spectrum of *relational exchanges* (which also involve distortions) including drives, food (or "phase-specific mana"), and needs: "physical needs (food, water, air, shelter), emotional needs (feeling, touching, contact, sex), mental-egoic needs (interpersonal communication, reflexive self-esteem, meaning), spiritual needs (God-communion, depth), and so on."

Wilber therefore recommends that "a comprehensive, unified, critical sociological theory might best be constructed around a detailed, multidisciplinary analysis of the developmental-logic and hierarchic levels of relational (psychosocial) exchanges that constitute the human compound individual." Accordingly, this type of integral or full-spectrum approach, which recognizes all the different levels of exchange, offers a superior critical analysis and integral theory ("a comprehensive critical theory in sociology") affecting both sociological (or collective) and psychological (or individual) consciousness studies.

CHAPTER 4. "TRANSLATION, TRANSFORMATION, TRANSCRIPTION" presents some general definitions needed to better understand a hierarchically ordered

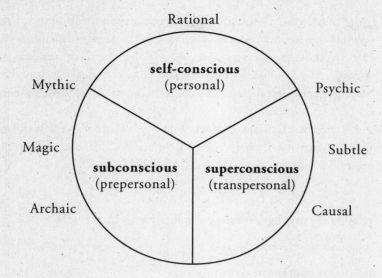

Rational

self-conscious
(personal)

Mythic

Psychic

Magic

Subtle

subconscious
(prepersonal)

superconscious
(transpersonal)

Archaic

Causal

**Three Domains of
Human Development**
FIGURE 2

universe seen within the developmental structural dynamics of Wilber's spectrum of consciousness model:

- **Deep structures** are "relatively ahistorical, collective, invariant, and cross-cultural"; they are "the basic levels of structural origination."

- **Surface structures** are "variable, historically conditioned, and culturally molded"; they are the surface forms of the various levels (or deep structures).

- **Translation** involves surface structures, which are "a horizontal or translative growth . . . of transcribing, filling in, or 'fleshing out' the surface structures of a given level," and whose function is "phase-specific mana" ("good mana"/"bad mana") coupled with "taboo."

- **Transformation** involves deep structures, which are "a vertical shift, a revolutionary reorganization of past elements and emergence of new ones . . . synonymous with transcendence," and it requires "death and rebirth on each level."

- **Transcription** is "the relationship between a deep structure and its surface structures, whose "dialectic of tensions" invariably contributes to and propels the "dynamic of development."

- **Immortality** symbols are generated from the various forms of "death denial."

- **Development** "in a sense, is a series of progressively shedding immortality projects by progressively shedding the layers of self these projects were designed to protect." That is, until ultimate awareness finally dawns "by transcending subject and object in *satori, moksha,* the supreme identity." At this stage, "according to the sages, all layers of self have been transcended—when all deaths have been died—the result is only God in final Truth, and a new Destiny beyond destiny is resurrected from the stream of consciousness."

CHAPTER 5. "SOME USAGES OF THE WORD 'RELIGION'" clearly differentiates among the current and varied uses (and thus confusions) of the word religion including:

1. "religion as non-rational engagement";

2. "religion as extremely meaningful or integrative engagement";

3. "religion as immortality project";

4. "religion as evolutionary growth";

5. "religion as fixation/regression";

6. "*exoteric religion,*" which includes belief and faith;

7. "*esoteric religion,*" which includes "the higher, inward, and/or advanced aspects of religious practice . . . or at least have as a goal, *mystical* experience";

8. "*legitimate religion,*" which "primarily validates translation";

9. "*authentic religion,*" which "primarily validates transformation."

Wilber maintains that "each of the preceding nine (or more) usages of the word 'religion' has its appropriate place—some 'religious' expressions are fixation/regressions, some are immortality projects, some are mana generators, some are legitimate, some are authentic."

These definitions, then, provide a means of determining the "degree of legitimacy" or the "horizontal scale; degree of translative smoothness and integrity, measured against the potential capacity of the given level itself," as well as the "degree of authenticity" or the "vertical scale; degree of transformative power, measured by the degree of hierarchical structuralization delivered by the transformation." Wilber then emphasizes that this type of integral methodology of analysis can be used to determine "illegitimate" or "legitimate" religions as well as "inauthentic" and "authentic" religions, including a number of historical examples showing that the variety of religions "have been both legitimate and authentic."

CHAPTER 6. "BELIEF, FAITH, EXPERIENCE, AND ADAPTATION" makes crucial distinctions between "religious belief, religious faith, religious mystical or peak experience, and religious structural adaptation (or actual adaptation to authentic-religious levels of development)." This type of differentiation and clarification is vital, Wilber points out, for "if they are all 'religious,' they are religious to differing degrees; the series itself shows increasing religious involvement."

In reviewing these "religious" phenomena, Wilber especially focuses on the importance of experience or an "actual encounter and literal cognition." This is especially true of an authentic "peak experience, a temporary insight into (and influx from) one of the authentic levels of religious structural organization (*psychic, subtle, causal*)," which Wilber also terms "a 'peek' experience" since they disclose a brief glimpse into the "higher realms of the person's as-yet unrealized structural potentials—psychic, subtle, causal [and ultimate]."

Wilber goes on to model how these higher transpersonal structures appear as an "influx," or as being "poured," into a person's "present level of structural adaptation . . . [which] seems to determine the form of its eventual expression—*magical, mythical, rational.*" Since the higher transpersonal structures can find expression in the lower prepersonal ones, this pre/trans insight is of immense importance to any integral sociology as it presents a way out of the common confusion between mythic religion and authentic spirituality. Indeed, as Wilber strongly recommends, "We should move on, as quickly as possible, from the *paradigm of peak experience* to the *paradigm of structural adaptation.*"

CHAPTER 7. "PRESENT-DAY SOCIOLOGY OF RELIGION" is the longest chapter in the book and points out that "modern development is marked by increasing rationalization" although, admittedly, the "process is far from complete," especially since it "only covers the first half of our proposed developmental scheme." Therefore Wilber briefly discusses the outdating of the "mythic-membership structure [since it] has reached the inherent limit of its integrative and truth-disclosing capacities."

Next, Wilber analyzes the work of a few prominent present-day sociologists (such as Robert Bellah, and Dick Anthony and Thomas Robbins); his main criticism is that they too fail to "explicitly distinguish legitimate and authentic," thus they misunderstood the qualities of mysticism or "the possible hierarchy of authentic religious adaptation—yogic, saintly, sagely." Instead, Wilber maintains, "If these levels of structural realization are not first distinguished, then any merely legitimate religion may be confused with genuinely authentic religion, and the dynamics of legitimacy may be likewise confused with the dynamics of authenticity."

One of his main points is that theorists need "to be careful to differentiate the hierarchical *types* of mystical union," including "authentic religious symbology," "authentic religious practice," and "authentic mystical unions (panenhenic, theistic, monistic, non-dual)."

Wilber also uses his theory of transcendental sociology to examine some of the "new religions," such as American civil religion, fundamentalistic mythic religion, and cultlike New Age religions, focusing on their regressive trends, or the "regressive consolation in various pre-rational immortality symbols and mythological ideologies." As he summarizes: "My point is simply that the new religions really involve at least two drastically different structural celebrations: *trans-rational*, on the one hand, and *pre-rational*, on the other."

Wilber lays out "the three great domains of human development," each with a "dominant psychological attitude":

1. *childish subconsciousness* and its "passive dependence";

2. *adolescent self-consciousness* with its "active independence";

3. *mature superconsciousness* with its "actively passive surrender."

He now has a tool for delineating the difference between, respectively:

1. the "clan-cult" with the "father figure/totem master" created from "passive dependence [that] is the disposition of the infant-child self-system";

2. the "emergence in adolescence of the critical, self-reflexive, self-conscious mentality" wherein "the adolescent mood of active independence is a phase-specific form of transcendence—the transcendence from subconscious dependence to self-conscious responsibility";

3. the "emergence of the mature disposition of actively passive surrender of isolated individuality to its own higher and prior nature, or radiant superconsciousness, in and as the entire world process at large."

Thus, with this type of integral approach based on the spectrum of consciousness there's a critical methodology "to distinguish child-like passive dependence from mature actively-passive surrender, with a correlative distinction between prepersonal cults and transpersonal sanghas," as well as between the "totem master" and "the guidance of an acknowledged spiritual master."

CHAPTER 8. "KNOWLEDGE AND HUMAN INTERESTS" gives the theoretical means for "extending sociology, especially a critical sociology," into one that is "capable of adequately embracing authentically spiritual or actually transcendental knowledge and interest." In a detailed discussion Wilber builds upon the work of Jürgen Habermas by adding the transpersonal modes of cognition, thus producing a model of five general modes of cognition:

1. *presymbolic awareness* is the body with its sensorimotor apprehension (instinctual interest);

2. *empirical-analytic cognition* is the mind's awareness of the physical world (technical interest);

3. *historical-hermeneutic* is the mind's knowledge of symbols (practical interest);

4. *critical-reflective* is the mind's ability to release "distortions and constraints of labor, language, or communication" (emancipatory interest);

5. *transsymbolic* is "spiritual gnosis, or spirit's direct and nonmediated knowledge of spirit as spirit" (liberational interest).

(See Figure 3: "Five General Modes of Cognition.")

In addition, Wilber further clarifies and summarizes each level of knowledge (or structure of consciousness) with their respective interests:

- **instinctual** is "bodily knowledge of the sensory world";

- **soteriological** is "the mind's attempt to reason about spirit";

- **liberational** is "the interest of gnosis, or spirit's knowledge of spirit as spirit, . . . in radical liberation (*satori, moksha, wu,* release)."

When all the interests and relational exchanges of the "human compound individual" are taken into account, then, Wilber concludes, "a truly critical and normative sociological theory" would embrace "the prepersonal, the personal, and the transpersonal dimensions of existence . . . in the observable, verifiable, inherently preferred direction of structural development and evolution, a direction that discloses itself in successive hierarchic emancipations that themselves pass judgment on their less transcendental predecessors."

CHAPTER 9. "METHODOLOGY, SUMMARY, AND CONCLUSION" provides a summary of the book, giving a "specialized example of the overall sociological methodology." Wilber suggests a structural analysis, a structural diagnosis, and a functional analysis (determination of legitimacy), all based upon the developmental-structural hierarchy and "structural-developmental-stage research." This is done in part by determining a group's "relative location on the developmental hierarchy

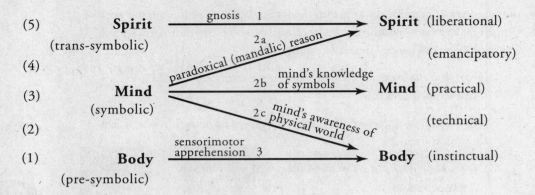

**Five General Modes
of Cognition**
FIGURE 3

of structuralization," to ascertain whether it is "archaic, magical, mythical, rational, psychic, subtle, causal."

In addition, the "refinement-sophistication of the developmental-structural hierarchies with regard to the higher and contemplative levels," will encourage, for example, the "careful and systematic hermeneutical reading of the various (esoteric) religious texts," and direct investigation or "actual data accumulation from populations of those genuinely engaged in superconscient development and adaptation."

After reviewing the three strands of verifiable knowledge accumulation (injunction, apprehension, and communal confirmation), where even "spiritual knowledge, like all other forms of valid cognitive knowledge, is experimental, repeatable, and publicly verifiable," Wilber incorporates a "verifiable gnosis." Thus he claims that "our methodological repertoire is completed." In conclusion, as he recommends, "The final contribution that transpersonal psychology can make to sociology is, if you want to know about the actually transcendent realms themselves, then take up a contemplative-meditative practice (*injunction*) and find out for yourself (*illumination*), at which point the all-inclusive community of transcendence may disclose itself in your case and be tested in the fire of the like-spirited (*confirmation*)." And when God is truly found and "ceases to be a mere symbol in your awareness . . . [but that] which you now recognize as your own true self," then, as Wilber proposes, we'll "find ourselves immersed in a sociable God, formed and forming, liberated and liberating—a God that, as Other, demands participation, and that, as Self, demands identity."

    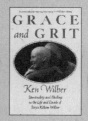

THE INTEGRAL VISION: SELF, LEVELS, & LINES

(1983–1994)

CHAPTER 7

Eye to Eye

The Quest for the New Paradigm

BY KEN WILBER

(Garden City, N.Y.: Anchor Press/Doubleday, 1983);

expanded, reprinted (Boston: Shambhala Publications, 1990);

The Collected Works of Ken Wilber, Vol. 3 (CW3) (Shambhala, 1999);
reprint paperback edition (Shambhala, 2001)

Preface

Eye to Eye: The Quest for the New Paradigm (1983) is a combination of mature Wilber/Phase 2 (evolutionary development) and early Wilber/Phase 3 (self, levels, and lines) emphasizing philosophy and psychology, therefore focusing on individual interior consciousness (Upper-Left quadrant) and the interior cultural worldviews (Lower-Left quadrant) in the Great Nest of Spirit and Kosmos, providing a strong critique of scientific reductionism, or scientism (which only emphasizes the Right-Hand exteriors).

Eye to Eye is a collection of related essays begun in the last years of the 1970s and finished in the early 1980s. Most of the chapters first appeared in the journal *ReVision* while Wilber was editor in chief, while others had been published earlier as journal articles.

Eye to Eye: The Quest for the New Paradigm was published in 1983 (Shambhala Publications); a reprint edition appeared in 1990 with an extra essay, "In the Eye of the Artist," which was later dropped from the 1996 reprint edition (Shambhala Publications); it is now part of *The Collected Works of Ken Wilber, Volume Three (CW3),* (Shambhala Publications, 1999); revised paperback edition (Shambhala Publications, 2001).

The **PREFACE** explains Wilber's intent to offer "an overall or 'comprehensive' knowledge quest—not with a view toward any sort of *finality* in knowledge, but with a view toward some sort of *balance* in the quest itself." However, he also contends that both orthodox psychology and New Agers are "terribly half-sighted," therefore, he wants "to expose and unravel some of the major obstacles to the emergence of such [a comprehensive or integral] paradigm." Wilber maintains that a truly all-embracing paradigm must take into account "a full-spectrum view of the human condition in its secular as well as divine possibilities."

CHAPTER 1. "EYE TO EYE" first explores the notion of a set of "supertheories" that would include, "beyond the physical sciences, the higher knowledge claims of philosophy-psychology and transcendental-mystical religion—a type of truly unified world view." Since this type of overview is starting to emerge in the world, Wilber recognizes that it must adequately address "its relation to empirical science," therefore, he examines "the nature of empirical science, the meaning of philosophical knowledge, and the essence of transcendental or spiritual knowledge" in order to "more easily envision the nature of a new and truly comprehensive paradigm, if such, indeed, exists." In order to support this endeavor, Wilber introduces the notion of epistemological pluralism based upon the Christian mystical metaphor of the three eyes of knowing, which correspond to the "three major realms of being described by the perennial philosophy":

1. **the eye of flesh,** "by which we perceive the external world of space, time, and objects" or the "gross (flesh and material)" realm;

2. **the eye of reason,** "by which we attain a knowledge of philosophy, logic, and the mind itself" or the "Subtle (mind and animic)" realm;

3. **the eye of contemplation,** "by which we rise to a knowledge of transcendent realities" or the "causal (transcendent and contemplative)" realm.

This nuanced understanding sheds light on a common fallacy in the modern world, particularly with scientism, which Wilber identifies as a category error, defined as "the attempt of one eye to usurp the roles of the other two," such as when science only addresses the gross world of flesh, or matter. In light of this critique, Wilber examines the history and rise of science, whereby "measurement, and virtually measurement alone, gives the data of scientific experiments." He summarizes: "Adam could name the stars, Pythagoras could count them, but Newton could tell you how much they weighed to the nearest pound." Wilber explains that "Religion *tried* to be scientific, philosophy tried to be religious, science tried to be philosophic—and all were, to just that extent, wrong. They were guilt of *category errors.*"

Wilber then discusses Kant and Nagarjuna, who both demonstrated that "pure reason is simply incapable of grasping transcendent realities, and when it tries . . . it generates only dualistic incompatibilities." He levels a strong critique at the reductionistic error and contradiction of scientism, which has robbed humanity of some of its long-treasured higher capacities gained through the eyes of reason and contemplation, which he reviews in detail. Therefore Wilber concludes: "An overall transcendental paradigm—or any comprehensive investigative paradigm—should *use and integrate all three eyes,* and so it is necessary, at the start, to delineate the respective roles of each. If they are not delineated, then our 'comprehensive paradigm' can be opened to scientism, to mentalism, or to spiritualism, each based on category error, each deadly in effect."

Wilber next considers what's necessary to verify valid knowledge since "all valid knowledge is essentially similar in structure, and thus can be similarly verified (or rejected)." He describes this process as the three strands of knowledge accumulation:

1. **injunction** is "an *instrumental* or *injunctive strand*," which means "a set of instructions, simple or complex, internal or external. All have the form 'If you want to know this, do this'";

2. **illumination** is "an *illuminative* or *apprehensive strand*," which is "an illuminative *seeing* by the particular eye of knowledge evoked by the injunctive strand";

3. **confirmation** is *"a communal strand"* since it is necessary to share "the illuminative seeing with others who are using the same eye" in order to arrive at a "communal or consensual proof of true seeing."

Wilber goes on to emphasize that "the secret to consensual validation in all three realms [eyes] is the same, namely: a *trained eye* is a *public eye*. . . . Even though contemplative knowledge is ineffable, it is *not* private: it is a shared vision." Therefore, most importantly, according to Wilber, "a balanced and integrated approach to reality" would need "to avoid the category errors: confusing the eye of flesh with the eye of mind with the eye of contemplation." Thus, he concludes: "a comprehensive-transcendental paradigm would draw freely on the eye of flesh and on the eye of reason; but it would also be grounded in the eye of contemplation," since "transcendent values are not empirical facts revealed to the eye of the flesh but contemplative and nonverbal insights revealed by the *lumen superius* in the cave of the Heart."

CHAPTER 2. "THE PROBLEM OF PROOF" is a very significant chapter in which Wilber examines in depth the important question: "How can we be sure that the 'knowledge' gained by any of these three modes [or eyes] of knowing—sensory, symbolic, and spiritual—is valid? Or conversely—and more significantly—on what grounds do we reject any 'knowledge' as being erroneous?" First he defines data as being "any directly apprehended experience" that is "found in the realms of flesh, mind, and spirit." Thus, he summarizes, there is real data to be found "in the realms of flesh, mind, and spirit" or the real object domains, named:

- **sensibilia,** which involves sensory data that's gathered by using our senses (or their extensions, e.g., microscopes, telescopes, etc.), thus they're apprehended through the eye of flesh;

- **intelligibilia,** which involves "a mental datum (or series of them)" that's grounded in one's "present, given, immediate mental experience," thus apprehended through the eye of reason;

- **transcendelia,** which involves "transcendental data directly perceived or intuited by the eye of contemplation," including "a single spiritual intuition, a mass illumination, a particular gnostic insight, or overall *satori*," thus they are "directly perceived or intuited by the eye of contemplation."

Wilber makes a careful distinction between the empirical, which he restricts "to its original meaning: knowledge grounded in sensory experience (sensibilia)," and experience, which is "simply synonymous with direct apprehension, immediate giveness, intuition—sensory, mental, and spiritual." Next, he reviews the verification procedures of "data accumulation in any realm," therefore offering a precise methodology for adequate verification, or nonverification," that can be equally applied to all three domains (sensibilia, intelligibilia, and transcendelia) and summarized as the three strands of valid data accumulation:

1. **instrumental injunction,** which means "If you want to *know* this, *do* this";

2. **intuitive apprehensions,** which means "a cognitive grasp, prehension, or immediate experience of the object domain . . . addressed by the injunction";

3. **communal confirmation,** which means "a checking of results . . . with others who have adequately completed the injunctive and apprehensive strands."

As a further clarification, Wilber adds that "although the same abstract strands operate in each [realm of sensibilia, intelligibilia, and transcendelia], the actual or concrete methodologies [of inquiry] are quite different (owing to the different hierarchical structures of the data or object domains themselves)":

- The *eye of flesh* uses an **empiric-analytic inquiry,** however "the only data with which it operates is in sensibilia—the eye of flesh or its extension," thus it's operative in the natural sciences; most importantly, Wilber points out, it has a "disproof mechanism" or "nonverifiability principle" (after Karl Popper).

- The *eye of mind* uses a **mental-phenomenological inquiry,** which is "the gathering of valid linguistic, noetic, or mental-phenomenological data," thus it's operative, for example, in mathematics, classic phenomenology, including the hermeneutic circle, and psychology, including Freudian psychoanalysis.

- The *eye of contemplation* uses a **transcendental inquiry,** which discloses "the facts or data . . . of the transcendental realm," thus, ultimately, "this direct, immediate, intuitive apprehension of Being . . . is *satori*," which is "a direct apprehension *of* spirit, *by* spirit, *as* spirit. . . ."

Wilber continues to present some practical examples, such as with Zen, which use the injunctive strand (*zazen* or causal-insight meditation), to reach intuitive

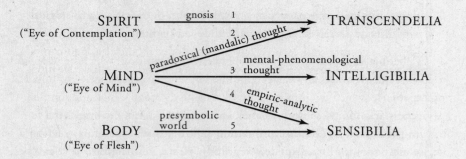

Epistemological Relationships
FIGURE I

apprehension (satori or *kensho*), and which is then given "a vigorous test" by adequately adapted individuals (the Zen master). He also reviews the category error that is made with the many rational "proofs" of God's existence, which will "simply delay the realization that there *is* an instrumental proof for the existence of God, but the instrument is contemplation, not reason, and the proof is direct, not mediate."

Wilber maintains that "if by 'science' one means the three strands of knowledge accumulation in any realm," then indeed there can be "the science of yoga, the science of being, or the science of meditation." This leads to an important discussion on theory and hypothesis, or theoretical knowledge, including an examination of the various epistemological relationships based on the spectrum of consciousness, including the fact that because mental data is actually "symbolic, intentional, reflective, and referential [it] can be used to point to, or represent, other data, from any other realms: sensibilia, intelligibilia itself, or transcendelia." (See Figure 1: "Epistemological Relationships.")

By following the "three eyes" approach, Wilber realizes that "transcendelia cannot be easily or adequately described in mental terms or maps," therefore, it can only be expressed "in the slippery, paradoxical, poetical terms of Mandalic Reason." For this reason, he suggests, it's possible to legitimately speak of a hierarchy of sciences:

- **monological sciences** or a science of sensibilia based upon an empiric-analytic inquiry, "when data comes from, or is grounded in, the object domain of sensibilia," such as with physics, chemistry, biology, astronomy, geology, etc.;

- **dialogical sciences** or a science of intelligibilia or the "rational, hermeneutical, semiotic sciences" based upon a mental-phenomenological inquiry, which is "when the data comes from, or is grounded in, the object domain of intelligibilia," such as with linguistics, mathematics, historic-hermeneutics, logic, etc.;

- **contemplative sciences** or a science of transcendelia or the "translogical, transcendental, transpersonal sciences" based on transcendental inquiry, which is "when the data comes from, or is grounded in, the object domain of transcendelia," such as with "openly experimental and contemplative disciplines," which can further be subdivided into:

- **mandalic sciences,** which include, however inadequately, "mental cartographies of the transmental realms" or mandalic maps, which are "paradoxical, translogical," though ultimately "Spirit as Spirit is not paradoxical; it is not characterizable at all in mental terms—but when put into mental terms, the result is paradoxical";

- **noumenological** or **gnostic sciences** or geist sciences, which are the actual methodologies and injunctions needed for "the direct apprehension of transcendelia as transcendelia; direct and intuitive apprehension of spirit, noumenon, Dharmakaya; based on gnosis."

Wilber is quite clear that "These gnostic sciences also perform *mandalic* sciences—they translate the higher realms (downward) into mental maps, cartographies, and so on, mostly for the use of beginners or outsiders, but they are very explicit about the limited functions of such mandalic maps—they are simply pictures of reality, not reality itself."

CHAPTER 3. "A MANDALIC MAP OF CONSCIOUSNESS" is an overview of the spectrum of consciousness model or synthesis that was presented in the first nine chapters of *The Atman Project* (1980). After introducing the concept of holism (after Jan Smuts) and a holon (after Arthur Koestler) in order to review the nature of development, Wilber summarizes: "As a general approximation, we may conclude that the psyche—like the cosmos at large—is many-layered ('pluridimensional'), composed of successively higher-order wholes and unities and integrations"; in other words, "the same force that produced humans from amoebas produces adults from infants." This observation is also confirmed by modern developmental psychology, which subscribes, in whole or part, "to the concept of stratified stages of increasing complexity," upon which Wilber bases "a fairly well-balanced and comprehensive model of the Spectrum of Consciousness":

- the **lower stages** and levels of the psyche are named in general terms as "instinctual, impulsive, libidinous, id-ish, animal, apelike";

- the **middle stages** are "socially adapted, mentally adjusted, egoically integrated, syntactically organized, conceptually advanced";

- the **higher stages** are known about from "higher-order personalities," the men and women who are "the world's great mystics and sages [and who] represent some of the very highest, if not the highest, of all stages of human development."

In the remainder of the chapter, Wilber reviews in detail the basic ontological structures involved in human development and existence. Various examples are drawn from developmental psychology, as well as from the perennial wisdom traditions (such as Vedanta, Buddhism, and the yoga chakra psychology), in which Wilber reviews in detail the basic realms in human development and existence:

- the **lower realms** involve the "somatic processes, instincts, simple sensations and perceptions, and emotional-sexual impulses," also called the body-ego or the typhonic self symbolized by the Typhon or the half-human, half-serpent (uroboros);

- the **intermediate realms** involve the mental-ego, which is when language and the mental or conceptual functions emerge, including concrete operational and formal operational thinking (after Piaget), as well as the shadow, persona, and total ego, until the self develops into an autonomous or self-actualized person, called the centaur. This is represented by "the great mythological being with animal body and human mind existing in a state of at-one-ment";

- the **higher realms** involve the subtle sphere, both low and high: the low-subtle is the psychic dimension, including "paranormal events . . . the lowest of the transcendental realms"; the high-subtle is when the self "extends within and beyond to various subphases of extraordinarily higher-order transcendence, differentiation, and integration";

- the **ultimate realms** involve the causal, low and high: the low-causal includes archetypal form, illumination, intuition, and beginning gnosis, until the realization of "God as an archetypal summit of one's own Consciousness"; the high-causal is "total and utter transcendence and release into Formless Consciousness, Boundless Radiance," traditionally known as enlightenment (or *sahaja samadhi*), in which "ultimate unity consciousness . . . completes that absolute gestalt toward which all manifestation moves."

CHAPTER 4. "DEVELOPMENT, MEDITATION, AND THE UNCONSCIOUS" condenses three of the most important chapters (10, 11, 12) from *The Atman Project,* examining the general principles operative in the form of development, i.e., when the developing self identifies with an emergent structure, then differentiates and transcends that structure, allowing each succeeding stage to operate on the previous level. Wilber also presents an in-depth discussion on the different types of the unconscious, including the ground-unconscious, archaic-unconscious, submergent-unconscious, embedded-unconscious, and emergent-unconscious, culminating in a recapitulation of meditation and the unconscious. He summarizes this developmental process of transformation: "Evolution then proceeds again, transformation by transformation, remembering more and more, unifying more and more, until every soul remembers Buddha, as Buddha, in Buddha—whereupon there is then no Buddha and no soul. And that is the final transformation." (See *The Atman Project* above-referenced chapter summaries herein for a more detailed presentation.)

CHAPTER 5. "PHYSICS, MYSTICISM, AND THE NEW HOLOGRAPHIC PARADIGM" is a review of the main premises found in the popular concept of the holographic paradigm, which, "in the final analysis, seems shot through with profound category errors," whereas the comprehensive-transcendental paradigm that Wilber proposes would "at least attempt to include monological sciences, dialogical sciences, mandalic sciences, and contemplative sciences." Wilber supports this conclusion by first reiterating the perennial philosophy (*philosophia perennis*) whose "most striking feature . . . presents being and consciousness as a *hierarchy of dimensional levels,* moving from the lowest, densest, and most fragmentary realms to the highest, subtlest, and most unitary ones," for which he gives the Hindu example of the various *koshas,* or "sheaths." Consequently, according to the perennial traditions, each level of this spectrum has an "appropriate field of study, which Wilber briefly outlines.

In addition, since "the various dimensional-levels are hierarchic," they exist as a "multidimensional interpenetration with nonequivalence" because "the higher transcends but includes the lower—*not* vice versa. That is, all of the lower is 'in' the higher, but not all the higher is in the lower." This can be accounted for with the perennial philosophy's notion of involution or the "movement from higher into the lower," combined with the scientific description of evolution or "the movement from the lower to the higher." Wilber summarizes: "The *ultimate aim of evolution* . . . is to awaken *as* Atman, and thus retain the glory of the creation without being forced to act in the drama of self suffering [known as the 'Atman-project']." By briefly reviewing our universe's history, beginning with the big bang, Wilber suggests, like Plotinus, that with the emergence of human beings "evolution is, as it were, half completed." However, he also claims that "in the past course of human history" some advanced-tip men and women have actively exercised "the evolutionary discipline of higher religion," therefore, in conclusion, "What remains is for the world to follow suit, via evolutionary or process meditation, into the higher realms, culminating at infinity."

For the most part, however, the essay focuses on critiquing any new paradigm that attempts to bring physics and mysticism together without understanding that "physics and mysticism are not two different approaches to the same reality. They are different approaches to two quite different levels of reality; the latter transcends but includes the former." In other words, although there may be a similarity of language, when the mystic speaks about the mutual interpenetration of all things, he or she is not speaking about the quantum level but the transcendent aspect of existence. Therefore Wilber reviews in detail the implicate order (after David Bohm), the holographic brain, the measurement problem based on problems of *uncertainty* and *probability*, and the mind and quantum mechanics, following which he concludes: "The perennial philosophy would agree that matter is created out of mind (prana), but through an act of precipitation and crystallization, not perception and measurement."

In sum, Wilber demonstrates that "If there is no conceivable physical test that would disprove the mystic view, and there isn't, then there is no conceivable one which would corroborate it either," especially since "the *existence* of higher states cannot be explained in terms of something that may or may not happen to a lower state." And since "mysticism itself is too profound to be hitched to phases of empirical scientific theorizing," then this marriage of science and religion suggested by "our understandable zeal to promulgate a new paradigm" is a dangerous approach, for "unwarranted and premature marriages usually end in divorce, and all too often a divorce that terribly damages both parties."

CHAPTER 6. "REFLECTIONS ON THE NEW AGE PARADIGM—AN INTERVIEW" covers a lot of ground as it presents another solid critique of the holographic paradigm and the "new physics" models presented in the proceeding chapter. In an interview with *ReVision* journal, Wilber points out that the holographic paradigm is "not totally wrong, just partial," because it only "covers the immanent but not the transcendent aspects of the absolute." Thus it's similar to "the problem of pantheism," which Wilber defines as "the mistake of confusing the whole world with Brahman," which unfortunately can become "a way to think about 'Godhead' without having to actually transform yourself."

Rather than just existing as one or two dimensions (such as an implicate/explicate order), Wilber points out there is a gradation in ontology composed of successive "levels of being and levels of knowing"(after Huston Smith). Thus, "evolution is hierarchical—rocks are at one end of that scale, God and the Omega is at the other, and plants, reptiles, mammals, human, and *bodhisattvas* fill up the middle, in that order. *And,* God is the very stuff, the actual essence, of *each* stage-level—God is not the highest level, nor a different level itself, but the reality of all levels." According to Wilber, "The problem with the popular holographic theories, as well as the general 'new physics and Eastern mysticism' stuff, is that they *collapse the hierarchy,*" and this will never work because "each higher level cannot be fully explained in terms of a lower level."

Therefore he refutes this argument of the pantheism/holographic paradigm by first positing the notion of a holoarchy, or a "mutually interdependent and interrelated" yet hierarchical model, which holds that "if the higher levels contain attributes not found on the lower levels, you simply can't have bilateral equivalence between them." He also presents the concept of involution, an idea that's "extremely well-developed in the traditional philosophies," and which states that "the absolute bliss of Brahman goes through a series of stepped-down versions, or dilutions, until it appears as the sexual thrill of orgasm."

The integral philosopher maintains that there's an epistemology available that's based on a hierarchy of knowledge or the three modes of knowing—sensory, symbolic, and contemplative, producing "a fundamentally different type of knowledge":

1. the **eye of flesh** (matter) or physical-sensory knowledge;

2. the **eye of reason** (mind) or the mental knowledge;

3. the **eye of contemplation** (spirit) or the spiritual knowledge.

Wilber then draws attention to the hermeneutic circle (after Heidegger) or where "meaning is a mental production and can be determined only by interpretation," and then to the operative subsets which makes up the knowledge domains of the eye of reason:

- the **sensory realm** (or matter) interpreted with empiric-analytic/technical knowledge;

- the **mental realm** (or mind) interpreted with hermeneutic-phenomenological/moral knowledge;

- the **spirit realm** (or ultimate reality) interpreted with paradoxical-mandalic/soteriological knowledge or mandalic reason, which is especially useful since "paradox is simply the way nonduality looks to the mental level."

(See Figure 2: "The Eye of Reason Interprets.")

Indeed, as Wilber carefully explains, since "Spirit itself is not paradoxical; it is not characterizable at all," then "whatever reality is, it can only, *only* be 'seen' upon *satori,* or via actual contemplative insight." In other words, he recognizes that

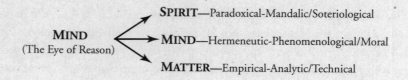

MIND
(The Eye of Reason)

SPIRIT—Paradoxical-Mandalic/Soteriological

MIND—Hermeneutic-Phenomenological/Moral

MATTER—Empirical-Analytic/Technical

The Eye of Reason
Interprets
FIGURE 2

"There is no way to directly understand spirit except by *radical spiritual transformation,* or the direct opening of the *eye of contemplation* in your own case." He also suggests that "we would expect spiritual processes to leave footprints in the biophysical substrate, either directly or in the mind," thus "these correlations, even though they are degenerate, are very important." Nevertheless, because "God can be verified as a transcendental reality by a community of transsubjective meditators," then, in essence, contemplative practices or "meditation itself is not a particular interpretation of spirit, but a direct and immediate identity with and as spirit."

After reviewing a wide range of other topics—from "wavicles" to Korzybski's famous utterance, 'Whatever you say a thing is, it isn't!'" to the double-bind theory, to Whitehead's philosophy, precognition, New Age theories and theorists, the Whorf-Sapir hypothesis, Wittgenstein's early work, a reductionism where "philosophy degenerates into only positivism, and psychology degenerates into only behaviorism"—Wilber summarizes: "An overall paradigm would have to include all the *modes of knowing* . . . and all the *correlative methodologies* . . . it would include an actual *summons to contemplative practice* . . . [and it] would demand a *social evolutionary stance,* a social policy geared to help human beings evolve through the stage-levels of existence." Yet, he also realizes since "transcendence cannot be forced . . . you can only force slavery; you can't force a person to be free," then "the only way you actually know the transmental is to actually *transform.*" Therefore, he suggests, "The only major purpose of a book on mysticism should be to persuade the reader to engage in mystical practice."

CHAPTER 7. "THE PRE/TRANS FALLACY" is probably one of the most important chapters in any of Wilber's works because it summarizes in detail his position on the pre/trans fallacy, (abbreviated as ptf). This critical breakthrough overturned the common "Romantic" error adopted in his earlier writings (in Wilber/Phase 1) and led to a greater emphasis on evolutionary development. First, Wilber succinctly states the standard definition of the pre/trans fallacy: "since the *pre*rational and *trans*rational are both, in their own ways, *non*rational, then they appear quite similar or even identical to the untutored eye." Throughout the essay, numerous theorists are presented who, in Wilber's judgment, make this theoretical error (such

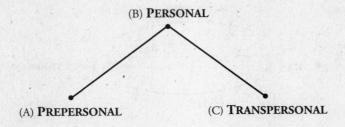

(B) **PERSONAL**

(A) **PREPERSONAL**   (C) **TRANSPERSONAL**

The Pre/Trans Sequence
FIGURE 3

as Freud, Jung, Reich, etc.), contrasted with those who do not (such as Aurobindo, Maslow, Baldwin, and Assagioli, etc.).

Wilber begins by emphasizing that the pre/trans fallacy is based solely upon the fact that "*all phenomena develop,* and thus true phenomenology is always evolutionary, dynamic, or developmental." This movement of evolution develops in at least three major stages comprising the overall sequence of development: from nature to humanity to divinity, from subconscious to self-conscious to superconscious, from prepersonal to personal to transpersonal. (See Figure 3: "The Pre/Trans Sequence.")

Next, Wilber explains that another theoretical tool is needed to understand involution/evolution since, "if the movement from the *lower to the higher* is evolution, then the reverse, the movement from *higher to the lower,* is involution." (See Figure 4: "Evolution/Involution.") This allows Wilber to summarize the pre/trans fallacy: "Since development moves from prepersonal to personal to transpersonal, and since both prepersonal and transpersonal are, in their own ways, nonpersonal, then prepersonal and transpersonal tend to appear similar, even identical, to the untutored eye. In other words, people tend to confuse prepersonal and transpersonal dimensions—and there is the heart of the ptf." This fallacy has two major forms: ptf 1 (or reductionism) is "the reduction of the transpersonal to the prepersonal," and ptf 2 (or elevationism) is "the elevation of the prepersonal to the transpersonal."

Consequently, Wilber explains, reductionism and elevationism create two opposed worldviews: reductionism or worldview one (WV 1) "sees development moving from a prepersonal source in nature, through a series of intermediate advances, to culmination in the 'high point' of evolution, that of human rationality." Elevationism or worldview two (WV 2) "sees development moving from a spiritual source ('in heaven') to a culmination in a 'low point' of alienation, that of a sinful humanity or of the individual and personal ego."

In order to demonstrate "how the pre/trans fallacy might be lurking behind various theories, personal and transpersonal," Wilber gives numerous examples of ptf in psychological theories. For example, as he showed in *The Atman Project,* Freud (WV 1) "reduced all spiritual and transpersonal experiences to the preper-

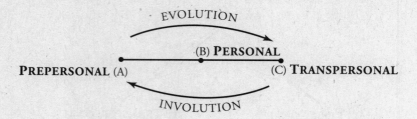

Evolution/Involution
FIGURE 4

sonal level," whereas Jung (WV 2) "tends to obscure the vast and profound differences between the lower collective unconscious and the higher collective unconscious." Consequently, Wilber asserts that both of these positions (Freudian and Jungian) tend to overlook the necessity and value of the ego, ego-strength, and ego-esteem (or what Meher Baba calls ego-centered integration) for "one must first strengthen ego, then transcend it."

In reviewing the ptf in sociology and anthropology, as he demonstrated in *Up From Eden,* Wilber explains that reductionists (WV 1), such as Darwin and his theory of natural selection, are examples of seeing "evolution as moving from lower to higher," yet they fail to acknowledge "the role played by Spirit in evolution." Conversely, elevationists (WV 2), such as Romantics rely on "the Eden corpus [where] Eden is interpreted as literal evolution instead of as prior involution . . . [thus] the necessary rise of self-conscious ego is then misinterpreted as a fall from a heavenly and spiritual estate, whereas it is simply an anxious halfway point on the way back from the lowest reach of self-alienation and subconsciousness to a real superconscious heaven in actualized Spirit." Therefore, Wilber criticizes the New Age enthusiasts whose ideas of "'nonegoism' usually conceals a mixture and confusion of pre-egoic fantasy with transegoic vision, of preconceptual feelings with transpersonal insight, of prepersonal desires with transpersonal growth, of pre-egoic whoopee with transegoic liberation."

Any overall developmental theory, however, would need to acknowledge that both views "may be partially right (and partially wrong)," therefore Wilber attempts "by taking out . . . ptf elements in each view, to make possible a general synthesis of all of them."

To that end, Wilber emphasizes that "The course of development is defined at every stage by increasing differentiation, integration, and transcendence" because "each stage of growth, no matter how lowly, transcends its predecessor to some degree by definition and by fact." However, as he explained in *The Atman Project,* "If development miscarries at any point, then instead of differentiation there is dissociation, instead of transcendence, repression." Wilber thus criticizes

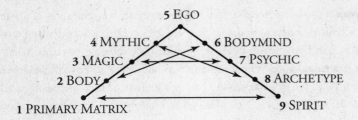

Western culture's current tendency to "cure the repression by regression," because, as he complains, "It is one thing to recontact the body so as to reintegrate it, quite another to recontact the body and stay there." Therefore he examines the primary matrix where the infant's early state is often elevated to "an identification with Self, an identification that is subsequently lost in development, and then regained in enlightenment," whereas in actuality, "what *is* lost in subsequent development is the relatively blissful ignorance of the subconscious, prepersonal, bio-material fusion." In other words, since "development goes from id to ego to Self," then, Wilber concludes, "Mysticism is not regression in service of ego, but evolution in transcendence of ego."

Wilber then goes on to give detailed explanations of a number of pre/trans confusions, such as claiming that "participation mystique is not a capacity; it is an incapacity"; that there's a profound difference between "a transpersonal community of *sangha* and a prepersonal clan or *cult*"; that spectrum psychology clarifies why both sides of the pre/trans fallacy either "see all psychotics as half-saints [elevationism] . . . [or] all saints as half-psychotic [reductionism]"; that ego-transcendence or ego-death (a trans-phenomenon) has often been confused with a nihilistic approach to life (a pre-phenomenon), yet it should be understood as a true desire for the release and the transcendence of the ego (separate self-sense), thus it's capable of ending psychological suffering, as exemplified in the practice of Buddhism; that pre/trans distinctions in human psychology help clarify the actual "order of phylogenetic and ontogenetic development," especially since "magic is almost always confused with psychic," or that "a similar confusion seems to exist with regard to myth and archetype." In a detailed discussion, Wilber suggests that since "Jung confused mythic image with transpersonal archetype" then "Jung's theories are in dire need of revision." (See Figure 5: "Pre/Trans Stage Confusions.")

Wilber closes by cautioning: "Since the general form of unwinding a ptf is to go from a bipole . . . to a tripole . . . it is important to remember that not every bipole conceals a ptf in need of teasing apart. Certain fundamental bipoles, such as yin/yang, heaven/earth, light/dark, left/right, active/passive, rest/motion, one/

many, good/evil—whatever else they may be, they are not examples of ptf-bipoles. They are dualities inherent in maya; they are transcended not by teasing one of the poles apart, but by uniting, integrating, and transcending both, equally, in the Tao." On a personal note, Wilber explains that he is quite aware of the care needed to be taken to avoid the pre/trans fallacy, especially since he too "once embraced those fallacies with enthusiasm . . . and, as Husserl observed at the turn of the century, one is most vehement against those errors that one recently held oneself." Instead, as he concludes, "a true marriage of science and religion" will demand that any "truly comprehensive paradigm . . . shall take the true from both and discard the false from both, or we shall continue to try to integrate the muddled half truths of each."

CHAPTER 8. "LEGITIMACY, AUTHENTICITY, AND AUTHORITY IN THE NEW RELIGIONS" is a summary of many of the principal topics in *A Sociable God*, and it later appeared as "The Spectrum Model," Wilber's contribution to *Spiritual Choices* (edited with Dick Anthony and Bruce Ecker, 1987). To properly evaluate the new religious movements of the Western (especially American) society, Wilber's thesis uses a developmental-structural approach, such as proposed by the spectrum of consciousness, to create a "believable scale or criteria for differentiating the more valid 'religious movements' from the less valid or even harmful."

Wilber's model includes at least three general realms or general structure-stages of development: 1) the prerational (subconscious); 2) the rational (self-conscious); and 3) the transrational (superconscious), which are further subdivided into seven corresponding worldviews: Archaic, Magic, Mythic, Rational, Psychic, Subtle, Causal, and Ultimate or "Spirit in the highest sense, not as Big Person but as the 'Ground of Being.'" By using this template and methodology, Wilber points out that it's necessary to be vigilant about the pre/trans fallacy (see previous chapter) so that neither the "transrational is reduced to the prerational (e.g., Freud), or the prerational is elevated to the transrational (e.g., Jung)." (See Figure 6: "The Pre/Trans Fallacy.")

Wilber then distinguishes between "the basic defining form of each level is its Deep Structure, whereas a particular element or component of each level is a Surface Structure. A change in deep structure we call Transformation; a change in surface structure, Translation." Thus he summarizes:

- a **Translation** of *Surface Structures* establishes "Legitimacy . . . a horizontal scale . . . a measure of the degree of integration, organization, meaning, coherence, and stability of or within a given level of structural adaptation or development";

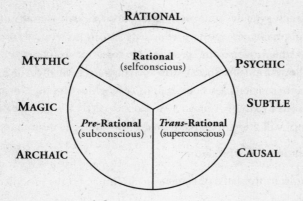

RATIONAL

MYTHIC — Rational (selfconscious) — PSYCHIC

MAGIC — SUBTLE

Pre-Rational (subconscious) — *Trans*-Rational (superconscious)

ARCHAIC — CAUSAL

The Pre/Trans Fallacy
FIGURE 6

- **Transformation** between *Deep Structures* establishes "Authenticity . . . a vertical scale . . . a measure of the degree of transformation offered by any particular psychosocial institution."

In relation to religious institutions, Wilber defines "any psychosocial institution that validates or facilitates translation we call Legitimate; any that validates or facilitates transformation we call Authentic." This combination of horizontal (legitimate) and vertical (authentic) scales is one of Wilber's primary tools of analysis. Problems usually arise when legitimacy and authenticity are confused, therefore it's very important to apply both of these two independent scales, that is, using both a developmental-structural analysis and a surface-functional analysis. This type of systematic procedure or methodology will "determine the group's level of authenticity, or its vertical degree of maturity and development," as well as its "degree of legitimacy, or its horizontal scale of integrative meaning and stability."

Next, Wilber introduces the different types of authority, remarking on the dualism between Good Authority or Bad Authority:

- Functional Authority, which is nonproblematic but involves "society's need to act as a pacer of development";

- Benign Authority such as a teacher;

- Compulsory Authority as necessary yet temporary;

- Phase-Specific Authority such as a teacher-student relationship.

Of course all of these types have their appropriate place, but Wilber's scheme outlines a way to distinguish the type of "authority which is not functional or phase-specific."

Wilber then provides some concrete examples, such as examining the "general pattern of problematic groups" which are usually prerational cults (Jonestown being a paradigmatic worst-case scenario). He concludes by presenting the research of Dick Anthony and Tom Robbins as a "corroborative scheme" since it offers even more criteria for assessing a proper analysis of religious groups. One of the important conclusions drawn by Anthony and Robbins is that "a positive, authentic [religious] group" will more than likely have at least the following characteristics:

1. "transrational, not prerational;

2. anchor legitimacy in a tradition;

3. phase-specific authority;

4. NOT headed by a Perfect Master;

5. NOT out to save the world."

CHAPTER 9. "STRUCTURE, STAGE, AND SELF" outlines the parameters of Wilber/Phase 3, which first appeared as an article in 1981 titled "Ontogenetic Development: Two Fundamental Patterns" (*The Journal of Transpersonal Psychology,* vol. 13, no. 1, 1981). Wilber concentrates on the two fundamental patterns in individual human ontogeny, and with supportive evidence from developmental psychology (such as Piaget, Kohlberg, etc.). He clearly defines and discusses the difference between:

- **transition-replacement structures** or the "stages and phases of consciousness," which "are essentially temporary, transition, replacements phases of consciousness," such as the "stages of self-moral development" and "cognitive maps or worldviews, that occur as successively new and higher structures emerge," which include: archaic (sensation, perception), typhonic (emotional-sexual), magic (early pre-op), Mythic (late pre-op, early con-op), rational (form-op);

- the **basic structures** or the "levels or structures of consciousness" which are "essentially permanent, enduring, basic components of consciousness," which include: physical, sensoriperceptual, emotional-sexual, phantasmic, rep-mind, rule/role mind, formal/reflexive mind, vision-logic, subtle, causal, and ultimate structures.

Wilber points out a clear differentiation between these enduring and transitional structures shows: "About half of development remains in existence (even if modified), and about half is lost or passes." In addition, Wilber explains that even though a worldview is transitional, this "is not to say that the old worldviews cannot in some cases be reactivated." Consequently, he explains: "The exclusive worldviews—archaic, typhonic, magic, mythic, and so on—are successively abandoned and replaced, but the basic structures themselves—preop, conop, formop, and so on—remain in existences, in awareness, functional and necessary."

The rest of the chapter places these structures in relation to the self-system, which is the vital link between them both because "in a sense, the basic structures form rungs in a ladder upon which the self-system then climbs, matter to body to mind to subtle to causal to spirit (generating certain self-transition stages in the process)." He examines both Eastern models, such as the "Buddhist notion of the five *skandhas* . . . the psychology of the yoga *chakras,* the Vedanta sheaths, and the Mahayana *vijnanas,*" as well as Western self psychology, developed by Hartmann, Sullivan, G. H. Mead, Erikson, Rogers, Fairbairn, Kohut, Loevinger, Maslow, and Branden, all of whom tend to see "the self as locus of appropriation" though in actuality "there *is* no self, only a 'stream of consciousness.'" Wilber generally summarizes his view of "the self as the locus of identification as well as the center of the sense of identity" seen as "the navigator of development," which is involved in a struggle between four forces: "preservation versus negation" and "ascent versus descent," since "the self does not merely float down the stream of consciousness—for better or worse, it pushes and pulls, holds on and lets go, ascends and descends, preserves and releases."

Wilber then sets out the self-stages of consciousness by looking in detail at "Kohlberg's moral development, Loevinger's ego development, and Maslow's needs hierarchy (to cite only three examples)," showing how their work is referring to the replacement-transition structures or exclusivity stages. In summary, Wilber states that "In attempting to integrate and synthesize Eastern and Western approaches (as well as various Western approaches themselves), the differences between basic structures and transitional-stages ought to be kept in mind, lest we end up comparing apples and oranges." Therefore he pointedly suggests that in the "search of a new and higher transcendental paradigm" it's extremely important for researchers of all types to not allow "stages [to] be confused with ontological structures (or vice versa)," a position that defines the main concerns of Wilber/Phase 3.

CHAPTER 10. "THE ULTIMATE STATE OF CONSCIOUSNESS" is a potent chapter for it masterfully discusses the mystical nondual worldview that claims, in essence, "The Absolute is both the highest state of being and the ground of all being; it is both the Goal of evolution and the Ground of evolution; the highest stage of development and the reality or suchness of all stages of development. . . ."

Wilber explains that this "paradox of instruction" must be fully taken into account: "if spirit is constantly transcendent, it is also completely immanent," therefore he's "firmly convinced that if a new and comprehensive paradigm is ever to emerge, that [transcendent-immanent] paradox will be at its heart." Then Wilber goes on to present quotes from the world's most sacred texts, uttered by some of the wisest saints and sages in humanity's tradition of spiritual wisdom, from Huang Po to Jesus Christ, from Johannes Scotus to Shankara, from Nagarjuna to Wittgenstein and others.

Wilber begins with the ancient seers of the Upanishads, who tell us "the Absolute is 'One without a second.'" Wilber also draws us into the secret that the Absolute is infinite which means spaceless, yet not "a very Big Space," therefore "since the infinite is present in its entirety at every point of space, *all* of the infinite is fully present right HERE"; and it is eternal, which means timeless, therefore "all of Eternity is already present right NOW." Thus, he concludes, "Point without dimension or extension, Moment without date or duration—such is the Absolute." Another striking paradox is that the Absolute is literally unattainable" simply because "it's impossible to escape It in the first place," therefore "the attempt to bring the soul and God together merely perpetuates the illusion that the two are separate." These paradoxical assertions, which are woven throughout Wilber's theories, are corroborated by statements from Western philosophers such as St. Bonaventure and Wittgenstein, and Eastern sages such as Shankara, Huang Po, and Sri Ramana Maharshi.

As our guide to the "Ultimate State of Consciousness," Wilber announces, "whereas union with God cannot be attained, knowledge of that union can be attained; that whereas we cannot manufacture the Supreme Identity, we can realize it." This is known as "the very Ultimate State of Consciousness, enlightenment, *satori, moksha, wu,* release, liberation," yet again, paradoxically, "the Ultimate State of Consciousness is in no way different from your ordinary state of consciousness or from any other state of consciousness you might have at this or at any other moment." Therefore, Wilber continues, "it's only because we keep insisting that the Ultimate State of Consciousness be different from the Present State of Consciousness that makes it so hard to admit to ourselves that we already know our Buddha Nature," hence, "all seeking, spiritual or otherwise, is ultimately irrelevant." In other words, "despite all the best assurances of the Masters," this nondual knowledge is difficult to realize yet impossible to deny: "Since you are Brahman, you obviously can't *see* Brahman, just as, for instance, an eye cannot see itself and an ear cannot hear itself." Once more, Shankara, Meister Eckhart, Alan Watts, Nagarjuna, and Hsuan-chueh, and many others, tell us precisely the same thing, as Wilber documents.

The "EPILOGUE" admits that "the possibility of a genuinely comprehensive paradigm is an alluring notion," however, he maintains, "the real point of this book . . . was not so much to present a final paradigm . . . as to point out some of the *major obstacles* now blocking its emergence." This includes "a half dozen or so: category error, the pre/trans fallacy, the confusion of legitimacy and authenticity, the confusion of structure and stage, the failure to grasp the paradox of spirit as goal and ground," all of which hamper today's theorists. Wilber did not want to give "a final view, but [rather] hints on how better to reach that view; not a final knowledge, but a balance in the quest itself; not a way to stop, but a way to carry on."

CHAPTER 8

Quantum Questions

Mystical Writings of the World's Great Physicists

EDITED BY KEN WILBER

(Boston: Shambhala Publications, New Science Library, 1984);

The Collected Works of Ken Wilber, Vol. 4 (CW4) (Shambhala, 1999);

revised paperback edition (Shambhala, 2001)

Quantum Questions: Mystical Writings of the World's Great Physicists was edited and compiled during Wilber's later Phase 2 and early Phase 3 period emphasizing modern physics (Right-Hand exterior quadrants) based on mystical writings by some of the early physicists on the limitation of science's "shadowy" system of mathematics (Left-Hand interior quadrants) in the Great Nest of Spirit or Kosmos.

Quantum Questions: Mystical Writings of the World's Great Physicists was published in 1984 (Shambhala Publications) under the New Science Library imprint; Wilber's contributions are now part of *The Collected Works of Ken Wilber, Volume Four (CW4),* (Shambhala Publications, 1999); paperback reprint edition (Shambhala Publications, 2001).

Quantum Questions offers a strong critique to the popular New Age interpretation of modern physics that uses it as a justification or proof for mysticism or a spiritual worldview. By presenting the actual writings culled from the founders of modern physics themselves—Heisenberg, Schrödinger, de Broglie, Jeans, Planck, Pauli, Eddington, and Einstein—all of whom were deeply concerned about these matters, this book shows unequivocally that "modern physics neither proves nor disproves, neither supports nor refutes, a mystical-spiritual worldview." This is because physics itself is based upon mathematics, which itself is nothing but a system of "shadow-symbols" (in the words of the physicists themselves); therefore these world-famous scientists understood it's absolutely necessary to use real mysticism to contact reality directly. The selections from *Quantum Questions* highlight the little-known fact that all these great physicists ultimately turned to mysticism for true knowledge of the world.

CHAPTER 9

Transformations of Consciousness

Conventional and Contemplative Perspectives on Development

BY KEN WILBER, JACK ENGLER, AND DANIEL P. BROWN

(Boston: Shambhala Publications, New Science Library, 1986);

The Collected Works of Ken Wilber, Vol. 4 (CW4) (Shambhala, 1999)

Foreword
Preface
About the Authors
Introduction by Ken Wilber, Jack Engler, and Daniel Brown

Transformations of Consciousness: Conventional and Contemplative Perspectives on Development is the essential Wilber/Phase 3 book emphasizing spectrum psychology, psychopathology, and psychotherapy or treatment modalities, therefore focusing on the development of individual interior consciousness (Upper-Left quadrant) in the Great Nest of Spirit or Kosmos.

Transformations of Consciousness is coauthored with Harvard professors Jack Engler and Daniel P. Brown and includes contributions by Mark Epstein, Jonathan Lieff, and John Chirban. Wilber's three essays were initially published in 1984, in *The Journal of Transpersonal Psychology*. These essays differentiate between enduring basic structures (waves) and transitional developmental lines (streams), which are balanced and navigated by the evolving self, or self-system. In these works Wilber demonstrates how to clearly delineate, correlate, and integrate the developmental spectrum of consciousness with a corresponding spectrum of psychopathology and the related spectrum of treatment modalities or therapeutic intervention.

Transformations of Consciousness: Conventional and Contemplative Perspectives on Development was published in 1986 (Shambhala Publications, New Science Library); it is now part of *The Collected Works of Ken Wilber*, Vol. 4 (CW4) (Shambhala Publications, 1999).

The "INTRODUCTION" by Ken Wilber, Jack Engler, and Daniel Brown presents the basic premises behind the full-spectrum model of human growth and its psychodynamic development by combining Western "conventional psychology and psychiatry" with "the world's great contemplative and meditative disciplines," especially those of the East. These conventional and contemplative approaches both "seem to point to a general, universal, and cross-cultural spectrum of human development, consisting of various developmental lines [streams] and stages [waves]." The authors explain that "One of the aims of this volume is to begin to flesh out this skeleton [model] by bringing together, for the first time, both of these major schools of development—conventional and contemplative" in order to create a full-spectrum model. Another major theme is that the different developmental stages are apparently "vulnerable to qualitatively distinct psychopathologies, which in turn yield to qualitatively different treatment modalities (or therapies in general) . . . the correlative or appropriate therapeutic intervention."

First, they acknowledge that each level and stage of the spectrum has both deep structures, which are the "recognizable similarities" of each level, and surface structures, which are specific to each culture and linguistic variation.

Next, the stage model, or the developmental-stage approach, is introduced as "one of the most widely used tools in [conventional] Western psychology." This includes research identifying a number of different developmental lines, such as "psychosexual, cognitive, ego, moral, affective, object-relational, and linguistic," all of which are generally claimed to be "largely invariant, cross-cultural, and 'quasi-universal.'" The authors point out that this "type of developmental-stage approach is also exemplified in the world's great contemplative and meditative disciplines," such as "the Mahamudra from the Tibetan Mahayana Buddhist tradition, the Vi-suddhimagga from the Theravada Buddhist tradition; and the Yoga Sutras from the Sanskrit Hindu tradition." They also give the example of "Aurobindo's version of overall development" with its overall life cycle, in which the first six stages are clearly similar to the developmental stages investigated by conventional psychology, whereas the higher stages tally those of contemplative development. Indeed, the authors claim: "The models are sufficiently similar to suggest an underlying common invariant sequence of stages, despite vast cultural and linguistic differences as well as styles of practice."

In summary, both conventional and contemplative developmental approaches seem to affirm "various strands or lines that are, in part, amenable to a stage conception; and both claim a general, universal, and cross-cultural validity." Nevertheless, the authors strongly maintain that "a rigidly linear and unidirectional model is not at all what we have in mind." Yet this attempt at a master template essentially adheres to the stage-model claim simply because "in any developmental sequence, certain classes of behavior stably emerge only after certain other classes." They also review "the nature and meaning of 'stages,' higher and lower," or the "relative 'before' and 'after' that constitutes one of the central claims of developmental theories." These "quasi-universal deep structures" or developmental stages, therefore, are typically invariant, and they "cannot be altered by environmental factors" or by "idiosyncratic surface structures." Nonetheless, the authors affirm that "there are no precise demarcation lines between stages," therefore these "invariant (quasi-universal) structures" are described as "snapshots" in a developmental process used to represent each "particular stage of development." The book's central theme specifies that the "different stages of development are vulnerable to qualitatively distinct psychopathologies."

Next, the authors, who "may differ on specific points . . . [though] all share a general consensus," define the "three broad ranges of overall development: prepersonal, personal, and transpersonal, each divided, for convenience, into three stages." Some of the chapters, therefore, will address these nine levels covered by both conventional and contemplative developments, which are then correlated to nine general levels of possible pathology:

1. **prepersonal** developments or "the three general levels of prepersonal object-relations development and their corresponding levels of psychopathology: psychotic, borderline, and psychoneurotic," as well as their corresponding therapeutic interventions;

2. **personal** developments or the "rational-individuated-personal selfhood," plus their corresponding pathologies and treatments, which are termed cognitive scripts, identity, and existential;

3. **transpersonal** developments called psychic, subtle, and causal, are where "meditative disciplines effect a transcendence of the normal separate-self sense," and they too have their own corresponding pathologies and treatments.

In summary, "This results in nine general levels (not lines) of overall development, with nine corresponding levels of potential psychopathology." The authors explain that another important factor to take into account in regard to transpersonal development is the prerequisite of a "strong, mature, well-differentiated psyche and a well-integrated self-structure with a sense of cohesiveness, continuity, and identity." Therefore, in Jack Engler's chapter, it's pointed out that a strong ego is needed for further transpersonal consciousness evolution or otherwise meditation itself can "produce side effects."

Daniel Brown's study of meditative stages is "perhaps the most complete, detailed, and sophisticated cartography of contemplative development yet to appear," thus the editors conclude that it should become "a standard in the field," as well as John Chirban's excellent review of the contemplative developmental stages exhibited by various Christian saints. These researchers all help to verify that with the synthesis and integration (or "mutually enriching dialogue") of both conventional and contemplative psychologies, we may finally have "the creation of a more integrated, full-spectrum model of human growth and development."

CHAPTER 3. "THE SPECTRUM OF DEVELOPMENT" (by Ken Wilber) is divided into two parts, with Part I offering a brief overview of the full-spectrum model, while Part II presents a concise summary of recent advances in psychoanalytic developmental psychology (including the work of Mahler, Kernberg, Blank & Blank, and Kohut). In fact, this chapter is a summary of Wilber's work in progress, a still unpublished textbook on transpersonal psychology referred to throughout as *System, Self, and Structure*.

Wilber begins by stating that his writings have "attempted to develop an over-all or Spectrum Model of Psychology, one that is developmental, structural, hier-archical, and systems-oriented, and that draws equally on Eastern and Western schools." Next, he defines the difference between "the basic structures and the tran-sition structures (each of which contain numerous different developmental lines)." Within this spectrum of consciousness, or "the spectrum model of development and pathology," Wilber identifies three major components:

1. **enduring basic structures**, or the levels of consciousness, which, "once they emerge in development, tend to remain in existence";

2. **temporary transition structures**, or the self-stages, which "are phase-spe-cific and phase-temporary structures that tend to be more or less entirely re-placed by subsequent phases of development";

3. **self-system**, or the self (sense of separateness or "I") that negotiates all of these different structures and developmental lines (as well as the states of consciousness); therefore Wilber defines it as "the locus of identification, vo-lition, defense, organization, and 'metabolism' ('digestion' of experience at each level of structural growth and development)."

First, the idea, based on evidence and observation, of "the basic structure or level of consciousness" is presented. Its notable feature is that "once it emerges in human development, it tends to remain in existence in the life of the individual during subsequent development." Based upon a structural model similar to the traditional Great Chain of Being (after Arthur Lovejoy and Huston Smith), Wilber describes a master template that contains several dozen levels, depending on the degree of sophistication. However, for this occasion, he presents nine or ten basic structures of consciousness development":

1. **sensoriphysical** are "the realms of matter, sensation, and perception";

2. **phantasmic-emotional** is "the emotional-sexual level";

3. **rep-mind** is "representational mind" or Piaget's preoperational thinking (pre-op);

4. **rule/role mind** is "Piaget's concrete operational thinking (con-op)";

5. **formal-reflexive mind** is "essentially Piaget's formal operational thinking (form-op)";

6. **vision-logic** is "a highly integrative structure; indeed, in [Wilber's] opinion it is the highest integrative structure in the personal realm";

7. **psychic** is "the culmination of vision-logic and visionary insight";

8. **subtle** is "the seat of actual archetypes, of Platonic Forms, of subtle sounds and audible illuminations, of transcendent insight and absorption";

9. **causal** is "the unmanifest source or transcendental ground of all the lesser structures; the Abyss, the Void, the Formless";

10. **ultimate** is when "consciousness is said finally to re-awaken to its prior and eternal abode as absolute Spirit, radiant and all-pervading, one and many, only and all the complete integration and identity of manifest Form with the unmanifest Formless."

In view of the transcendent-immanent paradox, Wilber points to the tenth structure itself, the ultimate or *tathata-sunyata* (the Buddhist term for "suchness-emptiness"), as actually being "not one level among others, but the reality, condition, or suchness of all levels." Or, "By analogy, the paper on which [the figure] is drawn represents this fundamental ground of empty-suchness." Wilber also presents another table, "Correlations of Basic Structures of Consciousness in Four Systems" (not pictured here), showing correspondences between Aurobindo, Mahayana Buddhism, yogic chakras, and the Kabbalah. (See Figure 1: "The Basic Structures of Consciousness.")

Next, Wilber considers the all-important transition stages or self-stages that tend "to be negated, dissolved, or replaced by subsequent development." This is the general pattern in development, and an important principle to recognize: "Each basic structure supports various phase-specific transitional structures or self-stages." Therefore, unlike Piaget's cognitive structures (which are basic structures), the self-stages include Kohlberg's moral stages, Loevinger's self identities, and Maslow's different self-needs.

To create a clearer picture, Wilber uses a simple metaphor of the self, or the self-system, as "the climber of the ladder," where each rung is a "level in the Great Chain of Being," and with each view from the ladder representing a "different view or perspective on reality, a different sense of identity, a different type of morality, a different set of self needs, and so on." As the climber moves up each rung (level), then "these changes in the sense of self and its reality, which shift from level to level, are referred to as Transition Structures, or, more often, as the Self-Stages." Therefore, Wilber defines that "the Basic Structures [levels] of consciousness are more or less enduring structures, but the Self-Stages [moving up the levels] are transitional, temporary, or phase-specific." Then he presents another table consisting of the "Correlations of Basic Structures of Consciousness with Three Aspects of the Self-

Stages" (not pictured here), which includes the work of Maslow (self-needs), Loevinger (self-sense), and Kohlberg (moral-sense).

Wilber explains that the self-system in part "possesses the following basic characteristics": identification, organization, will, defense, metabolism, navigation. In particular, navigation shows that "the self is faced with several different 'directional pulls'," here identified as the four drives: horizontally on a given level: "1) Preservation vs. 2) Negation, holding on vs. letting go," etc., vertically between levels: "3) Ascent vs. 4) Descent, progression vs. regression." These four drives are a reoccurring theme throughout Wilber's work and are pictured here in graphic form. (See Figure 2: "Four 'Drives' Affecting the Self-Stages.")

Wilber's summary of the form of overall development emphasizes that the basic structures emerge chronologically:

1. First the self will Identify with them, which is normal and phase-appropriate, until it's time "to ascend the hierarchy of basic structural development—to grow."

2. Then the self must "Release or negate its exclusive identification," or "die to that level," or disidentify with, or detach from that particular level,

3. in order "to ascend to the greater unity, differentiation, and Integration of the next higher basic level."

This developmental process of "preservation and negation (or life and death)," which operates at each level or basic structure, may exhibit:

- a "'healthy' or 'normal' preservation";

- a "morbid preservation," which is "nothing but fixation";

- a "healthy or normal negation," both horizontally (which "helps differentiate") and vertically (which "helps the disidentification");

- a "morbid negation" that is "simply repression."

Next, Wilber guides us through a survey of the developmental dimensions of psychopathology, based on recent developments in psychoanalytic ego psychology. They are presented with an overview of the work of some of the more important developmental psychologists, including the infant development research of Margaret Mahler, which is mostly based on "the development of the self-structure in infants (0–3 yrs)."

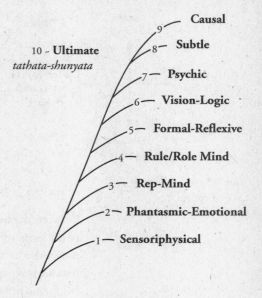

10 - **Ultimate**
tathata-shunyata

9 — **Causal**
8 — **Subtle**
7 — **Psychic**
6 — **Vision-Logic**
5 — **Formal-Reflexive**
4 — **Rule/Role Mind**
3 — **Rep-Mind**
2 — **Phantasmic-Emotional**
1 — **Sensoriphysical**

The Basic Structures of Consciousness
FIGURE I

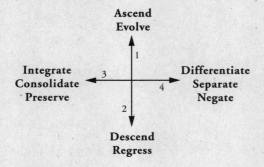

Ascend
Evolve

Integrate
Consolidate
Preserve

Differentiate
Separate
Negate

Descend
Regress

Four "Drives" Affecting
the Self-Stages
FIGURE 2

Importantly, the work of Blanck and Blanck is highlighted, especially their work on the "fulcrums of development," defined as the "critical nodal points of self-structuralization and self-differentiation." They demonstrated that each stage of self-development goes through a "separation-individuation phase" or "self-object differentiation." In light of this, Wilber suggests a full spectrum of developmental fulcrums that goes beyond the conventional ones proposed by developmental psychology by adding the contemplative or transpersonal realms of mysticism as well. Nevertheless, as he also emphasizes, the principles of development and differentiation remain the same.

Next, the work of Otto Kernberg is examined with his "conventional hierarchy of pathology" or the "malformations at each level of the fulcrums of self-development." His work is presented with numerous schematic figures, most of which are not pictured here. By fitting together these different psychological schools of thought, Wilber is able to dovetail conventional psychology with the contemplative approaches, and thus arrive at the major fulcrums of self-development. (See Figure 3: "Major Fulcrums of Self-Development.")

In a nontechnical summation Wilber concludes the chapter by emphasizing that the "emergence of a sense of self in the human being" proceeds through three general stages, or the "first three major fulcrums of self-development":

1. a **physical self** (0–1 year);

2. an **emotional self** (1–3 years);

3. a **mental self** (3–6 years), where each "self," respectively, "if disturbed, may result in a particular type (or level of pathology—psychoses, borderline, and neuroses)."

CHAPTER 4. "THE SPECTRUM OF PSYCHOPATHOLOGY" subdivides the overall spectrum of human development into three parts: "Prepersonal, Personal, and Transpersonal, each consisting of three major fulcrums of self-development and the corresponding pathologies." Therefore, this spectrum of nine major fulcrums (and their subphases) will be used to identify "the specific type(s) of pathology that are most characteristic of a developmental lesion at that phase or subphase [or fulcrum]." However, as Wilber warns: "The standard cautions and qualifications about using such hierarchical models of pathology should be kept in mind; i.e., no pure cases, the influence of cultural differences, genetic predispositions, genetic and traumatic arrests, and blended cases."

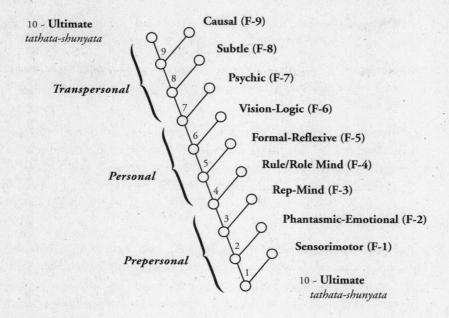

10 ~ **Ultimate**
tathata-shunyata

Causal (F-9)

Subtle (F-8)

Psychic (F-7)

Transpersonal

Vision-Logic (F-6)

Formal-Reflexive (F-5)

Rule/Role Mind (F-4)

Personal

Rep-Mind (F-3)

Phantasmic-Emotional (F-2)

Sensorimotor (F-1)

Prepersonal

10 ~ **Ultimate**
tathata-shunyata

**Major Fulcrums of
Self-Development**
FIGURE 3

Part I is a technical review of the psychological/psychiatric literature, viewed through the lens of Wilber's spectrum model. It begins with the various " 'prepersonal' or 'prerational' pathologies . . . so named because this range of development involves the stages leading up to the emergence of a rational-individuated-personal selfhood and its differentiation from prerational structures." Corresponding to the major fulcrums, the prepersonal psychopathologies include:

1. **Fulcrum-1** (F1) (sensorimotor): 1a) autistic psychoses, 1b) symbiotic infantile psychoses, most adult schizophrenia, and depressive psychoses;

2. **Fulcrum-2** (F2) (phantasmic-emotional): 2a) narcissistic personality disorders; 2b) borderline personality disorders;

2. **Fulcrum-3** (F3) (rep mind): 3a) borderline neuroses, 3b) psychoneuroses, including "Tragic Man" and "Guilt Man," resulting "in a tripartite structure of the Fulcrum 3 self: ego-superego-id."

Part II presents the intermediate or personal pathologies, based on recent research, beginning with the "higher or 'post-Oedipal' stages of development and their correlative vulnerabilities and dis-eases," and which include a "whole range of cognitive, identity, and existential concerns"; the personal psychopathologies include:

4. **Fulcrum-4** (F4) (rule/role mind): "the role self and cognitive-script pathology," including "script pathology" or "script neuroses";

5. **Fulcrum-5** (F5) (formal-reflexive): identity neurosis, which "specifically means all the things that can go wrong in the emergence of this self-reflexive structure";

6. **Fulcrum-6** (F6) (vision-logic): existential pathology, which "refers to a specific level of basic structure development ('vision-logic') and the correlative stage of self development ('centaur')," including the common syndromes of existential depression, inauthenticity, existential isolation and "uncanniness," aborted self-actualization, or existential anxiety often resulting in existential-level ennui.

Part III presents the transpersonal pathologies, in which, as Wilber points out, if the terms psychic, subtle, and causal don't work satisfactorily for you, then "substitute more neutral terms, such as *'beginning,' 'intermediate,'* and *'advanced'* stages." The recognition of these types of transpersonal psychopathologies permits a deeper understanding of consciousness evolution. There are, for example, at least three or four levels of development and pathology present in the transpersonal stages themselves. These transpersonal psychopathologies include:

7. **Fulcrum-7** (F7) (psychic): the psychic disorders, such as "spontaneous and usually unsought awakening of spiritual-psychic energies and capacities," (e.g., kundalini experiences) resulting in psychic inflation, the dark night of the soul, split life goals, pseudo-*duhkha* or the "realization of the painful nature of manifest existence itself"; *pranic* disorders or "a misdirection of kundalini energy in the early stages of its arousal," and "yogic illness" (after Aurobindo), which is basically due to the "great intensities of psychic and subtle energies," therefore putting a strain on the physical-emotional body;

8. **Fulcrum-8** (F8) (subtle): subtle disorders, such as integration-identification failure, which is a subtle fracture between self and archetypal awareness, including pseudo-nirvana or "simply the mistaking of subtle or archetypal forms, illumination, raptures, ecstasies, insights, or absorptions for final liberation," and pseudo-realization, "which involves an intense insight into the ultimately unsatisfactory nature of phenomena when viewed apart from noumenon . . . [and which] acts as the motivation to transcend all conceivable manifestation in nirvanic absorption";

9. **Fulcrum-9** (F9) (causal): causal disorders, which include "miscarriages" in the final integration of "the Formless or Unmanifest with the entire world

of Form, and the Manifest Realm," including the failure of complete self-differentiation or the "inability to accept the final death of the archetypal self. . . . The fall into the Heart is blocked by the subtlest contracting, grasping, seeking, or desiring; the final block: desire for liberation." There is also the failure to fully integrate with the world of forms, known as Arhat's disease, which can occur during classic *jnana samadhi, nirvikalpa samadhi,* and nirvana or when "no objects even arise in awareness." Yet, as Wilber observes, not until "this [causal] disjuncture is penetrated does the manifest realm arise as a modification of Consciousness, not a distraction from it. This is classic *sahaj-bhava samadhi,*" of which he has "read no text, nor heard any sage, that speaks of a level beyond this."

Wilber presents "a schematic summary of the discussion thus far: the basic structures of consciousness, the corresponding fulcrums of self-development, and the possible pathologies that may occur at each fulcrum." (See Figure 4: "Correlation of Structures, Fulcrums, Psychopathologies.")

CHAPTER 5. "TREATMENT MODALITIES" introduces the notion that since "qualitatively different pathologies are associated with qualitatively different levels of self-organization and self-development," then "a specific level of pathology would best respond to a specific type of psychotherapeutic intervention . . . tailored to each type or level of self-pathology." In a highly technical manner, Wilber evaluates the available literature regarding the various treatment modalities in both conventional and contemplative psychologies, each oriented to a particular level in the spectrum of consciousness.

This spectrum model, therefore, takes into account the characteristics and qualities of each fulcrum or milestone in the complete arc of self-development in the overall life cycle. Wilber first provides a short description of the particular psychopathology typical for each major fulcrum (introduced in the last chapter). He then suggests a particular treatment modality or set of modalities that would best apply to that particular level of development. First, there are the prepersonal treatment modalities (and psychopathologies) of the first three fulcrums:

1. **Fulcrum-1** (F1) (sensorimotor): psychoses: are of such a "primitive level of organization" that they often respond to a treatment of only pharmacological or physiological intervention;

2. **Fulcrum-2** (F2) (phantasmic-emotional): narcissistic-borderline: respond best to the treatment of structure-building techniques since with borderline pathologies "there is not enough structure to differentiate self and object rep-

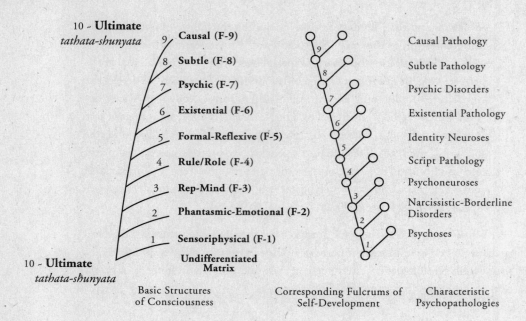

10 - **Ultimate**
tathata-shunyata

| Basic Structures of Consciousness | Corresponding Fulcrums of Self-Development | Characteristic Psychopathologies |

9 **Causal (F-9)** — Causal Pathology
8 **Subtle (F-8)** — Subtle Pathology
7 **Psychic (F-7)** — Psychic Disorders
6 **Existential (F-6)** — Existential Pathology
5 **Formal-Reflexive (F-5)** — Identity Neuroses
4 **Rule/Role (F-4)** — Script Pathology
3 **Rep-Mind (F-3)** — Psychoneuroses
2 **Phantasmic-Emotional (F-2)** — Narcissistic-Borderline Disorders
1 **Sensoriphysical (F-1)** — Psychoses

Undifferentiated Matrix

10 - **Ultimate**
tathata-shunyata

Correlation of Structures, Fulcrums, Psychopathologies
FIGURE 4

resentations . . . [therefore] the structure-building techniques aim at exactly that differentiation-and-integration";

3. **Fulcrum-3** (F3) (rep-mind): psychoneuroses: "once a strong-enough self-structure has formed (but not before), it can repress, dissociate, or alienate aspects of its own being"; in this case, treatment places an emphasis on "uncovering techniques" for they "are designed specifically to bring these unconscious aspects back into awareness, where they can be re-integrated with the central self."

Second, there are the personal treatment modalities (and psychopathologies) of the second three fulcrums:

4. **Fulcrum-4** (F4) (rule/role mind): script pathology: begins with "post-Oedipal development" as the self is concerned with conflicts that "are much more cognitive than psychodynamic in nature and origin, because at this point the self increasingly is evolving from bodily to mental levels"; in this case, the best treatment is "cognitive-script analysis" which assists in clarifying role confusion and in turn addresses role pathology and rule pathology," especially when "an individual's cognitive schemas, configurations, or rules are a major determinant of his or her feelings and action";

5. **Fulcrum-5** (F5) (formal-reflexive mind): identity neurosis: concerned with "the emergence and engagement of the formal-reflexive mind and its correlative, introspective self-sense (with its particular vulnerabilities and distresses)"; in this case, treatment is to use introspection and philosophizing, such as with "Socratic dialogue, which engages, simultaneously, the client's formal-reflexive mind . . . and its correlative self-sense."

6. **Fulcrum-6** (F6) (vision-logic): existential pathology: concerned with the "existential concerns of being-in-the-world" which may "begin to overwhelm the newly formed centauric self and freeze its functioning." Thus the centauric self must come to terms with authentic being and intrinsic meaning, in which case treatment is to "empty itself of egocentric, power-based, or inauthentic modes." Although this is the stated aim of the humanistic-existential psychologies, Wilber still argues that "according to the *philosophia perennis,* there lie above it the entire realms of the superconscient [transpersonal]."

In introducing the transpersonal realms, Wilber points out that these higher levels of "contemplative development in general possesses three broad levels or stages" and therefore they can be directly correlated with the psychic, subtle, and causal levels of consciousness. As an alternative to such names (including those below), if preferred, Wilber suggests using the "more neutral terms, such as *beginning, intermediate,* and *advanced;* or *ground, path,* and *fruition.*" In presenting corresponding treatment modalities, the transpersonal levels can be termed the psychic path of yogis, the subtle path of saints, and the causal path of sages (after Adi Da/Da Free John).

Next are the transpersonal treatment modalities (and psychopathologies) of the following three transpersonal fulcrums:

7. **Fulcrum-7** (F7) (psychic): the path of yogis (because it awakens kundalini energies) deals with psychic pathology, including "spontaneous and unsought awakening of spiritual-psychic energies," often associated with kundalini (yoga). This path also addresses other undesirable symptoms that may appear psychotic, such as the dark night of the soul, or psychic inflation, structural imbalance, split-life goals, pseudo-*duhkha, pranic* disorders, or yogic illness;

8. **Fulcrum-8** (F8) (subtle): the path of saints (because it awakens subtle-level contemplation) deals with subtle pathology, usually involving "some form of inquiry, overt or covert, into the contraction that constitutes the separate-self sense." This path also addresses "pseudo-nirvana," which is a "mistaking of archetypal forms for ultimate enlightenment," including a type of pseudo-realization;

9. **Fulcrum-9** (F9) (causal): the path of sages (because it "resides within the 'Heart' or causal/unmanifest realm") deals with causal pathology or the "final differentiation or detachment (i.e., from all manifest form)." This path addresses when "the separate-self 'falls' into the Heart," for even "this 'fall' into formless, unmanifest cessation or emptiness," which could, without a qualified teacher or guru, result in the ultimate pathology, a failure to integrate the manifest and unmanifest realms. This causal condition or failure to integrate must finally be overcome or transcended simply because, according to the perennial philosophy: "The re-union or re-integration of emptiness and wisdom are the 'supreme path,' the path of 'ordinary mind' (Maha Ati), 'open eyes' (Adi Da), and 'everyday mind' (Ch'an)—wherein all phenomena, high or low, exactly as they find themselves, are seen as already perfect expressions and seals of the naturally enlightened mind."

These observations are schematically presented with a "summary of the basic structures of consciousness, the corresponding fulcrums of self-development, their characteristic pathologies, and the correlative treatment modalities," (See Figure 5: "Correlation of Structures, Fulcrums, Psychopathologies, and Treatments.")

These considerations then lead to other related topics, such as emphasizing "the great care that should ideally be given to 'differential diagnosis,' particularly in light of the full spectrum of human growth and development," because "any effective and appropriate therapeutic intervention depends significantly on an accurate initial diagnosis." Importantly, an integral psychologist must use a "skilled understanding of the entire spectrum of consciousness" to take into account the pre/trans fallacy, which is "a confusing of pre-rational structures with trans-rational structures simply because both are non-rational," thus "a major therapeutic confusion."

Wilber affirms that his spectrum model is able to easily include within its theoretical structure what's known as COEX systems (after Stanislav Grof), which are systems of condensed experience that are "a dissociated pocket in the self-structure." The spectrum of consciousness sees pathological COEX systems as "a multi-layered unit of associated and condensed subphase malformations."

Wilber also discusses in depth the differing degrees of narcissism that can be diagnosed in a number of ways, from normal to subtle narcissism, however he emphasizes that it's important to recognize that "there are nine or so major levels of narcissism, each of which is less narcissistic (less selfcentric) than its predecessor(s)," indeed, "even into the subtle realm, according to Da Free John [Adi Da]. Narcissus (which is his term) is still present (although highly reduced) because there is still a subtle contraction inward on self and a consequent recoil from relationship."

Wilber adds a brief overview of a practical dream therapy and his theory of

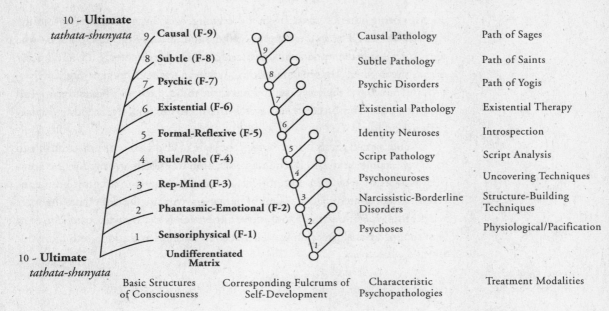

Basic Structures of Consciousness	Corresponding Fulcrums of Self-Development	Characteristic Psychopathologies	Treatment Modalities
10 ~ **Ultimate** *tathata-shunyata*			
9 **Causal (F-9)**	9	Causal Pathology	Path of Sages
8 **Subtle (F-8)**	8	Subtle Pathology	Path of Saints
7 **Psychic (F-7)**	7	Psychic Disorders	Path of Yogis
6 **Existential (F-6)**	6	Existential Pathology	Existential Therapy
5 **Formal-Reflexive (F-5)**	5	Identity Neuroses	Introspection
4 **Rule/Role (F-4)**	4	Script Pathology	Script Analysis
3 **Rep-Mind (F-3)**	3	Psychoneuroses	Uncovering Techniques
2 **Phantasmic-Emotional (F-2)**	2	Narcissistic-Borderline Disorders	Structure-Building Techniques
1 **Sensoriphysical (F-1)**	1	Psychoses	Physiological/Pacification
10 ~ **Ultimate** *tathata-shunyata* **Undifferentiated Matrix**			

Correlation of Structures, Fulcrums, Psychopathologies, and Treatments

FIGURE 5

dream interpretation. The viewpoint of the spectrum of consciousness naturally suggests "the way one might best deal with dreams is to start at the bottom and work up, resonating with the dream at each level."

Wilber then presents a short review of the practical benefits of meditation and psychotherapy, where meditation "aims at developing or moving consciousness into higher levels or dimensions of structural organization, [which] must break or disrupt the exclusive identification with the present level of development (usually mental-egoic)." Importantly, he considers how meditation can be used in conjunction with psychoanalysis or psychotherapy, in differentiating early fulcrum pathologies, something which meditation alone does not address well, and coupled with the fact that "meditation itself will probably facilitate, as a byproduct, the re-emergence or depression of various unconscious material, which can be worked on in therapy sessions." He therefore summarizes: "meditation is not a structure-building technique, nor an uncovering technique, nor a script-analysis technique, nor a Socratic-dialoguing technique. It cannot substitute for those techniques, nor should it be used as a way to 'spiritually bypass' any major work needed on those levels."

By following the development or evolution of consciousness, Wilber provides a simple formula: "increasing development = increasing interiorization = decreasing narcissism." This actually means "each higher level of consciousness is experi-

enced as being 'interior' to its lower or preceding level, but not as being 'inside' it."
In other words, "The soul is interior to the mind; it is not inside the mind—the
only thing inside the mind is thoughts, which is why introspecting the mind never
reveals the soul. As thoughts quiet down, however, the soul emerges interiorly vis-
à-vis the mind, and therefore can transcend the mind, see beyond it, escape it. And
likewise, spirit is not inside the soul, it is interior to the soul, transcending its limitations and forms."

Wilber's main thesis is that "Given the state of knowledge *already* available to
us, it seems ungenerous to the human condition to present any models less comprehensive—by which I mean, models that do not take into account both conventional *and* contemplative realms of human growth and development." In other
words, this type of integral full-spectrum approach is exactly what can help, or at
least support, transformation involved in consciousness evolution, both individually and collectively.

Spiritual Choices

The Problems of Recognizing Authentic Paths to Inner Transformation

EDITED BY DICK ANTHONY, BRUCE ECKER, AND KEN WILBER

(New York: Paragon House Publishers 1987);

The Collected Works of Ken Wilber, Vol. 3 (CW3) (Boston: Shambhala Publications, 1999)

Spiritual Choices: The Problem of Recognizing Authentic Paths to Inner Transforma-tion (1987) co-edited with Dick Anthony and Bruce Ecker, is a Wilber/Phase 2 work emphasizing human developmental evolution and sociology, therefore focusing on the relational exchanges or the interaction between individual interior consciousness (Upper-Left quadrant), interior cultural worldviews (Lower-Left quadrant), and exterior social techno-economic systems (Lower-Right quadrant) in the Great Nest of Spirit or Kosmos.

Spiritual Choices presents "the results of a major, year-long study conducted at the Center for the Study of New Religious Movements in Berkeley, California," which was led by Dick Anthony and for which Wilber was a consultant; it also contains contributions from numerous transpersonal psychologists in addition to prominent spiritual figures such as Ram Das (Richard Alpert), Werner Erhard, Claudio Naranjo, Jacob Needleman, Gary Rosenthal, Steven Tipton, Frances Vaughan, and John Welwood. Wilber's essay originally appeared in *Eye to Eye* (Shambhala Publications, 1983) as the chapter titled "Legitimacy, Authenticity, and Authority in the New Religions," here renamed "The Spectrum Model"; Wilber also participated in the dialogue "When Is Religion Transformative? A Conversation with Jacob Needleman" in the Part 4 "Overview."

Spiritual Choices: The Problem of Recognizing Authentic Paths to Inner Trans-formation was published in 1987 (Paragon House Publishers); Wilber's essay, as presented in *Eye to Eye,* is now part of *The Collected Works of Ken Wilber, Volume Three (CW3),* (Shambhala Publications, 1999).

Spiritual Choices further examines many of the issues begun in *A Sociable God,* which emphasized the difference between "legitimate" religions (which emphasize horizontal translation), and "authentic" spiritual paths (which emphasize vertical transformation). Through the writings of numerous spiritual authorities, the book also focuses on different spiritual groups as it provides some criteria for assessing contemporary spiritual choices. Overall, *Spiritual Choices* offers a valid approach, based upon the spectrum model, to verify authentic paths to inner transformation, and thus avoid the more mythic, cultic tendencies of the searching ego.

CHAPTER 11

Grace and Grit

Spirituality and Healing in the Life and Death of Treya Killam Wilber

BY KEN WILBER

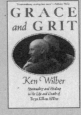

(Boston: Shambhala Publications, 1991; paperback edition, 1993);

The Collected Works of Ken Wilber, Vol. 5 (CW5) (Shambhala, 1999);

revised paperback edition (Shambhala, 2001)

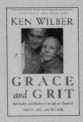

A Note to the Reader

Grace and Grit: Spirituality and Healing in the Life and Death of Treya Killam Wilber (1991) is a Wilber/Phase 2 book emphasizing the developmental evolution of the spectrum of consciousness (Upper-Left quadrant) supported by the perennial philosophy, yet because it is a personal and practical account of Wilber's life, it focuses on all four quadrants: behavioral, intentional, cultural, and social.

Grace and Grit tells the moving love story of Wilber's marriage to Terry (Treya) Killam in 1983 and then her five-year struggle with cancer, finally passing in 1989. The book was compiled from Treya's journals, with her blessing and specific suggestion to write a book about their story.

Grace and Grit: Spirituality and Healing in the Life and Death of Treya Killam Wilber was published in 1991 (Shambhala Publications); paperback edition (Shambhala Publications, 1993); it now appears as *The Collected Works of Ken Wilber, Volume Five (CW5),* (Shambhala Publications, 2000); reprint paperback edition (Shambhala Publications, 2001).

Grace and Grit—a phrase taken from Treya's last diary entry—is a narrative of the couple's arduous ordeal interspersed with interviews and brief descriptions of Wilber's spectrum model, the perennial philosophy, plus a few other topics that have appeared in his previous writings. There are considerations centered around issues of health ("why do we get sick?"), being a support person for the terminally ill, as well as discussions of some of the spiritual paths the Wilbers traversed on their perilous and blessed journey.

During this testing yet love-filled time, most of Wilber's concern and attention were focused on Treya (a nickname for Estrella, which is Spanish for "star"). At this time and afterward, he went through a nearly ten-year hiatus from writing (1984–1993) and publication (1986–1995). However, during this period Wilber did write one book, an eight-hundred-page tome titled *The Great Chain of Being: A Modern Introduction to the Perennial Philosophy and the World's Great Mystical Traditions,* which has since been shelved indefinitely. *Grace and Grit*'s popular success wonderfully attests to the fact that Treya's life story points to the unborn and undying Spirit. She learned to transcend death in the true Self, thus allowing countless others to gain strength and inspiration from her life of "passionate equanimity."

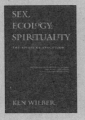    

FOUR QUADRANTS & THE POSTMODERN CRITIQUE

(1995–2000)

Sex, Ecology, Spirituality

The Spirit of Evolution

BY KEN WILBER

(Boston: Shambhala Publications, 1995);

The Collected Works of Ken Wilber, Vol. 6 (CW6) (Shambhala, 2000);

revised paperback edition (Shambhala, 2001)

Introduction

Sex, Ecology, Spirituality: The Spirit of Evolution (1995)—often called *SES*—is the first Wilber/Phase 4 work premiering a four-quadrant analysis that emphasizes an AQAL—or "all-quadrants, all-levels"—approach to integral studies, therefore focusing on the developmental tetra-interaction (or coevolution) of the Left-Hand interior quadrants with the Right-Hand exterior correlates in the Great Nest of Spirit or Kosmos.

Sex, Ecology, Spirituality, Wilber's magnum opus, was the culmination of a three-year meditation and research retreat from 1991 to 1994, thus ending a nearly ten-year absence from publication. Originally conceived as a smaller book titled *The Spirit of Evolution: Cosmos, Bios, Psyche, Theos,* the present version is now divided into two books, each of which could stand on their own, since it grew as a whole to over eight hundred pages (including two hundred pages of endnotes). *SES* became Volume One of a projected three-volume trilogy entitled *Kosmos* or *The Kosmos Trilogy* (Volumes two and three forthcoming).

Sex, Ecology, Spirituality: The Spirit of Evolution was published in 1995 (Shambhala Publications); in a revised edition, it now appears as *The Collected Works of Ken Wilber, Volume Six (CW6),* (Shambhala Publications, 2000); revised paperback edition (Shambhala Publications, 2001).

The "INTRODUCTION" begins by suggesting that science's answer "to Schelling's burning question, 'Why is there something rather than nothing?'" is based on nothing more than "the philosophy of 'oops.'" This is because science and the modern mind seem to claim "the universe just occurs, there is nothing behind it, it's all ultimately accidental or random, it just is, it just happens—oops!"

The other possibility Wilber alludes to "is that *something else is going on:* behind the happenstance drama is a deeper or higher or wider pattern, or order, or intelligence . . . this 'Deeper Order': the Tao, God, Geist, Maat, Archetypal Forms, Reason, Li, Mahamaya, Brahman, Rigpa." The main thesis of this book concerns a "possible Deeper Order. It is about evolution, and about religion, and, in a sense, about everything in between. It is a brief history of cosmos, bios, psyche, theos— a tale told by an idiot, it goes without saying, but a tale that, precisely in signifying Nothing, signifies the All, and there is the sound and the fury."

Wilber tells us this book is going to be "about *holons*—about wholes that are parts of other wholes, indefinitely. . . . We will be looking at holons in the cosmos, in the bios, in the psyche, and in theos; and at the *evolutionary thread* that connects them all, unfolds them all, embraces them all, endlessly." This grand task is accomplished by concentrating on "orienting generalizations" that show, beyond differences and disagreements, that there is "a great deal of agreement . . . from the various branches of knowledge (from physics to biology to psychology to theology), and if we string these orienting generalizations together, we will arrive at some astonishing and often profound conclusions." By working with these generalizations, Wilber explains, his work "delivers up a broad orienting map of the place of men and women in relation to Universe, Life, and Spirit," yet still, he continues, "this . . . map is nowhere near fixed and final." To further elucidate the details of these principles he has dedicated two more volumes of comparable size to *SES,* so that all three are simply called *Kosmos,* or *The Kosmos Trilogy.*

Although, in the final analysis, *Sex, Ecology, Spirituality* is a mystical book, Wilber claims that he's not just "doing metaphysics" because the work is in fact based on evidence gathered from every realm and study of existence. Modern reductionism, Wilber maintains, has not only "lost the Light and the Height; but more frightening, we have lost the Mystery and the Deep, the Emptiness and the Abyss," therefore "what follows is a cheerful parable of your being and your becoming . . . this is a chronicle of what you have done, a tale of what you have seen, a measure of what we all might yet become."

BOOK I, originally titled *Spirit-in-Action,* introduces a series of new terms (as does every Wilber book), such as *Kosmos, holons, holarchy, four quadrants, twenty tenets,* etc., while simultaneously chronicling the involutionary/evolutionary movement of Nondual Spirit. By relying on "orienting generalizations" gained from all human knowledge systems, this tome delineates the various developmental stages, or fulcrums, that exist in the co-evolving Great Nest of Spirit. All of these levels or dimensions can be seen as interacting with what Wilber calls the Big Three (a simplified version of the four quadrants), which are based on the principal differentiations of modernity: I/self, We/culture, and It/nature.

CHAPTER I. "THE WEB OF LIFE" introduces the ecological approaches of postmodern philosophy that are current in today's academic and professional world, including ecofeminism and deep ecology. According to Wilber, these theories are attempting to address the fractured worldview of modern life by propagating the understanding that the universe is essentially an "intricate web of patterns" seen as a "web of life." Such a perspective is further enlarged when a dynamic "evolutionary synthesis" is added or, as Wilber ironically points out, "It is one thing to merely have God on your side; quite another to have science on your side."

This type of advanced evolutionary view is even capable of resolving the classic "two arrows of time," the contradiction between entropy, or the universe's "winding down," and evolution, its "winding up." Wilber points out that many theorists claim that "a 'unity of science'—a coherent and unified worldview—is now possible," and his own integral vision is one of those unitive, integrating views.

By incorporating the system sciences of complexity, Wilber argues that the converse modern evolutionary synthesis has, in essence, "discovered basic regularities, patterns, or laws that apply in a broad fashion to all three 'Great Realms' of evolution:

- the **physiosphere** [matter, material, physical, cosmic];

- the **biosphere** [life, biological, biosocial];

- the **noosphere** [mind, psychological, historical, sociocultural]."

These nested domains have traditionally been seen as "one continuous and interrelated manifestation of Spirit, one Great Chain of Being, that reached in a perfectly unbroken or uninterrupted fashion from matter to life to mind to soul to spirit." Interestingly, although in a more limited sense than the Great Chain theorists intended, Wilber points out that today's systems sciences talk "openly and glowingly of hierarchy"—a word that originally meant "sacred governance," or "governing one's life by spiritual powers." The evolutionary sciences have, in a sense, "taken steps to 'temporalize' the Great Chain," since we now know that "evolution is irreversible. We may see amoebas eventually evolve into apes, but we never see apes turn into amoebas." Yet, as Wilber laments, in the postmodern world the notion of "hierarchy . . . has fallen on hard times."

He suggests that in order to get rid of "the problem of hierarchy" we should use instead Koestler's more holistic term, holarchy" (rooted in the ancient Greek word *holos,* or "wholeness"). In fact, "'*Hierarchy*' and '*wholeness*' are two names for the same thing, and if you destroy one, you completely destroy the other." In other words, holarchy actually reflects a "natural hierarchy" or an "actualization hierarchy." A heterarchy, on the other hand, is the horizontal arrangement of holons existing "within a given level of any hierarchical pattern." In brief: "within each level, heterarchy; between each level, hierarchy."

A holarchy itself is composed of *holons* (another Koestlerian term) meaning "whole/parts," which Wilber uses to mean "that which, being a *whole* in one context, is simultaneously a *part* in another. . . . The whole, in other words, is more than the sum of its parts, and that whole can influence and determine, in many cases, the function of its parts."

An important point Wilber always emphasizes is the fact that "these hierarchical networks necessarily unfold in a sequential or stage-like fashion . . . in other words, growth occurs in stages, and stages, of course, are ranked in both a logical and chronological order. The more holistic patterns appear later in development because they have to await the emergence of the parts that they will then integrate or unify." Wilber maintains that it's perfectly reasonable to speak of "higher" or "deeper" in this context since they "both imply a vertical dimension of integration not found in a merely horizontal expansion [heterarchy]." The value of the concept of "higher" is that it adds "something extra . . . relative to the previous (and less encompassing) stage." Indeed, according to Wilber, *the only way to get a holism is via a holarchy.*"

By acknowledging this nested yet ranked order of all things (holons), it's not only possible to better heal pathological or dissociated systems within a natural holarchy but it's also easier to recognize certain "qualitative distinctions" that, in turn, inevitably produce *value hierarchies*. Wilber points out that the notion of a mutually agreed-upon order of value and meaning is often denigrated by many modern/postmodern philosophers, such as "cultural relativists," "radical pluralists," "heterarchists," and the like. Yet, in opposition to their views, Wilber asserts that many of these contemporary theorists usually have their own ideological agenda, to such a degree they're often hiding their own "stealth hierarchy."

Wilber's integral vision, on the other hand, champions a universal pluralism that agrees in principle with "the broad conclusions of the cultural diversity movements: we do want to cherish all cultures in an equal light." Nevertheless, Wilber maintains that a true "universal pluralism is not a stance that all cultures agree with; that universal pluralism is a very special type of ranking that most ethnocentric and sociocentric cultures do not even acknowledge; that universal pluralism is the result of a very long history hard-fought against dominator hierarchies of one sort or another." Therefore he optimistically concludes: "If these various holarchies—in the sciences, in value judgments, in the great wisdom traditions—could in fact by sympathetically aligned with one another, a truly significant synthesis might indeed lie in our collective future." This type of "unifying and integrative move" or holarchical approach is the primary thesis of *Sex, Ecology, Spirituality,* and indeed, of Wilber's overall integral vision.

CHAPTER 2. "THE PATTERN THAT CONNECTS" introduces what Wilber calls the "twenty tenets" (although "there is nothing sacrosanct about the number 'twenty'"). Throughout this chapter, he presents the "twenty tenets (or conclusions) that represent what we might call 'patterns of existence' or 'tendencies of evolution' or 'laws of form' or 'propensities of manifestation.'" This list of twenty tenets, Wilber explains, are essentially "drawn from the modern evolutionary and system sciences . . . [but] not confined to these sciences." They're also based on principles of holarchy or hierarchical inclusiveness, thus creating "a genuine *uni-versum* ('one turn' or 'uni-verse'), or an emergent pluralism undergirded by common patterns—the 'patterns that connect.'"

Wilber discusses the **twenty tenets** at length, though he never systematically lists them. Hence the following numbering scheme is not his but simply a matter of convenience.

1. Reality as a whole is not composed of things or processes but of holons (wholes that are part of other wholes);

2. Holons display four fundamental capacities:

    a. self-preservation (or agency);

    b. self-adaptation (or communion);

    c. self-transcendence or self-transformation (or Eros);

    d. self-dissolution (or Thanatos);

3. Holons emerge;

4. Holons emerge holarchically;

5. Each emergent holon transcends but includes its predecessor(s);

6. The lower sets the possibilities of the higher; the higher sets the probabilities of the lower;

7. The number of levels that a holarchy comprises determines whether it is "shallow" or "deep"; and the number of holons on any given level we shall call its "span";

8. Each successive level or evolution produces greater depth and less span;

9. Addition 1: The greater the depth of a holon, the greater its degree of consciousness;

10. Destroy any holon, and you will destroy all of the holons above it but none of the holons below it;

11. Holarchies coevolve;

12. The micro is in relational exchange with the macro at all levels of its depth;

13. Evolution has directionality;

14. Evolution has increasing complexity;

15. Evolution has increasing differentiation/integration;

16. Evolution has increasing organization/structuration;

17. Evolution has increasing relative autonomy;

18. Evolution has increasing telos;

19. Addition 2: Every holon issues an IOU to the Kosmos;

20. Addition 3: All IOUs are redeemed in Emptiness.

Wilber stresses (Tenet 1) that "Reality is not composed of things or processes; it is not composed of atoms or quarks; it is not composed of wholes nor does it have any parts. Rather, it is composed of whole/parts, or holons." And again, "Reality isn't composed of quarks, or bootstrapping hadrons, or subatomic exchange; but neither is it composed of ideas, symbols, or thoughts. It is composed of holons."

Wilber here reintroduces the ancient Greek (Pythagorean) term *kosmos* in order to distinguish it from *cosmos* because, as he explains, in today's parlance *cosmos* usually only refers to the physical universe, whereas originally the kosmos (which Wilber spells with a capital *K*) was seen as "the patterned nature or process of all domains of existences, from matter to math to theos, and not merely the physical universe." And it's precisely in this pluridimensional, multileveled, interconnected sense that Wilber uses the term *Kosmos* to signify " 'the All' (which is the sum total of whole/parts [holons])," not just "the 'Whole' (which implies the ultimate priority of wholeness over partness)." Based on this holarchical understanding, Wilber defines the various levels or ontology of the universe as being composed of:

- **cosmos** (or physiosphere);

- **bios** (or biosphere);

- **nous** (or noosphere);

- **theos** (the theosphere or divine domain)—none of them being foundational (even spirit shades into Emptiness).

Wilber also acknowledges that since "the Kosmos is composed of holons, all the way up, all the way down," these emergent holons are therefore *transfinite,* or always part of even more embracing holons because "everything is a context within a context forever." In other words, the entire Kosmic "system is sliding—holons within holons. . . . It is unendingly, dizzifyingly holarchic." As a humorous simile for this nested chain of holons, Wilber mentions the ancient Chinese story that suggests that all of creation rests on "turtles all the way up, all the way down . . .

transfinite turtles." The twenty tenets, then, are meant to reflect the patterns that interconnect the nested capacity of holons as they extend to infinity.

In addition, Wilber discusses the four forces, or capacities, of a holon which are themselves in "constant tension" oscillating between "preserve or accommodate, transcend or dissolve—the four very different pulls on each and every holon in the Kosmos." These four forces "can be pictured as a cross, with two horizontal 'opposites' ([1]agency and [2] communion) and two vertical 'opposites' ([3] self-transcendence and [4] self-dissolution)."

Horizontally:

1. a holon's **agency** or *self-preservation* is its "capacity to preserve [its] individuality, to preserve [its] own particular wholeness or autonomy," thus "its self-asserting, self-preserving, assimilating tendencies—expresses its wholeness, its relative autonomy." Therefore "this intrinsic form or pattern is known by various names: *entelechy* (Aristotle), *morphic unit/field* (Sheldrake), *regime* or *code* or *canon* (Koestler), *deep structure* (Wilber)."

2. a holon's **communion** or *self-adaptation* is its capacity to function "as part of a larger whole, and in its capacity as a part it must adapt or accommodate itself to other holons," thus "its participatory, bonding, joining tendencies—expresses its partness, its relationship to something larger";

Vertically:

3. a holon's capacity for **self-transcendence** (or self-transformation or Eros) is its "vertical dimension that cuts at right angles, so to speak, to the horizontal agency and communion." This is "creativity" (after Whitehead) made in evolutionary "sudden leaps," or "symmetry breaks," which is the ability "to reach beyond the given and introduce some measure of novelty";

4. a holon's tendency of **self-dissolution** (or Thanatos) is a holon's capacity to "break down" since they're "built up (through vertical transformation) . . . in other words, that which is vertically built up can vertically break down, and the pathways in both cases are essentially the same."

Wilber also recognizes that "this constant horizontal battle between agency and communion extends even to the forms of pathology on any given level," resulting in either pathological agency (alienation and repression) or pathological communion (fusion and indissociation).

With agency and communion, "an excess of either will kill a holon immediately (i.e., destroy its identifying pattern); even an immoderate imbalance will lead to structural deformity." Wilber sees that "This primordial polarity runs through all the domains of manifest existence, and was archetypally expressed in the Taoist principles of yin (communion) and yang (agency)."

In continuing his review of these twenty "patterns that connect," Wilber is led to suggest that proper and important distinctions need to be made between "a vertical scale of deep versus shallow" or "depth/height versus shallow/flat," and "a horizontal scale of wide versus narrow" or "width versus narrowness."

This is also reflected in a holon's relatively stable deep structures, which obtain when "a holon's regime or deep structure governs . . . the types of worlds that it can respond to," especially since "greater depth pipes other worlds into this world, constantly . . ." and changing surface structures, which are the horizontal "variations within the deep structure." Moreover, a distinction must be drawn between the process of "translation [which] is a change in surface structures ('horizontal'), [and] transformation . . . a change in deep structures ('vertical')." Importantly, Wilber points out, "In transformation, new forms of agency emerge, and this means a whole new world of available stimuli becomes accessible to the new and emergent holon."

Wilber further states: "The relation between deep structures [vertical transformation] and surface structures [horizontal translation] I call 'Transcription.'" Or, more simply: since "translation shuffles parts [and] transformation produces wholes," then "evolution is first and foremost a series of transformations ('self-realization through self-transcendence')."

These principles are further elucidated in Addition 1: "The greater the depth of a holon, the greater its degree of consciousness." Thus Wilber clearly indicates "the spectrum of evolution is a spectrum of consciousness."

He goes on to address the fact that "evolution is not bigger and better, but smaller and better (greater depth, less span)," therefore one of the tenets holds that "greater depth always means less span, in relation to a holon's predecessor(s)." Importantly, this type of holarchical understanding helps to show that some holons (with less depth) are more fundamental, being a component of so many other holons, yet they're less significant, embracing so little of the Kosmos. Yet other holons (with greater depth) are less fundamental "because fewer other holons depend on it for their own existence," yet they're more significant "because more of the universe is reflected or embraced in that particular wholeness."

In reviewing this group of evolutionary principles (the twenty tents), Wilber is also in accord with the postmodern discovery suggesting that "holons do not simply reflect a pregiven world. Rather, according to their capacity, they select, organize, give form to, the multitude of stimuli cascading around them." By embracing postmodernism, the integral vision clearly claims: "You cannot point to any thing, to any holon, and say it's just *that* and nothing else, because every holon is simultaneously a superholon and a subholon: it is composed of holons and composes others (across both space and time); nothing is ever simply present."

By fully recognizing that all agency is agency-in-communion, Wilber acknowledges "the interdependence of microevolution and macroevolution," therefore making it clear that a distinction needs to be made between an individual holon and its social holon, or environment.

This principle also establishes that the coevolution of individual and social holons results in an enduring compound individual, "compounded of its junior holons and adding its own defining form or wholeness or canon or deep structure." Wilber here defines same level relational exchange as the condition in which "holons evolve, each layer of depth continues to exist in (and depend upon) a network of relationships with other holons at the same level of structural organization."

Telos is another Greek term used by Wilber to signify "the miniature omega-point pull of the end state of a holon's regime." He explains that "Limited contexts find resolution, not by anything that can be done on the same level, but only by transcending that level, by finding its deeper and wider context. Deeper and wider contexts exert a pull, a telos, on present limited contexts." Thus, when he asks whether there is a final Omega Point, he proposes the answer, "Who knows, perhaps telos, perhaps Eros, moves the entire Kosmos, and God may indeed be an all-embracing chaotic Attractor, acting, as Whitehead said, throughout the world by gentle persuasion toward love."

CHAPTER 3. "INDIVIDUAL AND SOCIAL" clarifies an important limitation to the "web of life" systems by recognizing that with these theories humans are usually reduced to being just another strand in the biosphere (biology). Therefore Wilber concludes that these types of systems theories can be "incredibly partial and lopsided." A central error of this approach is "a confusion and conflation of individual and social holons," and this is mostly because systems theorists construct hierarchies which almost always confuse the micro (individual) and macro (social) dimensions of holons.

Wilber recommends that "What is necessary, then, is to construct a series of true holarchies of compound individuals [or individual human holon] and then indicate, at the same level of organization, the type of environment (or social holon) in which the individual holon is a participant (and on whose existence the individual depends). And this needs to be done in all three of the great realms of evolution—physiosphere, biosphere, and noosphere."

Wilber then points out that this integral view has already been seen and articulated in part with the brilliant work of Erich Jantsch, who clearly distinguishes between microevolution (individual holons) and macroevolution (social holons). For example, when looking at the social holon of Gaia, the living earth, which is technically (Margulis and Lovelock) mostly composed of *prokaryotes* (cells with a nucleus), Wilber points out that naturally the simplest biospheric holons have the greatest span (or size) but the least depth (or levels). This means that "GAIA is indeed our roots and our foundation" because "the Gaia system is the largest living social holon on the planet (has the most units, or the greatest span), precisely because it is the shallowest (most primitive)." (See Figure 1: "Coevolution of Macro- and Microstructures.")

Wilber continues to discuss the differences between size, span, and embrace (depth), where, again, "increasing evolution produces Greater Depth (or greater embrace) and Less Span (or fewer holons capable of the greater embrace)." Wilber explains that the problem with size (span), then, is that it distorts and confuses the actual nature of the holarchical Kosmos, because it is, in reality, based upon greater embrace and greater depth (not span). He carefully notes, however, that "An individual holon can eventually *embrace the entire Kosmos*—its depth can go to infinity—but the actual number of holons (the span) that can realize this total embrace might be very, very few. Cosmic consciousness means cosmic embrace, it doesn't mean cosmic span."

Again, this theme, known as development is envelopment, specifies that "Any holon is fundamentally a compound individual and its same-level relational exchanges at *all* of its levels—a compound individual in a compound environment . . . a perfect expression of the self-transcending thrust of evolution, of creative emergence." Thus, Wilber concludes that "Love . . . like consciousness and creativity and self-transcendence, is built into the very *depth* of the Kosmos." Wilber further claims that by more accurately understanding these dynamics of emergent evolution, it's possible to more clearly differentiate not only individual (compound) holons from social holons but also to better identify their "same-level relational exchanges."

According to Wilber, this type of holarchical understanding offers a truer or more integral ecological philosophy since, in actuality, "The noosphere *depends* on the biosphere, which *depends* on the physiosphere—and that is true *precisely* because the physiosphere is a *lower* component of the biosphere, which is a *lower* component of the noosphere, and not the other way around." Therefore, Wilber contends, it's important for holistic theorists to fully recognize that "The biosphere is not in the physiosphere . . . the bios is not part of the cosmos, but just the opposite: the cosmos is a part of, a component of, the bios." This is ultimately because biology (life) added "something extra" beyond plain physical matter, there-

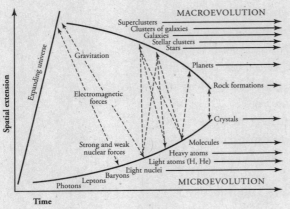

Cosmic Coevolution

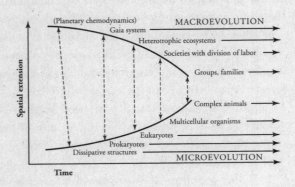

History of Life on Earth

Coevolution of Macro- and Microstructures (after Jantsch)
FIGURE 1

fore "The bios is a part of the *Kosmos* ["the All"], but not a part of the cosmos [the physical universe], and in that simple move we have forever disavowed reductionism." Wilber's integral vision, in other words, offers "a profoundly ecological orientation *without* regressively absolutizing the biosphere (nor the noosphere)."

As an example, by following the holarchical emergence and inclusive nature of the pyramid of development, an excellent example of a natural hierarchy, Wilber points out that "the brain of the human holon" follows the triune brain system (after Paul MacLean), which is compounded of:

1. a reptilian brain (or the brain stem), which is "the overall level of rudimentary sensorimotor intelligence and instinctive drives or impulses";

2. a paleomammalian brain (or the limbic system) which is "experienced as feelings and emotions, which become guiding forces for behavior";

3. a neomammalian brain (or the neocortex), which is "connected with the emergence of the noosphere." (See Figure 2: "The Human Holon: The 'Triune Brain.'")

Wilber's main point here is that with the human holon, the complex and nested triune brain moves beyond the biosphere into the noosphere and "the realm of sociocultural (and not just biosocial) evolution." These social holons, in other words, are the "social environment in which the triune-brained organisms existed." Wilber points out, "Just as matter had pushed forth life, the self-transcendent drive *within* biology pushed forth something *beyond* biology, pushed forth symbols and tools. . . . Kinship gave way to 'cultureship'." From this new emergent sphere of existence—the noosphere—the human holon produced villages, towns, cities, and states and more, therefore Wilber argues: "As far as we can tell, the human brain has remained virtually unchanged in the past fifty thousand years. . . . And yet the entire majesty and catastrophe of culture paraded across the scene, all on the same biological base, but a majesty and catastrophe that could not be reduced to, explained by, or contained in that base." Indeed, as we've seen, with the noosphere a whole new level "had been added to the evolutionary game." (See Figure 3: "The Social Holon: Emergent Geopolitical Systems Levels.")

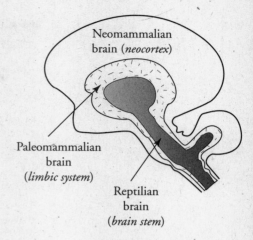

THE HUMAN HOLON
The "Triune Brain"
(after MacLean)
FIGURE 2

However, unlike some proponents of evolutionary progress, Wilber readily admits "The evolution of holons is not all sweet and light. . . . For the grim fact is that greater structural complexity—whether individual or social—means that more things *can* go horribly wrong." Accordingly, Wilber presents a fundamental principle: "The fact that evolution always produces *greater transcendence* and *greater differentiation* means that a factor of *possible* pathology is built into every evolutionary step." In other words, when transcendence goes too far it can become repression; when differentiation goes too far it becomes dissociation.

In summary: "Whenever there is *negation without preservation,* the result is pathology, of one sort or another, a pathology that, if severe enough, evolution sets about to erase in earnest."

Wilber then suggests that one possible way to deal with some of these pathologies may be with the so-called "regression in service of the ego" (a Freudian notion introduced by Ernst Kris). Nevertheless, Wilber maintains that this way of the retro-Romantic, who often "recommends regression, period," will usually, in the end, never be a fruitful model in a Kosmos generally governed by evolutionary progression. The integral theorist argues that as the Romantics push their "Way Back Machine" (after Sherman and Peabody) further and further back into history, they are "scraping layers and layers of depth off the Kosmos looking for a Garden of Eden that ever recedes into a shallower darkness." He contends that they are ultimately misguided in their attempt to undo the natural progression of the emerging human noosphere (including the modern mind), which is inherently accompanied by complex pathologies, as many theorists point out. In other words, Wilber's main point is that "It is one thing to remember and embrace and honor our roots; quite another to hack off our leaves and branches and celebrate that as a solution to leaf rot. So we will celebrate the new possibilities of evolution even as we gasp in horror—and try to redress—the multiplicity of new pathologies."

Ultimately, then, from Wilber's transpersonal point of view, the best thing the noosphere provides is interiority, or interior depth, a quality missed by the quan-

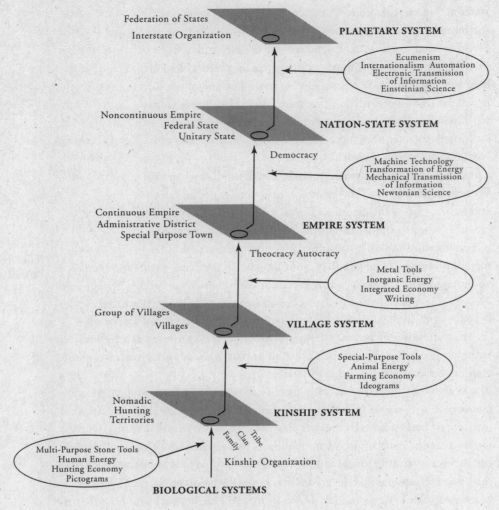

PLANETARY SYSTEM

Federation of States

Interstate Organization

Ecumenism
Internationalism Automation
Electronic Transmission
of Information
Einsteinian Science

Noncontinuous Empire
Federal State
Unitary State

NATION-STATE SYSTEM

Democracy

Machine Technology
Transformation of Energy
Mechanical Transmission
of Information
Newtonian Science

Continuous Empire
Administrative District
Special Purpose Town

EMPIRE SYSTEM

Theocracy Autocracy

Metal Tools
Inorganic Energy
Integrated Economy
Writing

Group of Villages

Villages

VILLAGE SYSTEM

Special-Purpose Tools
Animal Energy
Farming Economy
Ideograms

Nomadic
Hunting
Territories

KINSHIP SYSTEM

Tribe
Clan
Family

Multi-Purpose Stone Tools
Human Energy
Hunting Economy
Pictograms

Kinship Organization

BIOLOGICAL SYSTEMS

THE SOCIAL HOLON
Emergent Geopolitical
Systems Levels
(after A. Taylor)
FIGURE 3

titative measurements of physical-oriented system sciences, even if they're holistic. For example, by acknowledging interiors it's possible to know that "my mind is known interiorly 'by acquaintance,' but my brain is known exteriorly 'by description' (William James, Bertrand Russell)." In other words, Wilber recognizes "the brain is the outside, the mind is the inside." And, as a universal principle, this type of "exterior/ interior holds true for every holon in evolution."

CHAPTER 4. "A VIEW FROM WITHIN" is the first chapter to specifically introduce Wilber's concept of the four quadrants and the Big Three. Since humans holarchically embrace all the "preceding stages of evolution," he begins by pointing out that "we are all ultimately in each other, in various degrees." In other words, we may justifiably know "the within of things," and if we are cautious to take the anthropomorphic fallacy into account, as well as the tendency to retrotension (or "reading 'higher' thoughts and feelings into 'lower' forms simply because we humans feel them"), and also curb our presumptions somewhat, then Wilber proposes that "we can reasonably make correlations between outward form and interior perception."

With this type of integral understanding, and in agreement with numerous other theorists, Wilber argues that "the within of things, the interiority of individual holons, is in essence the same as Consciousness," thus he produces the following simple formulas:

- "The within of things is consciousness, the without of things is form";

- "the within of things is depth, the without is surface. But all surfaces are surfaces of depth, which means, all forms are forms of consciousness";

- Thus, stated as a general tenet, "The greater the depth of evolution, the greater the degree of consciousness."

Importantly, Wilber notes that it really doesn't matter "how far down (or not) you wish to push consciousness," since "the lowest or most primitive holons (quarks, for example) . . . have the least depth, the least consciousness, relatively speaking," yet, (in agreement with Whitehead) even they possess a form of "prehension."

Having made this distinction between interiority and exteriority, Wilber points out that "Interior holons have nothing to do with size or spatial extension," but instead "each new and emergent interior holon transcends but includes, and thus operates upon, the information presented by its junior holons, and thus it fashions something novel in the ongoing cognitive or interior stream." Wilber is expressing, in other words, Teilhard de Chardin's "law of complexity and consciousness," which, in essence, means Depth = Consciousness or, again, "greater depth, greater interiority, greater consciousness." (See Table 1: "The Without and the Within.")

He then offers a short review of holistic systems theories and the spheres or levels of evolution (physiosphere, biosphere, noosphere), each of which is seen as "transcending but including its predecessors." Wilber therefore presents a figure representing these three general domains of evolution from the viewpoint of a compound individual holon, thus showing their embracing nature. (See Figure 4: "The Nested Levels of Evolution in the Compound Individual Holon.")

Wilber turns to a close examination of "the evolution of the *within* of human

OUTWARD FORMS	FORMS OF CONSCIOUSNESS
atoms	prehension
cells (genetic)	irritability
metabolic organisms (e.g., plants)	rudimentary sensation
proto-neuronal organisms (e.g., coelenterata)	sensation
neuronal organisms (e.g., annelids)	perception
neural cord (fish/amphibians)	perception/impulse
brain stem (reptiles)	impulse/emotion
limbic system (paleomammals)	emotion/image
neocortex (primates)	symbols
complex neocortex (humans)	concepts

The Without and the Within
TABLE I

holons," beginning with the emergence of the first human animals. He gathers research from numerous sources and scholars, though most of the summary statements are by Jürgen Habermas and Jean Gebser (including Wilber's own previous work, especially in *Up From Eden*).

Based upon these findings, Wilber introduces at least "Four Major Epochs of Human Evolution, each anchored by a particular structure (or level) of individual consciousness that correspondingly produced (and was produced by) a particular social worldview . . . (the coevolution of macro and micro)."

These researchers claim that each structure of consciousness or worldview generates a variety of effects and characteristics unique to each worldview, by which Wilber means a "'Common Worldspace' in the broadest sense." Following Gebser, these are specifically called (I) the archaic, (II) the magic, (III) the mythic, and (IV) the mental worldviews, and (V) the integral:

The first of these five stages, the archaic, is defined by Wilber and Gebser as "a loose 'catchall' epoch that simply and globally represents *all* the structures of consciousness up to and including the first hominids."

Before these epochs are examined in further detail (in the next chapter), however, Wilber turns to an in-depth consideration regarding the four different strands of a holon, or what he calls the "four major quadrants or four major aspects to each and every holon." As a general rule, each quadrant "is intimately related and indeed dependent upon all the others, but none of which can be reduced to the others." These four quadrants are defined as follows:

1. "the **Upper-Right** (UR) . . . the exterior form or structure of an individual holon;

2. the **Upper-Left** (UL) . . . the interior form of an individual holon;

3. the **Lower-Right** (LR) . . . all the exterior forms of social systems;

4. the **Lower-Left** (LL) . . . the interiors of the social systems . . . [or the] culture, or the shared values that constitute the common worldviews of various social systems."

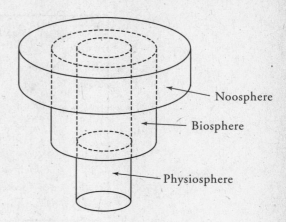

The Nested Levels of Evolution in a Compound Individual Holon
FIGURE 4

In order to present a summary of the four quadrants he provides another large schematic figure showing these multidimensional relationships that inevitably "leaves out more than it includes." (See Figure 5: "The Four Quadrants in Detail.")

Wilber's "balanced or 'all-quadrant' view" maintains that the Left-Hand (interior) and Right-Hand (exterior) approaches are both required in any model since "every holon has these four aspects or four dimensions (or four quadrants) of its existence, and thus it can (and must) be studied in its intentional, behavioral, cultural, and social settings." Most importantly, he continues, "none of the four quadrants can be privileged."

As an example of this four-quadrant scheme, Wilber clarifies their domain or "truth":

- the Upper-Left quadrant "emphasizes the importance of the notion of *sincerity*" and *truthfulness*;

- the Right-Hand (exterior) side "is fundamentally concerned with *propositional truth*" or determining whether something is true or false;

- the Lower-Left quadrant includes "the *shared cultural worldspace* necessary for the communication of any meaning at all," or of "cultural fit," thus it involves mutual understanding.

Wilber uses the four quadrants to critique any type of flatland reduction or reductionism, whether gross (atomistic) or subtle (holistic). A "modern flatland ontology," whether filled with "flatland atomists" or "flatland holists," must be avoided, according to Wilber, including "systems theorists and the structural/functionalists," and therefore "virtually all of the 'new paradigm' and 'ecological/holistic' theories."

He includes a strong critique of modernity's "fundamental Enlightenment

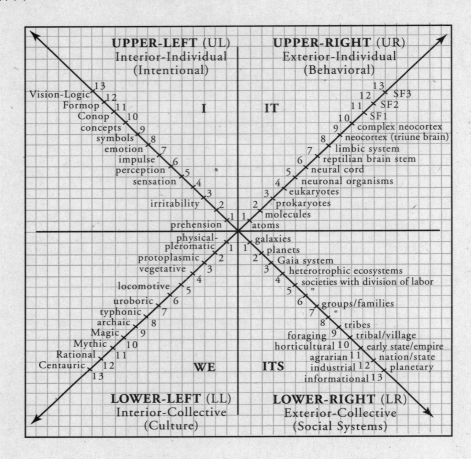

The Four Quadrants in Detail

FIGURE 5

paradigm," which Wilber heavily censures, especially its unwarranted demotion of "all degrees of interior depth to mere functions of exterior span." Indeed, as Wilber explains, "The holistic paradigm of the Enlightenment collapsed a Kosmos that was both vertically and horizontally holarchic . . . into a flatland cosmos . . . a flatland web that replaced vertical depth with the great universal system of [horizontal] interlocking span." Nevertheless, Wilber insists it's not so much that "systems theory and eco-holism is wrong" but rather they're just incomplete. Thus, again, Wilber calls for an elimination of both gross and subtle reductionism by actively recognizing and integrating all four quadrants so "that truth, truthfulness, meaning, and fit can be brought into a mutual harmony."

Wilber then introduces another way of describing the four quadrants, known simply as the **Big Three**:

1. Right-Hand exteriors or "**Its**";

2. Upper-Left individual interiors or "**I**";

3. Lower-Left collective interiors or "**We**";

Each domain has its own particular language system:

1. Right-Hand (exterior) quadrants use "**It-Language**";

2. Upper-Left (individual interior) quadrant uses "**I-Language**";

3. Lower-Left (collective interior) quadrant uses "**We-Language**";

In relation to the great wisdom tradition, or perennial philosophy, Wilber points out that the Big Three also correspond to Plato's concept of the True ("It"), the Good ("We"), and the Beautiful ("I"), and Buddhism's Three Jewels: dharma ("It"), Sangha ("We"), Buddha ("I"). Wilber further reveals that each domain also has its own validity criteria, namely:

1. **Right-Hand** ("It") or *propositional truth* (referring to an objective state of affairs, or it);

2. **Upper-Left** ("I") or *subjective truthfulness (or* sincerity);

3. **Lower-Left** ("We") or *normative rightness* (cultural justness or appropriateness; we).

As Wilber continues to emphasize, each quadrant has its own validity claim "and its own standards, and none of which can be reduced to the others." His conclusion, then, following other theorists, is that "if the great achievement of the Enlightenment (and 'modernity') was the necessary differentiation of the Big Three, the great task of 'postmodernity' is their integration." (See Figure 6: "The Four Quadrants (or the 'Big Three') of a Holon.")

Wilber ends this chapter by reviewing the controversial notion of onto-phylo parallels (an updated version of the simpler idea that "ontogeny recapitulates phylogeny") whereby the "the same basic structures of consciousness can be found in the individual self (UL) and its cultural setting (LL), that is, in the micro and macro branch of the evolution of consciousness." In other words, "It is the same basic structures of consciousness underlying both the micro and macro branch in both their ontogenetic and phylogenetic evolution, and it is the same developmental logic . . . that governs their evolution." Wilber also points out that these correlations are "onto/phylo parallels in the evolution of deep structures (not surface structures)."

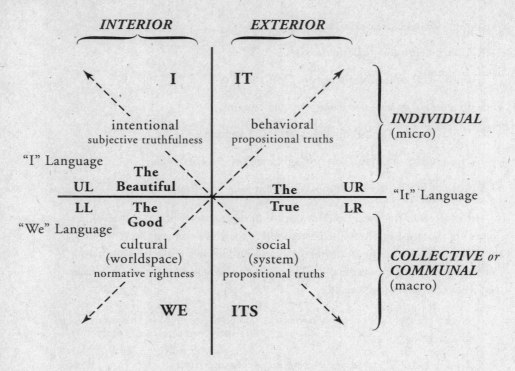

The Four Quadrants
(or the "Big Three")
of a Holon
FIGURE 6

Nonetheless, due to the controversy surrounding the traditional notion that ontogeny recapitulates phylogeny, Wilber assents to Silvano Arieti's position, which states: "This does not mean literally that in the psyche ontogeny recapitulates phylogeny, but that there are certain similarities in the [two] fields of development. . . ." With caution, then, onto-phylo parallels or homologies are best seen as a "series of abstract patterns," similar to Rupert Sheldrake's notion that "nature develops habits—morphic units with morphic fields, which he also calls holons." Indeed, Wilber suggests that we can actually observe these facts ourselves by looking into the "archeology of our own souls . . . enfolded in us as part of our own compound individuality, past interiors taken into our own present interiors, living on in the depths of our own being today, enriching us or destroying us, depending entirely on our own capacity to embrace and to transcend."

CHAPTER 5. "THE EMERGENCE OF HUMAN NATURE" is about phylogeny (situated mostly in the Lower-Left quadrant of the social holon) or the evolution of collective worldviews in "the emergence of human socio-cultural evolution." As we shall see, these collective worldviews of the average mode of consciousness emerged from the (I) archaic to the (II) magical-animistic to the (III) mythic to the mythic-rational to the (IV) egoic-rational, and, if successful, to today's highest average level (V) the integral-centaur.

I–II. Beginning with an inquiry into the important shift from the **archaic** to the magical (beginning approximately 500,000–100,000 B.P.* with the transformation of "hominids (or 'proto-humans') into true humans (Homo sapiens)." Wilber points out with the "emergence of Homo sapiens" that "the male and female values spheres . . . even in archaic hominid societies . . . were already beginning to differentiate, and often sharply." Wilber therefore agrees (following Habermas) that it was not the economy but "the novel emergence of the human family," especially "the role of the father," that linked "the two value spheres of the male and female" since this was "an emergent characteristic that is found nowhere else in evolution." These researchers suggest, in other words, that it's the "familialization of the male" within a family system that was the crucial integrating link, especially since "if evolution were to continue, a new integration was needed." Wilber concludes: "Thus began the one, single, enduring and nightmarish task of all subsequent civilization: the taming of testosterone."

Wilber goes on to explain in some detail that this important transition from the archaic stage to the magic means "right at the very defining transformation from hominids to humans, a sexual differentiation emerged, a differentiation that could dissociate into extreme sexual polarization." Therefore he discusses a number of important issues such as "male advantage and female advantage" which is "based largely on such simple biological factors"; the shift from matrifocal to patrifocal, the fact that "the 'patriarchy' was not something that could have simply and easily been avoided or bypassed," the different feminist responses to these "gender wars," as well as what can effectively facilitate both male and female liberation within the noosphere (or mind), though not the biosphere (nature, body). In other words, armed with a holarchical understanding, Wilber's evolutionary view maintains that "In the course of history and prehistory, it would take three or four major and profound cultural transformations to climb up and out of this biological destiny." It is only then, "when the noosphere and the biosphere were finally differentiated, biology was no longer destiny."

II. The **magical-animistic** epoch (beginning approximately 100,000 B.P.) emerged once "the familialization of the male, and emergence of the human socio-cultural evolution" had begun. This period is called magical because it parallels or correlates

---

* B.P. is a designation for "before the present"; B.C.E. means "before the common era"; C.E. means "common era." These dates are added, and are not necessarily given in the text of *SES;* they are only approximate.

with preoperational thinking (following Habermas, Gebser, Piaget) or when the "mind and body were still relatively undifferentiated, and thus mental images and symbols are often confused or even identified with the physical events they represent." In other words, in this worldview it appears that "the subject has special power over the object (*magic*) and the object has special subjective qualities (*animism*)."

In this regard, Wilber briefly touches on tribal kinship consciousness, including today's erroneous tendency of the "retro-Romantics . . . to turn back the clock and elevate this [magical] structure to a privileged status of integrative power it simply did not possess." He makes the point that this is especially true when considering that "tribes may or may not have known how to remain reverential of nature; it was *other* tribes they could not integrate." Nonetheless, he still maintains that since "primal tribes are literally our roots" then they should be rightly honored and necessarily integrated.

III. With the **mythic** or mythological worldview (beginning approximately 40,000 B.P., increasing after 10,000 B.P.), Wilber maintains that it was only with the "complex systems of mythology" that humans could finally become "transtribal" and "unify people beyond mere blood lineage," and therefore finally find "a way to transcend their isolated tribal kinship lineages." He points out (following Joseph Campbell) the rise of the first early states and the later "mythic-imperial empires (East and West, North and South), with their inherent dominator hierarchies" were "marked by an explosion of codified mythologies" (beyond the simpler myths of magical-animistic societies), especially since "these mythologies became a large part of the integrating structures for society (i.e., providing both cultural meaning and social integration)."

This transition moved human culture into the mythic-membership epoch (coming to fruition with "civilization" approximately 3500 B.C.E.) because it was a time when "personal identity switched to a role identity in a society of a common political (not genetically related) ruler." Importantly, however, Wilber emphasizes that "The average mode of the mythological epoch did not reach into the subtler and transpersonal dimensions, but remained grounded in a concrete-literal interpretation of myth."

At this point, Wilber propounds the important fact that all these epochs . . . refer only to the average mode of consciousness or the center of gravity "around which the society as a whole orbited." On the other hand, the most advanced form of consciousness evolution "began to penetrate not only into higher modes of ordinary cognition (the Aristotles of the time) but also into genuinely transcendental, transpersonal, mystical stages of awareness (the Buddhas of the time)." Therefore, according to Wilber, as the average mode of consciousness continued

SEX, ECOLOGY, SPIRITUALITY

to evolve, these epochs appear to correlate with the progressive evolutionary advances of the advanced-tip individuals. Thus he explains:

- "In the **Magical**, the most advanced mode seems to have been the Psychic (embodied in a few genuine shamans or pioneers of yogic awareness);

- in **Mythological** times the most advanced modes seems to have reached into what is known as the Subtle level (embodied in a few genuine saints);

- in **Mental-Egoic** times the most advanced modes reached into the Causal level (embodied in a few genuine sages)."

III–IV. The mythic-rational epoch (emerging during the first millennium B.C.E., declining after 1500 C.E.) is introduced with an extensive consideration of what exactly is meant by the word *rational* and *rationality*. Rationality is often linked with formal operational cognition (after Piaget) which simply means "the capacity not just to think, but to think about thinking." Wilber explains that with true rationality it's possible to:

- "reflect upon your own thought processes";

- "take perspectives different from your own";

- "entertain hypothetical possibilities";

- "become highly introspective."

However, rationality is mostly about "imagining all sorts of other possibilities," it offers a sound reasonableness that "tends to be universal in character," and is thus "highly integrative." With this definition, he concludes, "It is only rationality that allows the beginning emergence of a truly global or planetary network, which, freed from any particular society, can allow all societies their own unique and special place."

The next emerging structure is first recognized to be a hybrid that Wilber calls the mythic-rational, because the "old myths were propped up with rational reasons," or, technically, "the traditional mythological structures were at first rationalized." He then deduces: "And in one of the most difficult of all historical transformations, a universal and global reasonableness began to slowly replace local and divisive mythologies, mythologies that, precisely because they could not be universally argued and supported by shared evidence, could only be supported militarily and imperialistically."

IV. The **egoic-rational** structure of consciousness (beginning during the first millennium B.C.E., coming to fruition after 1500 C.E.) did fully not emerge as an average mode of awareness until "empires gave way to modern states," especially codified with separation of church and state. This involved the critical (and extremely difficult) "differentiation of the noosphere [rational mind] and the biosphere [magical-mythic body]." Wilber specifically identifies this transformation as a decidedly "new turn, a new transcendence" whereby humanity "discovered a new and deeper interior, with a new and higher consciousness, and that consciousness was to be found by looking within." This new rational emergent affected everything from politics to philosophy to religion (including the origination of "rational religions," such as Buddhism). All of this was precipitating a revolutionary "liberation in the noosphere," which facilitated recognition of the rights of the individual (such as with women, the abolition of slavery, equal protection under the law, etc., topics that Wilber discusses at length).

V. Vision-logic/planetary is the currently emerging yet struggling epoch associated with the highly anticipated global or world culture (after Frobenius). This worldview is based around the *integrated centaur*—"the mythic beast, half human and half horse"—which Wilber (following Benoit and Erikson) uses to represent "the integration of body and mind, or biosphere and noosphere." The centaur is associated with a kind of cognition . . . that Wilber calls vision-logic or network-logic, so "where rationality gives all possible perspectives, vision-logic adds them up into a totality." In other words, vision-logic not only can "reasonably decide the individual issues, but hold them all together at once in mind, and judge how they fit together as a truth-vision."

Wilber believes that only the centaur in vision-Logic (or the mature ego-rational) can possibly facilitate a planetary transformation simply because "it is vision-logic that drives and underlies the possibility of a truly planetary culture." Wilber also correlates the centaur's worldview with the integral-aperspectival mind (after Gebser) because it "adds up all the perspectives *tout ensemble,* and therefore privileges no perspective as final: it is aperspectival." However, Wilber warns, this awareness can lead to the postmodern dilemma of "aperspectival madness," which is a "leveling of perspectives" until, at times, a person is completely "lost in aperspectival space."

Nevertheless, Wilber concludes that since "centauric-integral awareness integrates the body and mind in a new transparency," then "the integral structure *can* integrate the physiosphere, the biosphere, and the noosphere," and thus the aperspectival world becomes "the culmination of the worldcentric vision started by rationality and completed by vision-logic." However, he points out, one of the principal difficulties with the emergence of this type of transnational worldview is the "global nature of this transformation," that is, global consciousness inherently involves the hard transition of "nations voluntarily surrendering some of their sovereignty for the global betterment."

The *dialectic of progress,* Wilber recalls, is "one of the defining aspects of evolution . . . [thus] it brings new and emergent possibilities and therefore new and potential pathologies." Wilber identifies a hierarchy of deficiency needs (following Maslow's needs hierarchy) in which "the emergence of a new level solves or 'defuses' some of the central problems and limitations of the previous stage (or else it wouldn't emerge), but it also introduces its own new problems and new scarce resources."

This gives Wilber an opportunity to look at multiculturalism in some detail, especially its postmodern error, which "confuses the fact that no perspective is final with the notion that all perspectives are therefore simply equal." Wilber's main point is that even multiculturalism is based "in the space of rational pluralism," which is, quite simply, "the only structure that will tolerate structures other than itself." In other words, this type of tolerance and rational pluralism must be extremely vigilant against lower structures (especially the mythic-imperialistic) because the mythic mind will literally "burn your tolerant tail at the stake in order to save your soul." Since mythic-ethnocentric intolerance is a very real and dangerous, Wilber argues that the only way a real planetary culture and tolerance will emerge is with "a correlative transformation in human consciousness." He maintains that the inherent "global nature of this transformation" leads to a transnationalism involving at least "three interrelated factors:

1. the necessity to protect the 'global commons,' the common biosphere that belongs to no nation, no tribe, no creed, no race;

2. the necessity to regulate the world financial system, which no longer responds to national borders;

3. the necessity to maintain a modicum of international peace and security. . . ."

In other words, at this time in human history, Wilber affirms, "the single greatest world transformation would simply be the embrace of global reasonableness and pluralistic tolerance—the global embrace of egoic-rationality (on the way to centauric vision logic)." As Wilber has shown, "The revolution, as always, will come from the within and be embedded in the without."

CHAPTER 6: "MAGIC, MYTHIC, AND BEYOND" is about ontogeny (situated mostly in the Upper-Left quadrant of the human holon) or the evolutionary emergence of the individual fulcrums (or milestones) of self-development. Wilber begins by reviewing the all-important pre/trans fallacy, which in essence means "since both prerational states and transrational states are, in their own ways, nonrational, they appear similar or even identical to the untutored eye. And once pre and trans are confused, then one of two fallacies occurs": reductionism, or when "all higher and transrational states are reduced to lower and prerational states"; or elevationism or when "one will elevate all prerational states to some sort of transrational glory."

Wilber suggests that "Freud was a reductionist, Jung an elevationist—the two sides of the pre/trans fallacy. And the point is that they are *both* half right and half wrong."

Wilber starts to "pick up the story of ontogeny" by first surveying the brilliant and detailed work of Jean Piaget, however, "without endorsing all of the Piagetian system." Piaget's four broad stages of mental or cognitive development correlate with the first few "fulcrums of development," a term (following Blank and Blanck) "representing a qualitatively new and distinct differentiation/integration (or transcendence-and-inclusion)." Therefore in order to correlate the social worldviews with the fulcrums, Wilber will "often hybridize Gebser's terminology to match Piaget's substages." The creative emergence of the fulcrums of self-development in the individual human holon are as follows:

(F1) Fulcrum-1 (*physical self*) (archaic and early archaic-magical) involves archaic fusion or "oceanic adualism" (Arieti) or "pleromatic fusion" (Jung) or "primary indissociation" (Piaget), which begins at birth when the infant is "embedded primarily in the physiosphere." This is the case until around the fifth or ninth month when the "infant transcends this archaic fusion state and emerges or hatches [following Mahler] as a grounded physical self." This sensorimotor period (zero to two years) "is thus predominantly concerned with differentiating the physical self from the physical environment." This is when early preoperational (pre-op) cognition or the archaic-magic worldview develops, therefore this early period is "one of 'magical cognitions' or 'magical proper,'" which includes "adherences," especially egocentrism (the extreme self-centeredness of an infant). In other words, Wilber summarizes, "As the mind begins to emerge with preop, the mental images and symbols themselves are initially fused and confused with the external world."

(F2) Fulcrum-2 (*emotional self*) (archaic-magical, magical, and early magic-mythic) involves the general period of pre-op (two to seven years), when the self "learns to differentiate its feelings from the feelings of others," or, in other words, "it transcends its embeddedness in the undifferentiated biosphere." It is during early pre-op (two to four years; "magic") that there emerges "the psychological birth of the infant" (after Mahler) or "the differentiation-and-integration of a stable emotional self." Wilber explains that "A developmental miscarriage at this critical fulcrum (according to Mahler, Kernberg, and others) results in the narcissistic and borderline pathologies."

By this time (around age three), Wilber continues, "language has begun to emerge, and development in the noosphere begins in earnest," yet still "magical cognitions continue to dominate the entire early preoperational period" which includes "adherences, or felt connections" (after Piaget), similar to the primary process (after Freud) with its magical displacement (objects are "linked") and condensation (objects are directly related). In other words, Wilber summarizes, "the first major layer of the noosphere is magical."

When the "shift from the magic to the mythic" occurs, the late pre-op child (four to seven years) realizes that "his or her thoughts do not egocentrically control, create, or govern the world [magic proper]." Wilber points out that it is from this magic-mythic structure that "so many of the world's classical mythologies seem in large part to issue." Therefore Wilber proceeds with a brief consideration of myth and archetype as seen by Freud and Jung, who both recognized them as archaic forms or archetypes, although, as Wilber points out, they both "differed profoundly over the actual nature of this archaic heritage." The integral theorist concludes: "All the world's great mythologies exist today in each of us, in me and in you. They are produced, and can at any time be produced, by the archaic, the magic, and the mythic structures of our own compound individuality (and classically by the magic-mythic structure)."

(F3) Fulcrum-3 (*self-concept*) (late magic-mythic and mythic) centers around the continual "emergence of the noosphere" (from images to symbols, then concepts) facilitated by the emergence of language. In this case, it's during the "terrible twos" that " 'No!' is the first form of specifically mental transcendence." This is the time of childhood when "a mental-linguistic self is beginning to emerge and beginning to exert some type of conscious will and conscious control over its spontaneous biospheric productions, and over its being 'controlled' by others as well."

However, as Wilber observes a "failure to differentiate mind and body" means that even though "the child can differentiate mind and body, differentiate the noosphere and the biosphere, that differentiation (as always) can go too far and result in dissociation." This leads to the psychopathologies of repression, psychoneurosis, and neurosis or neurotic symptoms, which are defined as when "repressed holons return in disguised forms," or, in other words, "every neurosis is a miniature ecological crisis." Wilber even suggests that this type of psychopathology relates to the "worldwide ecological crisis," which is really "a denial of our common ancestry, a denial of our relational existence with all of life." Healing comes "only as consciousness relaxes its repression, recontacts and befriends the biosphere that exists in its own being. . . . This is called 'uncovering the shadow,' and the shadow is . . . the biosphere."

(F4) Fulcrum-4 (*rule/role self*) (mythic-rational) involves concrete operational (con-op) cognition (seven to eleven years), and this is when the young self begins "to enter the world of other minds . . . so it must learn to take the role of other— a new, emergent, and very difficult task." This early mental self can also "work with mental rules," therefore Wilber also terms it the rule/role mind because of its higher "capacity to operate with both rules and roles." He explains that the "concrete operational world is sociocentric (centered not so much on a bodily identity as on a role identity)," which is also ethnocentric, therefore it's called mythic-membership.

Wilber distinguishes between early con-op as being mythic, and late con-op as being mythic-rational, since this structure still contains "'mythic' and 'anthropocentric' elements." Culturally, this worldview represents "the mythic-imperialism of the Great Empires, from the Greek and Roman to the Khans and Sargons to the Incas and Aztecs," which were only finally "deconstructed with the emergence of egoic-rationality (and formal operational cognition)."

(F5) Fulcrum-5 (*mature ego*) (egoic-rational) involves formal operational (form-op) cognition (eleven years onward) and since this is "a transformation from a role identity to an ego identity," Wilber first presents a detailed discussion on the various definitions of the ego, including the range of modern usage for the word:

- "a separate-self sense, isolated from others and from a spiritual Ground" (New Age writers);

- "the process of organizing the psyche" (psychologically oriented writers);

- the pure ego or transcendental ego (Kant, Fichte, Husserl).

Wilber's integral psychology uses the term *Ego* to mean "a rational, individual sense of self, differentiated from the external world, from its social role (and the superego), and from its internal nature (id)." At this fifth fulcrum, the ego involves "moving from a sociocentric to a worldcentric capacity," or as the self emerges through the "pre-egoic realms (particularly the archaic and magic)" to "the mythic state (as a persona or role) and then finally emerges in the formal operational stage, as a self clearly differentiated from the external world and from it various roles (personae)." Wilber emphasizes that this actually entails "a lessening of egocentrism as one moves closer to the pure Self . . . [because] the self becomes less and less ego-centric [or self-centered], and thus embraces more and more holons as worthy of equal respect . . . [until] the completely decentered self is the all-embracing Self (as Zen would say, the Self that is no-self)."

Again, fulcrum-5 involves formal operational awareness, which Wilber explains "brings with it a new world of feelings, of dreams, of wild passions and idealistic strivings . . . [because this is] the defining mark of reason: Reason is a space of possibilities," and only secondarily includes an "abstract understanding of mathematics, logic, and philosophy." Therefore Wilber gives some simplified equations:

- "formal operational = ecological" due to an "understanding of mutual relationships";

- "formal operational = understandings of relativity" since "all the various perspectives can be held in mind";

- "formal operational = non-anthropocentric," which essentially means "the multiculturalism of universal perspectivism," including the "rights (as an autonomous whole) and responsibilities (as a part of a larger whole— agency and communion, rights and responsibilities)."

Wilber acknowledges that the "characteristic pathology of this stage" is an identity crisis (after Erikson), which is "a failure to negotiate this painfully self-conscious phase (fulcrum-5)." Nevertheless, form-op is clearly defined as "the first structure that is:

- highly reflexive and highly introspective;

- it is experimental (or hypothetico-deductive) and relies on evidence to settle issues;

- it is universal as pluralism or perspectivism;

- it is propositional (can understand 'what if' and 'as if' statements;

- But all of these are just variations on the central theme: Reason is a space of possibilities."

Interestingly, Wilber explains that when Sigmund Freud's poorly translated German *das Ich*, "the I," is properly combined with "id" (which is Latin for "it" or the German Es), then Freud's groundbreaking book *The Ego and the Id* was really meant to convey "The I and the It.'" Wilber clarifies, "Freud's point was that people have a sense of I-ness or selfness, but sometimes part of their own self appears foreign, alien, separate from them—appears, that is, as an 'it.'"

Wilber enters into an in-depth discussion on Joseph Campbell's "pre/trans confusion." With admiration, Wilber still argues that Campbell tends "to elevate

myths," and therefore "commits the classic pre/trans fallacy" by not clearly distinguishing average-mode consciousness from the most-advanced or "those very, very
few individuals who do not take myth literally [as 'concrete myth'] but rather in
an 'as if' fashion . . . an 'as if' stance [which itself] is possible only with formal operational awareness." Wilber maintains that this type of pre/trans confusion, or
"the Romantic view of mythic-membership," can only be accurately countered by
a detailed evolutionary understanding, one which comes to an "inexorable conclusion: beyond mythology is reason, and beyond both is Spirit."

This is why there is a "battle of worldviews" going on in today's highly complex world. Nevertheless, Wilber concedes there is great "value to the mythological
approach" simply because "it can help us, of today's rational worldview, get in
touch with aspects of our roots, our foundations, some of the archeological layers
of our own present awareness." Nevertheless, in summary, he still suggests it's best
to avoid regression (to lower pre-egoic realms) since "each transformation upward
is a 'paradigm war'—a battle royale over how to exclusively view the world."

Therefore, according to Wilber, many of Carl Jung's collective archetypes—
"the magico-mythic motifs and 'archaic images'—should really be called 'prototypes'," because in agreement with Jung, "it is altogether necessary to contact and
befriend them, but it is finally necessary to differentiate and individuate from
them." However, in contradiction to Jung, Wilber maintains that "collective typical is not transpersonal." The real archetypes or "the true archetypes, the ideal
Forms—are the creative patterns said to underlie all manifestation and give pattern to chaos and form to Kosmos." The integral position, then, is that "a 'return to
roots,' is altogether appropriate and benign," that is, if the pre/trans confusion is
avoided by clearly understanding that "the 'hidden power' of myth is released when
it is taken up in the open space created by rationality . . . [for] it is reason, and reason alone, that frees the luminosity trapped in myth."

In assessing current social phenomena, such as the men's movement, Wilber
concludes: "The mythological structures themselves are now junior holons in the
person's own compound individuality, and should be honored as a rich source of
one's own being and one's own roots." However, he warns, "genuine spirituality
[generated from the transpersonal realms] is not . . . a product of the past (or of
past archetypes) . . . [but rather] they are Strange Attractors, lying in our future,
Omega Points that have not been collectively manifested anywhere in the past, but
are nonetheless available to each and every individual as Structural Potentials, as
future structures attempting to come down, not past structures struggling to come
up." In other words, Wilber assures us, "The great and rare mystics of the past
(from Buddha to Christ, from al-Hallaj to Lady Tsogyal, from Hui-neng to Hilde-

gard) were, in fact, ahead of their time, and are still ahead of ours. . . . They absolutely did not inherit the past, they inherited the future."

CHAPTER 7: "THE FURTHER REACHES OF HUMAN NATURE" is about the developmental journey of going within into the "interior castle" (after St. Teresa) or the depths of the human holon, which is situated within the context of the collective social holons (and thus all four quadrants). Wilber begins by stating again an important evolutionary principle: "Each stage of evolution, in whatever domain, involves a new emergence and therefore a new depth, or a new interiority, whether that applies to molecules or to birds or to dolphins; and that each new within is also a going beyond, a transcendence, a higher and wider identity with a greater total embrace. The formula is: going within = going beyond = greater embrace." As self-development proceeds, this increasing internalization means that the self's "relative autonomy—its capacity to stay inwardly focused—increases"; this understanding is expressed in another formula: "increasing development = increasing interiorization = increasing autonomy = decreasing narcissism (decentering)."

Meditation, for instance, "involves yet a further going within, and thus a further going beyond . . . thus meditation is one of the single strongest antidotes to egocentrism and narcissism (and geocentrism and anthropocentrism and sociocentrism)." In short, "every within turns us out into more of the Kosmos." Wilber then shifts again to the story of human development:

(F6) Fulcrum-6 (*centaur*) (holistic-integralism) involves the cognitive level of vision-logic or network-logic, which has been called dialectical, integrative, creative synthetic, and integral-aperspectival. Wilber explains that this centauric worldview "can integrate physiosphere, biosphere, and noosphere in its own compound individuality," thus this is an "overall integration" of the "bodymind-integrated self." Since the integrated self sets the stage for further transpersonal growth, Wilber clarifies that it's only "necessary to develop an adequate competence at that stage [or at any self-stage], in order for it to serve just fine as a platform for the transcendence to the next stage."

Nevertheless, "this beginning transcendence of the ego" has its own pathology, that of "a profound existential malaise," since the self will find that when all "consolations are gone[,] the skull will grin in at the banquet." Wilber reminds us, "the problems of one stage are only 'defused' at the next stage," therefore with "the transcendence of the centaur . . . we are here beginning to pass out of the noosphere into the theosphere, into the transpersonal domains, the domains not just of the self-conscious but of the superconscious."

On the subject of entering the transpersonal domains of self-development Wilber first discusses various philosophical objections to the transpersonal. Wilber argues that in actuality the religious or spiritual realms can only be adequately apprehended by direct spiritual experience. This evidence is only acquired when a person actually tries the experiment, in other words, "The experimenter must, in his or her own case, have developed the requisite cognitive tools."

Wilber claims that "the world's greatest yogis, saints, and sages . . . are not dogmatic; they are not believed in merely because an authority proclaimed them, or because sociocentric tradition hands them down . . . rather, the claims about these higher domains are a conclusion based on hundreds of years of experimental introspection and communal verification. . . . These spiritual endeavors, in other words, are purely scientific in any meaningful sense of the word, and the systematic presentations of these endeavors follows those of any reconstructive science."

Wilber next provides an in-depth exegesis of language and mysticism. He presents the authentic validity claims of mysticism, explaining that "these three strands . . . are the major components in any valid knowledge quest":

1. **injunction**, "which is always of the form, 'If you want to know this, do this'";

2. **illumination** or apprehension, where "you see or apprehend, via a direct experience, the disclosed data of the domain";

3. **confirmation** or communal confirmation where "in this community of peers, you compare and confirm—or reject—your original data."

Wilber emphasizes the importance of "social practices or social injunctions, [which] are crucial in creating and disclosing the types of worldspace in which types of subjects and object appear (and thus the types of knowledge that can unfold)." He also points out that a more accurate reading of Thomas Kuhn's word *paradigm* actually means "exemplary injunctions" or "actual practices." Wilber's crucial point is that the mystical traditions and their transpersonal "contemplative disclosures are open to the fallibilist criteria of all genuine knowledge, because the contemplative path [also] follows all three strands of valid knowledge accumulation."

Wilber stresses that although each mystical tradition has "their own particular and culture-bound trappings, contexts, and interpretations," they still demonstrate that "the deep structures of the contemplative traditions (but not their surface structures) . . . show cross-cultural similarities." Therefore Wilber concludes that it's totally valid, based on the work of many researchers and theorists (such as Grof, Walsh, Goleman, Washburn, Murphy, Adi Da, et al.) to use a developmental stage model in order to "rationally reconstruct the higher stages of transpersonal or con-templative development—stages that continue naturally or normally beyond the ego and centaur if arrest or fixation does not occur."

Wilber posits that a type of mysticism can be correlated with the "four general stages of transpersonal development, each with at least two substages (and some with many more)," with each archetypally represented by four individuals:

1. the **psychic** stage is associated with nature mysticism, represented by Ralph Waldo Emerson;

2. the **subtle** stage with deity mysticism, represented by Saint Teresa of Avila;

3. the **causal** stage with formless mysticism, represented by Meister Eckhart;

4. the **nondual** presence with nondual mysticism, represented by Sri Ramana Maharshi.

In the next chapter, Wilber will demonstrate that each advanced-tip individual "represents a form of tomorrow, a shape of our destiny yet to come. Each rode time's arrow ahead of us, as geniuses always do, and thus, even though looming out of our past, they call to us from our future."

CHAPTER 8. "THE DEPTHS OF THE DIVINE" begins by mentioning that "with the emergence of the Centaur . . . the border between the personal and the transpersonal," we have now entered into the general "domain of the Soul (that of the psychic and subtle)," as "the continuing evolutionary process of within-and-beyond brings new withins . . . and new beyonds [the causal and nondual]." Wilber notes that the word *transpersonal* is "somewhat awkward," therefore he clarifies that it actually "means 'personal plus,' not 'personal minus,'" since the previous personal levels are "negated and preserved, or transcended and included."

Wilber's interior tour of the transpersonal domains is accompanied by the four archetypal representatives referred to in the last chapter, who embody the characteristics of these transpersonal subdivisions:

(F7) **Fulcrum-7** (*psychic level*) (nature mysticism) is represented with quotes from the American scholar Ralph Waldo Emerson (1803–82), who describes this psychic level as a state in which "the soul knows no persons." This means, Wilber explains, "the observer in you, the Witness in you, transcends the isolated *person* in you and opens instead—from within or from behind, as Emerson said—onto a vast expanse of awareness no longer obsessed with the individual bodymind." Emerson called this awareness the Over-Soul (his famous "transparent eyeball") since it "is common in and to all beings . . . one and the same in all of us." This is also "experienced as the World Soul, since self and world are here finding a 'common fountain, common source.'"

In other words, "the Over-Soul is an experienced identity with all manifestation, it is an identity that most definitely and exuberantly embraces nature," therefore it involves a Kosmic consciousness where nature mysticism is based not on "ecocentric immersion or biospheric regression . . . [but] the realization that nature is not Spirit but an expression of Spirit."

Wilber therefore brings attention to the fact that theories of consciousness must "distinguish carefully and clearly between three quite different worldviews on the relation between Nature and Spirit:

1. The first is **magical indissociation**, where spirit is simply equated with nature (nature = spirit); predifferentiated; very 'this-worldly.'

2. The second is **mythic indissociation**, where nature and spirit are ontologically separate or divorced; very 'otherworldly.'

3. The third is **psychic mysticism**: nature is a perfect expression of spirit (or as Spinoza put it, nature is a subset of spirit; 'otherworldly' and 'this-worldly' are united and conjoined."

According to Wilber, with this "Eco-Noetic Self . . . [or] Over-Soul that is the World Soul" there is a new stage of development where a "new going within has resulted in a new going beyond," and a further development of a deeper moral sense takes place mostly because "the worldcentric conception gives way to a direct worldcentric experience, a direct experience of the global Self/World, the Eco-Noetic Self, where each individual is seen as an expression of the same Self or Over-Soul." Wilber is again emphasizing that morality and moral development are part of the evolutionary process, therefore "the whole point of the moral sequence, its very ground and its very goal, its omega point, its chaotic Attractor, is the drive toward the Over-Soul. . . . [Thus] in the light of the Over-Soul . . . I would see in an Other my own Self, with love driving the embrace, and compassion issuing the tenderest of mercies."

Wilber affirms that the true beauty and "mystery of the Over-Soul [is] allowing us to recognize ourselves in each other, beyond the illusions of separation and duality. . . . At the Psychic Level, the universalizing and global tendencies of reason and vision-logic come to fruition in a direct experience—initial, preliminary, but unmistakable—of a truly universal Self, common in and to all beings."

(F8) Fulcrum-8 (*subtle level*) (deity mysticism) is represented by the Spanish mystic St. Teresa of Avila (1515–82) who symbolizes the subtle level with the metaphor of the seven mansions or seven stages of growth presented in her book *Interior Castle,* which is, Wilber claims, "one of the truly great texts of subtle-level development." At this fulcrum of consciousness, Wilber explains that "This process of 'interiorization' or 'within-and-beyond" intensifies—a new transcendence with a new depth, a new embrace, a higher consciousness, a wider identity—and the soul and God enter an even deeper interior marriage, which discloses at its summit a divine union of Soul and Spirit, a union prior to any of its manifestations as matter or life or mind, a union that outshines any conceivable nature, here or anywhere else. Nature mysticism gives way to Deity Mysticism, and the God within announces itself in terms undreamt of in gross manifestation, with a Light that blinds the sun and a Song that thunders nature and culture into stunned and awestruck silence."

Most significantly Wilber and St. Teresa point to the transformative single experience of "complete cessation of all faculties, and in that pure absorption, the self tastes its primordial union with God (or what Teresa also calls Uncreated Spirit)." Wilber clarifies that in Vedanta this is the first "glimmer of *nirvikalpa samadhi* or formless absorption," which continues to be "the transformative event" in the later stages as well. St. Teresa speaks of this stage as a "silkworm" (the self or ego) emerging into a "butterfly" (the blessed soul) as it is transformed in the Fifth Mansion. In other words, "the ego dies and the soul emerges," so therefore "in the Sixth Mansion, Lover and Beloved, butterfly and God, soul and Uncreate Spirit, 'see each other' for extended periods of time."

The "possible pathology" at this subtle stage, Wilber explains, sometimes referred to as the dark night of the soul (after St. John of the Cross) is "that period after one has tasted Universal Being but before one is established in it, for one has now seen Paradise . . . and seen it fade." The Seventh Mansion, on the other hand, is "where actual Spiritual Marriage occurs, and vision gives way to direct apprehension or direct experience—'the union of the whole soul with God.'"

(F9) Fulcrum-9 (*causal*) (formless mysticism) is represented by the German Christian mystic Meister Eckhart (1260–1328), but Wilber begins by using both Eastern and Western terms to clarify that "in the subtle level, the Soul and God unite; in the causal level, the Soul and God are both transcended in the prior identity of Godhead, or pure formless awareness, pure consciousness as such, the pure Self as pure Spirit (Atman = Brahman)." In other words, this "pure formless Spirit is said to be the Goal and Summit and Source of all manifestation. And that is the *causal.*" Wilber goes on to discuss these matters in detail.

From the West, Meister Eckhart further illustrates the causal realm by emphasizing the necessity for "a transcendence or a 'breakthrough' (a word he coined in German)" so that one's own consciousness reveals a "a direct and Formless Awareness that is without self, without other, and without God." The Christian mystic specifically uses such terms as *Godhead* (or what Eckhart also calls *God beyond God*)," as well as *Abyss, unborn, formless, primordial origin, emptiness, nothingness.* Eckhart thus claims "God is void and free . . . [therefore] you should love God mindlessly." He refers (following Saint Dionysius) to this "pure formless awareness without mental intermediaries, as 'Divine Ignorance.'" This is fully appropriate, Wilber affirms, because "in this state of formless and silent awareness, one does not *see* the Godhead, for one *is* the Godhead, and knows it from within, self-felt, and not from without, as an object."

From the East, Sri Ramana Maharshi (1879–1950), "India's greatest modern sage," helps us to understand the causal realm by using Vedanta's formula: "the Self is 'not this, not that,' which in Sanskrit is the *'neti, neti'* . . . precisely because it is the pure Witness of this or that, and thus in all cases transcends any this and any that." Ramana further explains, "'I AM' is the name of God. Of all the definitions of God, none is indeed so well put as the Biblical statement I AM THAT I AM." Therefore, Wilber reminds us, "Ramana often refers to the self by the name 'I-I,' since the Self is the simple Witness of even the ordinary 'I.'" Thus, Wilber explains, the Indian sage "counsels us to seek the *source* of the mind . . . as one pursues this *'self-inquiry'* into the source of thoughts, into the source of 'I' and the 'world,' one enters a state of pure empty awareness, free of all objects whatsoever." In Vedanta this is "known as *nirvikalpa samadhi* (*nirvikalpa* means 'without qualities or objects')," and this is exactly "what Eckhart called 'the naked existence of Godhead.'" Ultimately, then, Wilber is in agreement with these great sages in that they see "the causal is a type of ultimate omega point . . . As the *Source* of all manifestation, it is the *Goal* of all development," however, as they all say too, the causal "is not the end of the story," nor "as Eckhart put it, the 'final Word.'"

(F10) Fulcrum-10 (*nondual*) (nondual mysticism) may be referred to as the tenth fulcrum, although this final awareness is not really a fulcrum per se, which is carefully noted: "This is not a particular stage among other stages—not their Goal, not their Source, not their Summit—but rather the Ground or Suchness or Isness of *all* stages, at all times, in all dimensions: the Being of all beings, the Condition of all conditions, the Nature of all natures." Nondual mysticism, in other words, reveals that "the Formless and the entire world of manifest Form—pure Emptiness and the whole Kosmos—are seen to be not-two (or nondual)." This awareness thus involves the extremely subtle "move from causal unmanifest to nondual embrace . . . [or] the development from *nirvikalpa* to *sahaj samadhi.*"

Paradoxically, Wilber maintains, there is "no entering this state, no leaving it;

it is absolutely and eternally and *always already the case:* the simple *feeling of being,* the basic and simple immediacy of any and all states, prior to the four quadrants, prior to the split between inside and outside, prior to seer and seen, prior to the rise of worlds, ever-present as pure Presence, the simple feeling of being: *empty awareness* as the opening or clearing in which all worlds arise, ceaselessly: I-I is the box the universe comes in." When seen from this enlightened perspective, Wilber explains that this spiraling Kosmic mystery "has never started, this nightmare of evolution, and therefore it will never end. It is as it is, self-liberated at the moment of its very arising. And it is only *this.* The All is I-I. I-I is Emptiness. Emptiness is freely manifesting. Freely manifesting is self-liberating."

When Wilber therefore asks, "Does history, then, have a Final Omega Point, the Omega of all previous and lesser omegas?" he brings up the popular notion of the so-called end of history, stimulated in part by Francis Fukuyama's international sensation *The End of History.* The West, Wilber observes, typically limits itself by only considering an "omega point of rationality," therefore Westerners typically like to think history ends with the completion of the "struggle for recognition" (after Fukuyama).

However Wilber contends, when asked if there is an absolute omega point, the only real answer is paradoxical because "It does exist, and we are not heading toward it." This understanding clearly and simply recognizes that "the Formless is indeed an ultimate Omega, an ultimate End, but an End that is never reached *in* the world of form." In other words, Wilber tries to explain that the ultimate Omega is actually "one's own Original Face, the Face one had before the Big Bang," yet still simultaneously, "evolution seeks only this Formless *summum bonum* . . . and it will *never* find it, because evolution unfolds in the world of form." Nondual mysticism thus demonstrates that "forms continue endlessly, holarchically— holons all the way up, all the way down—the universe as a self-reflexively infinite hall of mirrors." From this position, Wilber states that in the midst of this "endless dream" (where "the twenty tenets are the form and function, the structure and the pattern") the highest consciousness unanimously declares: "*Abide as Emptiness, embrace all Form:* the liberation is in the Emptiness, never finally in the Form (though never apart from it)."

BOOK II, originally called *Flatland,* is a critical response to the regressive state of postmodern cultural studies, especially in the universities. It takes on this task by addressing the modern "collapse of the Kosmos" into a flatland where only surfaces or exteriors predominate, whether atomistic (gross reductionism) or holistic (subtle reductionism). This rise of science or the "dominance of the descenders," as

Wilber points out, had been historically countered by the nineteenth-century Idealists (such as Schelling and Hegel) with their evolutionary philosophies of Spirit-in-action or God-in-the-making. However, in a philosophical analysis, Wilber concludes that in the end the Idealists offered "no yoga, no contemplative practices," therefore their grand theories degenerated into "mere metaphysics." In this case, Wilber argues, if the integral vision is to be truly effective in the world at large, then it must include and promote subjective transformation in order to gain a true and mutual global understanding that is thoroughly grounded in the "Love of the Kosmos itself."

CHAPTER 9. "THE WAY UP IS THE WAY DOWN" first introduces the "two legacies of Plato," which Wilber identifies as the "Descending Current" ("a descent of the One into the world of the Many") and the "Ascending Current" (the "return or ascent from the Many to the One"). Wilber's view emphasizes the nondual stance or "the Unifying Heart, the unspoken Word, that integrates both Ascent and Descent and finds Spirit both transcending the Many and embracing the Many." These principle currents are also correlated with wisdom (or Ascent) and compassion (or Descent) in the East, and in the West with Eros/Phobos or "the love of the lower reaching up to the higher" (and when they're not integrated, "Eros in flight from the lower instead of embracing the lower"); also Agape/Thanatos or "the love of the higher reaching down to the lower" (and when not integrated, "Agape in flight from the higher instead of expressing the higher"); as well as with the ideas of *Reflux* (return) and *Efflux* (creation) terms borrowed from the second-century philosopher Plotinus of Alexandria and Rome.

This leads Wilber into a disquisition on Plotinus (205–270 C.E.), labeling him the most divine of the Neoplatonists and "a synthesizing genius of unparalleled proportion." According to Wilber, his "nondual integration . . . [is] the great and enduring contribution of Plotinus, and it will always stand . . . as a luminous beacon to all those who tire of the violence and brutality of the merely Ascending or merely Descending trails."

CHAPTER 10. "THIS WORLDLY, OTHERWORLDLY" reaffirms the premise that "the great dualism of all dualisms . . . is between 'This World' [Descenders] and an 'Other World' [Ascenders]," therefore Wilber proceeds to give a short survey of Western philosophical history, which has created and maintained this division. From Plato's God ("both in the world and beyond it") and Aristotle's God ("only beyond it"), Wilber points out that this fracture or dualism was exploited by the Church and its "unearthly Trinity." By doing so, the Christian Church actively discouraged actual "causal-level realization" by declaring that Jesus was the "Only Ascended Son of God." This in turn, in the West, created what Wilber terms the "frustrated Ascenders," directly leading to "the coming dominance of the Descenders."

However, as Wilber notes, there has also been a nondual answer in the West reaching "from Augustine to Descartes, Spinoza, Berkeley, Kant, Fichte, Schelling, Hegel, Heidegger, and Sartre, to mention a few." Wilber calls this Western Vedanta, an esoteric form of Western philosophy based around the causal-level realization of "Basic Wakefulness, immediate consciousness . . . until there is *only* the Perfectly Divine in *all* perception, 'this world' and 'that world' being utterly irrelevant, and the way up and the way down meeting *in every single act* of loving and choiceless and nondual awareness."

CHAPTER 11: "BRAVE NEW WORLD" extends Wilber's analysis of Western philosophical history by using the concept of the dialectic of progress, to direct our attention to the "Good News" or the "Dignity of Modernity" (summarized after Voltaire's rallying cry "No more myths!"), while the next chapter will focus on the "Bad News" or the "Disaster of Modernity" (summarized as "No more Ascent!"). Wilber first focuses on the various positive characteristics that emerged with the Age of Reason (in the shift from mythic-rational to rational structures) as it accessed formal operational thought and the increased "space of possibilities." This increase of consciousness often sparked a sense of freedom from the "set of biological constants" therefore, he explains, it ignited social liberation movements.

These Enlightenment ideas are epitomized in a review of Immanuel Kant's three critiques, which are identified with the Big Three or the differentiated three spheres of science, morality, and art. Yet, Wilber concludes, without the proper distinction between the "literal-concrete myths" (prerational) and the "allegorical method" (transrational), the mythic "Church religion, across the board, became the laughingstock of the philosophers of the Age of Reason." As a consequence, the "birth of modernity" resulted in the dominance of science or "the dominance of the Descenders." Wilber explains that science's own research program was to examine the plentitude of nature, even searching for the so-called missing links. Nonetheless, theirs was "a purely Descended world, flatland to the core" since now the modern world believed, as Nietzsche proclaimed, "God is dead."

CHAPTER 12. "THE COLLAPSE OF THE KOSMOS" continues Wilber's survey of Western philosophical history by concentrating on the "Bad News" or the "Disaster of Modernity." He first reminds us that the mythic-rational structure, embodied in the official Church, had "locked the West into an almost exclusively Ascending Ideal for over a thousand years." In reaction to the mythic Church, the Age of Reason, he clarifies, "almost wholeheartedly threw itself over to the Path of

Descent and the glories of Creation and Efflux." However, the net effect was that the transpersonal domains were lost in the attempt to overthrow the mythic mind of the Church, and thus rational thinking pushed for the "collapse of the Kosmos" into a great "interlocking order of surfaces" (after Locke). This collapse or reductionism unfortunately allowed modernity's dignities (or the differentiation of the Big Three) to slide into dissociation where tragically "the Big Three were reduced to the Big One [exteriors only]." In reaction to this flatland worldview, postmodernity has justifiably attempted to overthrow the Big One by attacking the "so-called 'reflection or representation paradigm,'" yet they offered "no inner transformation, of any sort." Thus Wilber terms this "the archbattle of modernity and postmodernity" or simply "the battle between the Ego and the Eco."

In the revised edition of *Sex, Ecology, Spirituality* (2001), Wilber adds a diagrammatic overview with excellent illustrated figures and diagrams (not included here) of the four quadrants (and Big Three) in order to facilitate a consideration of "the Mind/Body Problem" or "the central problem of modernity." Wilber claims this predicament can be solved by understanding both the "body" and "mind" in their various relationships in the four quadrants, as well as understanding the various definitions of nature used by contemporary theorists. (See Figure 7: "The Ego and Eco Before the Collapse to Flatland.")

Wilber looks "more carefully at the strengths and the weaknesses of both the Ego and Eco camps" including:

- the "Ego-positive traits" or "genuinely enduring truths," such as freedom, worldcentric pluralism, and autonomy;

- the "Ego-negative" or "repression," "reductionism," and the "domination of rationality";

- the "Eco-positive" or "wholeness" epitomized by the Romantic movement;

- the "Eco-negative" or "regression," which involves the pre/trans confusion.

Wilber criticizes both approaches by calling "the Ego and the Eco the flatland twins locked in the dance of ironic self-destruction, both contributing equally to the failure of integration. The one absolutizes the noosphere, the other absolutizes the biosphere, neither of which alone can integrate the other." Later he calls this failure and fallacy the "paradox of damage."

CHAPTER 13. "THE DOMINANCE OF THE DESCENDERS" first encapsulates Wilber's analysis of modern Western philosophy, wherein he states: "The single greatest task facing modernity (and postmodernity) . . . [is] the integration of the

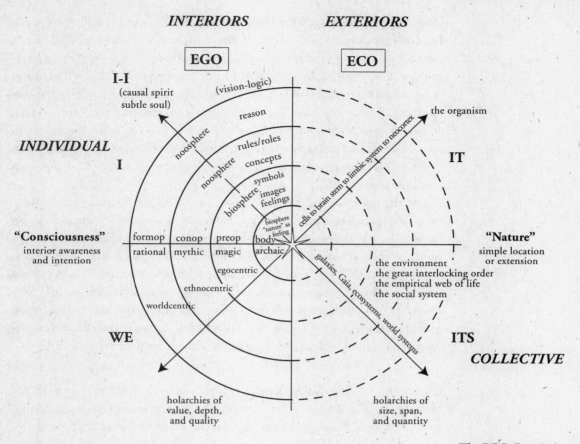

INTERIORS   EXTERIORS

EGO   ECO

I-I
(causal spirit
subtle soul)

INDIVIDUAL

I

(vision-logic)

reason

rules/roles

concepts

symbols

images
feelings

noosphere

noosphere

biosphere

biosphere
"nature" as
feeling

cells to brain stem to limbic system to neocortex

the organism

IT

"Consciousness"
interior awareness
and intention

| formop | conop | preop | body |
| rational | mythic | magic | archaic |

egocentric

ethnocentric

worldcentric

galaxies, Gaia, ecosystems, world systems

"Nature"
simple location
or extension

the environment
the great interlocking order
the empirical web of life
the social system

WE   ITS

COLLECTIVE

holarchies of
value, depth,
and quality

holarchies of
size, span,
and quantity

**The EGO (Interior)
and the ECO (Exterior)
Before the Collapse
to Flatland**
FIGURE 7

Big Three (person, culture, nature), now that they had been finally differentiated."
By summarizing both the Ego and the Eco camps' positive and negative traits,
Wilber launches into an in-depth analysis and critique of the "Eco-Romantic" ide-
ology and their regressive slide into subtle reductionism (a sensory-based interlocking whole) and sentiments regarding nature (with a small *n*). However, Wilber
explains that Nature with "a capital *N* (or Spirit as the nondual One)" is the meaning that the mystics (such as Plato and Plotinus) spoke about, whereas the Romantics offered only "a denatured nature in comparison with the Platonic/Plotinian
view." Wilber goes on to critique modernity's "obsession with sexuality" since, as he
explains, "when monological thought became God, sex became God's obsession."

These arguments allow Wilber to posit that since both the Ego and the Eco
camps were "at a theoretical standoff," then it would take the discovery of evolution
to propose a way to unite and integrate these two warring halves of monological

modernity. He then surveys the work of the nineteenth-century Idealists, especially Friedrich von Schelling (1775–1854) who, with his able student G. W. F. Hegel, used the dialectic to explain the evolutionary process of Spirit-in-action or God-in-the-making. The Idealists produced a "truly stunning vision" that Wilber claims is "a profound integration of Ego and Eco, of Spirit descending into even the lowest state and ascending back to itself, with Spirit nonetheless fully present at each and every stage as the process of its own self-realization and self-actualization, its own self-unfolding and self-enfolding development, a divine play of Spirit present in every single movement of the Kosmos, yet finding more and more of itself as its own Play proceeds. . . ."

Wilber sums up with the simple formula: "Plotinus temporalized = evolution." He continues to point out that Darwin and his theory of natural selection can only explain the process of "microevolution," not "macroevolution." In other words, Wilber is pointing out that Darwinian theory explains *how* (not *why*) evolution occurs, although he does note, Darwin himself "notoriously wavered" on this point (while the other discoverer of natural selection, Alfred Wallace, did not). Therefore "with the collapse of virtually any form of Idealism, the Western world nestled comfortably into the Descended domain of the naturalistic flatland" as scientific materialism became the dominant philosophy of the modern world.

CHAPTER 14. "THE UNPACKING OF GOD" offers an introductory view of the "coming of the World Soul . . . the Over-Soul, the transpersonal dawn, Homo universalis," which Wilber defines as "the integration of the physiosphere and biosphere and noosphere in each and every compound individual, not as a theory but as a central identity in consciousness." Nevertheless, this integration or emergence is not by any means guaranteed since, as always, "we have to make the future that is given to us." This is precisely why Wilber strongly believes that "the Descent of the all-pervading World Soul is facilitated, or hindered, to precisely the degree that we unpack its intuition adequately." Consequently humanity must exercise, he suggests, "a more graceful interpretation covering all four quadrants (because Spirit itself manifests as all four quadrants)." Therefore, as the integral theorist has tried to demonstrate, "The more you contact the Higher Self, the more you worry about the world, as a component of your Very Self, the Self of each and all." With this in mind, he presents two more additions to the twenty tenets:

- "Addition 2: *Every holon issues an IOU to the Kosmos*," which attempts to account for the fact that every holon (whole/part) is "Incomplete Or Uncertain" or an IOU, yet, nonetheless, "it is this incompleteness, this instability, that drives the agitated movement of the entire finite and manifest universe."

- "Addition 3: *All IOUs are redeemed in Emptiness*," which means that the only solution or answer for this dualism (or IOU) to be overcome, transcended, or liberated is via nondual Emptiness (*shunyata*) since "Emptiness is the reality of which all wholes and all parts are simply manifestations."

Again, we see, Wilber's integral vision is in harmony with the universal "message of the mystics, ever so simply put: Emptiness, and Emptiness alone, redeems all IOUs. In Emptiness alone, my debt is paid to the Kosmos, because in Emptiness, I-I am the Kosmos. . . . Not in Emptiness, but as Emptiness, I am released from the fate of a never-ending addition of parts, and I stand free as the Source and Suchness of the glorious display."

With this understanding, Wilber embraces but also moves beyond the legacy of the Idealists whose philosophy, he claims, will be "a necessary component in any sort of truly comprehensive worldview." However, he also criticizes the Idealists for relying too heavily on vision-logic or reason, and especially since they had "no yoga, no contemplative practices, no meditative paradigms, no experimental methodology to reproduce in consciousness the transpersonal insights of its founders." With the precipitous collapse of Idealism dismissed as "mere metaphysics," the reactive cry among most modern philosophers would become "Back to Kant!" This was epitomized by Feuerbach, the German philosopher, a student of Marx, who would soon "announce that any sort of spirituality, any sort of Ascent, was simply a projection of men and women's human potentials onto an 'other world' of wholly imaginative origins," and thus, Wilber observes, "the entire modern (and postmodern) world is, in effect, the followers of Feuerbach."

In response to "the paradox of damage" created by the warring of the Ego and Eco camps, and symbolized by the "two arrows of time" (entropy versus evolution), Wilber continues to argue that "Gaia's major problem" is mostly "how to get people to internally transform from egocentric to sociocentric to worldcentric consciousness." Thus he proposes an integral environmental ethics in which each and every holon possesses:

- **equal ground-value** since "all things and events, of whatever nature, are perfect manifestations of Spirit";

- **intrinsic value** reflecting its "wholeness" and "autonomy";

- **extrinsic value** reflecting its "partness" and "instrumental value."

In addition, Wilber contends, since today humankind is perched on "the edge of history" emerging into "a World Federation and a council of beings" with "the centaur anchored in world-centric vision-logic," we're "on the edge of transrational perception, a *Scientia Visionis*." Wilber suggests this is possible if we exercise both the "breakthrough to Nonduality . . . accomplished by Plotinus in the West and Nagarjuna in the East (and not them alone)," and the "evolutionary understanding of Nonduality . . . already won by Schelling in the West and Aurobindo in the East (and not them alone)."

With this type of enlightened and integral vision, Wilber ends his magnum opus by suggesting that the world must awaken to "see Spirit as the Life of Evolution and the Love of the Kosmos itself . . . [where] this Earth becomes a blessed being, and every I becomes a God, and every We becomes God's sincerest worship, and every It becomes God's most gracious temple."

A Brief History of Everything

BY KEN WILBER

(Boston: Shambhala Publications, 1996);

The Collected Works of Ken Wilber, Vol. 7 (CW7) (Shambhala, 2000);

revised paperback edition (Shambhala, 2001)

A Brief History of Everything (1996) is a Wilber/Phase 4 book emphasizing the AQAL all-quadrants, all-levels approach to integral studies, focusing on the developmental "tetra-interaction" (or coevolution) of the Left-Hand interior quadrants with the Right-Hand exterior correlates in the Great Nest of Spirit or Kosmos.

A Brief History of Everything was compiled as a study guide to *Sex, Ecology, Spirituality,* thus it's essentially a condensed version of *SES* set in a conversational or interview format, making it more accessible to a general audience. However, *Brief History* does contribute a number of new ideas not found in *SES,* such as industrial ontology, the culture gap, and a further elaboration of the basic moral intuition.

A Brief History of Everything was published in 1996 (Shambhala Publications); as a revised edition, it is now part of *The Collected Works of Ken Wilber, Volume Seven (CW7),* (Shambhala Publications, 2000); revised paperback edition (Shambhala Publications, 2001).

The "INTRODUCTION" begins with Wilber summarizing "the whole point of evolution: it always goes beyond what went before." Therefore, he concludes, there's "a common evolutionary thread running from matter to life to mind," and these are the "common patterns, or laws, or habits [that] keep repeating themselves in all those domains." Indeed, "Evolution is best thought of as Spirit-in-action, God-in-the-making, where Spirit unfolds itself at every stage of development, thus manifesting more of itself, and realizing more of itself, at every unfolding."

This type of multidimensional evolutionary view can more easily encompass both the Ascending and Descending currents of Spirit. Wilber maintains that this kind of approach can help heal the modern disaster of flatland, or the dominance of the Descenders, the scientific materialists who only affirm "this-world" of material particles. In addition, this overall view can help balance the opposite tendency of the Ascending Path to be "purely transcendental and otherworldly." As an alternative, Wilber's integral vision promotes "both transcendence and immanence, the One and the Many, Emptiness and Form, nirvana and samsara, Heaven and Earth."

Part I. Spirit-in-Action

CHAPTER I. "THE PATTERN THAT CONNECTS" explains that any brief history of everything must be based on "orienting generalizations," which are defined as the broad and general themes of agreement found across many fields of human knowledge. Wilber introduces some new terms, such as *holons* (or whole/parts), *holarchy* (or nested hierarchies), and focuses on the successive levels or embracing domains of the Great Nest of Being or the Kosmos (of cosmos, bios, nous, theos). All holons in the Great Holarchy are governed by basic evolutionary principles that he calls the twenty tenets or "the patterns that connect." (See Figure 1: "The Great Nest of Being: Greater Depth.")

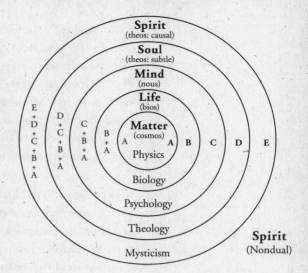

The Great Nest of Being: Greater Depth

FIGURE I

CHAPTER 2. "THE SECRET IMPULSE" is mostly concerned with the unfolding process of developmental evolution, even into the highest stages of self-development. This process, Wilber explains, is evolution's "secret impulse" in that it "transcends and includes." In other words, he claims, this *Telos* is the "basic drive of evolution to increase depth" and it creates a "spectrum of depth, a spectrum of consciousness," reaching all the way to Kosmic consciousness or Enlightenment. This concept of nested realms, Wilber notes, has also been universally recognized and expressed by the perennial philosophy or the "core of the world's wisdom traditions." In essence, Wilber claims, one of evolution's most relevant messages for humanity is "because the universe has direction, we ourselves have direction."

CHAPTER 3. "ALL TOO HUMAN" returns the discussion to the earlier evolutionary stages by highlighting the development of the noosphere or the human mind. Therefore Wilber takes the reader on a brief tour:

- **archaic-foraging epoch** or "the original tribal structure";

- the **agricultural epoch**, including horticulture based on the hoe, which is matrifocal with a magical worldview;

- the **agrarian**, based on the plow, which is a base for patriarchy with its mythic worldview;

- **industrialization**, which supports the rational worldview, and where gender roles began to expand "beyond biological givens."

CHAPTER 4. "THE GREAT POSTMODERN REVOLUTION" first points out that "the great postmodern discovery" began as an "attack" on modernity's "fundamental Enlightenment paradigm," which tends to promote "the mirror of nature, the reflection paradigm." Yet postmodernism also discovered that "worldviews develop—that neither the world nor the self is simply pregiven." Wilber uses his integral model to embrace this important postmodern discovery, emphasizing that the "different stages of consciousness growth present a different view of the world. The world looks different—is different at each stage."

CHAPTER 5. "THE FOUR CORNERS OF THE KOSMOS" introduces Wilber's revolutionary notion of the four quadrants, defined as "the inside and the outside of a holon, in both its individual and collectively forms." He cautions, however, that "We simply cannot reduce these quadrants to each other without profound distortions and violent ruptures." By taking such a comprehensive and integral approach, Wilber presents a way "beyond modernity," a way to "transcend and include modernity—or rational-industrialization." Only then, he suggests, can we create "what we might call sustainable rationality, sustainable industry."

CHAPTER 6. "THE TWO HANDS OF GOD" focuses on the fact that each of the four quadrants, including the interior (or Left-Hand quadrants) and exterior (or Right-Hand quadrants), has a different type of truth. Therefore, a genuine integral approach can only accept, he claims, "an 'all-quadrants' view, an interpretation from the context of the Kosmos in all its dimensions." From a more mystical point of view, Wilber identifies these interior and exterior domains as "the Right and Left Hands of God, how Spirit actually manifests in the world."

CHAPTER 7. "ATTUNED TO THE KOSMOS" considers the different meanings of "truth" or "degree of validity" in each quadrant. Wilber suggests that each quadrant has a corresponding validity claim:

- **propositional truth** (Right-Hand side or "It/Its");

- **truthfulness** (Upper-Left or "I");

- **justness** (Lower-Left or "We");

- **functional fit** (Lower-Right or "Its").

One reason for adopting such an integral view, Wilber explains, is these "validity claims force us to confront reality; they curb our egoic fantasies and self-centered ways; they demand evidence from the rest of the Kosmos; they force us outside of ourselves! They are the checks and balances in the Kosmic Constitution."

CHAPTER 8. "THE GOOD, THE TRUE, AND THE BEAUTIFUL" reduces the four quadrants into the Big Three of I, We, and It. Each domain essentially has its own "language":

- **"It-language"** (the Right-Hand side) or "the True" (science); the Dharma;

- **"I-language"** (the Upper-Left quadrant) or "the Beautiful" (art); the Buddha;

- **"We-language"** (the Lower-Left quadrant) or "the Good" (morals); the Sangha.

Thus these three general domains of the Big Three also correspond to Plato's "the Good (morals, the 'We'), the True (objective truths of 'Its'), the Beautiful (aesthetics . . . perceived by each 'I')." From the East he correlates these with the Three Jewels of Buddhism, i.e., the *dharma, sangha,* and Buddha, respectively, or what he calls "the Spiritual Big Three."

Wilber then goes on to explain that this "differentiation of the Big Three" of "art, morals, and science, or self, culture, and nature" was the good news or the "Dignity of Modernity." The bad news or the "Disaster of Modernity, on the other hand, is the dissociation of the Big Three, such as with scientific materialism. The task of postmodernity, he argues, involves integrating the Big Three, but without "regressing to mythic or magic indissociation." Only this type of integral approach, Wilber posits, can "honor science and morals and aesthetic equally and not simply reduce one to the other."

Part II. The Further Reaches of Spirit-in-Action

CHAPTER 9. "THE EVOLUTION OF CONSCIOUSNESS," primarily focuses on "the Upper-Left Quadrant, the interior stages of consciousness evolution." In this case, the ladder metaphor of ladder, climber, and view, while limited, can still be useful in explaining the fulcrums of self-development since the climber on each rung or stage of consciousness sees "a different view of self and other—a different Worldview."

Wilber maintains that a psychopathology results when "some aspects of the climber . . . get stuck at lower rungs." It is essential that all pathologies be addressed and healed, since the "genuinely spiritual or transpersonal stages of development depend for their development upon all the previous developments." Wilber therefore calls for the use of both a "depth" and "height" psychology, in view of the fact that "for the first time in history, we have access to both Freud and Buddha."

Chapter 10. "On the Way to Global: Part 1" traces the early stages in the developmental journey of the self, fulcrum by fulcrum, from

- **Fulcrum-0** or the basic perinatal matrices (BPM) to

- **Fulcrum-1** or the physical self to

- **Fulcrum-2** or the emotional self to

- **Fulcrum-3** or the conceptual self to

- **Fulcrum-4** or the rule/role self (continued)

Wilber explains in detail that each fulcrum of development has a corresponding pathology (birth trauma, psychosis, narcissism, psychoneuroses), and worldview (the primary matrix, archaic, magical, and mythical). In addition, he also stresses that there's often "retro-reading," or the tendency to erroneously look back at lower levels from higher or more developed levels, and thereby "distort what was actually occurring in the earlier periods [or fulcrums]."

Chapter 11. "On the Way to Global: Part 2" continues the self's developmental journey by first acknowledging that "the Telos of human development is towards less and less egocentric states," thus it's an important form of "transcendence of the shallower, a disclosure of the deeper." Wilber then moves on to

- **Fulcrum-4** or the sociocentric rule/role mind to

- **Fulcrum-5** or the worldcentric mature ego to

- **Fulcrum-6** or the centaur in vision-logic or network-logic, which is the realm of the authentic existential life (and also existential dread).

Chapter 12. "Realms of the Superconscious: Part 1" begins with Wilber reiterating that with the stage of the integrated centaur, consciousness is beginning to witness or observe the mind as an object, thus it begins to enter into the realms of the transpersonal or superconscious awareness. These higher stages, he emphasizes, will only unfold by engaging the "developed practices or injunctions or paradigms that would disclose these higher worldspaces." Wilber then considers:

- **Fulcrum-7** or the psychic realm of nature mysticism and the "World-Soul" or "Eco-Noetic Self" to

- **Fulcrum-8** or the subtle realm of deity mysticism and the true archetypes, thus here Wilber critiques Jung's collectively inherited images.

CHAPTER 13. "REALMS OF THE SUPERCONSCIOUS: PART 2" confirms that this process of transpersonal self-development is not just mere metaphysics because it's an imperative that you "perform the experiment and look at the data yourself." Wilber therefore continues with:

- **Fulcrum-9** or the causal domain of formless mysticism or "Emptiness" and the witness to

- **Fulcrum-10** or the nondual and nondual mysticism, which is impossible to describe, therefore Wilber reflects upon and repeats the essential wisdom of the nondual traditions: "Form is Emptiness and Emptiness is Form."

Indeed, the integral psychologist clarifies, to truly understand this paradoxical truth a person must practice and experience Enlightenment for oneself—yet at the same time, paradoxically, "you cannot engineer a way to get closer to God, for there is only God—the radical secret of the Nondual schools."

Part III. Flatland

CHAPTER 14. "ASCENDING AND DESCENDING" gives a brief précis of the previous chapters, thus recapitulating the brief history of evolution or Spirit-in-action, which, Wilber now reveals, can be seen as two principal currents: the Ascending or transcendent aspect, the "otherworldly" direction, and the Descending or immanent aspect, the "this-worldly" path.

These currents are the "faces" of God, according to Wilber, and they're represented traditionally, for example, by Plato's "two gods," Plotinus' Reflex (ascent) and Efflux (descent), the spiritual ideas of Eros (ascent) and Agape (descent), wisdom (ascent) and compassion (descent), *prajna* (ascended wisdom) and *karuna* (descended compassion), and with God (or the masculine face of Spirit) and the Goddess (or the feminine face of Spirit). Yet ultimately, the main point is to unite them both "in the nondual Heart of One Taste [which] is the source and ground of genuine spirituality."

CHAPTER 15. "THE COLLAPSE OF THE KOSMOS" explains both sides of modernity (via "the dialectic of progress") by reviewing the "Good News" or "the Dignity of Modernity," which includes the differentiation of the Big Three that liberated self, culture, and nature from being dominated by the others. This is contrasted with the "Bad News" or "the Disaster of Modernity," which includes the dissociation of the Big Three, especially when the exterior material domains dominate interior consciousness. This dissociation, according to Wilber, has generated for the modern worldview a descended grid of Flatland, which itself promotes an industrial ontology.

CHAPTER 16. "THE EGO AND THE ECO" contrasts and correlates the two opposing sides of modernity (its dignities or "good news" and disasters or "bad news") with the metaphors of the Ascending ego, which reflects "the fundamental Enlightenment paradigm," the "representational paradigm," or "the mirror of nature," and the Descending "Eco," expressed by the "Eco-Romantic rebellion."

Wilber's integral approach criticizes both programs of modernity, but especially the retro-Romantic or the Eco's tendency to send its "Way Back Machine" off in search of a Paradise Lost somewhere in the distant past. In actuality, Wilber maintains, the only hope is to unite them both and put an end to this "two-thousand-year-old battle at the heart of the West's attempt to awaken."

CHAPTER 17. "THE DOMINANCE OF THE DESCENDERS" suggests that an integral philosophy, such as the Idealist philosophy of Schelling's God-in-the-making or Spirit-in-action, is the only way to fully unite and integrate the modern discovery of evolution with the premodern emphasis on the Great Chain of Being. However, Wilber warns that there must be viable transpersonal practices to promote further development or the evolution of consciousness, otherwise, such noble theories will be condemned to be mere metaphysics, as was the case with the Idealists, who espoused the philosophy but had "no yoga."

CHAPTER 18. "THE UNPACKING OF GOD" maintains the critical importance of our spiritual intuitions being "adequately interpreted" or "unpacked" since only this approach will assist in their proper and healthy integration. Therefore, Wilber insists that all epochs (foraging, horticulture, agrarian, industrial, informational) must be constantly transcended yet included.

This is accomplished in part by encouraging an appropriate environmental ethics, which recognizes that all holons are anchored in the "equal Ground value" of Spirit. Then they include the rights of a holon based on its wholeness or autonomy (agency), balanced appropriately with the responsibilities of a holon based on its "partness" or communion with the whole.

According to Wilber, it's then possible to better exercise what he calls the *basic moral intuition* (BPM), which is "to protect and promote the greatest depth for the greatest span." Only this type of integral approach will help integrate "consciousness, culture, and nature [or the Big Three], and thus find room for art, morals, and science—for personal values, for collective wisdom, and for technical knowhow." With this integral vision, this genuine embracing of reality, Wilber reminds us "There in the Heart, where the couple finally unite, the entire game is undone, this nightmare of evolution, and you are exactly where you were prior to the beginning of the whole show."

CHAPTER 14

The Eye of Spirit

An Integral Vision for a World Gone Slightly Mad

BY KEN WILBER

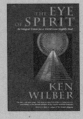

(Boston: Shambhala Publications, 1997; paperback edition, 1998);

The Collected Works of Ken Wilber, Vol. 7 (CW7) (Shambhala, 2000);

revised paperback edition (Shambhala, 2001)

Foreword by Jack Crittenden: What Is the Meaning of "Integral"?
A Note to the Reader: On God and Politics
Introduction: The Integral Vision: The Good, the True, and the Beautiful

The Eye of Spirit: An Integral Vision for a World Gone Slightly Mad (1997) is a Wilber/Phase 4 work emphasizing the AQAL approach to integral studies, focusing on the developmental tetra-interaction (or coevolution) of the Left-Hand interior quadrants with the Right-Hand exterior correlates in the Great Nest of Spirit or Kosmos.

The Eye of Spirit is a collection of essays, compiled and in some instances written in late 1996, some of which were in response to a series of articles that had appeared in *ReVision* (summer 1996), and that critiqued Wilber's work, often with an ideological bias. The new essays, therefore, included segments from recent introductions to reprinted books, articulating a more scholarly and detailed integral approach to the evolving four-quadrant Kosmos (including the spectrum of consciousness), while simultaneously offering a well-developed post-postmodern critical theory.

The Eye of Spirit: An Integral Vision for a World Gone Slightly Mad was published in 1997 (Shambhala Publications); paperback edition, (Shambhala Publications, 1998); as a revised edition, it is now part of *The Collected Works of Ken Wilber, Volume Seven (CW7),* (Shambhala Publications, 2000); revised paperback edition (Shambhala Publications, 2001).

A NOTE TO THE READER: "ON GOD AND POLITICS" presents Ken Wilber's views on how to integrate "the tradition of liberalism with a genuine spirituality," thus suggesting a spiritual humanism and integral vision where "integral means integrative, inclusive, comprehensive, balanced; the idea is to apply this integral orientation to the various fields of human knowledge and endeavors, including the integration of science and spirituality."

INTRODUCTION: "THE INTEGRAL VISION: THE GOOD, THE TRUE, AND THE BEAUTIFUL" summarizes Wilber's integral vision by introducing the four quadrants or the 1) interior and 2) exterior of the 3) individual and the 4) collective, which are modeled as holons situated within a holarchy manifesting as the Great Nest of Spirit at various levels. Therefore Wilber promotes the idea that integral studies must include the various "differentiations of modernity," which he characterizes as the Big Three, i.e., art, morals, and science, or self, culture, and nature, and which are expressed as "I," "we," "it," as well as the "three eyes of knowing," i.e., flesh, mind, and contemplation. (See Figure 1: "The Four Faces of Truth:

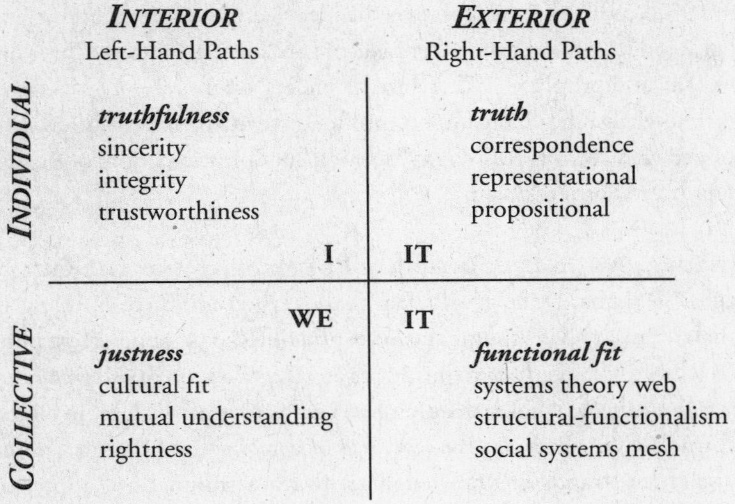

	INTERIOR Left-Hand Paths	**EXTERIOR** Right-Hand Paths
INDIVIDUAL	*truthfulness* sincerity integrity trustworthiness **I**	*truth* correspondence representational propositional **IT**
COLLECTIVE	**WE** *justness* cultural fit mutual understanding rightness	**IT** *functional fit* systems theory web structural-functionalism social systems mesh

Four Faces of Truth:
Validity Claims
FIGURE 1

Validity Claims") Wilber attempts this integration in order to present a master template depicting an expanded spectrum of consciousness situated within the four quadrants, which is therefore even capable of rectifying the "glaring deficiencies" of the premodern wisdom traditions or the perennial philosophy.

CHAPTER 1. "THE SPECTRUM OF CONSCIOUSNESS: INTEGRAL PSYCHOLOGY AND THE PERENNIAL PHILOSOPHY" updates some of the considerations first raised in *The Atman Project* in addition to including Wilber's new Foreword to the second edition. The chapter includes an essay originally titled "The Great Chain of Being" (in *Paths Beyond Ego,* Walsh and Vaughan, 1993). First Wilber appeals to the perennial philosophy, giving a few examples, to explain the tenet traditionally known as the Great Chain of Being, which represents the holonic nature of the Kosmos. Wilber once again affirms the significance of the pre/trans fallacy, and especially the role of involution and evolution, in defining the Atman project, in other words, the misguided but natural "attempt to find Spirit in ways that prevent it and force substitute gratifications."

CHAPTER 2. "IN A MODERN LIGHT: INTEGRAL ANTHROPOLOGY AND THE EVOLUTION OF CULTURES" updates some of the considerations first presented in *Up From Eden,* in addition to including the new Foreword to the second edition (1996), as well as including an article originally titled "The Neo-Perennial Philosophy" (first published in *The American Theosophist,* fall 1983, and *The Quest,* autumn 1992). Wilber's view promotes the idea that there is both an Ancient Wisdom that is indeed timeless and perennial, and an "ancient wisdom" that's only the "old, archaic, and primitive." Therefore he prefers a *neo-perennial philosophy* that would acknowledge the vitally important modern evidence of evolution, which in an expanded view sees the Kosmos as "nothing but Spirit-in-action, or the stages of Spirit's return to Spirit as Spirit."

CHAPTER 3. "EYE TO EYE: INTEGRAL PHILOSOPHY AND THE QUEST FOR THE REAL" is primarily the new Preface to the revised edition of *Eye to Eye* (1996, Shambhala), thus it reviews some the main principles of that book (first published in 1983) while updating them to introduce an integral vision or *integral studies* and an *integral philosophy* (whose "defining heart is the love of wisdom, in all its wondrous forms"). Wilber revisits the *three eyes of knowing* (flesh, mind, contemplation), the three strands of knowledge verification (injunction, apprehension, verification) in order to solve the "problem of proof." He also argues for the necessity to "engage the spiritual injunction," such as by meditation, since "in the smoking ruins that Kant left, the only possible conclusion is that all future metaphysics, to be genuine, must offer direct experiential evidence and data of the spiritual domain itself."

CHAPTER 4. "INTEGRAL ART AND LITERARY THEORY: PART 1" addresses how the integral approach can be effectively and pragmatically applied to such mental disciplines as art and literary criticism. By doing so, Wilber shows his mastery of postmodern philosophy, including interpretative hermeneutics, as well as presenting an insightful history of Western art and critical theory, and suggesting how they can all be included in the integral vision.

CHAPTER 5. "INTEGRAL ART AND LITERARY THEORY: PART 2" presents an example of how the process of art (or literary) interpretation and criticism can be accomplished in an integral manner since "an integral or holonic theory of art interpretation and literary criticism would include all of these various realms of the human unconsciousness." Wilber points out that "human intentionality is indeed 'onionlike': holons within holons of intentionality in an extraordinary spectrum of consciousness."

CHAPTER 6. "THE RECAPTURED GOD: THE RETRO-ROMANTIC AGENDA AND ITS FATAL FLAWS" is Wilber's answer to the criticisms and work of Michael Washburn and to the retro-Romantics in general. He does this mostly by underlining the need for an integral psychology at least to acknowledge the differences between:

THE EYE OF SPIRIT

- **basic structures**, which are the permanent, enduring structures;

- **transitional structures**, the temporary structures, such as worldviews, self-needs, moral stages, etc.;

- **self-system**, the self and "locus of identification" or simply "where the action is";

- **states of consciousness**, which are waking, dreaming, and deep sleep.

Wilber's integral psychology maintains that as the self undertakes its journey through the milestones of growth, or the *fulcrums of self-development,* it is critically necessary to precisely follow and model this overall development so as to make accurate distinctions between prepersonal and transpersonal phenomena and thus avoid pre/trans fallacies.

CHAPTER 7. "BORN AGAIN: STAN GROF AND THE HOLOTROPIC MIND" features Wilber's response to the work of Stanislav Grof and his holotropic paradigm, as well as to Grof's inaccurate critique of Wilber's work. In the process Wilber does concede the relative importance of Grof's basic perinatal matrices (BPMs), however Wilber maintains that in a developmental or involutionary/evolutionary view, Grof's concepts can possibly be better interpreted as an interplay between the "Frontal (Ego) and Deeper Psychic (Soul)" lines of development.

CHAPTER 8. "INTEGRAL FEMINISM: SEX AND GENDER ON THE MORAL AND SPIRITUAL PATH" provides Wilber with a platform to reply to a critique of his work by Peggy Wright (who, he believes tends, "to distort [his] overall view") in order to offer some ways that an *integral feminism* "can actually command the respect of both male and female theoreticians." Wilber shows an impressive command of feminist literature and research, situating each within the four quadrants. Nevertheless, he still concludes that "men and women both move through three broad hierarchical stages of Moral Development": the preconventional, conventional, and postconventional stages, or what Wilber has termed the egocentric, sociocentric, and worldcentric. This is especially true, he points out, because "genuine female mystics" have always claimed that "women, just like men, face years, and often decades, of blood, sweat, tears, and toil, in order to claim their birthright [of enlightenment]."

CHAPTER 9. "HOW STRAIGHT IS THE SPIRITUAL PATH? THE RELATION OF PSYCHOLOGICAL AND SPIRITUAL GROWTH" incorporates a review of the theoretical problems with Jenny Wade's *Changes of Mind* (1997), which, Wilber points out, is unfortunately based upon "David Bohm's extremely confused notions of implicate/explicate . . . a monological nightmare." Wilber is especially critical of this type of approach, since, as even Wade concedes, there is an "overall development unfolding" of a multilayered spectrum of consciousness. Any truly integral model, therefore, must include perhaps seventeen levels (or waves), "more than a dozen developmental lines" (or streams), the various states of consciousness, and a self-system (or "the poor lonely self") who is the "balancing act . . . at the center of the various streams and waves, levels and lines, structures and stages and states."

CHAPTER 10. "THE EFFECTS OF MEDITATION: SPEEDING UP THE ASCENT TO GOD AND THE DESCENT OF THE GODDESS" provides an appreciative consideration of the work of Harvard psychologist Charles Alexander and colleagues in order to discuss the role and effects of meditation in accelerating self development, especially into the transpersonal domains. In doing so, Wilber addresses the important question of whether "psychological development [is] necessary for spiritual development." Wilber affirms that any *integral transformative practice* (or ITP, after Michael Murphy and George Leonard) would, at the very least, put an equal emphasis on both body and mind at each and every stage of general evolution, gross bodymind to subtle bodymind to causal bodymind."

CHAPTER 11. "HEADING TOWARD OMEGA? WHERE EXACTLY IS THE GROUND OF BEING?" addresses some central issues brought up in various reviews and critiques of *Sex, Ecology, Spirituality.* In doing so, Wilber deprecates the Jungian notion of archetypes, which he claims would be better called *prototypes.* Wilber is therefore in agreement with Assagioli—an integral pioneer in his own right—that a distinction needs to be made between both "depth" (or prepersonal) and "height" (or transpersonal) psychologies. Such an approach will arrive at an integral theory of consciousness, one that should be based on the fact that consciousness is actually an all-level, all-quadrant affair.

CHAPTER 12. "ALWAYS ALREADY: THE BRILLIANT CLARITY OF EVER-PRESENT AWARENESS" reveals that the primary "realization of the nondual traditions is uncompromising: there is only Spirit, there is only God, there is only Emptiness in all its radiant wonder," and it is this enlightened awareness that "undoes the Great Search that is the heart of the separate-self sense." Thus Wilber suggests that when "the intrinsic potentials of the enlightened mind (the intrinsic potentials of your ever-present awareness) . . . combine with the native disposition and particular talents of your own individual bodymind . . . you are then motivated, not by the Great Search, but by the Gentle Compassion of these potentials."

CHAPTER 15

The Marriage of Sense and Soul

Integrating Science and Religion

BY KEN WILBER

(New York: Random House, 1998);

audio cassette (Audio Renaissance, 1998); paperback edition (Random House, 1999);

The Collected Works of Ken Wilber, Vol. 8 (CW8) (Boston: Shambhala Publications, 2000)

The Marriage of Sense and Soul: Integrating Science and Religion (1998) is a Wilber/ Phase 4 work that uses an AQAL, all-quadrants, all-levels, approach in order to explain how both science and religion or authentic spirituality can be integrated with the modern and postmodern worldview, therefore focusing on the developmental tetra-interaction (or coevolution) of the Left-Hand interior quadrants with the Right-Hand exterior correlates in the Great Nest of Spirit or Kosmos.

The Marriage of Sense and Soul was finished in the late fall of 1996 and originally titled *The Integration of Science and Religion: The Union of Ancient Wisdom and Modern Knowledge.* This two-hundred-page book was aimed at an audience of mainstream religious and scientific communities, not the New Age, new-paradigm crowd.

The Marriage of Sense and Soul: Integrating Science and Religion was first published in 1998 (Random House); audio cassette (Audio Renaissance, 1998); paperback edition (Random House, 1999); it is now part of *The Collected Works of Ken Wilber, Volume Eight (CW8),* (Shambhala Publications, 2000).

"A NOTE TO THE READER" introduces a "philosophical cold war of global reach" between science or the *scientific method* (which offers "value-free" facts or truth) and *religion* (which offers "value-laden meaning" or wisdom). Wilber explains that in the modern world both science and religion are locked in "a strange and grotesque coexistence, with value-free science and value-laden religion, deeply distrustful of each other, aggressively attempting to colonize the same small planet," especially true since "for literally billions of people around the world, religion provides the basic meaning of their lives." Therefore, in "integrating science and religion," Wilber's "primary prerequisite is that *both* science and religion must find the argument [for integration] acceptable in their own terms. For this marriage to be genuine, it must have the free consent of both spouses."

Part I. The Problem

CHAPTER I. "THE CHALLENGE OF OUR TIMES: INTEGRATING SCIENCE AND RELIGION" recognizes that since science discovers *truth* and religion generates *meaning,* then they "are at war in today's world." Wilber then introduces the core claim of spirituality or the premodern religious worldview as being the Great

Chain of Being or the Great Nest of Spirit, "a rich tapestry of interwoven levels, reaching from matter to body to mind to soul to spirit."

He then clarifies that the central claim of modernity is the "differentiation of the value spheres," which are defined as self, culture, and nature or art, morals, and science. This is the "good news" or the "dignity" of modernity, whereas the "bad news" or the "disaster" of modernity is its "dissociation, fragmentation, alienation," ending in a pathological "flatland" of scientific materialism (scientism). In this event, the integral theorist is out to demonstrate that the only way to "unite the best of premodern wisdom with the brightest of modern knowledge" is "to integrate the Great Chain of Being with the differentiations of modernity."

CHAPTER 2. "A DEADLY DANCE: THE RELATION OF SCIENCE AND RELIGION IN TODAY'S WORLD" reflects on the "antagonistic dance" between science and religion with Wilber defining "four or five major stances toward the relation of science and religion." These range from the fact that "science denies any validity to religion" to "religion denies any validity to science," from "plausibility arguments" to the "postmodern/paradigm," etc. In the end, the integral theorist declares that they're all inadequate, especially since, as he explained earlier, "The only way we can possibly integrate science and religion is by integrating the Great Chain with the major differentiations of modernity."

The integral approach, however, supports one of the "more sophisticated of the alternatives," which is basically some form of *epistemological pluralism* that uses at least three eyes of knowing:

1. the **eye of flesh** (empiricism);

2. the **eye of mind** (rationalism);

3. the eye of contemplation (mysticism) or the **eye of spirit**.

or even more levels, such as using five eyes: "material prehension, bodily emotion, mental ideas, the soul's archetypal cognition, and spiritual gnosis." Yet science, in this view, is usually "placed on the bottom rung of the great hierarchy," which is plainly not acceptable (especially since science doesn't even acknowledge the higher levels). Thus, perhaps the best solution is "in a more sophisticated integration, each of those levels (sensory, mental, spiritual) is also divided according to the differentiations of modernity (art, morals, and science)." This produces a "sensory science, mental science, spiritual science," so that "science is not under but alongside [religion], and this profoundly reorients the knowledge quest, placing premodernity and modernity hand in hand in the quest for the real, and thus bringing science and religion together in a most intimate embrace."

CHAPTER 3. "PARADIGMS: A WRONG TURN" examines in detail the fact that the popular use of Thomas Kuhn's word *paradigm* (from his groundbreaking book *The Structure of Scientific Revolutions,* 1962) is usually misinterpreted, and thus misapplied by many new-paradigm or New Age theorists. Wilber therefore argues that the new paradigm and postmodern theorists will never be able to integrate science and religion since they enact a "performative contradiction" or are "self-contradictory." They also are "monological to the core" (whether atomistic or holistic) and fail to realize that "all interpretations are not equally valid," the postmodern error.

Indeed, Wilber emphasizes, since real paradigms are "grounded in injunctions, exemplars, and social practices," then there must be a "demand for evidence—or validity claims" which, he continues, "simply means that one's ego cannot impose on the universe a view of reality that finds no support from the universe itself. The validity claims and evidence are the ways in which we attune ourselves to the Kosmos. The validity claims force us to confront reality; they curb our egoic fantasies and self-centered ways; they demand evidence from the rest of the Kosmos; they force us outside of ourselves! They are the checks and balances in the Kosmic Constitution."

Wilber again turns to the four levels (body, mind, soul, and spirit) with their four modes of knowing (sensory, mental, archetypal, and mystical), which can be shortened to the three eyes of knowing: the "languages" of the *monological* (eye of flesh), the *dialogical* (eye of reason), and the *translogical* (eye of contemplation). Therefore, unlike the new-paradigm theorists, the integral approach will definitely not "reduce translogical religion to a new monological paradigm," but rather expose all the eyes of knowing "to the differentiations of modernity (the differentiation of the value spheres of art, morals, and science)."

CHAPTER 4. "MODERNITY: DIGNITY AND DISASTER" defines what is generally meant by modernity or the clear "differentiation of the value spheres of Art, Morals, and Science," and the various trends in philosophy, art, science, cultural cognition, personal identity, political and civil rights, technology, and politics. On the other hand, postmodernity is distinguished in its narrow and extreme forms, such as the exaggerated "notion that there is no truth, only interpretations, and all interpretations are socially constructed." Wilber also identifies some of modernity's myriad of critics, such as the "premodern revivalist 'paradigm,'" the "postmodern 'paradigm,'" and the "global systems 'paradigm,'" yet he claims the key to modernity lies in the distinction "between differentiation and dissociation."

Wilber then goes into detail in regard to the "dignity of modernity" or the differentiation of the three value spheres, which range from "the Good, the True, and the Beautiful" (after Plato), to the languages of "We" (moral-ethical), "It" (objective-science), and "I" (expressive-aesthetic). He also gives a diagnosis of modernity's pathological "dissociation of the cultural value spheres," which he calls the disaster of modernity since, "put bluntly, the I and WE were colonized by the IT." This "scientific materialism" or "scientism" involves "the collapse of the Kosmos" into "Flatland" where, metaphorically speaking, "art and morals and contemplation and spirit were all demolished by the scientific bull in the china shop of consciousness." The integral theorist prescribes: "The cure for the disaster of modernity is to address the dissociation, not attempt to erase the differentiation."

CHAPTER 5. "THE FOUR CORNERS OF THE KNOWN UNIVERSE" suggests that the best way to escape the reductionistic disaster of modernity is to fully acknowledge not only the exteriors (Right-Hand side) but also the interiors (or Left-Hand side) of the Kosmos. These are the four types of hierarchies or "four faces of the Kosmos" or the four quadrants which "simply deal with the interior and the exterior of the individual and the collective."

Wilber's thesis is that these four quadrants correlate exactly with the differentiations of modernity or the "Big Three: I (Upper-Left), We (Lower-Left), It (Right Hand)" or the domains of art, morals, and science, respectively. He points out that modernity's disaster known as Flatland is precisely when "the Left-Hand or interior dimensions were reduced to their Right-Hand or exterior correlates" or simply when "Left collapsed to Right." This is what creates the great need for an integration since "unless we can find a way for *both* of those claims to be true—the transcendental and the empirical, the interior and the exterior—we will never genuinely integrate science and religion."

Part II. Previous Attempts at Integration

CHAPTER 6. "THE REENCHANTMENT OF THE WORLD" examines some of the recent attempts to resurrect the interior holons or "the interior dimensions of the Kosmos" which scientific materialism had "gutted and laid out to dry in the blazing sun of the monological gaze." Yet, since "the moment of truth of the scientific approach—a truth utterly lacking in premodern worldviews and among the Great Chain theorists—was that every Left-Hand event does indeed have a Right-Hand correlate," Wilber claims that when science "collapses the Left [interior] to the Right [exterior]" it also "likewise collapses *quality* to *quantity*, value to veneer, interior to exterior, depth to surface, dignity to disaster."

In reaction, Wilber outlines the postmodern revolt against flatland, beginning with the work of Immanuel Kant (1724–1804) and his three critiques, which address the Big Three of art, morals, and science. Kant was the first philosopher to fight against this modern collapse, as well as influencing the other four camps of subsequent Western philosophy: Romanticism, Idealism, Postmodern Poststructuralism, and Integralism, all of which will be examined independently in the following chapters.

CHAPTER 7. "ROMANTICISM: RETURN OF THE ORIGIN" considers the Romantic movement and its positive contributions, although, as Wilber complains, in their noble quest to return to nature they "often ended up recommending *anything* nonrational, including many things that were frankly prerational, regressive, egocentric, and narcissistic." This is because, according to the integral theorist, they succumbed to the *pre/trans fallacy*. To correct this confusion is to understand "the overall arc of consciousness evolution" from "prepersonal to personal to transpersonal" or "id to ego to God."

Wilber critiques the view of the Romantics or the retro-Romantics, such as ecofeminists or ecomasculinists, who want to ride their "Regress Express" or "Way Back Machine" to a premodern primal paradise. However, because "premodern societies . . . were largely *pre*-differentiated, not trans-differentiated," Wilber argues that "they cannot serve as cogent models for the integration of the Big Three." Instead, like the Idealists, "it is to tomorrow, not yesterday, that our vision must be turned. . . . The God of tomorrow, not the God of yesteryear, comes to announce our liberation."

CHAPTER 8. "IDEALISM: THE GOD THAT IS TO COME" is a fascinating account of the nineteenth-century "Idealist Vision [which] was alive to the currents of development (or evolution)," unlike the tenets of premodern religion, which always tended to see that "history is devolution" or a "Fall" from the Source and Origin. To counter this, the Idealists, such as Fichte, Schelling, and Hegel, accurately suggested that nature was more like "slumbering Spirit" since "Spirit evolves from objective Nature to subjective Mind." This Spirit-in-action or God-in-the-making (after Schelling) was a "lustrous vision [that] saw the entire universe—atoms to cells to organisms to societies, cultures, minds, and souls—as the radiant unfolding of a luminous Spirit, bright and brilliant in its way, never-ending in its liberating grace."

Nonetheless, as Wilber points out, the Idealists "possessed no yoga—that is, no tried and tested practice for reliably reproducing the transpersonal and superconscious insights that formed the very core of the great Idealist vision," therefore "the glory of the vision" was relegated to "mere metaphysics." In addition, with the

"continuing collapse of the Kosmos . . . under the reign of it-science . . . combi
with it-industrialization," then "the Left-Hand interior dimensions were being r.
idly colonized and enslaved by the aggressive Right-Hand domains." Thus, '
short, the Big Three were rudely collapsed into the Big One of material monism
The integral approach, however, based on an understanding and acceptance of sc
ence, evolution, and religion (or authentic spirituality), fully recognizes and a
knowledges that "one of the crucial ingredients in any integration of science an
religion is the integration of empirical evolution with transcendental Spirit."

CHAPTER 9. "POSTMODERNISM: TO DECONSTRUCT THE WORLD" explains
that the postmodern movement was "attempting to undermine science in its own
foundations," since Romanticism and Idealism had both failed "by arguing for
higher modes of knowing." Postmodernity, then, did this by clearly recognizing
and proving that "interpretation is an intrinsic feature of the fabric of the universe."
However, as Wilber quickly notes, their "moment of truth . . . was taken to absurd
and self-defeating extremes." Nevertheless, he embraces the need to acknowledge
their "important truths," especially after the "linguistic turn in philosophy" of
Saussure where "language speaks," leading to the "postmodern poststructuralists,"
reviewed in depth:

- **constructivism**, which says that reality is not simply given but is
  a construction;

- **contextualism**, which says that "meaning is context-dependent";

- **integral-aperspectival** awareness or vision-logic, which maintains that
  "cognition must privilege no single perspective."

Unfortunately, as Wilber points out, with most postmodern movements
"depth takes a vacation" so there's "no value, no meaning, and no qualitative distinctions of any sort," which creates a "disenchanted" modern world that's thrown
into "the twilight zone known as the disqualified universe." In other words, with a
postmodern philosophy promoting "no within, no deep," people can be lost forever in what Wilber calls aperspectival madness, "the contradictory belief that no
belief is better than any other—a total paralysis of thought, will, and action in the
face of a million perspectives all given exactly the same depth, namely, zero."
Nonetheless, he still optimistically concludes the only way out is "to introduce the
within, the deep, the interior of the Kosmos, the contours of the Divine."

Part III. A Reconciliation

CHAPTER 10. "THE WITHIN: A VIEW OF THE DEEP" proclaims that since "a modern and postmodern spirituality has continued to elude us," if there's to be a true integration of science and religion then "spirituality must be able to stand up to scientific authority." In order to do this, Wilber suggests that "spirituality must be able to integrate the Big Three values spheres of Self, Culture, and Nature, not merely attempt to dedifferentiate them in a premodern slide or deconstruct them in a postmodern blast." He therefore continues: "The integral approach attempts just that—an integration, just as they are, of the Big Three. . . . All that is required is that each begin to harbor the suspicion that its truth is not the only truth in the Kosmos."

In other words, Wilber suggests, by fully taking into account "the compelling evidence for the existence of all Four Quadrants, which themselves have an enormous amount of data," and by relying on the scientific method's three basic strands of knowing (injunction, apprehension, confirmation/rejection), "it can be shown that the genuine interior modes of knowing also follow these same three strands." Since science is correct but only partial, then the best way for there to be a viable "resurrection of the interior" is for science to move beyond "the myth of the given, the myth that the sensorimotor world is simply given to us in direct experience and that science carefully and systematically reports what it finds there." Yet science will still "investigate the interiors" because "interior spaces and structures . . . can be investigated in their own right." Therefore "science [as scientism] cannot reject a mode of knowing merely because it is interior." It's this type of integral approach that will permit "an opening to the deep."

CHAPTER 11. "WHAT IS SCIENCE?" answers this question by calling for a real science, or one that would use "a methodology that could legitimate the interiors with as much confidence as the exteriors." Then, after assessing the scientific method and the two types of empiricism, i.e., very broad and very narrow, Wilber defines the "essential aspects of scientific inquiry," which are based upon the three strands of valid knowledge:

- an **instrumental injunction** or "an actual practice, an exemplar, a paradigm, an experiment, an ordinance";

- a **direct apprehension** or "a direct experience or apprehension of data";

- **communal confirmation** (or rejection) or "a checking of the results . . . with others who have adequately completed the injunctive and apprehensive strands."

Wilber shows that these three strands also relate to

1. "the strength of empiricism" by being grounded in evidence;

2. to Thomas Kuhn's notion of paradigms or exemplars, which are grounded in "an actual practice, an injunction," and to

3. Sir Karl Popper's "falsifiability principle," which is "operative in every domain, sensory to mental to spiritual."

The integral theorist suggests that if science and religion will each "give a little," then real science must "expand from narrow empiricism (sensory experience only) to broad empiricism (direct experience in general)," and real religion "must open its truth claims to direct verification—or rejection—by experiential evidence . . . [and therefore] engage the three strands of all valid knowledge and anchor its claims in direct experience."

When this is all taken into account, Wilber concludes: "science and religion would fast be approaching a common grounding in experiential data that finds the existence of rocks, mathematics, and Spirit equally demonstrable."

CHAPTER 12. "WHAT IS RELIGION?" looks at "real religion" by first offering Wilber's strong critique of the mythological element still present in most religions, the leftovers from the premodern era (and the mythic level of consciousness), which shrinks from any sort of actual evidence and validity claims. In addition, he claims that "Mythology will not stand up to the irreversible differentiations of modernity; it confuses prerational with transrational; it fosters regressive ethical and cognitive modes," therefore, in conclusion: "If religion is to survive in a viable form in the modern world, it must be willing to jettison its bogus claims, just as narrow science must be willing to jettison its reductionistic imperialism."

In other words, the integral approach is "claiming that when it comes to a modern science of spirituality (a science of direct spiritual experience and data), those mythological themes—and mythology itself—will form no essential part of authentic spirituality." As he explains, with the integral approach "Real science and real religion are actually allied against . . . bogus science and bogus religion [which] means each camp must jettison its narrow and/or dogmatic remnants, and thus accept a more accurate self-concept, a more accurate image of its own estate."

Counter to mythic religion, Wilber argues that *authentic spirituality* "can no longer be mythic, imaginal, mythological, or mythopoetic: it must be based on falsifiable evidence . . . it must be, at its core, a series of direct mystical, transcendental, meditative, contemplative, or yogic experiences." In other words, these spiritual experiences also need to be "rigorously subjected to the three strands of all valid knowledge." Next, in a synopsis of the "contemplative core" of religion, Wilber points out that "religion's great, enduring, and unique strength is that, at its core, it is a science of spiritual experience (using 'science' in the broad sense as direct experience, in any domain, that submits to the three strands of injunction, data, and falsifiability)." In fact, this is exactly what the actual "founders of the great traditions," or the major world religions, gave to their disciples: "not a series of mythological or dogmatic beliefs but a series of practices, injunctions, or exemplars," or more simply, "if you want to know this Divine union, you must do this."

Wilber therefore emphasizes that "in the spiritual sciences, the exemplar, the injunction, the paradigm, the practice is: meditation or contemplation." It's through this type of "training in spiritual science" that the "the eye of contemplation" is opened as a person becomes "adequate to the injunction." This process is exactly what demonstrates the real "proof of God's existence" since, as Wilber confides: "The great and secret message of the experimental mystics the world over is that, with the eye of contemplation, Spirit can be seen. With the eye of contemplation, God can be seen. With the eye of contemplation, the great Within radiantly unfolds."

CHAPTER 13. "THE STUNNING DISPLAY OF SPIRIT" affirms that when science escapes its "narrow empiricism" (confined to only sensory experience) it may then legitimately expand into a broad science or a deep science based on a "broad empiricism" that can sufficiently apply the "three basic strands of knowing . . . to any and all direct experience, evidence, and data." This approach harmoniously integrates all four quadrants or the Big Three—art, objective science, and morals, and therefore gives the modern world "a broad science of each quadrant:

- **Upper-Right** ("It") or natural sciences: "the sciences of the exteriors of individual holons: physics, chemistry, geology, biology, neurology, medicine, behaviorism, and so forth"; pioneers include Skinner; Watson, Locke, etc.

- **Lower-Right** ("Its") or systems sciences and sociology: "the sciences of the exteriors of communal holons: ecology, systems theory, exterior holism, sociology, and so on"; pioneers include Comte, Marx, Parson, Luhmann, etc.

- **Lower-Left** ("We") or worldviews or shared cultural meanings: "the interiors of communal holons": "the intersubjective signs, values, shared cultural meanings and worldviews of a given culture"; pioneers include Kuhn, Dilthey, Gebser, Weber, Gadamer, etc.

- **Upper-Left** ("I") or personal psychology and transpersonal development: "the contours of the interiors of individual holons": logic, mathematics, depth psychology, etc., yet including "the higher stages of interior develop-

INTERIOR INDIVIDUAL (UL)	EXTERIOR INDIVIDUAL (UR)
* Interpretative * Hermeneutic * Consciousness	* Monological * Empirical, Positivistic * Form

Sigmund Freud C. G. Jung Sri Aurobindo Plotinus Guatama Buddha	logic mathematics psychology art and aesthetics mental phenomena spiritual experiences	physics chemistry biology geology medicine neurology behaviorism	B. F. Skinner John Watson John Locke Empiricism Behaviorism

INTENTIONAL   *BEHAVIORAL*

CULTURAL   *SOCIAL*

Thomas Kuhn Wilhelm Dilthey Jean Gebser Max Weber Hans-Geor Gadamer	shared cultural meanings worldviews values intersubjective signs cultural "glue"	ecology systems theory sociology population economics infrastructure dietary patterns	Talcott Parson Auguste Comte Karl Marx Gerhard Lenski

INTERIOR COLLECTIVE (LL)	EXTERIOR COLLECTIVE (LR)

Broad and Deep Sciences of the Four Quadrants (and Their Theoretical Pioneers)
FIGURE I

ment, [where] genuinely spiritual or mystical experiences begin to unfold";
pioneers include Freud, Jung, Adler, Piaget, Emerson; St. Teresa of Avila,
Plotinus, Shankara, and Gautama Buddha.

(See Figure 1: "Broad and Deep Sciences of the Four Quadrants (and Their Theoretical Pioneers.")

This integral approach is a path of "unity-in-diversity," yet one that still clearly
recognizes "the 'diversity' part of the unity-in-diversity, [because] this diversity is
every bit as important as the unity." And importantly, this includes the transpersonal or the spiritual domains since "there appear to be at least four higher stages of
consciousness development," referred to by Wilber as "the psychic, the subtle, the
causal, and the nondual . . . [and, respectively,] associated with . . . nature mysticism, deity mysticism, formless mysticism, and nondual mysticism."

Indeed, Wilber is fascinated that these "deep sciences" are actually "the meeting of premodern and modern" because "the Great Chain is now firmly situated

within the differentiations of modernity, something that had never happened in any premodern culture." Yet for the premodern wisdom traditions, "the Great Chain, apart from its lowest level, actually covers only the Upper-Left quadrant," therefore, historically "the modern and differentiated disciplines of [science] . . . tore into the premodern and predifferentiated worldview with a vengeance, and neither the Great Chain, nor the spiritual worldviews associated with it, ever recovered."

This is precisely why Wilber wants "to find some scheme that could accommodate both premodern and modern worldviews, and thus integrate religion and science." As we've seen, the integral approach is able "to integrate the Great Chain with the four quadrants" so that "the Great Chain of Being can take its rightful place within the differentiations of modernity." In other words, he concludes: "It is only by acknowledging, honoring, and including all four quadrants that the long-sought integration of premodern religion and modern science might finally become a reality."

Part IV. The Path Ahead

CHAPTER 14. "THE GREAT HOLARCHY IN THE POSTMODERN WORLD" again emphasizes that since the modern West was the "first significant culture to radically deny the Great Nest of Being," then this "disaster of modernity" created "the disqualified universe of flatland holism," the "disenchantment of the world," the "modern wasteland." Yet, if we "distinguish between the dignity and the disaster of modernity," then "it is not necessary to attempt to integrate spirituality with the collapsed Kosmos or with the disaster of modernity," but rather to only "integrate the Great Chain with the four quadrants."

By doing so, this approach integrates or fully acknowledges both the "vertical levels (the traditional Great Chain)" as well as the "horizontal dimensions present on each and every level (the four quadrants)," in which case there are four levels with three dimensions each:

- the art, morals, and science of the *sensory realm*;

- the art, morals, and science of the *mental realm*;

- the art, morals, and science of the *spirit realm*.

Wilber then presents some practical examples from "the four levels we are using, in this simplified account, the sensorimotor, the mental, the subtle soul, and the causal spirit" where "each level, as always, transcends and includes its predecessors," in order to show what this type of integration might look like. Thus he gives brief examples from the levels of art (as the Beautiful), the levels of morals (as the Good), and the levels of science (as the True), by which Wilber means the "levels of objective, exterior, sensory-empirical science." This allows a deep science to actually measure or register the Right-Hand quantitative aspects of the exterior correlates (such as with EEG brain-state research), although empirical measurements will never register the Left-Hand qualitative aspects of the interiors states (in other words, they cannot reveal meaning).

This integral embrace is critically important because "empirical science is accessing the exterior modes of all of the higher levels as well," which is only natural, since in actuality "the higher levels themselves are not above the natural or empirical or objective, they are within the natural and empirical and objective. Not on top of, but alongside of. Spirit does not physically rise above nature (or the Right-Hand world); Spirit is the interior of nature, the within of the Kosmos. We do not look up, we look within." In other words, this capacity to "thoroughly 'ground' or 'embody' metaphysical or transcendental claims, in effect providing a seamless union of transcendental and empirical" is a type of "transcendental naturalism or naturalistic transcendentalism—a union of otherworldly and this-worldly, ascending and descending, spiritual and natural—a union that avoids, I believe, the insuperable difficulties of either position taken alone." Only this approach will allow all the faces of Spirit to be included and embraced, for then "Spirit seen subjectively is Beauty, the I of Spirit. Spirit seen intersubjectively is the Good, the We of Spirit. And Spirit seen objectively is the True, the It of Spirit."

CHAPTER 15. "THE INTEGRAL AGENDA" recapitulates the previous chapters, which suggested how "the three strands of Deep Science (injunction, apprehension, confirmation; or paradigm, data, falsifiability)" operate in both the exterior and interiors realms; how the Great Holarchy (Great Chain) will be "coupled with the differentiations of modernity and submitted to the tests of deep science"; how "religions the world over will have to bracket their mythic beliefs"; how the "esoteric core of premodern religion" is not really "a series of mythic beliefs and non-falsifiable beliefs, but a series of contemplative practices, actual interior experiments in consciousness, grounded in direct experience"; and how "most religions will continue to offer sacraments, solace, and myths (and other translative or horizontal consolations), in addition to the genuinely transformative practices of vertical contemplation."

Wilber insists that "religion will also have to adjust its attitudes toward evolution in general," which he contends shouldn't be too difficult since "evolution is actually the Great Chain temporalized." When evolution in general is added to the integral agenda, such as proposed by the Idealists or Aurobindo, it's apparent that "each epoch, each era, each stage of cultural evolution brings with it important truths, valuable insights, and profound revelations." Thus, unlike in the retro-Romantic view, each epoch "then adds its own, emergent, novel truths, thus both including and transcending its predecessors." Indeed, this understanding paves the way for an evolutionary spirituality since, according to Wilber, "an evolutionary view is the most viable chariot for a truly integrative stance, extending an embrace that, by any other name, is genuinely compassionate."

Then Wilber turns to "deep science research" which would "attempt to investigate the various phenomena in each of the four quadrants—subjective states, objective behavior, intersubjective structures, and interobjective systems—and correlate each with the others, without trying to reduce them to the others." This integral view "is a harmonization of the broad sciences of all the levels in each of the quadrants: thus, 'All-Level, All-Quadrant.'" In addition, this AQAL approach would naturally include "the deep science of the higher stages of development or evolution in the Upper-Left quadrant," thus "it would give real religion—genuine spirituality and the deep sciences of the interior—an unprecedented role as the vanguard of evolution, the growing tip of the universal organism, growing toward its own highest potential, namely, the ever-unfolding realization and actualization of Spirit."

Since the all-level, all-quadrant approach "is the direct result of the harmonization of premodern religion (all-level) with the differentiations of modernity (all-quadrant)," it will also address and effect politics. That's because, as Wilber explains, "if there is to be a genuine integration of modern science and premodern religion, it will have political dimensions sewn into its very fabric . . . so the political integration of modernity and premodernity would involve the integration of the Enlightenment of the West with the Enlightenment of the East": the Enlightenment of the West or "the best of modernity" recognizes that "the core of the liberal Enlightenment was the assertion that the state does not have the right to legislate or promote any particular version of the good life." The "Enlightenment of the East" or "the best of premodernity" which includes and "simply means any genuine spiritual experience, whether East or West. . . . The *summum bonum* of the Good Life. . . ."

Since the integral approach differentiates between prerational mythic belief and transrational awareness, "genuine spiritual experience (or spiritual Enlightenment)" will embrace "the general tenets of rational political liberalism (not prerational mythic reactionism)." In other words, "through the powers of advocacy and example, encourages others to use their liberal freedom—the Enlightenment of the West—in order to pursue spiritual freedom—the Enlightenment of the East."

   This approach includes both the premodern worldview represented by traditional conservatism as well as the "rational differentiations of modernity" represented by traditional liberalism, thus "the integration of premodern religion with the differentiations of modernity would open up the possibility of a significant reconciliation of conservative and liberal views." Yet spiritual realization will always be "thoroughly transliberal, bringing together the Enlightenment of the East with the Enlightenment of the West." Then, perhaps, with "political freedom joined with spiritual freedom," as Wilber realizes, we may all "witness the liberation of all sentient beings without exception. And on the distant, silent, lost horizon, gentle as fog, quiet as tears, the voice continues to call."

One Taste

Daily Reflections on Integral Spirituality

BY KEN WILBER

(Boston: Shambhala Publications, 1999; paperback edition, 2000);

The Collected Works of Ken Wilber, Vol. 8 (CW8) (Shambhala, 2000)

A Note to the Reader

January	May	September
February	June	October
March	July	November
April	August	December

One Taste: Daily Reflections on Integral Spirituality (1999) is a mature Wilber/Phase 4 work offering a personal and practical account of Wilber's integral vision from the all-quadrants, all-levels approach to integral studies.

One Taste, originally subtitled "The Journals of Ken Wilber," was suggested as a project by Shambhala Publications, Wilber's principal publisher, therefore during the year of 1997 he kept a nearly day-by-day chronicle of his activities and ideas, thus giving him an opportunity to reflect on the spectrum of life itself from an integral perspective in the space of a year, including a few essays written during that period.

One Taste: Daily Reflections on Integral Spirituality was published in 1999 (Shambhala Publications); paperback edition (Shambhala Publications, 2000); it is now part of *The Collected Works of Ken Wilber, Volume Eight (CW8),* (Shambhala Publications, 2000).

One Taste begins with Wilber's search to find a mainstream publisher for *The Marriage of Sense and Soul* (written in 1996–97 and published by Random House in 1998), and broadens to cover nearly everything, from nipple-piercing to the Witness consciousness, from the year's favorite movies and music to appreciative accounts of architecture, literature, and high fashion, all seen from a variety of meditative states and from within a circle of good friends (and tasty dinners), spiced with some sexual adventures with Wilber's future wife, Marci Walters.

One Taste is interspersed with a few short essays reviewing Wilber's AQAL approach to consciousness studies, including an "integral psychograph" of the individual self that incorporates the developmental lines of consciousness. Throughout the book the reader gets a real taste of what an integral practice is about in personal terms, one that anybody can aspire to, one that attempts "to simultaneously exercise all the major levels and dimensions of the human bodymind—physical, emotional, mental, social, cultural, spiritual." Ultimately, however, we discover that this type of integral practice is mostly about the "One Taste" of nondual consciousness, the enlightened presence where "transcendence restores humor" and where empathy and compassion embrace all.

 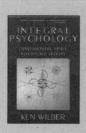  

INTEGRAL AQAL APPROACH (NEW MILLENNIUM)

Standing in the doorway of a new millennium, Ken Wilber was finding that his all-quadrants, all-levels, all-lines schema, begun with *Sex, Ecology, Spiritually* in 1995 and culminating at the century's end, had led some people to suggest that he was entering Phase 5. He was relying more on the language of fluid mechanics and movement to loosen the perceived rigidity of his linear-stage model, (although Wilber had never intended his developmental model to be perceived as strictly linear). Thus the AQAL model now had "waves" instead of "levels" or "structures," "streams" instead of "developmental lines," "nests" instead of "chains" or "ladders," and it involved "spirals of development," the "great River of Life," and so on. Also, by the close of the twentieth century Wilber was advocating a more incisive critique of the perennial philosophy in general (actually started back in 1983), even assailing the premodern spiritual traditions themselves, although, naturally, not their universal and transpersonal wisdom but rather their sociocultural limitations and premodern orientations.

In addition, there was his increased insistence on including not only the *levels* (or waves) and *lines* (or streams) in the spectrum but also clearly differentiating the various *states, types,* and *worldviews* of consciousness—in other words, a fully AQAL approach. In Wilber's integral psychology, all of these various aspects of consciousness are intimately involved in the dynamic development of *the self,* or the separate self-sense (proximate, distal, witness). In doing so, he was uniting the premodern view of *all-levels* (represented by the Great Chain of Being) with the modern and postmodern view of *all-quadrants* (represented by the differentiation of the Big Three, or the value spheres of culture, art, and nature; morals, self, and science), and thus presenting a genuine "marriage of modern science and ancient religion."

There was also Wilber's recent acknowledgment of the evidence gathered by the memetic value system of Spiral Dynamics and its numerous color-oriented value memes that recast the collective evolution of worldviews (which in turn heavily influences the sense of self and its individual development), which Wilber's work has already ably documented. All of these developments began to suggest to some of his students that Wilber had moved considerably beyond the basic four-quadrant model initiated by *SES.*

Moreover, with the impending release of Volume Two of *The Kosmos Trilogy* it seemed not only logical but necessary to acknowledge another emerging phase in Wilber's work. Nonetheless, after initially rejecting the idea and downplaying the significance of another phase, Wilber now maintains that any possible Phase 5 would have to involve what he calls *integral post-metaphysics* and its practical corollary of an *integral methodological pluralism.* Indeed, since it's this emphasis on post-metaphysics that denotes his shift into a Phase 5, it is notable with the publication of his next series in *The Collected Works,* i.e., *CW9: A Theory of Everything, CW10: Boomeritis,* and *CW11: Kosmic Karma and Creativity.* From Wilber's personal perspective, he's been privately thinking in these terms for at least a couple of decades; it's just taken him this long to more fully articulate his vision to the public after laying the foundations with the work of Phase 4 (or the AQAL approach).

In the end, all of these discussions of different phases are only academic since the phase designations are only intended to act as guides or maps for the ever-growing oeuvre of Ken Wilber, though they can be instructive. As already mentioned, the four or five phases in Wilber's publications stand united in their fundamental theory and approach for they all recognize evolutionary development for both the individual and the collective as a dynamic, interactive, and unfolding process of transcendence and inclusion ultimately driven by Eros or love. This body of work represents a comprehensive embrace of reality that can be pictured as a nested mandala, a morphogenetic matrix, or a graded holarchy of Spirit (the Great Nest of Being) reaching from dust to Deity, from dirt to Divinity.

However for some readers, this vast integral model, which uses a *holonic indexing system* or an *integral methodological pluralism* to examine and map the grand spectra of the Kosmos, has grown into an incredibly complex artifice. Wilber's integral model, however, retains the distinction of being the simplest presentation of its type, incorporating and integrating as it does a vast range of disciplines and study, embracing and reaching from premodern mysticism to the rational brilliance of the modern sciences to the critical concerns of the postmodern mind. Wilber believes that the importance of an integral approach is monumental, for if humanity wants to actually utilize the profound wisdom of premodern metaphysics without succumbing to the devastating liabilities of the modern/postmodern currents, then it must come to terms with "modern Kantian and postmodern Heideggerian thought." If it fails to do so, spirituality can't hope to survive with any intellectual credibility. Simultaneously, an AQAL approach attempts to bring depth or interior reality back to the debased, reductive philosophy of scientific materialism and flatland modernity. In other words, besides setting up and facilitating the Integral Institute (I-I) and Integral University (IU), which is harvesting the pragmatic applications generated from the intellectual insights of AQAL methodology, one of Wilber's primary campaigns of the twenty-first century is to help "spirituality be post-metaphysical in some sense." This will help establish an intellectual foundation where an authentic religious or spiritual or transpersonal reality can better "survive in a modern and postmodern world." By bringing metaphysics into the world of modern scientific knowledge, Wilber is once again bridging the gap between the premodern and modern/postmodern worlds, between the ancient East and the scientific West.

With "a more integral map," it may then be possible for humanity to better use the inner-world cartographies of premodern religion, yet bring to spirituality the insightful precision of a *broad science* or *deep science* that uses investigative methods based upon verifiability. Thus Wilber's new project of actively applying the AQAL metatheory, which is basically a refinement and expansion of his original spectrum of consciousness model, now more fully includes the sociocultural and exterior domains of reality or all four-quadrants (not just interiors). In addition, he's attempting to establish real religion and authentic spirituality "without relying on any pregiven archetypal, or independently existing ontological structures, levels, planes, etc."

At the dawn of the new millennium, then, Wilber is proclaiming that "The leading edge of consciousness evolution stands today on the brink of an *integral millennium*—or at least the possibility of an integral millennium—where the sum total of extant human knowledge, wisdom, and technology is available to all. And sooner or later we will have, of course, a Theory of Everything to explain it all." Such a grand integral vision will be stabilized by the practical applications generated by an integral approach that can create "a cross-cultural mapping of all of the states, structures, memes, types, levels, stages, and waves of human consciousness. This overall map . . . then becomes the psychological component of a possible Theory of Everything, where it will be supplemented with findings from the physical, biological, cultural, and spiritual dimensions." And pushing at the leading edge of this integral movement will be the newly formed and funded Integral Institute and its collolary, Integral University, Wilber's other major project initiated during the first years of the new century. This is a worldwide collection of other integral thinkers and visionaries who understand the viability of the AQAL approach and are already preparing texts for publication and developing additional projects for pragmatic application.

Since all of Wilber's books have stayed in print over decades, Shambhala decided to publish *The Collected Works of Ken Wilber, Volumes One–Eight,* a unique tribute to a living philosopher who turned fifty years old in 1999. Presented in beautifully crafted hardbound volumes, *The Collected Works* originally contained Wilber's principal writings from 1977 to 2000, as well as including some unpublished works, most of his articles, several interviews, many of his book forewords, plus a few revised editions of some recent Wilber/Phase 4 works (i.e., *Sex, Ecology, Spirituality, A Brief History of Everything,* and *The Eye of Spirit*). *The Collected Works* will continue to release further volumes as Wilber continues to write and publish (with volumes 9–11 appearing in 2004). Thus, at the start of the millennium, the world was treated to a massive collection of over five thousand densely packed pages of Ken Wilber's collected writings. Wilber took the opportunity to review many of his original intentions and their effects, thus providing reflective introductory essays that placed each one of his books in a mature, post-metaphysical perspective of the recently christened Wilber/Phase 5.

One of the previously unpublished gems contained within Volume Four of *The Collected Works* was *Integral Psychology: Consciousness, Spirit, Psychology, Therapy*, a condensed version of *System, Self, and Structures* (the unfinished psychology textbook often mentioned in *Transformations of Consciousness*). Written during the spring of 1999 and released the next spring as a single paperback edition, *Integral Psychology* was originally intended to be a guided tour through the various comparative charts (these appear in the book's back matter) which Wilber had compiled from hundreds of researchers and various developmental systems. This book has become the epitome of Wilber's integral model.

Integral Psychology provides a more refined and updated explication of Wilber's holonic modeling system than any other book he's produced to date. In other words, practically every major theme he's ever considered throughout his career has been artfully integrated into this compact volume. In addition, Wilber addresses nearly every major critique that's been aimed at his work, especially those concerns arising in the wake of *Sex, Ecology, Spirituality*, showing his willingness to modify or expand his views.

Within *Integral Psychology*, in a series of succinct chapters, Wilber summarizes not only his psychological model but also his philosophical positions concerning premodernity, modernity, and the "great quest" or "bright promise" of postmodernity, i.e., to recover from the flatland disaster of the modern world (including scientific materialism) and the regressive postmodern slide into deconstructive nihilism. In response, Wilber offers his own post-postmodern philosophy, or a "constructive postmodernity." This type of integral metatheory forms the basis for his Theory of Everything—from consciousness studies to marketplace business, from international politics to science, from ecophilosophy to gender studies, from cultural to social infrastructures, from mythic religion to authentic spirituality, and so on. *Integral Psychology* was succeeded by an even more concise and practical book, *A Theory of Everything*, published the same year the paperback edition of *Integral Psychology* came out.

In the fall of 2000, *A Theory of Everything: An Integral Vision for Business, Politics, Science, and Spirituality* (Shambhala Publications, 2000; paperback edition, 2001) appeared, and further established the practical application of the integral vision, applying it to a variety of fields, as the subtitle indicates. At this time, *A Theory of Everything* is perhaps the best short introduction to Wilber's lifelong body of work. This brief guide suggests how his integral approach can affect numerous disciplines and studies. By the turn of the century entering into the new millennium, Shambhala announced that Wilber is the most widely translated academic author in America.

In *A Theory of Everything,* as he had begun with *Integral Psychology,* Wilber was incorporating the model of human development called "Spiral Dynamics," based on the pioneering work of Clare Graves (and currently carried forward by visionaries like Donald Beck and Christopher Cowan). Spiral Dynamics models the evolution of the various sociocultural worldviews, or the spiral of development, through a series of "value memes" which are represented by a spectrum of colors (beige, red, purple, blue, orange, green, yellow, turquoise, coral). These memes closely correlate with Wilber's spectrum of worldviews (situated in the Lower-Left quadrant), thus this gave him the impetus to adopt Spiral Dynamic's language system into his integral metatheory.

What also impressed Wilber was the wealth of Spiral Dynamics' empirical evidence and its practical application from governments to corporations. Yet, according to Wilber, even Spiral Dynamics must become four-quadrant in their approach in order to be truly integral. Beck has accordingly recently modified his system into "Spiral Dynamics integral" (SDi) or a 4Q/8L (four quadrants, eight levels) approach. Thus, as only one example among many, Wilber's theory of everything is informing and influencing even the leading visionaries of the emerging integral culture. This, indeed, is the stated goal and crucial task of the Integral Institute, which intends to promote and encourage integral ideas in the coming decades.

Wilber's writings continue to emerge practically nonstop even as he engages in all his other activities. During the years surrounding the turn of the new century a couple of excellent essays summarizing the mature Wilber/Phase 4 AQAL position appeared in the newly founded *Journal of Consciousness Studies,* beginning in 1997 with "An Integral Theory of Consciousness" (now published in *CW7*), and then in November/December of 2000 with "Waves, Streams, States and Self" (now in the revised edition of *The Eye of Spirit*).

However, during these years, Wilber was wrestling not just with the founding of the Integral Institute and Integral Univeristy and other business ventures such as the cutting-edge Web site Integral Naked (www.integralnaked.com), but also with his first novel, *Boomeritis: A Novel That Will Set You Free* (Shambhala Publications, 2002). Wilber had periodically worked for several years on this book before it was finally finished in the form of a critical postmodern novel supplemented with over a hundred pages of endnotes (even he remarked, "a novel with endnotes?") and hundreds of pages of sidebars and postings found on the Shambhala Publications Web site (www.wilber.shambhala.com). Wilber purposefully intended to level a strong critique at the narcissistic tendencies of his own generation of baby boomers and the magical-mythic regressive tendencies of the New Age. What started out as an academic treatise morphed into the more user-friendly novel.

The basic narrative structure of *Boomeritis* is a wild postmodern ride through a series of integral lectures as perceived through the erotic imagination of its protagonist, a twenty-two-year-old character named Ken Wilber (in typical boomeritis fashion, how narcissistic can a writer get?) who was either searching for AI (artificial intelligence) or trying to find an orgasm as big as God. This book was Wilber's tongue-in-cheek way to present his integral position without appearing too mean-spirited or overly critical. Yet, by emphasizing the importance of human development and its tendency to degenerate into the different forms of psychopathology at each level, he's also trying to prescribe a type of therapy for those of us in the modern/postmodern world who are infected with boomeritis, or the tendency to be self-centered and narcissistic (after all, the boomers have often been criticized as being the "Me generation").

Boomeritis is a critical look at the "green meme" or the dominance of relative pluralism and extreme postmodernism, often in the form of "political correctness" and the "victim syndrome," which have recently run rampant in the popular culture and throughout the Western world's intelligentsia and academia. Wilber's sharp analysis is both a hilarious and cutting commentary on the ironic and nihilistic tendency of the postmodern mind. Indeed, Wilber claims, it is the "mean green meme (MGM)," or the pathological side of green (the "sensitive self") that is the greatest obstacle to the continuing emergence of a truly integral culture.

Instead, as an alternative, Wilber's vision offers a genuine *universal pluralism* initiating the "quantum leap to second-tier awareness," which embraces both holism and holarchy, pluralism and elitism, feminine and masculine values, left- and right-wing politics, or, in other words, the entire spiral of possible worldviews. Both Wilber and Spiral Dynamics claim that only "an integral jump to second-tier awareness"—which acknowledges the correct but partial position of each lower worldview or meme without absolutizing any one of them—has the capacity to engender a worldcentric tolerance that accepts *the entire* spiral of development, and thus every worldview. This "prime directive" of second-tier awareness, or of centauric vision-logic, honors each level with compassionate care, yet ultimately it transcends all worldviews, personal or collective, in the nondual understanding of One Taste.

Revisions and restatements notwithstanding, nearly thirty years after the publication of his first book, and after absorbing the extensive censure of his critics, Wilber still asserts: "I have found [my work's] basic framework to be as sturdy and solid as ever; if anything, subsequent research, evidence, and theory have actually increased its plausibility." Nevertheless, he is constantly ready to modify and further articulate his integral vision when the evidence demands it, another hallmark of clear and unbiased thinking and an orientation toward truth. Therefore, all the phases of Wilber's prolific output unite in presenting a model of evolutionary development that pictures an unfolding process of transcendence and inclusion in both interiors and exteriors, all nested as a Kosmic Mandala or AQAL matrix grounded in the radiant Divine Domain. Yet, as this summary review book demonstrates, each one of these phases has its own unique theoretical implications as well as its own literary brilliance and mystical insight. However, Wilber's work is best apprehended by actually reading selections from his comprehensive oeuvre, a record that's sure to expand and evolve in the coming years, an inspiring testament to the dynamic activity of Spirit-in-action.

The Collected Works
of Ken Wilber

Volumes I–VIII

BY KEN WILBER

(edited by Kendra Crossen Burroughs)

(Boston: Shambhala Publications, hardcover, CW1–CW4, 1999, CW5–CW8, 2000)

VOLUME ONE: (CW1)	*The Spectrum of Consciousness* (1977); *No Boundary: Eastern and Western Approaches to Personal Growth* (1979); plus selected essays;
VOLUME TWO: (CW2)	*The Atman Project: A Transpersonal View of Human Development* (1980); *Up From Eden: A Transpersonal View of Human Evolution* (1981); plus the biographical essay "Odyssey: A Personal Inquiry into Humanistic and Transpersonal Psychology";
VOLUME THREE: (CW3)	*A Sociable God: Toward a New Understanding of Religion* (1983); *Eye to Eye: The Quest for the New Paradigm* (1983);
VOLUME FOUR: (CW4)	*Transformations of Consciousness: Conventional and Contemplative Perspectives on Human Development* (1986); *Integral Psychology: Consciousness, Spirit, Psychology, Therapy* (1999); selections from *The Holotropic Paradigm and Other Paradoxes; Quantum Questions; Spiritual Choices;* plus numerous forewords to various books, selected essays on transper-

sonal psychology, including "Sociocultural Evolution" (1983, previously unpublished);

VOLUME FIVE: *Grace and Grit: Spirituality and Healing in the Life and Death*
(CW5) *of Treya Killam Wilber* (1991);

VOLUME SIX: *Sex. Ecology, Spirituality: The Spirit of Evolution* (1995, 2000
(CW6) revised edition);

VOLUME SEVEN: *A Brief History of Everything* (1996, 2000 revised edition);
(CW7) *The Eye of Spirit: An Integral Vision for a World Gone Slightly Mad* (1997); plus the essay "An Integral Theory of Consciousness";

VOLUME EIGHT: *The Marriage of Sense and Soul: Integrating Science and Religion* (1998);
(CW8) *One Taste: Daily Reflections of Integral Spirituality* (1999); plus one foreword.

The Collected Works of Ken Wilber: Volumes One–Eight (1999, 2000) present the books and major essays of Ken Wilber in his first four phases covering his publishing career up to the new millennium, beginning with the spectrum of consciousness premiered in 1975 through the four quadrants premiered in 1995.

The Collected Works include important journal articles, essays, interviews, and book forewords, as well as new indexes and reflective introductions for each volume that reviews, from Wilber's own perspective, the breadth of his writings.

The Collected Works of Ken Wilber: Volumes One–Four also premiered two unpublished books in Volume Four: *Integral Psychology: Consciousness, Spirit, Psychology, Therapy* as the most current statement of Wilber's integral theory, and *Sociocultural Evolution,* a lengthy essay written at the same time as *A Sociable God* (*CW3*).

The Collected Works of Ken Wilber: Volumes Five–Eight, published in 2000 (Shambhala Publications), contained the revised editions of *Sex, Ecology, Spirituality (CW6), A Brief History of Everything (CW7),* and *The Eye of Spirit (CW7),* released as paperback editions in 2001, plus *Grace and Grit (CW5),* and Wilber's other books written and published during the period from 1995 to 2000.

All of Ken Wilber's books have stayed in print since the time he began publishing over twenty-five years earlier, therefore this high demand for his written works prompted Shambhala Publications to take on the monumental task of compiling the collected writings of "one of the most widely read and influential American philosophers of our time."* As "the most widely translated academic writer in America," with his fourteen books having been translated into over thirty languages, Wilber was accorded the honor, at only age fifty, of being the first psychologist or philosopher in history to have his collected works published while still alive.

The popular reception of *The Collected Works,* packaged in handsomely bound hardcover volumes totaling slightly over 5000 pages, is further testament to Wilber's prolific output and wide-ranging influence. Shambhala observes that "In these collected works, Wilber's integral vision embracing the essential truths of East and West is applied to a wide range of fields—from art to psychoanalysis, from medicine to sociology, from religion to evolutionary theory." Perhaps Wilber himself explained his intent best when he said: "I therefore sought to outline a philos-

---

* Blurb from *The Collected Works of Ken Wilber.*

ophy of universal integralism. Put differently, I sought a world philosophy—or an integral philosophy—that would believably weave together the many pluralistic contexts of science, morals, aesthetics, Eastern as well as Western philosophy, and the world's great wisdom traditions. Not on the level of details—that is finitely impossible; but on the level of orienting generalizations . . . a holistic philosophy for a holistic Kosmos, a genuine Theory of Everything." This central theme of an all-embracing integral vision runs through every page of Ken Wilber's writings, from the first chapters he wrote in his early twenties, to his most recent work composed during the dawn of the new millennium. Grand theories and philosophies abound, from ancient times to the modern age, from scientific studies to the realms of mysticism, yet his words tug beautifully at the heart and awaken the mind, in an achievement of inclusiveness unprecedented in the history of philosophy.

Integral Psychology
Consciousness, Spirit, Psychology, Therapy

BY KEN WILBER

(Boston: Shambhala Publications, 2000; paperback edition, 2001);

The Collected Works of Ken Wilber, Vol. 4 (CW4) (Shambhala, 1999)

Integral Psychology: Consciousness, Spirit, Psychology, Therapy (2000) is a fully mature Wilber/Phase 4 work emphasizing the AQAL approach to integral studies, therefore focusing on the developmental tetra-interaction (or coevolution) of the Left-Hand interior quadrants with the Right-Hand exterior correlates in the Great Nest of Spirit or Kosmos.

Integral Psychology was written in about a month during the spring of 1999, and was initially intended as a condensed version of *Self, System, Structure* (the unfinished transpersonal psychology textbook begun in the mid-1980s, and still a projected two-volume set). It was also conceived as an explanation of the comprehensive charts placed at the book's end, drawn from numerous premodern, modern, and postmodern theorists. At the turn of new millennium, when it was first published, Wilber claimed that "*Integral Psychology* is at this time the definitive statement of my general psychological model, and my other writings in the field should be coordinated with its views."

Integral Psychology: Consciousness, Spirit, Psychology, Therapy was published as part of *The Collected Works of Ken Wilber, Volume Four (CW4),* (Shambhala Publications, 1999); single paperback edition published in spring 2000 (Shambhala Publications).

NOTE TO THE READER: "A DAYLIGHT VIEW" takes a brief look at Ken Wilber's "hidden history" of Western psychology, for he confides that "somebody has got to tell." This is because what the traditional textbooks on psychology don't explain is that "the roots of modern psychology lie in the spiritual traditions, precisely because the psyche itself is plugged into spiritual sources. In the deepest recesses of the psyche, one finds not instincts, but Spirit—and the study of psychology ought ideally to be the study of all of that, body to mind to soul, subconscious to self-conscious to superconscious, sleeping to half-awake to fully awake." Wilber reminds us that the definition of *psychology* implies "the study of the psyche, [for] the word *psyche* means mind or soul."

We're introduced to "the commanding figure of Gustav Fechner" who the orthodox textbooks claim is one of the founders of psychology (along with people like Wilhelm Wundt), yet when Wilber found one of Fechner's books, *Life after Death* (1835) in a "wonderful old-book store," he discovered that Fechner had also designed an integral system of psychological development back in the nineteenth century, which moved "from body to mind to spirit, the three stages of the growth of consciousness." In other words, Wilber informs us, "Fechner's approach to psychology was thus a type of integral approach: he wished to use empirical and scientific measurement, not to deny soul and spirit but to help elucidate them." And since the "the textbooks [did] not bother to tell us *that*," Wilber informs us he was prompted to write a "history of psychology and philosophy." Wilber's deep understanding of the history of Western psychology illuminates the fact that many of the founding fathers, such as Fechner (1801–1887), William James (1842–1910), and James Mark Baldwin (1861–1934), were all initially working "when the newly emerging science of psychology was still on speaking terms with the ancient wisdom of the ages—with the perennial philosophy, with the Great Nest of Being, with the Idealist systems . . . [thus] these pioneering modern psychologists managed to be both fully scientific and fully spiritual, and they found not the slightest contradiction or difficulty in that generous embrace."

Wilber's presentation is precisely such an integral psychology because, while it's "attempting to include the best of modern scientific research on psychology, consciousness, and therapy, it also takes its inspiration from that integral period of psychology's own genesis." He states that "the major aim of this book is to help start a discussion, not finish it; to act as a beginning, not an end." Yet he shows "the briefest outline of what one type of integral psychology might look like . . . [as] it attempts to include and integrate some of the more enduring insights from premodern, modern, and postmodern sources, under the assumption that all of them have something incredibly important to teach us. And it attempts to do so, not as a mere eclecticism, but in a systematic embrace, with method to the madness." Therefore, Wilber believes "that integral psychology (and integral studies in general) will become increasingly prevalent in the coming decades, as the academic world gropes its way out of its doggedly night view of the Kosmos," and will instead lead us into "a daylight view," which is why Wilber dedicates the book to "dear Gustav."

PART I. GROUND: "THE FOUNDATION" first defines *psychology* as "the study of human consciousness and its manifestations in behavior":

- "The Functions of consciousness include *perceiving, desiring, willing,* and *acting*;

- The Structures of consciousness, some facets of which can be *unconscious,* include *body, mind, soul,* and *spirit*;

- The States of consciousness include normal (e.g., *waking, dreaming, sleeping*) and altered (e.g., *nonordinary, meditative*) [states];

- The Modes of consciousness include *aesthetic, moral,* and *scientific*;

- The Development of consciousness spans an entire spectrum from *prepersonal* to *personal* to *transpersonal,* subconscious to self-conscious to superconscious, id to ego to Spirit;

- The Relational and Behavioral aspects of consciousness refer to its *mutual interaction* with the objective, *exterior world* and the *sociocultural world* of *shared values* and *perceptions.*"

Wilber suggests that the different schools of psychology "all possessed true, but partial, insights into the vast field of consciousness," therefore, he announces "the endeavor to honor and embrace every legitimate aspect of human consciousness is the goal of an integral psychology." With Wilber's "integral psychology—a subset of integral studies in general—we have an enormous wealth of theories, research, and practices, all of which are important trees in the integral forests." It's with this type of integral embrace that Wilber intends to draw upon "premodern, modern, and postmodern sources, with a view to a reconciliation."

CHAPTER 1. "THE BASIC LEVELS OR WAVES" is one of the longest chapters in the book. It first introduces the "premodern or traditional sources" that would "be a crucial ingredient of any truly integral psychology." Therefore Wilber refers to "the perennial philosophy, or the common core of the world's great spiritual traditions," which is basically "the view that reality is composed of various *levels of existence*—Levels of Being and of Knowing—ranging from matter to body to mind to soul to spirit. Each senior dimension transcends but includes its juniors, so that this is a conception of wholes within wholes within wholes indefinitely, reaching from dirt to Divinity." This nested idea has been traditionally termed the Great Chain of Being but Wilber prefers to call it a "'Great Nest of Being' [or 'Great Nest of Spirit'] with each senior dimension enveloping and embracing its juniors, much like a series of concentric circles or spheres." (See Figure 1: "The Great Nest of Being").

Wilber's integral psychology uses "all three terms—Basic *Levels* or Basic *Structures,* and Basic *Waves*—interchangeably, as referring to essentially the same phenomenon; but each has a slightly different connotation that conveys important information:

- '**Level**' emphasizes the fact that these are *qualitatively* distinct levels of organization, arranged in a nested hierarchy (or holarchy) of increasing holistic embrace (each level transcending but including its predecessors).

- **'Structure'** emphasizes the fact that these are enduring *holistic patterns* of being and consciousness (each is a holon, a whole that is part of other wholes).

- **'Wave'** emphasizes the fact that these levels are not rigidly separate and isolated, but, like the colors of a rainbow, infinitely shade and grade into each other. The basic structures are simply the basic colors in that rainbow."

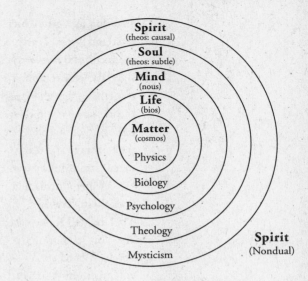

The Great Nest of Being
FIGURE I

In response to postmodern concerns, Wilber contends that these various basic waves (or levels and sub-levels) are "the codification of direct experiential realities, reaching from sensory experience to mental experience to spiritual experience," not constructed from abstract metaphysical speculation. In other words, since "we live in a patterned Kosmos, these richly textured patterns can be—and were—spotted by intelligent men and women in almost every culture," than they've also been "communally generated and consensually validated." In addition, according to these advanced-tip individuals: "Radiant Spirit transcends and includes absolutely everything. Spirit is thus both the very *highest wave* (purely *transcendental*) and the *ever-present ground* of all the waves (purely *immanent*), going beyond All, embracing All. The Great Nest is a multidimensional latticework of Love—*eros, agape, karuna, maitri*—call it what you will, it leaves no corner of the Kosmos untouched by care nor alien to the mysteries of grace."

Wilber urges that it's imperative that this "wisdom of premodernity" be combined and integrated with the "many refinements (and sometimes corrections) offered by modernity and postmodernity." By following the "general contours of the various levels" of this Great Nest, he suggests, we'll find the best way to construct a truly integral view, one that will "affirm our continuity with the wisdom of the ages; a way to acknowledge our own ancestors; a way to transcend and include that which went before us, and thus flow with the current of the Kosmos."

Wilber's integral psychology is aligned with the enduring core of the perennial philosophy. He observes that "human beings have available to them an extraordinary Spectrum of Consciousness, reaching from prepersonal to personal to transpersonal states . . . a richly textured rainbow of consciousness, spanning subconscious to self-conscious to superconscious." This also includes "the higher (transpersonal) stages," or the "upper reaches of the spectrum of consciousness" where, as Wilber explains, "orthodox Western psychological research begins to abandon us, and we increasingly must draw on the great sages and contemplatives, East and West, North and South." Although Wilber assures us that "a general cross-cultural *similarity* of these higher, transrational, transpersonal stages is a sure sign that we are photographing some very real currents in a very real River," he nonetheless emphasizes that "the Great Nest is a potential, not a given," even with the higher levels, and especially on a collective scale. Yet he relies on evidence showing "the fact that the great yogis, saints, and sages have *already* experienced many of the transpersonal realms," therefore "the fact remains that *right now* we have at least these extraordinary transpersonal realms already available to us."

Wilber affirms that the *basic waves* themselves are not "permanently fixed and unchanging essences," like rigid philosophical ideals or "eternally unchanging archetypal molds." Rather, they're more like the "habits of evolution," or "a Kosmic memory," or "evolutionary grooves" that exist as "a great morphogenetic field or developmental space—stretching from matter to mind to spirit—in which various potentials unfold into actuality." And although existing as a nested holarchy, Wilber specifies that "overall development is absolutely not a linear, sequential, ladder-like affair. It is a fluid flowing of many streams through these basic waves." He again points to the charts, which outline the various correlations of the basic waves as being a "master template taken from premodern, modern, and postmodern sources, using each to fill in the gaps in the others." Yet still he qualifies, "In all the charts, the correlations I have given among the various stages and theorists are very general, meant only to get us in the right ballpark (and initiate more refined and careful correlations)."

In regard to the charts in the book's Appendix, Wilber explains that they're "based on the textual reports of some three thousand years of meditative experience, coupled with recent psychological research; but they are always open to revision and clarification." However, they present the Great Nest of Spirit in "a slightly more sophisticated version: matter, sensation, perception, exocept, impulse, image, symbol, endocept, concept, rule, formal, vision-logic, vision, archetype, formless, nondual." Nevertheless, these "enduring holistic patterns" are "not rigidly separate and isolated," rather they're "very fluid and flowing," such that "overall development is a very messy affair!"

Next, in order to better clarify the slippery distinction between the *structures* and *states* of consciousness, Wilber links his integral system with "the most classic, and probably the oldest, of the sophisticated versions of the Great Nest . . . that of Vedanta [Hinduism] which also includes the extremely important distinctions between states, bodies, and structures":

I. "A **Body** is the *energetic support* of the various states and levels of mind, of which Vedanta gives three:

1. the **Gross Body** of the *waking state* (which supports the material mind);

2. the **Subtle Body** of the *dreaming state* (which supports the emotional, mental, and higher mental levels);

3. the **Causal Body** of *deep sleep* (which supports the spiritual mind)."

II. "A **Structure** is a *sheath* or *level* of consciousness, of which the Vedanta gives five of the most important:

1. the Material level;

2. the Biological level;

3. the Mental level;

4. the Higher Mental;

5. the Spiritual. "

In short, structures are "the *holistic patterns* that are found in both the *levels* of development and the *lines* of development," thus they're "stable patterns of events," which are distinguished as two major types:

1. **Basic Structures** are "in the basic levels of consciousness (such as sensation, impulse, image, rule, form-op, vision-logic, psychic, subtle, etc.)";

2. **Developmental Lines** are structures "of consciousness such as the stages of cognition, affect, needs, morals, and so on).

In addition, following his previous work, Wilber points out that "Psychological Structures can be divided and subdivided in numerous ways:

- *Deep* and *Surface* [structures or features];

- *Levels* and *Lines* [or basic waves and developmental streams];

- *Enduring* and *Transitional* [or permanent and temporary structures]."

III. "A **State** is a *state* of consciousness, such as *waking, dreaming,* and *deep sleep*," therefore "the major states are also of two [or three] general types":

1. **Natural States** of consciousness, such as waking (gross ego), dreaming (subtle soul), and deep sleep (causal spirit); Wilber subdivides these states into the various forms of mysticism (nature, deity, formless, nondual). He also explains that "The importance of these three (or four) natural states is that every human being, at no matter what stage of structure or level of develop-

ment, has available the general spectrum of consciousness—ego to soul to spirit—at least as temporary states, for the simple reason that all humans wake, dream, and sleep."

2. **Altered States** are nonordinary or non-normal states of consciousness that are always temporary, including peak experiences, which range from "drug-induced states to near-death experiences to meditative states," such that "Peak experiences can occur to individuals at almost any stage of development." However, Wilber importantly explains, "The way in which those states or realms are experienced and interpreted depends to some degree on the stage of development of the person having the peak experience," therefore Wilber's integral psychology creates "a grid of around sixteen very general types of spiritual experience: psychic, subtle, causal, and nondual states *poured into* archaic, magic, mythic, and rational structures."

3. **Meditative States,** on the other hand, "access these higher [transpersonal] realms in a deliberate and prolonged fashion," therefore, Wilber points out that "*Temporary states* must become *permanent traits*. Higher development involves, in part, the conversion of altered states into permanent realizations . . . [where] the transpersonal potentials that were only available in temporary *states* of consciousness are increasingly converted into enduring *structures* of consciousness (states into traits). This is where meditative states becomes increasingly important" because as the higher "basic structures in the Great Nest of Being . . . emerge permanently in an individual's development, their potentials, once available only in passing states, become enduring contours of an enlightened mind."

This type of integral psychology shares many important similarities with other theoretical systems, including the Eastern "chakra system, the Vedanta sheaths and states, the Buddhist vijnanas, the Kashmir Shaivite vibratory levels, and Aurobindo's superconscient hierarchy," as well the Western "Neoplatonic tradition, represented by currents from Plotinus to Kabbalah to Sufism to Christian mysticism. . . ."

Wilber brings up the traditional concept of "Seven Ages of a Person," where "each of the seven stages is said to take seven years," therefore (in his charts) the integral model also maps the approximate "dates of emergence of the basic waves," or the "average ages of emergence of the basic structures of consciousness." However, he admits, "exactly how to divide and subdivide the number of colors in a rainbow is largely a matter of choice." In an endnote, Wilber indicates that he's also "subdivided many of the basic structures into early, middle, and late," although he prefers and tends to use "low" and "high." The integral theorist recognizes "around seven to ten Functional Groupings [or 'orienting generalizations'] which reflect easily recognizable Stages" of human growth:

1. **sensorimotor** [0–18 months];

2. **phantasmic-emotional** (or emotional-sexual) [1–3 years];

3. **rep-mind** (short for representational mind, similar to general preoperational thinking, or 'pre-op') [3–6 years];

4. **rule/role mind** (similar to concrete operational thinking, or 'con-op') [7–12 years];

5. **formal-reflexive** (similar to formal operational, or 'form-op') [12–21 years];

6. **vision-logic** [open ages, 21–28 years];

7. **psychic** [28–35 years];

8. **subtle** [35–42 years];

9. **causal** [42–49 years];

10. **nondual** [49 years–]."

Wilber carefully explains that the development of the spectrum of consciousness is not exactly the same as the range of cognitive development, although they may be similar. This is especially true since cognition in Western psychology has been reduced by "the world of scientific materialism" to exclude the stages of higher "postformal development," especially the "transmental domains (of psychic, subtle, causal, or nondual occasions—transrational and transpersonal)." As a general rule, then, Wilber maintains that "cognitive development is necessary (but not sufficient) for these other developments" since in actuality cognition is only one "relatively independent" developmental line among the many others.

The charts and the text recapitulate the current research by showing that "Cognitive Development moves through the three or four major stages (with numerous substages)":

- **sensorimotor** (*physical-biological; preconventional; egocentric*) "stages usually occur in the first two years of life, and result in a capacity to perceive physical objects."

- **concrete** (*preformal, magic/mythic; conventional; sociocentric; ethnocentric*) stage occurs when "cognition then slowly begins to learn to represent these objects with names, symbols, and concepts. . . . [For] there is a world of difference between mythic symbols taken to be *concretely* and *literally* true . . . and mythic symbols imbued with *metaphor* and *perspectivism,* which only come into existence with formal and postformal consciousness." However, most "concrete operations are carried out by *schemas* and *rules,* which also allow the self at this stage to adopt various *roles* in society, and thus move from the egocentric/preconventional realm to the sociocentric/conventional."

- **formal** (*reason/rationality; postconventional; worldcentric*) is when "consciousness further develops and deepens, these concrete categories and operations begin to become more generalized, more abstract (in the sense of being applicable to more and more situations), and thus more *universal.* Formal operational consciousness can therefore begin to support a postconventional orientation to the world, escaping in many ways the ethnocentric/sociocentric world of concrete (and mythic-membership) thought." Rationality (or "reason in the broad sense"), what Gebser calls *perspectival reason,* supports critical thinking because it is "highly reflexive" and "allows sustained introspection. And it is the first structure that can imagine 'as if' and 'what if' worlds: it becomes a true dreamer and visionary."

- **postformal** (*vision-logic; mature postconventional*) includes "the existence of yet higher *postformal* stages of cognition—or a higher reason—which takes even more perspectives into account. . . . [This] bringing together [of] multiple perspectives while unduly privileging none is what Gebser called *integral-aperspectival,* which involves a further deepening of worldcentric and postconventional consciousness." Wilber also confirms that there is general agreement that these *postformal* or "Vision-Logic" developments involve at least two or three major stages:

1. **early vision-logic** is when "growing beyond abstract universal formalism (of formop), consciousness moves first into a cognition of dynamic relativity and pluralism";

2. **middle to late vision-logic** proceeds "further into a cognition of unity, holism, dynamic dialecticism, or universal integralism."

Nonetheless, as Wilber points out, "As 'holistic' as these vision-logic developments are, they are still mental realm developments. They are the very highest reaches of the mental realms, to be sure, but beyond them lie supramental and properly transrational developments."

In summary, Wilber's full-spectrum cognitive developmental model presents "around sixteen waves in the overall spectrum of consciousness, but these can be condensed or expanded in numerous ways." Again he reminds us that "the Great Nest is simply a great morphogenetic field that provides a developmental space in which human potentials can unfold . . . [while evolving] through these general waves in the great River, some two dozen different developmental streams will flow, all navigated by the self on its extraordinary journey from dust to Deity."

CHAPTER 2. "THE DEVELOPMENTAL LINES" clearly distinguishes between the basic waves or the basic structures or levels of the Great Nest and the psychological concept of the "relatively independent" developmental lines, also called developmental streams (after Howard Gardner). These streams all run through the basic waves "at different rates, with a different dynamic, and on a different time schedule." The *developmental lines,* in part, include:

- morals
- affects [feelings]
- self-identity
- psychosexuality
- cognition
- ideas of the good
- role taking
- socio-emotional capacity
- creativity
- altruism
- spiritual (including several lines such as care, openness, concern, religious faith, meditative stages)

- joy
- communicative competence
- modes of space and time
- death-seizure
- needs
- worldviews
- logico-mathematical competence
- kinesthetic skills
- gender identity
- empathy

Wilber states that "overall development—the sum total of all these different lines—shows no linear or sequential development whatsoever. . . . However, the bulk of research has continued to find that each developmental line itself tends to unfold in a sequential, holarchical fashion: higher stages in each line tend to build upon or incorporate the earlier stages, no stages can be skipped, and the stages

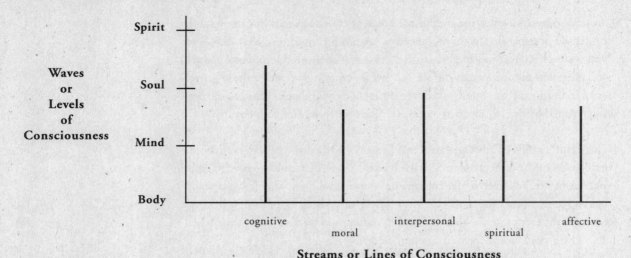

Waves or Levels of Consciousness

Spirit —

Soul —

Mind —

Body

cognitive   moral   interpersonal   spiritual   affective

Streams or Lines of Consciousness

The Integral Psychograph
FIGURE 2

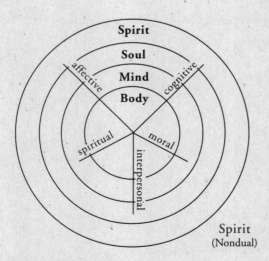

The Integral Psychograph
as a Holarchy
FIGURE 3

emerge in an order that cannot be altered by environmental conditioning or social reinforcement." In this case, the developmental streams develop "in a relatively independent manner" as they evolutionarily "migrate through" this Great Nest, which, as we've seen, "is most basically that morphogenetic field or developmental space." Wilber concludes, "The individual potentials that emerge in human development . . . tend to follow the current in the great River of Life, they follow the waves in the Great Holarchy."

Wilber introduces the notion of an *integral psychograph* to more accurately represent this complex process since "a person can be highly evolved in some lines, medium in others, and low in still others." This integral psychograph depicts a graph where "the levels in the Great Nest are shown on the *vertical axis,* and through those levels run the various *lines.*" (See Figure 2: "The Integral Psychograph.")

However, Wilber explains, "Since the Great Nest is actually a *holarchy,* we can more accurately represent the integral psychograph" with the developmental streams portrayed as lines radiating throughout the nested concentric circles which represent the basic waves or structures of consciousness. (See Figure 3: "The Integral Psychograph as a Holarchy.")

Wilber then clarifies the important distinctions between:

- **Hierarchy** or "increasing holistic capacity . . . the relation *between* levels, which each senior level transcending and including its juniors, but not vice versa . . . and that 'not vice versa' established an *asymmetrical hierarchy of increasing holistic capacity.*"

- **Heterarchy** or "nonhierarchical interaction among mutually equivalent elements . . . *within* each level, most elements exist as mutually equivalent and mutually interacting patterns. Much of development—at least half of it—involves various types of nonhierarchical, heterarchical processes of competence articulation and application."

- **Holarchy** is "a *balance* of both *hierarchy* (qualitatively *ranked* levels) and *heterarchy* (mutually *linked* dimensions). Theorists who attempt to use only one or the other of those types or relations have consistently failed to explain development at all."

CHAPTER 3. "THE SELF" continues to examine the central items of an integral model of psychology by turning attention *to the self* or the "navigator" of both the basic waves and the developmental streams. Wilber specifies that "an amalgam of all these 'selves' . . . and all of them are important for understanding the development or evolution of consciousness" which comprise the *overall self:*

- **Proximate self** or the "I" or the "closer" self-sense is "some sort of *observing self* (an inner subject or watcher)" that is the *"aspect of the self [which] does undergo relatively sequential or stage-like development,"* yet, because "the overall self contains several different *streams* (and all sorts of *subpersonalities*), the overall self does *not* show a sequential stage-like development." This *proximate self-development* (similar to Loevinger's ego development) is, Wilber claims, "at the very heart of the evolution of consciousness. *For it is the proximate self that is the navigator through the basic waves in the Great Nest of Being.*"

- **Distal self** or "me," "or even 'mine,'" or the "farther away" self-sense is "some sort of *observed self* (some *objective* things you can see or know about yourself—I am father, mother, doctor, clerk; I weigh so many pounds, have blond hair, etc.)"

- **Witness** or "the transcendental Self, antecedent Self, or 'I-I'" is that aspect of the self where "according to the mystics, you are one with God as ultimate Subject or pure Consciousness—a pure Emptiness that, as absolute Witness, I-I, or Seer, can never itself be seen, and yet paradoxically exists as Everything that is seen: the Spirit that transcends all—and thus can never be seen—and includes all—and thus is everything you are looking at right now."

Wilber then reviews the general patterns involved in the form of development (see: *The Atman Project,* 1980, Chapter 10) which is what occurs when "the self (the proximate self) encounters a new level in the Great Nest." By doing so, the self "goes through a Fulcrum (or a milestone) of its own development" as it evolves through a "1-2-3 Process" of transformation:

1. "first [the self] identifies with [that level] and consolidates its;

2. then disidentifies with it (transcends it, de-embeds from it); and

3. then includes and integrates it from the next higher level."

In this unfolding sequence, Wilber explains, the proximate self ("I") at each fulcrum must deal with "a difficult life-death battle ['literally, as a type of death-seizure'], involving the death (or the disidentifying with, or the transcendence) of each level, which can often be quite traumatic." Indeed, "the only reason the self eventually accepts the *death* of its given level is that the *life* of the next higher level is even more enticing and ultimately satisfying." Finally, "when all deaths have been died, the result is only God, or what the Sufis call the Supreme Identity of self and spirit."

In addition, the self has a certain amount of "fluid access," since "to say that the self has identified with a particular wave in the Great Rainbow does not, however, mean that the self is rigidly stuck at that level. On the contrary, the self can be *all over the place* on occasion. Within limits, the self can temporarily roam all over the spectrum of consciousness—it can regress, or move down the holarchy of being and knowing; it can spiral, reconsolidate, and return." Yet still, Wilber confirms, "the self's Center of Gravity, so to speak, tends to hover around one basic level of consciousness at any given time."

In summary the proximate self "is the navigator of the *waves* (and *streams*) in the great River of Life . . . as the self navigates from egocentric to sociocentric to worldcentric to theocentric waves (or precon to con to postcon to post-postcon levels of overall development)—an identity that ranges from matter to id to ego to God." In other words, Wilber defines the proximate self as "the central navigator through the Great Nest, the self is the locus of such important functions of the self" or *functional invariants:*

• **"identification** (what to call 'I');

• **will** (or choices that are free within the constraints and limitations of its present level);

- **defenses** (which are laid down hierarchically);

- **metabolism** (which converts states into traits), and most important of all;

- **integration** (the self is responsible for balancing and integrating whatever elements are present)."

In conclusion, Wilber claims it's important to realize that "the self as navigator is a juggling act of all the elements that it will encounter on its extraordinary journey from subconscious to self-conscious to superconscious." Or, more precisely: "What each of us call an 'I' (the proximate self) is both a *constant function* and a *developmental stream.* That is, the self has several *functional invariants* that constitute its *central activity* . . . and this self (with its functions) also undergoes *its own development* through the basic waves in the Great Nest (the stages): material self to bodily self to mental self to soul self to selfless Self. Especially significant is the fact that, as the locus of integration, the self is responsible *for balancing and integrating all of the levels, lines, and states in the individual.*"

CHAPTER 4. "THE SELF-RELATED STREAMS" opens with the *overall self* navigating "through the basic waves of the Great Nest by using the self's capacity to identify with each wave and ride it to some sort of completion." Wilber describes "the self's identifying with a particular level of consciousness" as its "exclusive identification," which is specifically when "The proximate self's center of gravity is predominately at one general *functional grouping* (which generates a corresponding *fulcrum* of self-development)." In other words, as Wilber explains, when "the self's center of gravity orbits around a new level of consciousness . . . [it has] a new and different outlook on life . . . a different architecture, the self at each level *sees a different world:* it faces new fears, has different goals, suffers new problems. It has a new set of needs, a new class of morals, a new sense of self."

Technically, Wilber calls these subsets of developmental lines in general *self-related* lines or streams, defined as those "developmental lines that are especially and intimately associated with the self, its needs, its identity, and its development." In other words, "The self-related stages . . . are most intimately connected with [both] *self identity,* and *morals and perspectives,* or the different types of outlook (and *worldview*) that the self has at each of the basic levels of consciousness." He concludes: "Each stage of development sees a different world—with different needs, different tasks, different dilemmas, different problems, and pathologies. Instead of reducing all of life's problems to something that went wrong in the first age of a person, there are six or seven other ages, equally important, sometimes more important."

After analyzing numerous researchers' work, Wilber summarizes their developmental message since they all tell a similar story of consciousness going through various self-stages.

The *self-related streams* also include the important developmental lines, which show that as the self expands to "a new sense of identity, it has a new and higher view of the world, with a wider and more encompassing set of morals and perspectives." A number of significant researchers are introduced, many of whom are included in the charts. Although "these different self-related developmental streams still retain a relatively independent character," Wilber points out that these researchers all see "a general view of morals and perspectives evolving from: preconventional to conventional to postconventional (to post-postconventional)—yet more general evidence for the Great Nest and its often universal currents." Nonetheless, the self-related streams are "necessary but not sufficient" for further development in the other developmental lines. Therefore, Wilber explains, "even though most of the individual developmental lines undergo a sequential holarchical unfolding, overall development itself does not."

According to the evidence, Wilber maintains, there actually are universal patterns representing invariant sequences, although a number of critics object that this type of developmental work may be biased and "inherently Eurocentric, marginalizing, sexist," which are important concerns. Wilber's schema, however, suggests that the stages are essentially "surfing the waves of the nonrelativistic Great Holarchy . . . flowing across a morphogenetic field and developmental space that spans insentient matter to superconscient spirit, while remaining, at every stage, fully grounded in that Spirit which is the suchness and isness of the entire display."

In order to present some concrete evidence from other researchers that confirms the viability of his developmental model, Wilber gives an extensive review of Spiral Dynamics based on the work of Donald Beck, Christopher Cowan, and Clare Graves and their so-called waves of existence. These eight basic waves of existence or "eight general value memes or deep structures" literally create the "'different worlds' available to the self as it develops along the great spiral of existence, driven by both its own internal dynamics and shifting life conditions." Paraphrasing Beck, Wilber refers to "all eight waves, the percentage of the world population at each wave, and the percentage of social power held by each":

The first six levels are subsistence levels that indicate first-tier thinking:

- **archaic-instinctual** (beige) or *uroboric*; with 0.1 percent of the adult population, 0 percent power; beige is "basic survival . . . uses habits and instincts just to survive . . . forms into survival bands to perpetuate life. . . ."

- **animistic-tribalistic** (purple) or *typhonic-magic*; with 10 percent of population, 1 percent of the power; with purple, "thinking is animistic; magical spirits, good and bad, swarm the earth leaving blessings, curses, and spells that determine events. Forms into ethnic tribes. . . ."

- **power gods** (red) or *mythic-magic*; with 20 percent of the population, 5 percent of the power; red is the "first emergence of a self distinct from the tribe; powerful, impulsive, egocentric, heroic. Mythic spirits, dragons, beasts, and powerful people . . . The basis of feudal empires—power and glory. . . ."

- **conformist rule** (blue) or *mythic-membership*; with 40 percent of the population, 30 percent of the power; with blue, "Life has meaning, direction, and purpose, with outcomes determined by an all-powerful Other or Order . . . Basis of ancient nations. Rigid social hierarchies . . . Law and order . . . concrete-literal and fundamentalist belief. . . ."

- **scientific achievement** or **individualistic achiever** (orange) or *rational-egoic*; with 30 percent of the population, 50 percent of the power; with orange, "The self 'escapes' from the 'herd mentality' of blue, and seeks truth and meaning in individualistic terms—hypothetico-deductive, experimental, objective, mechanistic, operational—'scientific' in the typical sense. . . . The laws of science rule politics, the economy, and human events. . . . Basis of corporate states. . . ."

- **sensitive self** or **relativistic network self** (green) or *early vision-logic*; with 10 percent of the population, 15 percent of the power; with green, "communitarian, human bonding, ecological sensitivity, networking . . . Against hierarchy; establishes lateral bonding and linking . . . Emphasis on dialogue, relationships. Basis of collective communities (i.e., freely chosen affiliations based on shared sentiments) . . . Strongly egalitarian, antihierarchy, pluralistic values, social construction of reality, diversity, multiculturalism, relativistic value systems; this worldview is often called pluralistic relativism. . . ."

With "second-tier thinking," Wilber explains (following Beck) that there's a "revolutionary shift in consciousness," or a "momentous leap" (Graves), so that "with the completion of the green meme, human consciousness is poised for a *quantum jump* into . . . Second-Tier Consciousness, [where] one can think both vertically and horizontally, using both hierarchies and heterarchies; one can, for the first time, *vividly grasp the entire spectrum of interior development,* and thus see that each level, each meme, each wave is crucially important for the health of the overall spiral."

- **systematic-integrative** (yellow) or *middle vision-logic* (Wilber); with "1 percent of the population, 5 percent of the power"; with yellow, "Life is a kalei-

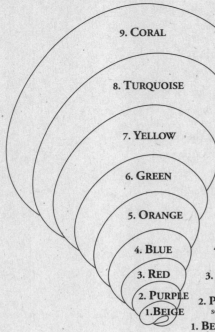

THIRD-TIER THINKING

9. **CORAL:** PSYCHIC / Integral-Holonic (and beyond to the transpersonal)
(slowly emerging); beginning of transpersonal waves

SECOND-TIER THINKING

8. **TURQUOISE:** HOLISTIC / Whole View / Late Vision-Logic / Centaur
synergize & macromanage entire spiral; grand unification (T.O.E.); universal

7. **YELLOW:** INTEGRATIVE / Flex Flow / Middle Vision-Logic
integrate and align systems; natural hierarchies (holarchies)

FIRST-TIER THINKING

6. **GREEN:** NETWORK SELF / Human Bond / Early Vision-Logic
explore inner self, equalize others; pluralistic relativism

5. **ORANGE:** SCIENTIFIC-INDIVIDUALISTIC / Strive Drive / Formal-Rational
analyze and strategize to prosper; corporate states; worldcentric

4. **BLUE:** CONFORMIST RULE / Truth Force / Mythic-Membership
find purpose, bring order, insure future; ancient nations; ethnocentric

3. **RED:** POWER GODS / Magic-Mythic
express impulsively, break free, be strong; feudal empires; egocentric

2. **PURPLE:** MAGICAL-ANIMISTIC / Kin Spirits / Magic-Typhon
seek harmony and safety in a mysterious world; ethnic tribes

1. **BEIGE:** INSTINCTUAL / Survival Sense / Archaic
sharpen instincts and innate senses; survival bands

THE SPIRAL OF
DEVELOPMENT
(Transcend-and-Include)
*Adapted by permission from
Don Beck and Chris Cowan,
Spiral Dynamics: Mastering
Values, Leadership, and
Change (1995)*

FIGURE 4

doscope of natural hierarchies [holarchies], systems, and forms. Flexibility, spontaneity, and functionality have the highest priority. Differences and pluralities can be integrated into interdependent, natural flows. . . . The prevailing world order is the result of the existence of different levels of reality (memes) and the inevitable patterns of movement up and down the dynamic spiral."

- **global-holistic** (turquoise) or *late vision-logic* (Wilber); with turquoise, "Universal holistic system, holons/waves of integrative energies; unites feeling with knowledge [centaur]; multiple levels interwoven into one conscious system . . . Uses the entire spiral; sees multiple levels of interaction; detects harmonics, the mystical forces, and the pervasive flow-states that permeate any organization."

(See Figure 4: "The Spiral of Development (Transcend-and-Include)."
Counter to the emphasis on vertical waves (or structural levels), Wilber explains that "horizontal typologies" such as Jungian types, the Enneagram, Myer-Briggs, and so on are "not vertical levels, stages, or waves of development, but rather different types of orientations possible at each of the various levels." There-

fore, they only represent the "types of personalities that may—or may not—be found at any of the stages," especially since "they simply outline some of the *possible* orientations that may, or may not, be found at any of the stages, and thus their inclusion is based more on personal taste and usefulness than on universal evidence."

Again, in summary, it's the *proximate self* who navigates all the "multiple waves and streams—and types—that can be found in the great River of Life. None of them have the final answer; all of them have something important to tell us." Once more, Wilber emphasizes that the self's journey transcends and includes the entire spectrum of consciousness by "honoring and embracing each and every wave and stream in the Great Nest of Being."

Interestingly, Wilber notes that "The vast majority of modern researchers do not include, or even acknowledge, the higher, transpersonal, spiritual levels." This is especially striking because since premodern times there have always been very rare souls, humanity's "highly evolved yogis, saints, and sages [who have] had access to the transrational, transpersonal, transcendental realms—they embraced, in their own way and in their own terms, the entire Great Nest of Being, subconscious to self-conscious to superconscious." Indeed, he emphasizes that the "Wisdom of Premodernity was embodied in the Great Nest of Being . . . whereas Modernity, for the most part, denies [these levels] altogether." In fact, he bemoans, the bleakness of scientific materialism acts as if "these higher, transpersonal, spiritual realms" were some sort of "massive collective hallucination," while arrogantly proclaiming the "extraordinary journey from matter to body to mind to soul to spirit" is "nothing but arrangements of frisky dirt." And worse, he ironically notes, everything's supposedly run and created by "dumb chance and dumb selection, as if two dumbs would make a Shakespeare."

The integral vision, on the other hand, claims that this modern "cultural catastrophe is 'horrifying,'" yet, nevertheless, it cannot stop the "inherent potentials of the bodymind" which are essentially grounded in "the mystery of transcendence, ecstasy and liberation, radiant God and beloved Goddess." This is exactly why any truly multidimensional psychology will fundamentally insist that *integral* means, "if it means anything, the integration of all that is given to humanity; and if modernity insists instead on trashing everything that came before it, then the integral enterprise is derailed from the start." In other words, according to Wilber, an "integral psychology (or any sort of integral studies)" will have to adamantly maintain that "If we are to move forward to the bright promise of an integral approach, we need a way to honor *both* the strengths and the weaknesses of *both premodernity* and *modernity.* If we can find a coherent way to honor truths both *ancient* and *modern,* a truly integral approach might become more than a passing dream."

PART II. PATH: "FROM PREMODERN TO MODERN" mentions that the "great systems of spirituality . . . are part of the legacy of premodernity," whereas modernity has "specifically defined itself as 'anti-religion.'" Therefore, Wilber says that "a truly integral psychology would surely wish to include the religious or spiritual dimensions of men and women," in which case it would surely need "to embrace the enduring insights of both 'religious' premodernity and 'scientific' modernity." Nonetheless, he concludes, it would only be able to do so by "jettisoning their limitations," for this is the only way to foster a truly integral or "constructive postmodern approach" which can both "appreciate the strengths of the ancient traditions" while simultaneously "understanding the important contributions of modernity."

CHAPTER 5. "WHAT IS MODERNITY?" focuses on the "widespread loss of meaning," as well as "the ideals of equality, freedom, and justice, regardless of race, class, creed, or gender; modern medicine, physics, biology, and chemistry; the end of slavery; the rise of feminism; and the universal rights of humankind" in modern life.

After explaining that the *triumph of modernity* is best seen as the "differentiation of art, morals, and science," Wilber introduces his conception of the *four quadrants* or the four general classes" representing "the interior and the exterior of the individual and the collective." In turn, these four aspects "can be summarized as the 'Big Three' of I, we, and it." And since, Wilber continues, the truly integral approach is intended "to reintroduce consciousness, the within, the deep, the spiritual, and thus move gently toward a more integral embrace," then the integral task is "to take the strengths of both premodernity and modernity, and jettison their weaknesses."

CHAPTER 6. "TO INTEGRATE PREMODERN AND MODERN" emphasizes the integrative conclusion of *The Marriage of Sense and Soul* that "In order to integrate premodern and modern, we need to integrate the Great Nest with the differentiations of modernity. This means that each of the levels in the traditional Great Nest needs to be carefully differentiated according to the four quadrants. To do so would honor *both* the core claim of ancient spirituality—namely, the Great Nest—and the core claim of modernity—namely, the differentiation of the value spheres [art, culture, science]. And this would offer a foundation that might help us move toward a more Integral Psychology."

In other words, Wilber is summarily suggesting an "all-level, all-quadrant" (AQAL) approach to integral studies that would entail:

- the very best of Premodernity (which was *all-level*);

- the best of Modernity (which was *all-quadrant*);

- the best of Postmodernity (which involves their *integration*).

Only this type of integral "marriage would allow us to move forward to the bright promise of a Constructive Postmodernity: the integration of art, morals, and science, at every level of the extraordinary spectrum of consciousness, body to mind to soul to spirit." (Wilber further explores these themes in Chapter 13: "From Modernity to Postmodernity" in *Integral Psychology*.)

CHAPTER 7. "SOME IMPORTANT MODERN PIONEERS" reviews Wilber's integral approach, which "allows us to map the exterior correlates of interior states, without attempting to reduce one to the other." This is a *tracking* of "the interior waves of the full spectrum of consciousness, as they appear in an individual—from body (feelings) to mind (ideas) to soul (luminosity) to spirit (all-pervading) . . . These cannot be reduced to material dimensions (because, unlike matter, they do not possess simple location). Nonetheless, feelings, mental ideas, and spiritual illuminations all have physical correlates that can be measured by various scientific means, from EEG machines to blood chemistry to PET scans to galvanic skin responses." (See Figure 5: "Correlations of Interior (Consciousness) States with Exterior (Material) States.")

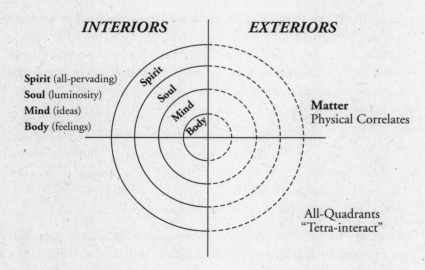

Correlations of Interior (Consciousness) States with Exterior (Material) States

FIGURE 5

Nonetheless, the integral approach posits that "none of those Right-Hand correlates have any *value gradations,* which are the essence of the Left-Hand domains themselves." Therefore, in contradistinction to flatland reductionism or scientific materialism, it's not necessary to "erase value, meaning, depth and Divinity from the face of the Kosmos itself." Wilber argues that it's perfectly valid to see "that some levels and stages of growth are better, higher, deeper, more encompassing, and more liberating—moving from egocentric to sociocentric to worldcentric—and although all of those interior waves have *exterior correlates* in organic brain functions (which can and should be studied), they cannot be reduced to those correlates without completely destroying the very factors that define them."

He suggests that an all-quadrant, all-level approach is a method by which "science could supplement (not replace) religion, spirituality, and psychology." In order to more convincingly demonstrate this point, Wilber points to "some important modern pioneers" as exemplars of this integral approach, especially since they "increasingly had access to scientific data on evolution, and thus increasingly understood something about the Great Nest that the premodern pioneers usually did not: it shows development not just in individuals, but in the species; not just ontogenetically, but phylogenetically." Wilber assesses some of these integral pioneers:

- James Mark Baldwin (1861–1934) "came to see consciousness as developing through a half-dozen qualitatively distinct stages, each of which hierarchically differentiates and reintegrates the lower elements on a higher level," thus Baldwin offered "one of the first, and still one of the most sophisticated, accounts of the stages of religious development."

- Jürgen Habermas (born 1929) is "the most comprehensive developmental philosopher now working. However, lamentably, he leaves out and totally ignores any of the stages of I, we, and it consciousness beyond those of vision-logic. . . . Nonetheless, for the ground it covers . . . no integral view can hope to succeed that ignores his profound contributions."

- Sri Aurobindo (1872–1955) is "India's greatest modern philosopher-sage" and was "one of the first truly great sages to have access to the evolutionary record (disclosed by the differentiations of modernity)." This, according to Wilber, allowed him to develop a very sophisticated "integral yoga . . . India's first great synthesis of the truths of the premodern Great Nest with the truths brought by the differentiations of modernity."

- Abraham Maslow (1908–1970) is "a developmentalist . . . [and] one of the first to gather substantial empirical and phenomenological evidence suggesting that each level in the Great Nest has a different need, that these needs emerge hierarchically and prepotently, and that each of us carries the potential for all of these levels-needs."

Nevertheless, as inspiring as these pioneers' work surely is, Wilber goes on to point out that "Each new generation has a chance to move the integral vision forward in a substantial way, simply because new information, data, and discoveries are constantly being made," guiding "us to even further integral visions."

PART III. FRUITION: "AN INTEGRAL MODEL" begins with an overview of the previous chapters by again stating that a true integral psychology would include:

- "the very best of Premodernity (the Great Nest);
- Modernity (the differentiation and evolution of the value spheres);
- Postmodernity (their integration across all levels in the Great Nest)."

In this section, Wilber presents the outcome of an all-level, all-quadrant approach.

CHAPTER 8. "THE ARCHEOLOGY OF SPIRIT" is the longest chapter in the book, and is packed with detail describing the various *fulcrums* or "milestones" in the development of the proximate self, which Wilber metaphorically titles the Archeology of Spirit.

Wilber begins by encapsulating his current integral view (presented in the foregoing sections) by stating "in short: *waves, streams, states, self*, and *self-streams* . . . Thus, in the simplest of terms, we can say that *development* comes down to *waves, streams*, and *self.*" These are the "major components of an Integral Model" which comprehensively integrates the best of modern evidence with "the best of the perennial philosophers, to arrive at a master template of a Full-Spectrum Developmental Space, reaching from matter to body to mind to soul to spirit . . . [all being] basic waves of being and knowing through which the various developmental streams will flow, all of which are balanced and (ideally) integrated by the self in the remarkable journey from subconscious to self-conscious to superconscious." Wilber also reminds us that when these "basic structures, levels, or waves in the Great Nest of Being and Knowing" are "taken together, the basic levels in virtually every major system, ancient and modern, Eastern and Western, simply describe a vast morphogenetic field or developmental space, and one that is migratory—it grades holarchically, transcending and including, nests within nest indefinitely, inviting a development that is envelopment."

Wilber then focuses on *nine correlative fulcrums* [including Grof's birth fulcrum, F-0, which makes ten] "that the self goes through in a complete evolution or development through the entire Great Nest . . . [or] the self's journey from conception to enlightenment." He specifies that "Each time the self (the proximate Self) steps up to a new and higher sphere in the Great Nest, it can do so in a relatively healthy fashion—which means it smoothly differentiates and integrates the elements of the level—or in a relatively pathological fashion—which means: it either *fails to differentiate* (and thus remains in *fusion/fixation/arrest*) or it *fails to integrate* (which results in *repression, alienation, fragmentation*)."

Wilber explains, "The differentiation-and-integration process can go wrong at each and every self-stage (or fulcrum), and the *level* of the fulcrum helps determine the *level* [not just *type*] of pathology." This is because "A failure at any of those points results in a *pathology*—a malformation, crippling, or narrowing of the self in its otherwise ever-expanding journey." Indeed, Wilber concludes, "The one thing we learn from the existence of the multiple levels of the spectrum of consciousness is just how many different dimensions of existence there are, and how a sensitivity to these *multiple dimensions* demands a *multiplicity of* treatment modalities." In addition, a number of crucial factors are outlined:

- "Each level of self development has different types of defenses. The self, at every level, will attempt to *defend* itself against pain, disruption, and ultimately death, and it will do so *using whatever tools are present at that level.*"

- "In short, the level of defenses, the level of self development, and the level of pathology—all are facets of the same migratory unfolding across the qualitatively distinct waves in the Great Nest."

- "Each level of the Great Nest has a qualitatively *different architecture,* and thus each wave of self-development, self-pathology, and treatment likewise has a qualitatively different tone."

The bulk of the chapter contains Wilber's presentation of a simplified summary or what he calls "the archeology of the self": "an archeology of depth," or "the archeology of Spirit." He uses this metaphor of the archeology of Spirit to show that "as the more superficial layers of the Self are peeled off to expose increasingly deeper and more profound waves of consciousness . . . this involves the *emergence* of *ever-greater potentials,* which therefore leads us forward, not backward, and shows us *future evolution* and *growth,* not past evolution and regression. This is an archeology of depth, to be sure, but a depth that plumbs the future, not the past; that reaches into a greater tomorrow, not a dusty yesterday; that unearths the hidden treasures of involution, not the fossils of evolution. *We dig in order to go beyond, not back.*"

In a later section, Wilber gives an overview of the "equally lovely" metaphors of *depth* and *height* since he points out (following Huston Smith) that "the traditions usually refer to greater Levels of Reality as *higher,* and greater Levels of the Self as *deeper,* so that the *higher* you go on the Great Nest of Being, the *deeper* you go into your own selfhood."

Nevertheless, Wilber emphasizes that "In the final analysis levels of reality and levels of consciousness are two phrases for the same thing." This allows Wilber to define the difference between *depth psychology,* which includes "anything *lower* than the ego (archaic impulses, vital emotions, magic-mythic fantasies)" therefore it "actually means lower, primitive psychology"; and *height psychology,* which includes "anything *higher* than the ego (soul and spirit)."

In addition, these two metaphors of depth and height allow Wilber to define some crucial evolutionary principles:

- **"Evolution** is the *ascent of consciousness* from matter to body to mind to soul to spirit";

- **"Involution** is the *descent of consciousness* through any of those vehicles";

- **"Regression** is moving *backward* in the line of evolution";

- **"Development** is moving *forward* in that line [of evolution]."

In other words, Wilber is picturing the Great Nest as "degrees of interior depth . . . since the higher spheres are experienced as being interior to, and deeper than, the lower, which are experienced, in comparison, as superficial, shallow, and exterior"; therefore:

- "the **Body** is experienced as being *inside the physical environment;*

- the **Mind** is experienced as being *inside the body;*

- the **Soul** is experienced *interior to the mind;*

- and deep *within the soul* is **Pure Spirit** itself, which *transcends all* and *embraces all* (thus transcending inside and outside)."

Using this depth metaphor, Wilber describes the development of the self as "slowly abandoning the pale and primitive surfaces, becoming less narcissistic, less of the shallows, less of the surface, and diving instead into the deep, where individual selves are increasingly united in that common Self which shines throughout the entire display . . . [where] the heart of the all-encompassing Self is increasingly intuited." By using the height metaphor he also concludes: "To move from *ego-centric* to *ethnocentric* to *worldcentric* to *theocentric* is to ascend into greater and wider and higher spheres of release and embrace, transcendence and inclusion, freedom and compassion." (See Figure 6: "The Archeology of Spirit: Layers of the Self.")

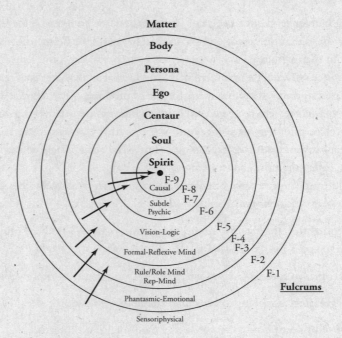

Matter
Body
Persona
Ego
Centaur
Soul
Spirit

F-9
Causal   F-8
            F-7
Subtle
Psychic   F-6
Vision-Logic   F-5
               F-4
Formal-Reflexive Mind   F-3
                      F-2
Rule/Role Mind
Rep-Mind   F-1
                   Fulcrums
Phantasmic-Emotional

Sensoriphysical

The Archeology of Spirit:
Layers of the Self
FIGURE 6

To briefly present this archeological expedition, it's necessary to abridge numerous sections of Wilber's detailed account, including his descriptions of each fulcrum or milestone of the self with their corresponding treatment for the "different pathologies faced by the self on its jostling journey through the great River":

Lower Fulcrums and Pathologies (F-0 to F-3):

(F-1) Fulcrum-1 (*sensoriphysical*) continues when "somewhere during the first year, the infant . . . differentiates its body from the environment, and thus . . . if the self does not correctly differentiate from, and integrate its images of, the physical environment, the result can be psychosis (the individual cannot tell where his body stops and the environment begins, he hallucinates, and so on)." "The *worldview* of this stage is Archaic, and this archaic consciousness, if not differentiated (transcended) and integrated (resolved), can lead to primitive pathologies." Treatment for "the earliest fulcrums (F-0 and F-1) have, until recently, resisted treatment (except for *medication/pacification*), precisely because they are so primitive and difficult to access."

(F-2) Fulcrum-2 (*phantasmic-emotional*) is when "Identity switches from fusion with the material world [fulcrum 1] to an identity with the Emotional-Feeling

Body (which begins fulcrum-2). . . . If the emotional *bodyself* has difficulty differentiating itself from others, the result can be *narcissism* (others are treated as extensions of the self) or *borderline disorders* (others are constantly invading and disrupting the self's fragile boundaries)." "The *worldview* of this stage is Magical—the self can magically order the world around in omnipotent fantasy, the environment is full of animistic displacements . . . *fixation* at this magical level (and magical subpersonalities) is a large part of the cognitive repertoire of the borderline and narcissistic conditions." Treatments for "the borderline level of pathology (F-2) . . . [are] called *structure building:* they attempt to build up the self's boundaries and fortify ego strength. . . . These F-2 approaches include aspects of *object-relations therapy . . . psychoanalytic ego psychology . . . self psychology* . . . and numerous integrations of those approaches."

(F-3) Fulcrum-3 (*rep-mind*) is when "The conceptual mind begins to emerge and develop (especially around 3 to 6 years), the child eventually differentiates the conceptual mind and the emotional body (this is fulcrum 3). . . . [A] failure to differentiate leaves a *fusion* with the labile emotional self, whereas a failure to integrate leads to a *repression* of the emotional self by the newly emerging mental-egoic self (classic psychoneurosis)." "The conceptual self is frightened of, and overwhelmed by, the feelings of the body (especially sex and aggression), and in its misguided attempt to defend itself against these feelings, merely ends up sending them underground (as impulsive subpersonalities), where they cause even more pain and terror than when faced with awareness." Treatment for "typical *neurosis* (F-3) . . . involves relaxing and undoing the repression barrier, recontacting the repressed or shadow feelings, and reintegrating them into the psyche, so that the ongoing flow of consciousness unfolding can more smoothly continue."

Wilber tells us "These therapeutic approaches are generically called *uncovering techniques* because they attempt to uncover and reintegrate the shadow. [However] this 'regression in service of the ego' . . . this healing regressive spiral . . . [or] Curative Spiral is not a regression to a higher ground, but to a lower one, which helps reset the foundations for a surer transcendence." (See Figure 7: "The Curative Spiral.")

Intermediate Fulcrums and Pathologies (F-4 to F-6):

(F-4) Fulcrum-4 (*rule/role mind*) "begins to emerge (typically ages 6–12) and the self's center of gravity starts to identify with that wave . . . [as it] begins to take the *role of others,* and therefore begins to shift from egocentric/preconventional to *sociocentric/conventional.* If something goes wrong at this general wave, we get a 'script pathology'—all of the false, misleading, and sometimes crippling scripts, stories,

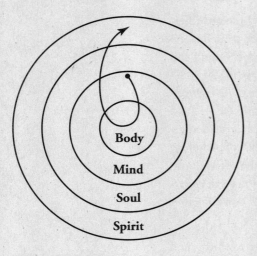

Body

Mind

Soul

Spirit

The Curative Spiral
FIGURE 7

and myths that the self learns." "The worldview of both late F-3 and early F-4 is Mythic, which means that these early roles are often those found displayed in the mythological gods and goddesses, which represent the *archetypal roles* available to individuals." Treatment or "therapy (such as *cognitive therapy*) helps the individual to uproot these false ideas about itself and replace them with more accurate, healthy scripts."

At this stage, Wilber presents a brief critique of the Jungian view. He distinguishes between the few "high archetypes" or "symbols of the transpersonal domains" and the "mythic roles" that "are simply part of the many (sub)personalities that can exist at this preformal mythic level of consciousness development; they are preformal and collective, not postformal and transpersonal."

(F-5) Fulcrum-5 (*formal-reflexive mind*) is "when the Self-Reflexive Ego emerges, and the center of gravity begins to shift from conventional/conformist to postconventional/individualistic, the self is faced with 'identity versus role confusion'"; therefore "problems at this stage (F-5) often center around the incredibly difficult transition from conformist roles and prescriptive morality, to universal principles of conscience and postconventional identities. . . . Erikson's 'identity crisis' is a classic summary of many of the problems of this stage."

(F-6) Fulcrum-6 (*centaur*) is when "the panoramic view of Vision-Logic brings *existential* issues and problems to the forefront, along with the possibility of a more fully integrated bodymind or Centauric Self"; therefore "as vision-logic begins to emerge, postconventional awareness deepens into fully universal, existential concerns: life and death, authenticity, full bodymind integration, self-actualization, global awareness, holistic embrace—all summarized as the emergence of the centaur (e.g., Loevinger's autonomous and integrated stages)."

Here, at the border to the transpersonal, Wilber summarizes: "In the *archeological journey to the Self*, the personal realm's exclusive reign is coming to an end, starting to be peeled off a radiant Spirit, and that universal radiance begins increasingly to shine through, rendering the self more and more transparent."

Higher Fulcrums and Pathologies (F-7 to F-9):

(F-7) Fulcrum-7 (*psychic*) is when "the Transpersonal Domains begin to come into focus, not simply as passing peak experiences, but as new and higher structures—with new and higher possible pathologies."

(F-8) Fulcrum-8 (*subtle*) is when "experienced previously only in peak experiences, or as a background intuition of immortality, wonder, and grace, the Soul begins now to emerge more permanently in consciousness. Not yet infinite and all-embracing, no longer merely personal and mortal, the soul is the great intermediate conveyor between pure Spirit and individual self." With profound insight into the full spectrum of the human being, Wilber recognizes "A sickness of the soul is sickness indeed. The pathologies that beset psychic and subtle development are numerous and profound. . . . But in all of these cases, understanding the experience depends upon understanding both the level *from which* the experience originates (psychic, subtle, causal, nondual) and the level *at which* it is experienced and interpreted (archaic, magic, mythic, rational, centauric)"; treatment involves being "increasingly attuned to the diseases of the soul, using the techniques of both traditional spiritual disciplines and modern psychotherapy . . . [or] the more traditional techniques—which are also part of any integral therapy":

- the **path of shamans**/yogis (psychic/nature mysticism);

- the **path of saints** (subtle/deity mysticism);

- the **path of sages** (causal/formless mysticism);

- the **path of siddhas** (dealing with psychic, subtle, causal, and nondual).

(F-9) Fulcrum-9 (*causal*) is when "we are at the point where the soul has emerged from the interior depths of the mind and pointed the way to a greater tomorrow. . . . When the soul itself grows quiet, and rests from its own weariness; when the Witness releases its final hold, and dissolves into its ever-present ground; when the last layer of the Self is peeled into the purest emptiness; when the final form of the self-contraction unfolds in the infinity of all space; then Spirit itself, as ever-present awareness, stands free of its own accord, never really lost, and therefore never really found. With a shock of the utterly obvious, the world continues to arise, just as it always has."

The amazing journey of self-development, which "is reached by a simple technique: turn left at mind, and go within," Wilber further explains in detail and profundity: "As usual, the more we go within, the more we go beyond. In the extraordinary archeology of Spirit, the deeper the level, the wider the embrace—the within that takes you beyond. . . . In the archeology of the self, deep within the personal lies the transpersonal, which takes you far beyond the personal: always within and beyond." Until, finally, we penetrate, "in the deepest within, the most infinite beyond. In ever-present awareness, your soul expands to embrace the entire Kosmos, so that Spirit alone remains, as the simple world of what is . . . the sun shines from inside your Heart and radiates out into the world, blessing it with grace; supernovas swirl in your consciousness, the thunder is the sound of your own exhilarated heart . . . here in the obvious world of crystalline One Taste, where inner and outer are silly fictions and self and other are obscene lies, and ever-present simplicity is the sound of one hand clapping madly for all eternity. In the greatest depth, the simplest what is, and the journey ends, as it always does, exactly where it began."

With an integral full-spectrum therapy approach, Wilber asserts that "Most adults' center of gravity is somewhere around *mythic, rational,* or *centauric;* and they have occasionally had psychic or subtle peak experiences (which they may or may not have trouble integrating). Therefore, today, typical individual therapy tends to involve:

- *strengthening boundaries* (F-2);

- contacting and *befriending shadow feelings* (F-3);

- *cognitive rescripting* (F-4); and

- *Socratic dialogue* (F-5 and F-6);

- with specific issues of *getting in touch with one's feelings* (F-3);

- dealing with *belongingness needs* (F-4);

- *self-esteem* (F-5); and

- *self-actualization* (F-6).

Sometimes these are accompanied by issues of *integrating* peak experiences and spiritual illuminations (*psychic, subtle, causal,* or *nondual*), which need to be carefully differentiated from prerational magic and mythic structures . . . [or] differentiating between preformal magic and mythic and postformal psychic and subtle."

The basis of Wilber's entire integral psychological system revolves around the fact that the "common thread to all these levels of treatment . . . is this: *awareness in and of itself is curative. . . .* This is *curative* for a basic reason: *by experiencing these facets fully,* consciousness can genuinely acknowledge these elements and thereby let go of them: see them as an object, and thus differentiate from them, de-embed from them, *transcend them*—and then integrate them into a more encompassing, *compassionate embrace.* The curative catalyst, in every case, is bringing awareness or consciousness to bear on an area of experience that is (or has been) denied, distorted, falsified, or ignored. . . . In each case, those alienated facets remain as 'stick points' or lesions in awareness, split off or avoided—a fragmentation that produces pathology, with the type of pathology depending in large part on the level of the fragmentation. Contacting (or recontacting) those facets, meeting them with awareness, and thus experiencing them fully, allows consciousness to differentiate (transcend) and integrate (include) their important voices in the overall flow of evolutionary unfolding."

In addition, Wilber includes the various numerous *subpersonalities* or the "different vocal and subvocal voices in one's inner dialogue" since "authorities on subpersonalities point out that the average person often has around a dozen or more. . . ." And when mapping them on an *integral psychograph* it's vitally important to take into account the fact that "each of these subpersonalities can be at a different level of development in any of its lines." In other words, subpersonalities can form at virtually any of the fulcrums:

- archaic subpersonalities (F-0, F-1);

- magical subpersonalities (F-2, F-3);

- mythic subpersonalities (F-3, F-4);

- rational subpersonalities (F-5, F-6); and even

- soul subpersonalities (F-7, F-8)."

This means *not* that "a person is simply at one stage, with one type of defense, one type of pathology, one type of need, and one type of treatment . . . [but] that the individual has numerous types and levels of needs, defenses, and pathologies (e.g., from borderline to neurotic to existential to spiritual), and will therefore respond to a wide variety of therapeutic endeavors." Once again, Wilber stresses that "The *curative catalyst* is to bring awareness to bear on these subpersonalities, thus objectifying them, and thus including them in a more compassionate embrace." Thus, as usual, "no matter how numerous the subpersonalities, it is the task of the proximate self to fashion some sort of integration or harmony in the chorus of voices, and thus more surely wend its way to the Source of them all."

Once this "archeology of the Self" is better understood, Wilber points out that a *full-spectrum therapy* can be applied since an authentic "full-spectrum therapist is an archeologist of the Self" who "works with the body, the shadow, the persona, the ego, the existential self, the soul and spirit, attempting to bring awareness to all of them, so that all of them may join consciousness in the extraordinary return voyage to the Self and Spirit that grounds and moves the entire display."

This chapter concludes by proposing a four-quadrant or integral therapy since "All four quadrants mutually interact (they are embedded in each other), and thus *all* of them are required in order to understand pathologies in *any* of them." This is especially true since "A malformation—a pathology, a 'sickness'—in any quadrant will reverberate through all four quadrants, because every holon has these four facets to its being." It's therefore vitally important to honor the four-quadrant circle: "cripple one quadrant and all four tend to hemorrhage." Therefore, Wilber suggests that "a *truly integral therapy* is not only *individual* but *cultural, social, spiritual,* and *political.*"

Wilber highly recommends that each individual take up their own integral practice, which will "simultaneously exercise all the major capacities and dimensions of the human body mind—*physical, emotional, mental, social, culture, spiritual*" and "The general idea of integral practice is clear enough: *Exercise body, mind, soul, and spirit in self, culture, and nature.* . . . Practice them diligently, and coordinate your integral efforts to unfold the various potentials of the bodymind—until the bodymind itself unfolds in Emptiness, and the entire journey is a misty memory from a trip that never even occurred."

CHAPTER 9. "SOME IMPORTANT DEVELOPMENTAL STREAMS" starts by reminding us that it is "up to the self to integrate all these various streams [developmental lines]." This chapter examines "some of the more important lines that the self has to balance on its overall journey." Indeed, Wilber reminds us, "the self is learning to be at home in the Kosmos" therefore "an individual's psychograph . . . is actually a graph of one's 'at-home-ness' with the world. The deeper each stream, the more of the Kosmos it embraces, until it embraces the All, and is thus released into the Ground and Suchness of the entire display." Wilber discusses these important developmental streams, linking them with their appearances in the charts (see Appendix 1):

- **Morals** (charts 1A and 5C) "refers to the "stream of moral development," which, "as with most streams, runs from egocentric to ethnocentric to worldcentric to theocentric (or, more accurately, 'pneumocentric,' or spirit-centered, so as not to confuse the transpersonal realms with mythic theism). Each of those *increasingly greater moral depths* encompasses within itself a large *moral span* (from 'me' to 'us' to 'all of us' to 'all sentient beings'). . . . This *expanding identity* is directly reflected in *moral awareness* (subjective identity is reflected in intersubjective morals: not just organism and environment, but self and culture). . . . [I]dentity can span the entire spectrum of consciousness, matter to body to mind to soul to spirit, with each expansion bringing a greater *moral embrace,* until the All itself is embraced with passionate equanimity."

- **Motivation:** Levels of Food (or Need) (chart 1B) "refers to the levels of *need, drive,* or *fundamental motivation* (which may be conscious or unconscious) . . . [generating] a system of Relational Exchange with the same level of organization in the world at large, resulting in a Holarchy of 'Food'—*physical food, emotional food, mental food, soul food.* . . . Although we may discern many different types and levels of needs, all genuine needs simply reflect the *interrelationships* necessary for the life of any holon (at any level)."

- **Worldviews** (chart 1B) "refers to the way the world looks at each of the basic waves in the Great Nest. . . . A worldview unfolds in a particular culture with its specific (and often local) *surface features* [worldspace]. . . . In general, 'worldview' refers to the Lower-Left quadrant. . . . Worldviews are particularly important because all individual, subjective consciousness *arises within* the clearing created by cultural or intersubjective structures. . . . The point is that *subjectivity* and *intersubjectivity*—in fact, all four quadrants—are mutually arising and mutually interdependent."

- **Affect: Emotions/Feelings** (chart 1B) "refers to the developmental line of *affects, or 'emotion' and 'feelings'* in the broadest sense," thus Wilber distinguishes between two somewhat different meanings of the word *emotion*:

  1. the "specific level of consciousness: the *pranamayakosha,* or the level-sheath of *emotional-sexual energy* (the basic structure of *'impulse/emotion'*)"; and

  2. "the *energetic feeling tone* [or 'affective tone'] of any and all of the basic structures across the entire spectrum. . . . Consciousness itself is more of a *'feeling awareness'* than it is a 'thinking-awareness,' and there are levels of that feeling-awareness, or experiential vividness, across the Great Nest."

- **Gender: Gender Identity** (chart 1B) "follows the development of gender from its:

  1. *biological roots* (which are biological givens, not cultural constructions), through

  2. *conventional formations* (which are cultural constructions, mostly) into

  3. *transgender orientations* (which are largely transdifferentiated and transconventional)."

- **Aesthetics: Art** (chart 8) "refers to levels of *aesthetic experience* . . . you can analyze [with a 'dual analysis'] a given activity (such as art) on the basis of both:

1. the level it *comes from* and

2. the level it *aims at*—or the level producing the art and the level depicted in the art. . . . The resultant artwork is thus a combined product of the structures that are producing the art and the structures that are depicted in the art (i.e., the *level of self* producing the art, and the level of reality depicted in the art)."

- **Types of Cognitive Lines** (chart 3B) follows "cognitive development" by moving away "from a monolithic one-axis model to an integral model of states, waves, and streams," therefore "based primarily on the fact of *natural states of consciousness* [waking, dreaming, deep sleep] . . . we could trace the development of different types of cognition (*gross, subtle,* and *causal*) as they appear throughout a person's life":

a. Gross-Reflecting Line of Cognition "takes as its objects the sensorimotor realm . . . [which] runs from sensorimotor to preop to conop to formop and trails off at vision-logic."

b. Subtle Cognition "takes as its object the world of thought, or the mental and subtle realms altogether. This developmental line also begins in infancy (and probably in prenatal states; it is said to be the main cognitive mode of the bardos, as well as sleep with dreams and meditative states of *savikalpa samadhi* [ecstasy with form]. . . . [It has] available to it the same basic waves as most other streams: preconventional, conventional, postconventional, and post-postconventional (or egocentric, sociocentric, worldcentric, and pneumocentric)."

c. Causal Cognition "is the root of attention (and the capacity for Witnessing). This line, too, can be traced to early childhood, although it comes increasingly to the fore in the postformal stages." In essence, "that which obscures the realization of the nondual domain is precisely the subject/object dualism, and this dualism first arises in the causal domain as a constriction or *contraction* in *consciousness* (namely, as the dualism between subject and object, in this case, the unmanifest world of empty consciousness and the manifest world of objects). . . . In order to reverse this 'fall,' an individual has:

1. *first* to reestablish the *capacity for Witnessing* (by strengthening the capacity for attention, equanimity, and detachment—or disidentification from the objects of awareness, including the body, the ego, and the soul);

2. *second,* to then *dissolve the causal Witness*—and the root of attention—into pure nondual One Taste."

This consideration leads Wilber into clarifying that the "three great realms—gross, subtle, and causal—are home to three different lines of self" or the three major self lines generically called:

- **frontal line** or *ego* (gross realm);
- **deeper psychic** or *soul* (subtle realm);
- **Witness** or *Self* or (causal realm).

By doing so, Wilber continues to radically break with the traditional view which tends to see the self as "one stream [of development since it] might actually be several different streams, each developing relatively independently." Therefore he observes "they do not develop one after the other, but alongside each other." In other words, "the realms of gross, subtle, and causal can develop, to some degree, independently of each other; and thus the frontal, the soul, and the Self can develop, to some degree, alongside each other."

Wilber then discusses each *self-stream* (chart 4B):

I. **Frontal** (or *ego*) "includes all of the self-stages that *orient consciousness to the* gross realm (the material self, the bodyself, the persona, the ego, and the centaur—all of which can be generically called 'the ego'). . . . The *frontal* is therefore the self-stream responsible for orienting and integrating consciousness in the gross domain."

II. **Deeper psychic** (or *subtle soul*) "includes all the self-streams that adapt consciousness to the many facets of the subtle sphere. The soul is the self that depends on the subtle line of cognition (which includes . . . imagination, reverie, daydreams, creative visions, hypnogogic states, etheric states, visionary revelations, hypnotic states, transcendental illuminations, and numerous types of *savikalpa samadhi* [ecstasy with form]), and thus the soul is the self-stream that orients and integrates consciousness in the subtle domain." Wilber concedes that there is a type of "U-development that the subtle sometimes seems to go through: present early in development (as 'trailing clouds'), then fading out as frontal (egoic) development starts to get under way, only to reassert itself in the postformal stages."

III. Witness (or *causal self*) "is the self that depends upon the *causal line of cognition* (the capacity for *attention, detached witnessing, equanimity* in the face of gross and subtle fluctuations, etc.), and thus it is the self that orients and integrates consciousness in the causal domain." It includes the "causal and nondual" where he also points out (in an endnote) that the causal sheath is "the root source, and thus the 'cause,' of all the other levels of consciousness and reality . . . the root of attention, which is a constriction [or a '*contraction* in consciousness'] around the Heart, and appears in the form of the Witness, or the pure Subject split from the world of objects." In addition, "just as important, this Self is responsible for the *overall integration* of all the other selves, waves, and streams . . . held together, and drawn together, by the radiant Self, the purest Emptiness that can impartially reflect, and therefore embrace, the entire manifest domain." He also mentions in an endnote that naturally "the pure transcendental Self or Witness does not itself develop, since it is sheer formlessness; however, access to this Self does develop. . . ."

In summary, Wilber says: "Although with higher development, the *center of gravity* of consciousness increasingly shifts from ego to soul to Self, nonetheless all of those are the necessary and important vehicles of Spirit as it shines in the gross, subtle, and causal realms. Thus, all three of them can be, and usually are, simultaneously present in various proportions throughout development, and the highest development itself simply involves their seamless integration as a chorus of equally valued voices of Spirit in the world." (See Figure 8: "Three Major Self Lines.")

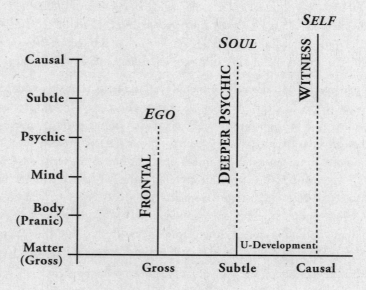

THREE MAJOR SELF LINES
The Development of the Frontal or Ego, the Deeper Psychic or Soul, and the Witness or Self
FIGURE 8

These distinctions once again allow Wilber to claim, as the "simplest generalization," that *integral psychology* "involves *waves, streams,* and *states, ego, soul,* and *spirit.*" This means that integral therapy encourages the therapist to "be alert to ways to recognize and strengthen the *soul* and *spirit* as they increasingly make their appearance, not simply after the *ego,* but within it and alongside it. Integral and transpersonal therapy works *concurrently* with the *frontal, soul,* and *spirit,* as they each unfold alongside each other, carrying their own truths, insights, and possible pathologies. Attunement to these different dimensions of consciousness can facilitate their more graceful unfolding." Nevertheless, he cautions that "without a strong ego as a foundation, the higher realms cannot be carried as a permanent, stable, integrated realization."

Wilber is openly calling for a full-spectrum realization where "the center of gravity [of the self] continues to shift holarchically toward the deeper layers of the Self (ego to soul to spirit), and around these deeper waves consciousness is increasingly organized. . . . All of the lower selves, as *functional capacities,* continue to exist, holarchically enfolded in higher waves; they all continue to serve functional capacities, face their own problems, respond to their own treatments; but they increasingly lose their power to commandeer consciousness and claim it for their own. Thus, for an overall integral development, the *center of gravity* of consciousness still moves through the nine fulcrums in the Great Nest, but it is a cacophony of many voices, many streams, often overlapping, always intertwining. But none of the major waves of consciousness can be totally bypassed on that account. . . . All these waves and streams are headed toward the ocean of only One Taste, pulled through that great morphogenetic field by the force of 'gentle persuasion toward Love'—pulled, that is, by Eros, by Spirit-in-action, by the Love that moves the sun and other stars."

CHAPTER 10. "SPIRITUALITY: STAGES OR NOT?" begins by acknowledging that the exact definition used for *spirituality* is what will determine "whether spirituality itself necessarily unfolds in stages." Wilber gives "five very important aspects of the broad phenomenon we call 'spirituality,' and all of them deserve to be included to some degree in any integral model":

1. "*Spirituality involves the highest levels of any of the developmental lines* . . . [which] basically means the *transpersonal,* transrational, post-postconventional levels of *any* of the lines. . . . In this usage, spirituality (or this particular aspect of spirituality) definitely follows a sequential or stage-like course."

2. "*Spirituality is the sum total of the highest levels of the developmental lines* . . . [where] even though the individual lines unfold hierarchically, the *sum to-*

tal of the highest stages of those lines would show no such stage-like development . . . Every person's spiritual path, in other words, is radically individual and unique, even though the particular competences themselves might follow a well-defined path."

3. "*Spirituality is itself a separate developmental line* . . . in this case spiritual developmental would show some sort of stage-like unfolding, since a developmental line, by definition, shows development. . . . This includes most of the various meditative paths East and West. In all of these cases, these aspects of spirituality show holarchical sequential development (although again, that does not preclude regressions, spirals, temporary leaps forward, or peak experiences of any of the major states). . . . These *stages of spirituality* are deeply important, whether they appear East or West, North or South, and no account of spirituality is complete without them."

4. "*Spirituality is an attitude (such as openness or love) that you can have at whatever stage you are at.* . . . This is probably the most popular and common definition . . . it has proven very difficult to define or even state in a coherent fashion."

5. "*Spirituality basically involves peak experiences* . . . (or *altered states* of consciousness). . . . [These] do not usually show development or stage-like unfolding. They are temporary, passing, transient . . . [therefore] at virtually any stage of development, temporary peak experiences of the transpersonal realms are possible. However, to the extent these *temporary states* are converted to *enduring traits,* they become structures that show development."

Based on these definitions, Wilber is able to conclude that "because the developmental lines themselves can unfold independently, an individual can be at a very high spiritual stages (transpersonal or post-postcon) in one line and still be at a very low personal or psychological stage (con or precon) in others." Therefore it depends on how we define those terms that the question "does psychological development [have] to be completed before spiritual development can begin?" can be more accurately answered.

This leads directly to "the importance of spiritual practice" since, whether "stages or not, authentic spirituality does involve practice. . . . [A]s the testimony of the world's great yogis, saints, and sages has made quite clear, authentic spirituality can also involve direct *experience* [not just "belief, faith, or religious mythology," all of which are important] of a living Reality, disclosed immediately and intimately in the heart and consciousness of individuals, and fostered by diligent, sincere, prolonged spiritual practice." Importantly, then, "Authentic spirituality is not about *translating* the world differently, but about *transforming* your consciousness." Wilber stresses that "the 'new paradigm' approaches to spirituality" are in error when they suggest that you "would simply have . . . [to] change the way you think about the world."

Because of these considerations, Wilber claims that "The ecological crisis—or Gaia's main problem . . . is that not enough human beings have developed to the postconventional, worldcentric, global levels of consciousness, wherein they will automatically be moved to care for the global common." In other words, Wilber maintains "The *primary cure* for the *ecological crisis* is not learning that Gaia is a Web of Life, however true that may be, but learning ways to foster these many arduous waves of *interior growth,* none of which are addressed by most of the new-paradigm approaches." Therefore, he points out, "Sadly, in claiming to offer a completely 'holistic' view of the world, they often prevent or discourage people from taking up a genuine path of interior growth and development, and thus they hamper the evolution of just that global consciousness that they otherwise so nobly espouse."

CHAPTER 11. "IS THERE A CHILDHOOD SPIRITUALITY?" revisits the question by way of the previous five definitions of spirituality (first presented in Chapter 10 of *Integral Psychology*):

- Definition 1: when "spirituality is the highest level in any line";

- Definition 2: when "spirituality is the sum total of the highest levels in all the lines," which if they're defined "as transrational supramental, postformal, superconscious, and post-postconventional, then those are not significantly present in childhood";

- Definition 3: when "spirituality is a separate line of development," thus suggesting "we should not conclude that infants are saints or sages, or permanently in touch with authentic spiritual realities, but rather are on a long road to authentic spirituality via higher development";

- Definition 4: when "spirituality is an attitude such as openness or love," thus suggesting that infants or childhood "can be in touch with the attitude that defines spirituality (openness, love, fluidity). . . . [However] if your idea of spirituality is feeling good, then childhood might be Eden, but if your idea also involves doing good, by taking the role of others, and projecting your consciousness through multiple perspectives and pluralistic outlooks so as to include compassion, caring, and altruism, then childhood is a realm of diminished expectations, no matter how wonderfully fluid and flowing its egocentrism";

- Definition 5: spirituality as "peak experiences" which "offers a credible definition and a modest amount of evidence that at least some children have some types of spiritual experiences," however, they are "peak experiences of the psychic, subtle, causal, or nondual realm interpreted through an archaic, magic, mythic, or rational outlook—for most children, that means magic or mythic."

One of the ways Wilber is able to explain the spiritual "aspect of infancy and childhood" is that they may be "trailing clouds of glory" ("from Wordsworth: 'Not in entire forgetfulness . . . but trailing clouds of glory do we come . . .'") since with "the Deeper Psychic (or Soul) dimension, some evidence tentatively suggests, is present from prenatal through the early years, but then fades as Frontal (or Egoic) development gets under way. The 'trailing clouds of glory' refers in general to all the deeper psychic (or soul) awareness that the individual brings to this life and which is therefore present in some sense from conception forward." This more credible option (since the Romantic "deeper ground or potential . . . seems to be largely inadequate in both theory and data") involves the bardo realms where the "deeper psychic being is increasingly submerged and forgotten as frontal or egoic development gets under way," therefore, sometimes "this deeper psychic being emerges (which often brings flashbacks of childhood)." However, Wilber maintains, "whatever this deeper psychic capacity is, it is *not* the resurrection of a prerational infantile structure, but the discovery of a transrational structure."

CHAPTER 12. "SOCIOCULTURAL EVOLUTION" begins with Wilber stating that if the Great Chain or the perennial philosophy is to be brought "into the modern and postmodern world," then there must be recognized at least "four major inadequacies to the Great Chain as it was traditionally conceived":

1. "The four quadrants were very seldom *differentiated* on an adequate scale. . . . This left the Great Chain open to devastating critiques from the Enlightenment . . . all of which demonstrated that consciousness is not merely a disembodied, transcendental noumenon, but is deeply embedded in contexts of objective facts, cultural backgrounds, and social structures."

2. "The level of mind itself needs to be *subdivided* in the light of its *early developments*. Here the contributions of Western psychology are decisive. . . . Precisely because the infantile and childish origins of the preformal levels of *magic* and *mythic* were not clearly understood, the traditions often confused them with the postformal states of *psychic* and *subtle,* and this pre/post fal-

lacy haunts most of the perennial philosophy, injecting it not only with truly enlightened wisdom, but substantial stretches of superstition."

3. "Because the traditional Great Chain theorists had a poor understanding of the early, infantile, prerational stages of human development, they likewise failed to grasp the types of *psychopathologies* that often stem from complications of these early stages. . . . Meditation—which is a way to carry development forward into the transpersonal—will not, as a rule, cure these prepersonal lesions."

4. The Great Chain's "lack of understanding evolution," although, Wilber points out, "if you tilt the Great Chain on its side and let it unfold in time—instead of being statically given all at once, as traditionally thought—you have the outlines of evolution itself. Plotinus temporalized = evolution." This means that "What the perennial philosophy took to be eternally unchanging archetypes can better be understood as *formative habits* of evolution, 'Kosmic memories,' as it were, and not pregiven molds into which the world is poured."

After taking into account the inadequacies listed above, set within the context of the four quadrants, Wilber goes on to differentiate between the principle forms of collective evolution, as opposed to individual evolution:

- **Social** "refers to the Lower-Right quadrant (the *interobjective* dimension, including forms of the techno-economic base, social systems, institutions, and physical structures)";

- **Cultural** "refers to the Lower-Left quadrant (the *intersubjective* dimension, including collective worldviews, ethics, values, and meaning)."

Wilber is thus able to look at all the various theorists of both social and cultural evolution, or sociocultural evolution, and conclude that "A genuine or *integral holism* would include both the [social] *exterior holism* of systems theory and the [cultural] *interior holism* of phenomenal consciousness, morals, values, waves, streams, and states, all embraced in their own terms, not forced into the molds of the others." Therefore, after reviewing the groundbreaking work of sociocultural evolutionists such as Jean Gebser and Jürgen Habermas, Wilber maintains that "since evolution is one of the crucial ingredients—some would say *the* crucial ingredient—of the modern scientific worldview, and if we truly wish an *integral embrace* of *premodern, modern,* and *postmodern,* then we need a way to put the theory of evolution in a context that both honors its truths and curtails its abuses."

In order to do so, Wilber provides five important hints or a set of tenets that can "explain both advance and regression, good news and bad news, the ups and downs of an evolutionary thrust that is nonetheless as active in humans as it is in the rest of the Kosmos." Only then can humanity "rehabilitate Cultural Evolution in a sophisticated form," one which will need at least these five "central explanatory principles" for "any balanced account of history":

1. "The Dialectic of Progress" suggests that "each stage solves or defuses certain problems of the previous stage, but then adds new and recalcitrant—and sometimes more complex and more difficult—problems of its own"; in other words, "The more stages of evolution there are—the greater the depth of the Kosmos—the more things that *can* go wrong."

2. "The *distinction* between Differentiation and Dissociation" is "one of the most prevalent forms of evolutionary pathology, and occurs when *differentiation* goes too far into *dissociation,* whether ontogenetically or phylogenetically."

3. "The *difference* between Transcendence and Repression" reveals that "each new and higher stage has exactly this choice: transcend and include, befriend, integrate, honor; or transcend and repress, deny, alienate, oppress."

4. "The *difference* between Natural Hierarchy and Pathological Hierarchy" establishes that "that which transcends can repress and thus normal and natural hierarchies can degenerate into pathological hierarchies, into dominator hierarchies."

5. "Higher Structures can be Hijacked by Lower Impulses" such as when "the advanced technologies of rationality, when hijacked by tribalism and its ethnocentric drives, can be devastating [such as during wars]."

However, taken together, Wilber believes it is possible "to reconstruct the evolution of human consciousness in a much more satisfactory and compelling fashion, a fashion that can clearly account for the undeniable advances as well as the undeniable disasters of human history." This is especially true since human beings "are part and parcel of a single and all-encompassing evolutionary current that is itself Spirit-in-action, the mode and manner of Spirit's creation."

Another of Wilber's distinctions, first presented in *Up From Eden,* is that it's possible to trace "cultural developments in both the Average Mode and the Most Advanced Mode that typically defined a given era." Indeed, Wilber contends, only with this distinction is it possible to realize that "both the average and the most advanced modes of development continued to deepen with subsequent evolution"; thus he gives a brief overview of this general idea:

- "When the *average* level of consciousness of a given culture, is, say, Magical . . . the *most highly evolved* mode was generally shamanic . . . (reaching at least to the Psychic domain). . . . The Magical/Shamanic Mode was the dominant form of consciousness for the largest period of humanity's stay on earth thus far, reigning from perhaps as early as 500,000 years B.C.E. to around 10,000 B.C.E. with its peak period probably from around 50,000 to 7000 B.C.E." The shaman was "the first great discovery of, and exploration of, the transpersonal domains [nature mysticism]" and although "it was a magic-level peak experience of the psychic domains . . . it retained preformal imprints and interpretations, heavily involved, as magic often is, with power drives and needs."

- "As the *average* mode evolved from magic into Mythic (beginning roughly around 10,000 B.C.E.), and nature elementals and polytheistic figments increasingly gave way to a conception of one God/dess [subtle] underlying the manifold world, the figure of the Saint eventually became the dominant spiritual realizer. . . . The great conveyor of *growing-tip* consciousness as it moved within and beyond nature mysticism to Deity Mysticism . . . disclosed depths of the soul, and heights of reality, that altered the very nature of consciousness at large, and left the world profoundly altered in its very structure."

- "As the *average,* collective mode of consciousness evolved from mythic to Mental (beginning around the sixth century B.C.E.), the *most advanced* mode evolved from subtle to Causal, and the Sage, more than the saint . . . whereas the saint experienced divine interior luminosity, grace, love, and ecstasy, the sage experienced nothing. . . . But far from being a literal 'nothing' or stark blankness, Emptiness is the creative ground of all that is (hence 'causal'). . . . Whereas, in the subtle, the soul and God find a communion or even union, in the causal, the soul and God disappear into Godhead . . . and deity mysticism gives way to Formless Mysticism . . . the Consciousness that is infinitely within and beyond the manifest world altogether."

- "The great Nondual Traditions began around 200 C.E., especially with such figure as Nagarjuna and Plotinus; but these traditions, particularly in their advanced forms as Tantra, began to flower in India around the eighth to the fourteenth century (coincident with the first collective or *average-mode* glimmers of Vision-Logic, exemplified in the West with Florence and the rise of Humanism, circa fourteenth century). It was during this time that Ch'an

Buddhism saw its extraordinary rise in Tang and Song China (the seventh through thirteenth centuries), and Padmasambhava brought Tantra to Tibet, which began its unparalleled flowering (especially the eighth through the eighteenth centuries)."

Wilber explains that "among other things, distinguishing between *average* and *most advanced* allows us to avoid assuming that all the products of one era were generated by the same wave of consciousness," a tendency of the Romantic theorists. In other words, this understanding will help to prevent the *Romantic fallacy* because it is "all too easy to assume that evolution has gone steadily downhill from these wonderful ancient days of rampant spirituality, whereas—if we actually follow the growing tip itself—spirituality has in many ways continued to deepen profoundly over the ages." Wilber maintains that "scholars who mistake magic and mythic for authentic spirituality" don't actually understand that "the most advanced figures of the past were plumbing the depths of the transpersonal levels, and those lie in our collective future, not our collective past. . . . They are figures of the deepest layers of our own true Self, layers that whisper to us from the radiant depths of a greater tomorrow."

CHAPTER 13. "FROM MODERNITY TO POSTMODERNITY" is a general overview of Wilber's penetrating philosophical discussions about *postmodernity* or the general trend of philosophy following in the wake of modernity. (These views were first presented by Wilber in *Sex, Ecology, Spirituality,* Book II, *A Brief History of Everything,* and *The Eye of Spirit,* (and most fully in *The Marriage of Sense and Soul.*)

He begins by restating his position that "no epoch is without its geniuses, its wisdom, its enduring truths," therefore, he claims that a sane integral approach "would surely attempt to honor, acknowledge, and incorporate these enduring truths in the ongoing sweep of consciousness evolution." To do this, we must integrate all the wisdom and knowledge from:

- the *premodern heritage,* which is "the Great Nest of Being and Knowing . . . a road map to Spirit, not in a pregiven way, but as a morphogenetic field of gentle persuasion";

- the *modern heritage,* which is "the need to recognize and honor art, morals, and science [the Big Three], and let each pursue its own truths without violence from the others" as well as "the modern discoveries of evolution in the quadrants";

- the hopeful prospect of a *constructive postmodernity* "which involves the integration of the best of premodernity (the Great Nest) and modernity (the differentiation and evolution of the Big Three), resulting in a more integral all-level, all-quadrant" approach.

Throughout much of the chapters, Wilber presents an excellent history of postmodernity or the "genealogy of postmodernism," especially "the bright promise of a constructive postmodernity [which unfortunately] slid into a nihilistic deconstructive postmodernity when the pluralistic embrace turned into a rancid leveling of all qualitative distinctions. Postmodernity, attempting to escape flatland, often became its most vulgar champion." Wilber differentiates between:

Postmodernity's Good News:

- "Interpretation *is an intrinsic feature of the fabric of the universe:* there is the crucial insight at the heart of the great postmodern movements." This provides, Wilber suggests, "three important core assumptions" of postmodernity:

    1. **constructivism**—"reality is not in all ways pregiven, but in some significant ways is a construction, an interpretation";

    2. **contextualism**—"meaning is context-dependent, and contexts are boundless";

    3. **integralism** or *integral-aperspectivism*—"cognition must therefore unduly privilege no single perspective."

- "The linguistic turn in philosophy—the general realization that language is not a simple representation of a pregiven world, but has a hand in the creation and construction of that world." (Here Wilber gives an in-depth appraisal of Saussure's work since "most forms of postmodern poststructuralism trace their lineage to the work of the brilliant and pioneering linguist.")

- Vision-logic or network-logic, or what Gebser called the integral-aperspectival worldview, "adds up all the perspectives, privileging none, and thus attempts to grasps the integral, the whole, the multiple contexts within contexts that endlessly disclose the Kosmos, not in a rigid or absolutist fashion, but in a fluidly holonic and multidimensional tapestry."

Postmodernity's Bad News:

- "Language collapses" since "any mode of knowing can be collapsed and confined merely to surfaces, to exteriors, to Right-Hand occasions."

- "No within, no deep" or "depth takes a vacation" since "there are only sliding chains of signifiers, everything is a material text, there is nothing under the surface, there is only the surface," therefore "to collapse the Kosmos to Right-Hand surfaces is thus to step out of the real world and into the Twilight Zone known as the disqualified universe."

Nonetheless, Wilber concludes, "The enduring contributions of the Post-modern era—the world is in part a *construction* and *interpretation; all meaning is context-dependent;* contexts are *endlessly holonic*—are truths that any comprehensive view would surely wish to embrace." This is why he proposes that "Any integral theory would be wise to include *constructive, contextual,* and *integral-aperspectival* dimensions in its own makeup." In other words, a genuine "constructive post-modernism takes up the multiple contexts freed by pluralism, and then goes one step further and weaves together into mutually interrelated networks" thus creating, by whatever name, an "integral-holism" or "unity-in-diversity" or "universal integralism." Indeed, Wilber claims, "The integral psychology that I am presenting is offered in the spirit of a constructive postmodernism."

CHAPTER 14. "**THE 1-2-3 OF CONSCIOUSNESS STUDIES**" first tackles the *mind-body problem* or what's called the "world-knot" (after Schopenhauer). Essentially Wilber believes the problem centers around how "mind" and "body" are defined. This is especially true since "a good deal of the mind-body problem is a product of flatland [or scientific materialism]" which derives from either of these solutions:

- the *dualist* (or interactionism) position, which maintains "There are at least two realities in the world: *consciousness* and *matter.* Neither can be reduced to the other; instead, they *'interact'* . . . but then the dualist faces the age-old dilemma: how can two fundamentally different things influence each other?"

- the *physicalist* (or the materialist) approach, which claims that "There is only the physical universe described best by physics and other natural sciences . . . and therefore those 'interiors' are simply illusions (or, at best, byproducts without any genuine reality)."

Thus Wilber maintains that to move beyond "the theoretical terms of flatland" would involve using "an 'all-level, all-quadrant' approach," in which case, "mind" and "body" have "two very different meanings, showing that there are really four problems hidden in one":

- "Body" (with a capital *B*) (or the Upper-Right quadrant) is "*the biological organism as a whole,* including the brain (the neocortex, the limbic system, reptilian stem, etc.)," therefore this means "the brain is in the Body, which is the commonly accepted scientific view";

- "body" (or the Upper-Left quadrant) can also mean (for the average person) "the *subjective feelings,* emotions, and sensations of the felt body . . . in this common usage, 'body' means the lower levels of one's own interior";

- "mind" (or the Upper-Right quadrant) can mean only "brain" since "many scientific researchers simply identify 'mind' with 'brain,' and [thus] they prefer to speak only of brain states, neurotransmitters, cognitive science, and so on";

- "mind" (or the Upper-Left quadrant) also means "the upper levels of [one's] own interior."

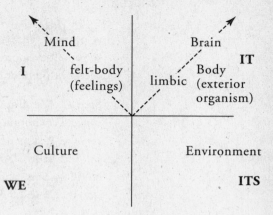

Meanings of "Mind" and "Body"

FIGURE 9

(See Figure 9: "Meanings of 'Mind' and 'Body.'")

With these definitions, Wilber suggests, "Here is the world-knot, *the inherent paradox of flatland:* the body [feelings] is in the mind [interior], but the brain [exterior] is in the Body [exterior organism]." In other words, as he explains, "The materialist reduces the mind to the brain . . . [yet] the dualist, on the other hand, acknowledges as real both consciousness and matter, but generally despairs of finding any way to relate them."

Wilber's solution, however, suggests "This is where the *transrational stages of development* have so much to offer this discussion" for with "the disclosure known as satori it becomes clear that the subject and object are two sides of the same thing, that inside and outside are two aspects of One Taste." Nevertheless, he cautions: "This genuinely nondual solution is not something that can be fully grasped at the *rational* level. . . . Therefore the 'proof' for this nondual solution can only be found in the *further development of consciousness* of those who seek to know the solution . . . nonetheless it is the only acceptable form of the solution according to a genuinely integral paradigm." Once more, Wilber's developmental solution "involves an 'all-level, all-quadrant' view, which plugs the mind back into its own body and intimately relates the mind to its own Body. And it does so, in the final analysis, through the disclosures of the postrational, nondual stages of consciousness development. That means that part of this solution involves the existence of higher stages of development," thus Wilber proposes "two general phases for unsnarling the world-knot or Mind-Body Problem":

Step 1. The all-quadrant approach holds that "it is not enough to say that organism and environment *coevolve;* it is not enough to say that culture and consciousness *coevolve.* All four of those 'tetra-evolve' together [*tetra* is Greek for 'based on four']." In other words, "All four quadrants—organism, environment, consciousness, and culture—cause and are caused by the others: they 'tetra-interact.'" Wilber's solution therefore "allows an equal inclusion of:

1. First-Person [*subjective*] phenomenal accounts ('I'),

2. Second-Person *intersubjective* backgrounds ('We),

3. Third-Person [*objective/scientific*] physical systems ('It')

that we will call 'the 1-2-3 of Consciousness Studies.'" This is because with Wilber's integral language: "The 1) *subjective* features of consciousness (waves, streams, states) are intimately interrelated with the 3) *objective* aspects of the organism (especially the brain, neurophysiology, and various organ systems in the individual), with 2) background *cultural* contexts that allow meaning and understanding to be generated in the first place, and with the 3) *social* institutions that anchor them."

Step 2. The all-level approach involves recognizing "the transpersonal domains of consciousness," which many researchers are currently doing in greater numbers. However, Wilber points out, "One is hard-pressed to find in many of those authors a full appreciation of the stage conceptions of consciousness development." They need to "move from being merely all-quadrant to being *all-level, all-quadrant.* Or *1-2-3 across all levels.*"

With this type of comprehensive approach, Wilber is emphasizing that "A staggering amount of evidence—premodern, modern, and postmodern—points most strongly to an integral approach that is all-quadrant, all-level. The sheer amount of this evidence inexorably points to the fact that we stand today on the brink, not of fashioning a fully complete and integral view of consciousness, but of being able to settle, from now on, for nothing less."

CHAPTER 15. "THE INTEGRAL EMBRACE" concludes the book by stating that "To embrace the best of premodern, modern, and postmodern . . . might allow a genuinely integral psychology to emerge." This means, in other words, "While attempting to set aside the distortions of each epoch, we seek to honor their truths, for they are all truths of the human potential. To ignore past truths—in either phylogeny or ontogeny—is the very definition of pathology. Therefore, an integral approach—a sane approach—attempts to honor, acknowledge, and incorporate the enduring truths into the ongoing sweep of consciousness, for they are the truths of our very own Self, even here and now":

- from *premodernity*: "From the premodern heritage, we have learned of the Great Nest of Being and Knowing, and found that it is a road map to Spirit, not in a rigid and predetermined fashion, but as *a flowing morphogenetic field of gentle persuasion*. . . . Each senior level *transcends and includes* its juniors, so that this Great Nest is a holarchy of extended love and compassionate embrace, reaching from dirt to Divinity, with no corner of the Kosmos left untouched by grace or care or luminosity. The ancient sages taught us that, precisely because reality is multilayered—with physical, emotional, mental, and spiritual dimensions—reality is not simply a one-level affair lying around for all and sundry to see: you must be *adequate* to the level of reality you wish to understand. . . . You must grow and evolve in your capacity to perceive the deeper layers of your Self, which disclose higher levels of reality: the great within that is beyond: the greater the depth, the higher the reality."

- from *modernity*: "From modernity we take the enduring truth of the *differentiation* and *evolution* of the Big Three (the Good, the True, and the Beautiful)"; further, "From modernity, we learn that each of the levels in the Great Nest needs to be differentiated into the four quadrants (or simply the Big Three), and done so on a widespread scale. From modernity we also learn that *each of those quadrants evolves, and thus an integral psychology follows those developments as they appear in any individual. . . . It is the job of an integral psychology to track all of these various waves and streams as they unfold in any given individual.*"

- from *postmodernity*: "Modernity's differentiation of the value spheres allowed postmodernity to see exactly how interrelated the four quadrants are. . . . Contextualism means consciousness doesn't merely reflect the world, it helps construct it. Contextualism means that holons are nested, indefinitely. Integral-aperspectivism means that as many perspectives as humanly possible must be included in an *integral embrace*. That the Kosmos is endlessly holonic—there is the message of postmodernism."

It is the combination of all these enduring truths that allows Wilber to propose an *integral studies* that takes "great care to ensure that the important differentiations of modernity are in fact integrated, that the Big Three do not fly apart; that subtle reductionism does not creep into the picture, yielding a flatland holism; and that any approach to consciousness is indeed a 1-2-3 approach, including and equally honoring *first-person, second-person,* and *third-person* accounts of consciousness." The transpersonal theorist continues, "The result is an '*all-level, all-quadrant' approach to integral studies,* across the spectrum of disciplines— science, history, religion, anthropology, philosophy, psychology, education, politics, business."

Wilber thus ends on a positive note: "This is the dawning of the Age of Vision-Logic, the rise of the network society, the postmodern, aperspectival, internetted global village. Evolution in all forms has started to become conscious of itself. . . . Evolution, as Spirit-in-action, is starting to awaken on a more collective scale. Kosmic evolution is now producing theories and performances of its own integral embrace. This Eros moves through you and me, urging us to include, to diversify, to honor, to enfold. . . . This Eros is the same Spirit-in-action that originally threw itself outward to create a vast morphogenetic field of wondrous possibilities (known as the Great Nest). . . . From subconscious to self-conscious to superconscious, the great Play continues and the grand River flows, with all of its glorious streams rushing to the ocean of One Taste, never really lost, never really found, this sound of the rain on the temple roof, which only alone is."

A Theory of Everything

An Integral Vision for Business, Politics, Science, and Spirituality

BY KEN WILBER

(Boston: Shambhala Publications, 2000; paperback edition, 2001)

A Theory of Everything: An Integral Vision for Business, Politics, Science, and Spirituality (2000) is a fully mature Wilber/Phase 4 (or early Wilber/Phase 5) work summarizing the AQAL all-quadrant, all-level, all-lines approach to integral studies, focusing on the developmental tetra-interaction (or coevolution) of the Left-Hand interior quadrants with the Right-Hand exterior correlates in the Great Nest of Spirit or Kosmos.

A Theory of Everything is a short book that clarifies Wilber's integral vision and its attempt to embrace or integrate body, mind, soul, and spirit as they appear in self, culture, and nature.

A Theory of Everything: An Integral Vision for Business, Politics, Science, and Spirituality was released in late 2000 (Shambhala Publications); paperback edition (Shambhala Publications, 2001); it is Wilber's first book published after (and therefore not included in) *The Collected Works of Ken Wilber.*

A Theory of Everything is, at this time, perhaps the best short introduction to Wilber's AQAL approach, especially in its more sophisticated phase of applying the theory more pragmatically, such as in business, politics, science, and spirituality. This manner of embracing the entire spectrum of consciousness in all four quadrants comes as close as anything has come so far to a genuine "theory of everything."

As he has done recently, such as in *Integral Psychology,* Wilber continues to make extensive use of the Spiral Dynamics model based on the developmental work of Clare Graves, and carried forward by Donald Beck and Christopher Cowen. Since this system closely correlates with Wilber's own spectrum model, at least up to the stages of centaur vision-logic, he explains how Spiral Dynamics uses the developing "value memes" (or vMemes), symbolized by a rainbow of colors, to describe the "spiral of development" in human sociocultural worldviews. According to the available evidence, this spiral grows to embrace all the various worldviews of humankind eventually evolving to second-tier consciousness. He also critiques the various forms of "boomeritis," or the tendency of the baby-boomer generation to be self-centered. Indeed, he identifies the "green meme," or the postmodern sensitive self of relative pluralism, as being under the influence of boomeritis, while also claiming this is one of the major obstacles to the emerging integral culture.

Throughout the book, Wilber evaluates the work of scores of contemporary theorists working in various fields of research, thus verifying to some degree that there's now an emerging "integral revolution" penetrating the various strata of society. However, he adamantly encourages them all to use a more all-quadrant, all-level approach to combat deconstructionism and its slide into ironic nihilism. *A Theory of Everything* also announces the formation the Integral Institute (I-I), which is composed of several "branches of integral medicine, integral psychology, integral spirituality, integral business, integral ecology, integral education, integral art, and integral politics, with more branches in the planning (media, diplomacy, law)." Nonetheless, the founder and president of the board informs us that "Members of Integral Institute do not necessarily agree with all the details of my version of integralism, but they do share a deep interest in a more integral, balanced, comprehensive vision, spanning the spectrum from matter to mind to spirit, exercised in self and culture and nature."

Since Wilber's integral model promotes the viability of the entire spiral of development without privileging any particular level—its "prime directive"—it simultaneously embraces the lower memes, or worldviews, as well as encouraging growth into the higher, transpersonal domains. Therefore, the integral approach attempts to align the global culture with what Wilber defines as both "good science" (as opposed to scientism) and "deep spirituality" (rather than mythic religion). Since this methodology not only considers the *interior* dimensions of consciousness, it also addresses their practical uses and physical correlates or "footprints" in the *exterior* "real world." To this end, Wilber presents some pragmatic applications of the AQAL model that can be used in the world of politics, business, medicine, education, ecology, etc. This type of integral vision gives humanity a true world philosophy, a universal stance that fully honors unity-in-diversity, an ever-expanding *"unitas multiplex"* of greater and greater embrace. The approach presents a truly comprehensive approach to life as a whole by including yet transcending all the spheres of human consciousness and existence, high and deep, inside and out, scientific and religious, masculine and feminine, prepersonal, personal, transpersonal, and so on. Thus, in the end, as Wilber is wont to remind us, the AQAL approach always already sees the whole Kosmos or the Great Nest of Spirit existing *in* and *as* the blissful One Taste of Divine Realization or God-Only.

Boomeritis

A Novel That Will Set You Free

BY KEN WILBER

(Boston: Shambhala Publications, 2002);

paperback edition (Shambhala, 2003)

Omega_Doom@FutureWorld.org

SEMINAR_1@PROBLEMCHILD.COM

1. Cyber_Rave@XTC.net
2. The_Pink_Insides_of_
   Cyberspace@LookingGlass.org
3. The_Lay_of_the_Within
   @SpiralDynamics.org
4. And_It_Is_Us@FuckMe.com

SEMINAR_2@BOOMERITISRULES
.COM

5. Subvert_Transgress_Deconstruct
   @FuckYou.com
6. Dot-com_Death_Syndrome
   @ReallyOuch.com

7. The_Conquest_of_Paradise
   @MythsAreUs.net
8. The_New_Paradigm
   @WonderUs.org

SEMINAR_3
@BEYONDTHEMEGENERATION.COM

9. Pluralism_Falls_Apart
   @DisIntegrationCity.com
10. The_Integral_Vision@IC.org
11. Cosmic_Consciousness
    @OriginalFace.org
12. Happily_Ever_After
    @HereAndNow.com

Boomeritis: A Novel That Will Set You Free is a fully developed Wilber/Phase 4/5 postmodern novel that mostly uses his Phase 2 model emphasizing the developmental evolution of the spectrum of consciousness and cultural worldviews yet including all four quadrants (behavioral, intentional, cultural, and social) in the Great Nest of Spirit.

Boomeritis began as an academic treatise in late 1998 titled *Boomeritis: A Strange Case of Arrested Development,* and then later was changed to *Boomeritis: The Pig in the Python and Other Gruesome Tales* (*CW7,* 2000), but finally, in 2001, it was modified into a novel, in order to cleverly critique the baby boomer generation's narcissistic tendencies as well as the flatland approach of extreme postmodernism that's so prevalent in academia and New Age circles. Wilber also wrote and posted on Shambhala's Web site one hundred fifty pages of endnotes and four hundred pages of scholarly sidebars and postscripts of explanatory and background material, including "The Deconstruction of the World Trade Center," in order to clarify his more current AQAL ("all quadrants, all levels") position.

Boomeritis: A Novel That Will Set You Free was published in June 2002 (Shambhala Publications); paperback edition (Shambhala Publications, 2003); it will be part of *The Collected Works of Ken Wilber, Volume Nine (CW9),* (Shambhala Publications, forthcoming).

Boomeritis is Wilber's name for a "dis-ease" or psychopathological condition that he claims is rampant in the baby boomer generation or in people who have evolved to the "green meme" (a stage of natural development) also called the network self (after the Spiral Dynamics developmental model of sociocultural worldviews), alternatively known as the "cultural creatives" (after Paul Ray). The green meme is supposedly found in approximately 25 percent of the population in the modern/postmodern world, particularly in the United States. Wilber's thesis, then, is that a bad case of narcissism has penetrated the decades-long attempt by the green meme (and cultural studies in general) to be more pluralistic and inclusive. Regrettably, the green meme has attempted this, as he explains, with a flatland pluralism or the inability to acknowledge or account for any real depth and meaning in the Kosmos (or the other memes in the overall spectrum of consciousness).

Wilber claims that the green meme's extreme form of subjectivism ("I do my thing and you do your thing") combined with an inflated egocentricity ("Nobody tells me what to do!") have become pathological obstacles in boomers' attempts to make a better world. The only way out, according to the integral psychologist, is for boomeritis, this insidious form of narcissism, to be recognized and released from its extreme condition and to be healed with a more integrative and holarchical understanding. This will develop into the more appropriate integral transformation known as *second-tier awareness* or the yellow (integrative) and turquoise (holistic) memes.

Each chapter, therefore, specifically critiques several identifications or fixations of the green meme, such as the fascination with new paradigms, the deconstruction of any conventional worldview, UFO abductions, astrology, the abuse excuse, the hundredth monkey, the indigenous mind and its primal Paradise, the extreme forms of the ecology movement and feminism, etc.—in order to assist boomers and others to disidentify with the green worldview's narcissistic tendencies while integrating the positive aspects of its pluralistic inclusiveness. Thus, Wilber honors the healthy qualities of the green meme, such as its networking or sensitive self, human bonding, ecological sensitivity, cultural diversity, and egalitarian values. Yet by releasing the self-centered extremes of the green (i.e., the "MGM" or "mean green meme"), Wilber contends that it should then be easier to progressively develop into the higher or more embracing memes of second-tier thinking and ultimately further into the transpersonal third-tier.

As an intentionally constructed postmodern novel, full of lively and obnoxious characters, and resplendent with double meanings and blurring of the line between fact and fiction, *Boomeritis* also strongly critiques the postmodern atmosphere that has infected today's academia, including many New Age theorists. Thus Wilber directly addresses the widespread pervasion of "endless irony" that claims no true value system, judgments, or meaning exist; thereby causing the inadvertent subversion and nullification of any truly progressive political agenda. However, instead of a nihilistic future, a worldwide crisis, the endless dilemma of diversity, the destruction of the environment, and the end of civilization as we know it, Wilber suggests that another better way is possible: an integral way that includes all the partial truths of each and every meme existing in the entire rainbow or spectrum of consciousness.

Wilber believes this transformation into second-tier thinking will probably happen more readily with the younger generations (the Gen-Xers and Millennials, or the "geeks"), as well as holding out the possibility for aging boomers (or the "geezers"). This is because these opposite ends of the human lifespan are usually the ones most open to consciousness transformation (i.e., the development between levels or memes) instead of just processing middle-aged translations (i.e., which occur within a level or meme). In other words, as the boomer generation approaches the second half of life, they're once again open to further transformation or growth. Wilber claims that the times are still ripe for the green worldview to move into the "Big Picture" of second-tier thinking, promoting an evolution from *relative pluralism* (green) to *integral universalism* (yellow/turquoise), thus moving beyond the clash of worldviews into a healthier embrace that honors the entire spectrum of development.

Wilber ironically casts himself in *Boomeritis* as a fictitious twenty-two-year-old "mini-me" protagonist (i.e., showing how narcissistic a boomer writer can get) while the "real" Wilber's current integral AQAL position is expounded by the various professors at Harvard's Integral Center (a takeoff on Wilber's real-world Integral Institute). Perhaps his character is embodied most directly in the brilliant Mark Jefferson (the character is also partially based on an Afro-American friend), although in an interview he claims his deepest identification is with the voice of Joan Hazelton (see "*Boomeritis* Character Chart" below).

The young, bemused, and naive Ken has a technodigital vision that human intelligence, or even consciousness itself, can be downloaded into silicon chips as artificial intelligence, that is, until he stumbles upon the Integral Center and learns about the complex, interacting levels of consciousness and the evolutionary necessity for each level to transcend and include its predecessors. Along with the young Ken, the reader learns about the entire spectrum or spiral of development—including all the various color memes and their worldviews (beige, red, purple, blue, orange, green, yellow, turquoise, and coral)—as we zigzag through a montage of complicated university lectures, exotic fantasy sequences with Ken's naked girlfriend, comic asides, and other assorted trips devoted to sex, drugs, and rock 'n' roll, including a good dose of meditation and spiritual enlightenment. Here, by the story's end, is revealed the central tantric message of the book.

Like young Ken, therefore, the reader is invited to understand his or her own narcissism and thus openly encouraged to think more integrally, i.e., to "think yellow" (second-tier), by recognizing each level or meme in the spiral to be exactly what it is—a phase-specific stage of development. Indeed, this type of integral embrace is called the *prime directive:* "The health of the *entire* spiral is the prime directive, not preferential treatment for any one level." This is especially true and relevant since each and every human being is always "born at beige," the lowest meme, thus starting afresh the grand spiral of development from the lower to the higher memes in the ever-flowing River of Life. With this vast all-embracing integral vision, according to Wilber, it's only by making the quantum leap to *second-tier vision-logic t*hat the world as a whole will continue its natural evolutionary development and thus be better prepared to unfold *third-tier consciousness* or the transpersonal levels of Spirit Itself.

BOOMERITIS CHARACTER CHART

(taken from a Shambhala interview with Ken Wilber: "On the Release of *Boomeritis* and the Completion of Volume 3 of *The Kosmos Trilogy*," 2002)

Boomeritis CHARACTER	REAL LIFE PERSON
Ken Wilber	Ken Wilber as a 22-year old student
Derek Van Cleef	"An extraordinarily brilliant man I knew, who ended up killing himself."
Stuart Davis	Stuart Davis, modern musician, with such releases as *Kid Mystic* and *Bright Apocalypse* among others
Chloe	Based partly on Marci, Wilber's ex-wife
Mark Jefferson	"Based loosely on a good friend of mine, a young black man named Mark Palmer."
Joan Hazelton	"Joan is the voice that I talk to myself with"; described as a combination of Ken and Treya.
Lesa Powell	"Lesa is very loosely based on a really extraordinary woman named Maureen Silos," an Afro-American scholar.
Margaret Carlton	"I can't say."
Charles Morin	"I can't say."
Carla Fuentes	"A composite. Carla is part Hispanic and part Native American. The Hispanic part is based loosely on a professor I once knew, and the Native part on my friend Sra Bates, who is Wolf Clan Cherokee."
Kim, Jonathan, Carolyn, Scott, Beth, Katish, Vanessa (the young students)	"Most of it is just made up."

Integral Philosophy

By deeply, profoundly, uninterruptedly inquiring into the Witness of all knowledge, this specific type of philosophical inquiry [*jnana* yoga] opens onto contemplative awareness: the mind itself subsides in the vast expanse of primordial awareness, and *philosophia* gives way to *contemplatio*.

The heart of Integral Philosophy, as I conceive it, is primarily a mental activity of coordinating, elucidating and conceptually integrating all the various modes of knowing and being, so that, even if Integral Philosophy itself does not *deliver* the higher modes, it fully acknowledges them, and then allows and invites *philosophia* to open itself to the practices and modes of *contemplatio*.

Integral Philosophy is also, by virtue of its comprehensiveness, a powerful *critical theory*, critical of all less encompassing approaches—in philosophy, psychology, religion, social theory, and politics.

And, finally, it is a *theoria* that is inseparable from *praxis*, on all levels, in all quadrants.

—Ken Wilber, *The Eye of Spirit*

Epilogue

THE GLOBAL INTEGRAL VISION

THE MAP IS NOT THE TERRITORY: A CALL TO CHANGE THE MAPMAKER!

A theory of *everything*? "Well, of course not," confesses his publisher Shambhala Publications in an on-line ad for *A Theory of Everything,* "but when leaders in fields as diverse as business, psychology, medicine, international development and politics . . . want to understand their work in a wider context, they turn to philosopher and author Ken Wilber."

There is always a risk, in work this complex and multilayered, of confusing the map with the territory itself. But Wilber has in fact recognized this very dilemma by embracing its implications from his earliest book, *A Spectrum of Consciousness,* whose first chapters clearly distinguish between the systems of symbolic or dualistic knowledge (the "map") and the "nondual mode of knowing" (or the real "territory" of Reality). Contrary to the accusations of some critics, Wilber is not interested in just making neat, orderly maps for their own sake. Instead, as plainly stated on those opening pages written back in his early twenties, he has always insisted that the best objective is to *engage* in injunctive practices, i.e., do the yoga so that ultimate Reality (or the "territory" of God or nondual Spirit) is actually discovered and truly known directly for oneself. With this radical, yet practical, understanding the various maps or guides are finally dispensed with and Reality itself is *directly* experienced. Distinguishing between what's traditionally known as the "two truths" (i.e., relative truths and Absolute Truth), this paradoxical concern has been an overriding theme throughout all of Wilber's works. He clearly stated as much in his 1977 debut, *The Spectrum of Consciousness:*

> Now in itself, there is nothing particularly damaging or misleading about symbolic maps—they are of immense practical value and are quite indispensable to a civilized society. As Schröedinger pointed out, however, the problem comes as soon as we forget that the map is not the territory, as soon as we confuse our symbols of reality with reality itself. Reality, so to speak, lies "beyond" or "behind" the shadowy symbols that are, at best, a second-hand facsimile.

Even in regard to his own intricate modeling systems, Wilber has always conceded that "a dualistic map of nondual territory just has to be booby-trapped," thus this fact must be accounted for. Nevertheless, he maintains that by "working with broad orienting generalizations, we can suggest a broad orienting map for the place of men and women in relation to Universe, Life, and Spirit." The integral vision therefore, is nothing more than *a very reliable map* based on the received wisdom of both East and West, the ancient and modern worlds, yet, as always, it's always open to further revision.

The warning against confusing the map with the territory or journey is similar to the Zen admonition not to confuse the finger pointing at the moon for the moon itself. Wilber's first book begins in this spirit by suggesting that it's only by using a combination of psychotherapy and mystical insight that we can be persuaded into "seeing our maps as maps," for only then we'll be "in a position to go beyond them to the territory itself, to relinquish the hold these social dreams exercise over us . . . for as a person divides Reality, he so acts."

Nearly twenty-five years later, the fifty-year-old integral philosopher consistently echoes the same practical wisdom, as he does in every one of his books: "Although most of my books attempt to offer a genuinely integral vision, they almost always end with a call for some sort of *integral practice*—a practice that exercises body, mind, soul, and spirit in self, culture, and nature (all-level, all-quadrant)." The ultimate perfection of practice is the present realization of mystical enlightenment (God-Realization) or One Taste. As Wilber muses, "There is only One Taste in the entire Kosmos, and that taste is Divine, whether it appears in the flesh, in the mind, in the soul." Wilber's concludes, in *A Theory of Everything,* that everyone must ultimately abandon any and all theories, even "theories of everything":

> The integral vision, having served its purpose, is finally outshined by the radiance of a Spirit that is much too obvious to see and much too close to reach,

and the integral search finally succeeds by letting go of the search itself, there to dissolve in a radical Freedom and consummate Fullness that was always already the case, so that one abandons a theory of everything in order to simply be Everything, one with the All in this endless awareness that holds the Kosmos kindly in its hand. And then the true Mystery yields itself, the face of Spirit secretly smiles, the Sun rises in your very own heart and the Earth becomes your very own body, galaxies rush through your veins while stars light up the neurons of your night, and never again will you search for a mere theory of that which is actually your own Original Face.

With Wilber's all-quadrants, all-levels or holonic approach, he has placed an added emphasis on championing the postmodern position, which demonstrates "the intrinsic role that interpretation plays in human awareness . . . *Interpretation is an intrinsic feature of the fabric of the universe:* there is the crucial insight at the heart of the great postmodern movements." Thus, he too (like postmodernists in general) heavily criticizes the "fundamental Enlightenment paradigm" of modernity (known as the myth of the given) because reality is not simply given but rather "in some significant ways is a construction, an interpretation" created by people who are always set within a particular historical and sociocultural milieu. Wilber goes on to suggest that by using a holonic AQAL approach "it is not necessary to picture the basic structures or basic holons as being permanently fixed and unchanging essences. . . . They can, in part, be understood as *habits of evolution,* more like a Kosmic memory than a pregiven mold." The integral philosopher is accounting for the shifting conditions and holistic processes of evolution by presenting a dynamic map of reality that applies the postmodern critique which contends that it's impossible to perfectly reflect back the true nature of reality (the "mirror of nature"). Nonetheless, Wilber still contends that this integral philosophy honors wisdom's greatest task:

> The task of philosophy, as it were, is not simply to clarify the maps and *correct* their deviations from reality, but to *elucidate* these deeper currents from which thought couldn't deviate even if it wanted to! In Zen there is a saying, "That which one can deviate from is not the true Tao." In other words, in some ways our knowledge is indeed a matter of correcting our inaccurate maps; but also, and at a much deeper level, there is a Tao, a Way, a Current of the Kosmos, from which we have not, and could never, deviate. And part of our job is to find this deeper Current, this Tao, and express it, elucidate it, celebrate it.

By employing a radical post-postmodern approach, yet one tempered with an integral metatheory that recognizes the importance of all quadrants (personal, behavioral, social, and cultural) as well as all levels in the Great Nest of Being, Wilber is insisting that our philosophies or world maps must account for "the mapmaker" or the subject ("I") who is making the maps:

> Genuine philosophy . . . is not merely a matter of making pictures of the objective world, but rather of investigating the structures in the subject that allow the making of the pictures in the first place. Because, put bluntly, the mapmaker's fingerprints are all over the maps he makes. And thus the secret to the universe is not just in the objective maps but in the subjective mapmaker.

This certainly includes Wilber's own sophisticated integral maps, as well as any other of your favorite maps, from myths to sutras, from the Bible to the Koran, from science to religion, from conservatism to liberalism, from the political left to the right—they must all be ultimately seen as personal limitations and liabilities superimposed on the living nature of an ultimately loving and spiritual Kosmic Mandala radiating as the nondual dance of the unqualifiable and Absolute Divine.

In an interview given during the first year of the new millennium, Wilber plainly admits "a lot of what I'm saying could be wrong," and yet, he contends, "clearly nobody wants to confuse the map with the territory, but just as well you don't want a fucked-up incomplete map."* In fact, this is one reason why Wilber's many books never cover precisely the same aspects of the "territory" as did his previous ones, because he's attempting to map out new venues, so to speak, articulate even greater possibilities of comprehensiveness. Yet overall, each of the phases in his career is still united in purpose: to provide a comprehensive cartography of both the "insides" and "outsides" of the Divine Kosmos.

In order to comprehend the vastness of Wilber's integral vision, he suggests that a reader should try a minimum of two or three books in order to grasp the comprehensive territory. Then, he suggests, "See if they make sense to you; see if you can improve them; see in any event if they help you bring forth your own integral ideas and aspirations. . . . It is not a fixed or final theory, simply one that has served its purpose if it helps you get to a better one." He himself has always found useful the advice given by one of his professors who suggested that a good theory is "one that lasts long enough to get you a better one."

---

* "An Enlightenment Interview with Ken Wilber: Fifth Interview Segment" by Jordan Gruber @www.enlightenment.com; see also: Ken Wilber interview, "Speaking of Everything CD" (www.enlightenment.com, 2002).

Perhaps one of his most persuasive statements regarding this type of flexible approach was made back in 1986 on the last pages of his contribution to *Transformations of Consciousness,* which, I believe, is worth quoting in full:

> I would like to be very clear about what this presentation has attempted to do. It has not offered a fixed, conclusive, unalterable model. Although I have at every point attempted to ground it in the theoretical and phenomenological reports of reputable researchers and practitioners, the overall project is obviously metatheoretical and suggestive, and is offered in that spirit. But once one begins to look at the full spectrum of human growth and development, an extraordinarily rich array of material becomes available for metatheoretical work; a variety of connections suggest themselves which were not apparent before, and a wealth of hypotheses for future research become immediately available. Moreover, different analytical, psychological, and spiritual systems, which before seemed largely incompatible or even contradictory, appear closer to the possibility of a mutually enriching synthesis or reconciliation.
>
> This presentation has offered one such full-spectrum approach, more to show the strong possibilities than the final conclusions; if this type of model is useful in reaching better ones, it will have served its purpose. My point, rather, is that given the state of knowledge *already* available to us, it seems ungenerous to the human condition to present any models *less* comprehensive— by which I mean, models that do not take into account both conventional *and* contemplative realms of human growth and development.

As a post-postmodernist Wilber constantly reminds us that our perceived reality is not pregiven but is actively evolving or developing as the Great Nest of Spirit. Therefore, in actuality, Wilber is only sharing his particular vision for others to consider. He suggests that we too must at least try to include these evolutionary patterns of life and consciousness in a greater integral embrace by actively practicing and exhibiting a "correct but partial" or "partial but true" attitude of inclusiveness, one where, in essence, "everybody is right." In fact, Wilber is so committed to this type of inclusive approach that he has said: "And on my tombstone, I dearly hope that someday they will write: He was true but partial. . . ."

His guiding principle throughout the development of his work has been: "I have a general rule: *Everybody is right.* Every single system ever offered has *some* degree of truth in it."* In further explanation of his true purpose, he said in *A Theory of Everything:*

---

* op. cit.

The real intent of my writing is not to say, you must think in this way. The real impact is to enrich: here are some of the many important facets of this extraordinary Kosmos; have you thought about including them in your own worldview? . . . In this Theory of Everything, I have one major rule: *Everybody* is right. More specifically, everybody—including me—has some important pieces of truth, and all those pieces need to be honored, cherished, and included in a more gracious, spacious, and compassionate embrace, a genuine T.O.E.

Wilber affirms that something more than just an integral map is needed. We also require a *true integral practice* in order to eventually adapt to the higher transpersonal levels of evolution whose ultimate estate is enlightenment. This capacity, Wilber claims, is inherent in all of us, enfolded as innate structural potentials that will develop and evolve as our own personal odyssey reaches from infancy to adulthood in the unfolding of a spiritually realized person. According to Wilber's integral AQAL perspective "the major implications of an all-level, all-quadrant approach to spirituality is that physical, emotional, mental, and spiritual waves of being should be simultaneously exercised in self, culture, and nature (i.e., in the I, we, and it domains)." This great unfolding or evolutionary potential becomes, as Wilber's collected writings demonstrate, the ultimate purpose of any genuine integral enterprise: "to change the mapmaker!" Wilber argues, in *A Theory of Everything*, "What is required, in my opinion, is not simply a new integral theory or a new T.O.E., important as that is, but also a new *integral practice*. Even if we possessed the perfect integral map of the Kosmos, a map that was completely all-inclusive and unerringly holistic, that map itself would not transform people. We don't just need a map; we need ways to change the mapmaker."

In other words, and in perfect harmony with the world's perennial philosophy, or the wisdom tradition taught by the world's greatest shamans, saints, sages, and siddhas, Wilber claims that ultimately the challenge is really up to us: to practice, to discover and directly experience the truth of reality for ourselves, and then to share our insights with others as much as possible, in a compassionate and enlightened embrace. Yet, as he is wont to remind us: "As always, we have to make the future that is given to us." Indeed, Wilber already expressed similar sentiments back in the first years of his career, in *No Boundary:*

This is a simple but arduous practice, yet its results constitute nothing less than liberation in this life, for the transcendent self is everywhere acknowledged as a ray of the Divine. In principle, your transcendent self is of one nature with God (however you might wish to conceive it). For it is finally,

ultimately, profoundly, God alone who looks through your eyes, listens with
your ears, and speaks with your tongue. . . . At the bottom of your soul is the
soul of humanity itself, but a divine, transcendent soul, leading from bondage
to liberation, from enchantment to awakening, from time to eternity, from
death to immortality.

This understanding gives us the impetus to further evolve—to live life fully
in all its dimensions! Morally, as Wilber often points out, this includes the necessity
to develop through the preconventional and postconventional (and even post-
postconventional) stages or waves that are evolving from egocentric to sociocentric
to worldcentric to the bodhisattvic embrace with an enlightened and compassionate inclusion, yet transcendence, of all phenomena. Wilber suggests that the entire spiral of development must be honored and protected, nurtured and cared for,
and this is the "prime directive" and "basic moral intuition" of his integral philosophy. Thus Wilbur reminds us, in *A Theory of Everything:*

> Human beings are born and begin their evolution through the great spiral of
> consciousness, moving from archaic to magic to mythic to rational to per-
> haps integral, and from there perhaps into genuinely transpersonal domains.
> But for every person that moves into integral or higher, dozens are born into
> the archaic. The spiral of existence is a great unending flow, stretching from
> body to mind to soul to spirit, with millions upon millions constantly flow-
> ing through the great river from source to ocean. . . . But the major problem
> remains: not, how can we get everybody to the integral wave or higher, but
> how can we arrange the health of the overall spiral, as billions of humans con-
> tinue to pass through it, from one end to the other, year in and year out?

If properly applied and understood, Wilber's integral maps should motivate
readers to find a true teacher of the transpersonal realms, just as we study with university professors in order to master the realms of the rational mind.

THE LOGIC OF SEEING WITH VISION (VISION-LOGIC)

Second-tier awareness is the worldcentric stage of consciousness that emerges after the mental-rational structure has adequately developed and the lower levels of
consciousness have been integrated. As Wilber proclaimed in *Sex, Ecology, Spirituality,* "what rationality has put asunder, vision-logic will unite." Vision-logic, in
other words, is an integrative structure of consciousness with an intellectual capacity that's also heartfelt and intuition based (or body-integrated). Therefore it

stands at the threshold of the higher transpersonal realms. Wilber, following other theorists such as Jean Gebser and Broughton and Benoit, represents this integral stage of development with the mythic centaur, the half-horse, half-human creature of ancient Greek mythology, to symbolize the healthy integration yet differentiation of the body (animal nature) and the mind (human nature). This stage of mature development, in the terms of Spiral Dynamics, permits the shift into second-tier awareness, or the so-called yellow and turquoise memes. Wilber acknowledges that vision-logic is a natural capacity of human consciousness that all people, at least in potential, have in common, to greater or lesser degrees.

Wilber sees his own body of written work as being principally an intellectual approach set within a spiritual vision—as a vision-logic or network-logic—one that's "intentionally written in the centaur-level language of depth." This type of approach offers humanity an integral vision, a cognitive gestalt that networks the numerous pieces of the puzzle together to create a "big picture" of the Kosmos. In other words, "You can't honor various methods and fields without showing how they fit together. That is how to make a genuine world philosophy." By using "orienting generalizations" to create "a broad orienting map," the integral vision brings together all the information and experiences of humankind in a way that forms an intellectually cohesive whole. Wilber constructs as deep and wide a model as possible, based upon the largest amount of available evidence.

Wilber's work may be challenging, even daunting at times. Vast amounts of diverse data are synthesized as a harmonious unity, though embraced in a way that is so elegant and simple and comprehensive. Wilber himself has been personally evolving, and so too his writings and philosophy have expanded. The integral philosopher continues to study and write, sometimes in collaboration with like-minded pioneers at the Integral Institute. In doing so, he explores further refinements in the overall modeling of the spectrum of consciousness. But subtle revisions notwithstanding, more than twenty years after the publication of his first book, Wilber reports: "I have found [my model's] basic framework to be as sturdy and solid as ever; if anything, subsequent research, evidence, and theory have actually increased its plausibility." Nevertheless, he is always ready to modify and further refine his integral vision when new evidence warrants it.

THE INTEGRAL VISION: A WORLD PHILOSOPHY

Although Wilber was the first theorist to bring the spectrum idea into contemporary psychology (particularly into consciousness studies), his integral approach is not solely the record of one individual's evolution. All the "eyes of knowing" (sensory, mental, spiritual) may be opened by anyone, for, as we've discussed, they are our own innate structural potentials. Accordingly, he urges every person from every culture and persuasion to realize some type of integral vision, to engage in authentic spiritual practice, and awaken to the One Taste of the Divine. The integrative linking of this vast spectrum of the scientific and spiritual domains is a grand coup of intellectual reconciliation and integrative capacity. Yet, this is a universal vision that can be used by anyone willing to take the time and effort to transform by following the current of love or Eros in a compassionate embrace of all manifestation. Wilber's vision (*theoria*) calls us to an integral practice (*praxis*), which includes contemplation and meditation (*contemplatio*) exercised in all quadrants, on all levels; thus he explains, in *The Eye of Spirit,* using the language of *philosophia*:

> The heart of integral philosophy, as I conceive it, is primarily a mental activity of coordinating, elucidating and conceptually integrating all the various modes of knowing and being, so that, even if integral philosophy itself does not *deliver* the higher modes, it fully acknowledges them, and then allows and invites *philosophia* to open itself to the practices and modes of *contemplatio.* Integral philosophy is also, by virtue of its comprehensiveness, a powerful *critical theory,* critical of all less encompassing approaches—in philosophy, psychology, religion, social theory, and politics. And, finally, it is a *theoria* that is inseparable from praxis, on all levels, in all quadrants.

As we've seen, Wilber's integral vision expresses an extraordinary scope, uniting the duality and relativity of opposites, of the physical as well as metaphysical, including the "insides" and "outsides" of the Kosmos, embracing feminine and masculine values, recognizing the unconscious, subconscious, and conscious domains, marrying the teachings of East and West, of premodern, modern, and postmodern, secular and sacred wisdom traditions, movement and stillness, Creation and Emptiness. No wonder historian Jack Crittenden has included Ken Wilber in an expansion of Alasdair MacIntyre's well-known choice between Aristotle and Nietzsche, the Root architects of the modern and postmodern view, respectively, but rather "the twenty-first century literally has three choices: Aristotle, Nietzsche, or Ken Wilber."

The integral vision, with its full embrace of reality, its inclusive pluralism, openly promotes a type of evolution revolution. This ethical orientation involves the compassionate notion of basic moral intuition, which is "to protect and promote the greatest depth [of evolution] for the greatest span [or number of holons]." This care is based upon an evolutionary understanding of transcendence-yet-inclusion, grounded in nondual spiritual awareness. It is similar to the Spiral Dynamic's prime directive: "The health of the entire spiral [of development] is the prime directive, not preferential treatment for any one level." This view leads Wilber to suggest that any Integral Age will certainly involve a tolerant integral embrace in which people consciously acknowledge that "this Great Nest is a holarchy of extended love and compassionate embrace, reaching from dirt to Divinity, with no corner of the Kosmos left untouched by grace or care or luminosity." This is the essence of Wilber's integral message, extending all the way to complete enlightenment or God-Realization.

Indeed, in today's global New Age of change and transition the integral visionary and spectrum psychologist continues to announce the possibility of an emerging Integral Age:

> For the fact is, this is the dawning of the age of vision-logic, the rise of the network society, the postmodern, aperspectival, internetted global village. Evolution in all forms has started to become conscious of itself. Evolution, as Spirit-in-action, is starting to awaken on a more collective scale. Kosmic evolution is now producing theories and performances of its own integral embrace. This Eros moves through you and me, urging us to include, to diversify, to honor, to enfold. The love that moves the sun and other stars is moving theories such as this, and it will move many others, as Eros connects the previously unconnected, and pulls together the fragments of a world too weary to endure.

The dawn of a New Age notwithstanding, Wilber somberly cautions us in *Up From Eden* to curb our narcissistic tendencies personified by the modern malaise of boomeritis:

> While I am encouraged by the glimmerings of a New Age, I conclude with a sober appraisal: we are nowhere near the Millennium. In fact, at this point in history, the most radical, pervasive, and earth-shaking transformation would occur simply if everybody truly evolved to a mature, rational, and responsible ego, capable of freely participating in the open-exchange of mutual self-esteem. *There* is the "edge of history." There would be a *real* New Age. We are nowhere near the stage "beyond reason," simply because we are nowhere yet near universal reason itself.

Over twenty years later, standing at the promising outset of a new millennium still full or terrors and possibilities, Wilber expounds, in *A Theory of Everything*, on the necessity for a more embracing integral vision that will create a deeper revolution by acknowledging the entire spiral of evolution:

I believe that the real revolutions facing today's world involve, not a glorious collective move into transpersonal domains, but the simple, fundamental changes that can be brought to the magic, mythic, and rational waves of existence. . . . In other words, most of the work that needs to be done is work to make the lower (and foundational) waves more healthy in their own terms. . . . An integral vision is one of the least pressing issues on the face of the planet. . . . *Nonetheless,* the advantage of second-tier integral awareness is that it more creatively helps with the solutions to those pressing problems. In grasping big pictures, it can help suggest more cogent solutions. . . . In all these ways and more, we could indeed use an integral vision for a world gone slightly mad.

Yet even though realistic, the visionary Wilber still sees a more positive, integral future as part of Spirit's evolutionary play, thus in *A Theory of Everything* he tells us in prophetic language:

So it is that the leading edge of consciousness evolution stands today on the brink of an integral millennium—or at least the possibility of an integral millennium—where the sum total of extant human knowledge, wisdom, and technology is available to all.

Such is his vast vision of the present and future: the promotion of integral approaches to education, medicine, business, politics, science, and spirituality, all with a heightened emphasis on evolutionary development. This is indeed a genuine way to honor and acknowledge all four quadrants of the universe. Wilber elucidates the primary motivation behind his writings, when addressing his eight-hundred-page magnum opus *Sex, Ecology, Spirituality:*

I sought a world philosophy. I sought an *integral* philosophy, one that would believably weave together the many pluralistic contexts of science, morals, aesthetics, Eastern philosophy, and the world's great wisdom traditions. Not on the level of details—that is finitely impossible; but on the level of orienting generalizations: a way to suggest that the world really is one, undivided, whole, and related to itself in every way: a holistic philosophy for a holistic Kosmos: a world philosophy, an integral philosophy.

Wilbur cordially speaks and interacts with any who read his books and seek him out in an honest attempt to understand what he's saying. But in the end, the mystic-philosopher tells us, in *Collected Works, Volume Eight:*

When all is said and done, and argument and theory come to rest, and the separate self lays its weary head on the pillow of its own discontent, what then? When I relax into I-I, and the infinite spaciousness of primordial purity drenches me in Being; when I relax into I-I, and the eternal Emptiness of ever-present awareness saturates the self, fills it with a Fullness that cannot even be contained; then all the agitated anxieties of life return to their source in God and Goddess, and I-I alone shine in the world that I-I alone created. . . .

Let us, then You-and-I, recognize together who and what we are. And I will be with you until the ends of the world, and you will be with me, for there is only One Self, which is the miracle of Spirit.

It's up to us, then, to see for ourselves what Wilber has to tell us by reading some of his numerous books, articles, and essays, especially his most recent and fully articulated AQAL approach in *Integral Psychology* and *A Theory of Everything,* in order to better understand the possibilities of an integral vision in this modern age and postmodern times. Wilber's depth of insight, his inclusive embrace of One Taste, allow him to gently nudge us to realize the same unity and divine oneness of Spirit:

Just so, the same Spirit-in-action has written this book, and it is the very same Spirit-in-action who is now reading it. From subconscious to self-conscious to superconscious, the great Play continues and the grand River flows, with all of its glorious streams rushing to the ocean of One Taste, never really lost, never really found, this sound of the rain on the temple roof, which only alone is.

But perhaps one of Spirit's great gifts at this turn into the new millennium is that it offers the emerging world culture an integral vision that's been magnified through the brilliant mind and spirit of Ken Wilber. Since this gift has been given in a prolific series of exquisitely articulated writings, it's really up to us to now better understand his integral message and AQAL approach, to see the inclusive glory of this vision, to feel the heart of its truth. In this way we can deepen the capacity of our own intelligence and compassion to more fully embrace the vastness and mystery of Spirit's radiant display and ultimate transcendence. Perhaps we'll then see that one of Wilber's greatest gifts is the motivation his work provides to change the mapmaker—us!—by conveying a persuasive call to psychological growth and development. We shall see, as history continues to unfold through the third millennium's coming decades, if we are up to the task of applying an integral approach in order to embrace the family of humanity and to extend loving care and compassion to all things in the Great Nest of Spirit.

Acknowledgments

I humbly acknowledge, first of all, my debt to all my teachers and spiritual guides, both living and deceased but alive in the pages of human history and sacred texts. To all my friends throughout the years who have financially, emotionally, psychologically, mentally, and spirituality served me and my evolution. I give thanks and remembrance, for I couldn't have done it without you. Particularly, I would like to mention my life's love and lady, Ellie Staples; my dear friend and supporter; Iris Lawton; and my brother-friends, Mark Schillinger, Frank Marrero, John Burton, and Terry Patton—thank you, I love you, bless you all forever.

A special mention of grateful thanks to my literary agent, John White, who's diligent and tireless efforts have made this book become real and to who I owe much—thank you for not giving up. I also wish to thank the excellent team at Jeremy P. Tarcher, a division of the Penguin Group, including Mitch Horowitz, executive editor; Ashley Shelby, assistant editor; David Walker, art director; Deborah Miller, copyeditor; you did an excellent job and brought a dream into the real world—thank you for completing a massive and difficult project.

To my brothers, mother, and family—thank you for your support and love.

A sincere acknowledgment and thanks goes to Ken Wilber, a man and friend who has been generous to me and my work, and don't we hope the integral evolution revolution is successful! Mostly, a heartfelt acknowledgment to my Guru and Spiritual Master, Ruchira Avatar Adi Da Samraj, Who affirmed and taught me the Way of the Heart and self-transcending God-Communion; I love You. Ultimately, and truthfully, I owe it all to God—in endless praises and thanks.

Correlative Charts Compiled by Ken Wilber

from *Integral Psychology* (2000)

Integral Psychology (2000) presents Correlative Charts compiled by Wilber himself in the late 1990s, comparing his well-defined *basic waves* or structures of consciousness with hundreds—probably thousands—of researchers. This evidence is part of the massive amount of data that Wilber comprehensively uses to base his work—his integral vision—on. Since these charts are a basic guideline or outline to Wilber's integral or AQAL (all quadrants, all levels, all lines, all states, etc.) approach, they effectively present partial definitions of many of his terms, if only by a comparative analysis. Therefore, I thought it would be useful to include a few descriptive explanations scattered throughout the text of *Integral Psychology* to explain Wilber's conception of the Correlative Charts as a whole.

First, Wilber explains that these "General Waves of Self-Development are not rigidly discrete rungs in a ladder, but overlapping streams of self unfolding and they exist as *functional subholons* in subsequent development (barring pathology, such as being split off into dissociated subpersonalities)." (108–9) This means that the Charts themselves focus on diachronic elements, or changes that occur over a period of time, whereas only a few of the *functional invariants*, or the functions of the proximate self, such as identity, will, cognition, integration, and metabolism, are included. Nevertheless, Wilber quickly agrees that "the self and its functions seem to be absolutely crucial in any integral psychology." (226, 9n)

In regard to the number of levels, Wilber clarifies (in an endnote): "I have suggested around sixteen major waves, which can be condensed into *nine or ten functional groupings* (all shown in the Charts), but all such cartographies are simply different approaches to the many waves in the great River of Life, matter to mind to spirit, which is the most precious legacy of the ancient wisdom." (190) Once again, he refers to the fluid nature of any type of numbering scheme, therefore countering the rigid or linear system his critics often accuse him of adhering to. Thus, as he technically explains, "depending on how and what you count as a 'level,' I have listed anywhere from sixteen Basic Structures [or Waves] (in boldface) to thirty (counting sublevels); as functional groupings, I usually give nine or ten (i.e., sensorimotor, emotional-sexual, rep-mind, con-op, form-op, vision-logic, psychic, subtle, causal, nondual). . . . I should say that what we count as a stage depends first and foremost on empirical and phenomenological evidence, and as that evidence becomes richer, our stage conceptions become clearer. . . . The sixteen or so basic structures/stages presented in the Charts are based on the textual reports of some three thousand years of meditative experience, coupled with recent psychological research; but they are always open to revision and clarification." (219–20, 2n)

Wilber also openly concedes that this broad "spectrum of evidence" focuses mostly on the "Upper-Left quadrant of subjective consciousness"; nonetheless, he still confidently concludes: "the Charts . . . are a startling testimony to the fact that, even if there are millions of details yet to be worked out, the broad contours of the Spectrum of Consciousness have already been significantly outlined. The general similarities in all those Charts are most suggestive, and, from a bird's-eye view, hint that we are at least in the right ballpark." (184) In this case, the Comparative Charts are a strong graphic presentation outlining in brief form the wealth of evidence incorporated by and correlated with Ken Wilber's comprehensive integral model of consciousness and Kosmos, the Great Holarchy of Being and Knowing.

Chart 1a. Wilber Correlations

Correlative Basic Structures	General Self-Sense	Specific Aspects	Defenses	Possible Pathology	Fulcrum	Treatment	Moral Span (those worthy of moral consideration)
matter (subatomic, atomic, molecular, polymer), sensation, perception, exocept — *sensorimotor*	material self	pleromatic	distortion, delusional proj. hallucination, wish fulfillment	psychosis	BPM: F-0	intense regressive therapies	—
	bodyego	uroboric		psychosis	F-1 (physical self)	pacification (Gedo: pacification)	autistic, symbolic, self-only
impulse/emotion, image, symbol — *phantasmic-emotional*		axial-body, pranic-body (typhonic), image-body (magical)	selfobject fusion, projection, splitting	borderline	F-2 (emotional self)	structure-building (Gedo: unification, optimal disillusion)	impulsive, magical, narcissism, hedonic (egocentric)
endocept, concept — *rep-mind*		name-self, concept-self	isolation, repression, reaction form., displacement	neurotic	F-3 (self-concept)	uncovering (Gedo: interpretation)	safety, power
rule/role early, late; transition — *conop*	persona	membership-self (mythic) early, middle, late	duplicitous transaction, covert intentions	script	F-4 (role self)	script analysis	mythic-membership, conformist (sociocentric)
formal early, late; transition — *formop*	ego	mature ego	suppression, anticipation, sublimation	ego	F-5 (mature ego)	introspection (Gedo: introspection)	rational-reflexive (worldcentric)
vision-logic early, middle, late — *postformal*	centaur	centaur (existential, integrated self)	inauthenticity, deadening, aborted self-actualization, bad faith	existential	F-6 (centaur)	existential therapy	universal-global
psychic early (vision), late	soul	psychic self	psychic inflation, split-life goals, pranic disorder, yogic illness	psychic	F-7 (psychic)	path of yogis	panenhenic, all earthly beings (yogic) (shamanic)
subtle early (archetype), late		subtle self (archetypal)	failed integration, archetypal fragmentation	subtle	F-8 (subtle)	path of saints	panentheistic, all sentient beings in all realms (saintly) (bodhisattvic)
causal early (formless), late	spirit	Pure Self (Witness)	failed differentiation, Arhat's disease	causal	F-9 (causal)	path of sages	always already (sage/siddha) (Buddhic)
nondual early, middle, late		Nondual			Ground		

Moral Span — Locus / Moral reach:

- Locus of bodily self — "me"
- Locus of mythic-membership — "us" (family, group, tribe, nation)
- Locus of rational universal pluralism — "all of us" (all humans without exception)
- Locus of World-Soul — all earthly beings without exception
- Locus of Brahma-lokas — all sentient beings in all realms without exception
- self-liberation in primordial awareness — all manifest and unmanifest reality

Moral stages: preconventional → conventional → postconventional → post-postconventional

Chart 1b. Wilber Correlations

Correlative Basic Structures	(developmental stratum)	Affect	Levels of "Food" (relational exchange)	Gender Identity	Worldviews — name	Worldviews — general characteristics	(sociocentric scope)
matter: -subatomic, -atomic, -molecular, -polymer	sensorimotor	• reactivity		• morphological-genetic givens		• undifferentiated, pleromatic	
sensation	sensorimotor	• sensations	material exchange	• undifferentiated	archaic		
perception	sensorimotor	• physiostates:	-food				egocentric
exocept	phantasmic-emotional	touch, temperature, pleasure, pain	-labor		archaic-magical	• hallucinatory wish fulfillment, subject-object fusions	egocentric
impulse/emotion	phantasmic-emotional	• protoemotions: tension, fear, rage, satisfaction	emotional exchange	• differentiated basic-gender identity	magical	• "selfobject"	egocentric
image	phantasmic-emotional	• 2° emotions: anxiety, anger, wishing, liking, safety	-sex		magic-mythic	• egocentric, word magic, narcissistic; locus of magic power = ego	egocentric
symbol	rep-mind	belongingness	-safety, power		mythic	• omnipotence of ego challenged; security; ego omnipotence transferred to gods	ethnocentric
endocept	rep-mind	• 3° emotions: love, joy, depression, hate,	-belongingness, care	• gender conventionality	mythic (literal)	• concrete-literal myths	ethnocentric
concept	rep-mind		mental exchange	• gender consistency (norms)	mythic-	• locus of magic power = deified Other	ethnocentric
rule/role — early	conop	• 4° emotions: universal affect, global justice, care, compassion, all-	-membership		rational	• rationalization of mythic structures	worldcentric
rule/role — late	conop		discourse			• demythologizing, formalizing	worldcentric
formal — transition / early	formop		-self-reflective exchange	• gender (rational)	formalism	• static universal formalism	worldcentric
formal — late / transition	formop	• human love, world-centric altruism	-autonomous exchange		pluralistic	• static systems/contexts	worldcentric
vision-logic — early	postformal		exchange	• androgyny (trans-differentiated)	relativism	• pluralistic systems, dynamic-multiple contexts/histories	worldcentric
vision-logic — middle	postformal				holistic	• integrates multiple contexts, paradigmatic	worldcentric
vision-logic — late	postformal				integralism	• cross-paradigmatic; dialectical developmentalism as World Process	worldcentric
psychic — early (vision) / late		• awe, rapture, all-species love, compassion	soul exchange: -psychic vision		psychic (shamanic, yogic)	• union with World Process; nature mysticism; gross realm unity	theocentric
subtle — early (archetype) / late		• ananda, ecstasy love-bliss, saintly commitment	-God communion, -God union	• archetypal gender union (tantra)	subtle (archetypal, saintly)	• union with creatrix of gross realm; deity mysticism; subtle realm unity	theocentric
causal — early		• infinite freedom-release, boddhisattvic-compassion	spiritual exchange: -Godhead identity	• beyond gender	causal	• union with source of manifest realms; formless mysticism; causal unity	theocentric
(formless) late					(formless, sage)		theocentric
nondual — early / middle / late		• one taste	-sahaja		nondual (siddha)	• union of form and formless, Spirit and World Process nondual mysticism	theocentric

Chart 2a. Basic Structures in Other Systems

Basic Structures	Huston Smith levels (planes)	Plotinus	Buddhist Vijnanas	Stan Grof	John Battista	Chakras	General Great Chain	James Mark Baldwin
matter -subatomic			(levels of csness)	BPM: oceanic to birth		1. material	matter	
-atomic	body (terrestrial)	matter						
-molecular								prelogical
-polymer							body	
sensation		sensation	1-5 five senses	somatic	sensation			
perception		perception			perception			
exocept								
impulse/emotion		pleasure/pain		aesthetic	emotion	2. emotional-sexual		
image		images						
symbol				psychodynamic Freudian COEX systems			mind	
endocept	mind (intermediate)	concepts, opinions				3. intentional-mind, power		
concept					cognition			
rule/role early		logical faculty	6. manovijnana (gross-reflecting mind)			4. community-mind, love		quasi-logical
late								
transition						5. verbal-rational mind		
formal early		creative reason			self-aware			logical
late								
transition								
vision-logic early		world soul	7. manas (higher mind)	existential death-rebirth (cf BPM)				extra-logical
middle						6. psychic-mind, ajna (vision)		
late								
psychic early (vision)	soul (celestial)			astral-psychic extra-human			soul	hyper-logical
late								
subtle early (archetype) late		nous	8. tainted alayavijnana (archetypal)	identifications archetypal deity, luminosity	unition	7. sahasrara, transcendental csness, light (higher shabd chakras, to cessation)	spirit	
causal early (formless) late	spirit (infinite)	absolute one	9. nondual consciousness as suchness	universal mind supracosmic void	absolute			
nondual early middle late				ultimate		(release of all chakras in the Real)		

sensorimotor → phantasmic-emotional → rep-mind → conop → formop → postformal

391

Chart 2b. Basic Structures in Other Systems

Basic Structures	General Great Chain	Aurobindo	Kabbalah	Vedanta (state)	Vedanta (body)	Vedanta (sheaths)	William Tiller	Leadbetter (Theosophy)	Adi Da
matter-atomic (-subatomic, -molecular, -polymer)	matter	physical	malkhut	waking	gross	1. material (anna-mayakosha)	physical	physical	1. physical body
sensation		sensation					etheric	etheric (fine physical)	
perception	body	perception							
exocept									
impulse/emotion		vital-emotional	yesod			2. emotional-sexual (prana-mayakosha)	astral	astral (emotional)	2. emotional body
image									
symbol	mind	lower-mind	netzach/hod				m-1 (lower mind)		
endocept					subtle				
concept		concrete mind		dreaming		3. middle mind (mano-mayakosha)	m-2 (intellectual mind)	mental	
rule/role early		logical mind (reasoning)	tiferet						3. lower mind / will-power / gross-mind
rule/role late									
transition									
formal early									
formal late									
transition		higher mind (systems)				4. higher mind (vijnana-mayakosha)	m-3 (spiritual mind)		
vision- early			chesed/gevurah					causal (higher mind)	4. higher mind / psychic opening
logic middle									
late									
psychic early (vision)	soul (psychic and subtle)	illumined mind	chokhmah/binah	deep sleep	causal			buddhic (illumined mind)	
(vision) late									
subtle early (archetype)		intuitive mind	keter			5. bliss mind (ananda-mayakosha)	spirit	atmic (universal spirit)	5. supramental / psychic/subtle
(archetype) late		overmind	ayn						
causal early	spirit (causal and nondual)	supermind	ein sof	turiya	turiya	Brahman-Atman (turiyatita)		monad/logos	6. formless cessation, nirvikalpa
(formless) late									
nondual early		satchitananda							7. sahaja bhava
nondual middle									
late									

Developmental-line labels (lower axis): sensorimotor — phantasmic-emotional — rep-mind — conop — formop — postformal

Chart 3a. Cognitive Development

Average age of emergence	Correlative Basic Structures	Piaget	Commons & Richards	Kurt Fischer (level)	Alexander (levels of mind)
	-subatomic				
	matter -atomic / -molecular / -polymer				
0-18 months (sensorimotor)	sensation				
	perception	sensorimotor	1a sensorimotor actions	1. single sensorimotor set (3-4 months)	1. sensorimotor
	exocept		1b sentential actions	2. sensorimotor mapping (7-8 months)	
	impulse/emotion (phantasmic-emotional)			3. sensorimotor system (11-13 months)	2. prana - emotion-desire
1-3 yrs	image	preconceptual	2a nominal actions	4. single representational set (20-24 months)	
	symbol	preoperational			
3-6 yrs (rep-mind)	endocept	intuitive (conceptual)	2b preoperational actions	5. representational mapping (4-5 yrs)	3. representational mind
	concept	preoperational			
7-8 (conop)	rule/role early	concrete operational – substage 1	3a primary actions	6. representational system (6-7½ yrs)	
9-10	rule/role late	– substage 2	3b concrete operations		
11-12	transition	transition [late conop/early formop (substage 1)]			
13-14 (formop)	formal early	formal operational – substage 2	4a abstract	7. abstract set (10-12)	4. abstract mind
15-19	formal late	– substage 3	4b formal	8. abstract mapping (11-15)	
19-21	transition	(transition – late formop/early polyvalent)			
open (postformal)	vision-logic early	(polyvalent logic – systems of systems)	5a systematic	9. systems (19-21)	
	logic middle		5b meta-systematic	10. systems of systems (24-26)	
	logic late		6a paradigmatic		
[21-28]	psychic early		6b cross-paradigmatic		
[28-35]	(vision) late				
[35-42]	subtle early				5. transcendental intuition
	(archetype) late				
[42-49]	causal early				6. root mind
	(formless) late				7. pure Self
[49-]	nondual early				8. Brahman-Atman
	nondual middle				
	nondual late				

earliest expectable →

Chart 3b. Cognitive Development

Michael Basseches	1a preformal; 1b formal; 2 intermediate postformal; 3 general advanced; 4 advanced dialectical thinking
Jan Sinnott	sensorimotor; preoperational; concrete; formal; relativistic; unified-theory
Gisela Labouvie-Vief	symbolic; intra-systemic; inter-systemic; autonomous
Patricia Arlin	sensorimotor; preoperational; 2a low concrete; 2b high concrete; 3a low formal; 3b high formal; 4a postformal; 4b-e late; postformal (dialectical)
Sri Aurobindo	physical; vital-emotional; lower mind; concrete mind; logical mind (reasoning); higher mind (systems); illumined mind; intuitive mind; overmind; supermind; satchitananda
Herb Koplowitz	formal; systems; general systems; unitary concepts; →
Pascual-Leone	sensorimotor; preoperational; late concrete; early formal; formal; late formal; pre-dialectical; dialectical; transcendental-thinking
overall cognitive lines	gross; gross-reflecting; subtle; causal; nondual
Correlative Basic Structures	matter (subatomic, atomic, molecular, polymer); sensation; perception; exocept; impulse/emotion; image; symbol; endocept; concept; rule/role (early, late); formal (transition, early, late, transition); vision-logic (early, middle, late); psychic/vision (early, late); subtle/archetype (early, late); causal/formless (early, late); nondual (early, middle, late)

Bottom scale: sensorimotor — phantasmic-emotional — rep-mind — conop — formop — postformal

Chart 4a. Self-Related Stages

Correlative Basic Structures	Jane Loevinger (ego stages)	John Broughton (self epistemology)	Sullivan, Grant, and Grant (self-integration)	Fulcrums (Wilber)	Jenny Wade	Michael Washburn	Erik Erikson
matter -subatomic / -atomic / -molecular / -polymer				**F-0** pre and perinatal; deeper psychic trail	pre, peri, neonatal (possible transcendental)		
sensation / **perception**	presocial, autistic			F-1	1. reactive	original embedment	trust vs. mistrust
exocept			1. differentiation of self & nonself				
impulse/emotion	symbiotic			F-2	2. naive	bodyego	autonomy vs. shame and doubt
image							
symbol	impulsive		2. manipulative-demanding			primal repression	
endocept							
concept	self-protective	0. self "inside," reality "outside" / 1 big-person mind, little-person body / 2. naïve subjectivism, mind and body differentiated	3. power: a. rules- "cons"	F-3	3. egocentric	mental ego	initiative vs. guilt & anxiety
rule/role early / late	conformist	3. persona vs. inner self	b. rules- conformist	F-4	4. conformist		industry vs. inferiority
transition		4. dualist or positivist cynical, mechanistic	4. early individuation				
formal early	conscientious-conformist	5. inner observer differentiated from ego	5. continuity	F-5	5. achievement/ affiliative		identity vs. role confusion
formal late	conscientious		6. self-consistency				
transition							
vision- early	individualistic	6. mind and body experiences of an integrated self	7. relativity-integration	F-6	6. authentic	regression in service of transcendence	intimacy/ isolation
vision- middle / late	autonomous						
logic early / late	integrated			F-7			generativity/ stagnation; integrity/despair
psychic early / (vision) late				F-8	7. transcendent	regeneration in spirit	
subtle early / (archetype) late							
causal early / (formless) late				F-9	8. unitary	integration	
nondual early / -middle / late				nondual			

(Developmental bands along left axis: sensorimotor, phantasmic-emotional, rep-mind, conop, formop, postformal)

Chart 4b. Self-Related Stages

Correlative Basic Structures	Major Self Line	Neumann — mythological stages	Neumann — psychological stages	Scheler (structural hardware)	Pascual-Leone (ego development)	Karl Jaspers	Rudolph Steiner	Don Beck (spiral dynamics)
-subatomic								
matter -atomic / -molecular -polymer		pleroma	pleromatic					instinctive
sensation		uroboros	uroboric fusion / alimentary uroboros	organismic survival			physical body	
perception			uroboric Mother					
exocept		the Great Mother	wish-fulfillment	instinctual effects			etheric body	animistic-tribalistic
impulse/emotion			magic / maternal incest / bodyself narcissism				astral (emotion) body	
image		separation of the World Parents	Oedipus/Electra	associative memory	stages of self development beyond phenomenological ego or ordinary adult ego = stages of transcendental ego (Kant, Husserl) or "ultraself" {	level-types of existential-phenomenological reduction, or meditative thinking {		power-gods
symbol		dragon fight	cs/uncs overcoming instincts				sensation-soul	
endocept		birth of the Hero / slaying of Mother	emergence of ego	practical intelligence				absolutist-religious
concept			differentiation of anima					
rule/role — early / late		slaying of Father	differentiation of animus		1. existential self	1. empirical	rational-soul	individualistic
transition		captive and treasure	mature ego	creative-spiritual intelligence	2. duality self	2. conceptual		achiever
formal — early / late					3. dialectical self	3. temporal		relativistic
transition		Transformation	ego/self integration		4. realized self (quaternity thinking) →	4. true meditative thinking	consciousness-soul	systematic-integrative
vision- — early								
logic — middle / late								
psychic — early / late (vision)	Witness (or Self) — deeper psychic (or soul) — frontal (or ego)						spirit-self	global-holistic
subtle — early / (archetype) late							spirit-life	
causal — early / (formless) late							spirit-man	
nondual — early / middle / late								

sensorimotor · phantasmic-emotional · rep-mind · conop · formop · postformal

Chart 4c. Self-Related Stages

Correlative Basic Structures	(developmental level)	Cook-Greuter: perspective	Cook-Greuter: self-sense	Cook-Greuter: characteristics	Clare Graves (ego types)	Robert Kegan	Fulcrums (Wilber)
-subatomic	sensorimotor						F-0
matter -atomic -molecular -polymer							
sensation							
perception		none	presocial	autistic, undifferentiated	1. autistic	0. incorporative	F-1 physical
exocept							
impulse/emotion	phantasmic-emotional	none / 1st person	symbiotic	confused, confounded	2. magical animistic	1. impulsive	F-2 emotional
image			impulsive	rudimentary			
symbol	rep-mind	2nd person	self-protective	self-labeling, basic dichotomies, concepts	3. awakening/fright; 4. aggression/power	2. imperial	F-3 mental: self-concept
endocept							
concept		3rd person	rule-oriented; conformist	early roles, simple roles	5. sociocentric	3. interpersonal	role-self
rule/role early / late	conop		self-conscious; goal-oriented	introspection, historical self, many roles	6. individualism (aggressive)	4. formal-institutional	F-4 (persona)
transition		4th person	conscientious	relativity of self, self as system	7. individualism		F-5 ego (rational reflexive)
formal early / late	formop		individualistic; autonomous		(integrated)	5. postformal-interindividual	integrated:
transition		5th person	ego-witnessing; construct-witnessing	self as construct, self transparent ego			F-6 centaur
vision-logic early / middle / late	postformal	6th person; global	universal	transcendence			
psychic (vision) early / late		cosmic	cosmic				F-7 soul: psychic
subtle (archetype) early / late							F-8 subtle
causal (formless) early / late							F-9 spirit: causal
nondual early / middle / late							nondual: nondual

Note: preconventional brackets 1st–2nd person; conventional brackets 3rd–4th person; postconventional brackets 5th–6th person.

Chart 5a. The Self-Related Stages of Morals and Perspectives

Correlative Basic Structures	Kohlberg (moral judgement)	Torbert (levels of action-inquiry)	Blanchard-Fields (socioemotional development)	Kitchener & King (reflective judgement)	Deirdre Kramer (social-cognitive stages)	William Perry (self-outlook)
matter —subatomic —atomic —molecular —polymer						
sensation						
perception						
exocept						
impulse/emotion						
image						
symbol	0. magic wish	1. impulsive	1. one perspective	1. concrete category	1. undifferentiation	1. dualistic
endocept						
concept	1. punishment/obedience					
rule/role early						
rule/role late	2. naive hedonism	2. opportunist	2. dualist-absolutist	2. representational relations	2. preformism	2. early multiplicity
transition						
formal early	3. approval of others	3. diplomat	3. multiple outcomes	3. personal impressions	3. formism/mechanism	3/4. multiplicity
formal late	4. law and order	4. technician	4. early multiple perspectives	4. abstractions	4. static relativism, pluralism	
transition	4/5. transition					5. relativism, pluralism
vision-logic early	5. prior rights/ social contract	5. achiever	5. multiple perspectives	5. relativism, contextualism	5. static systems	
vision-logic middle			6. integrative multiple perspectives	6. early synthesis	6. dynamic relativism, contextualism	commitment: 6/7. early
vision-logic late		6. existential		7. synthesis	7. dynamic dialecticism ("integration of cultural and historical systems into evolving social structures")	8/9. middle, late
psychic (vision) early	6. universal ethical	7. ironist (transcendental)				
psychic (vision) late						
subtle (archetype) early	7. universal spiritual					
subtle (archetype) late						
causal (formless) early						
causal (formless) late						
nondual early middle late						

Kohlberg scale brackets: preconventional — conventional — postconventional — [post-postconventional]

Basic structures lower axis: sensorimotor · phantasmic-emotional · rep-mind · conop · formop · postformal

Chart 5b. The Self-Related Stages of Morals and Perspectives

Top bands (perspectives): egocentric → ethnocentric → worldcentric → theocentric

Moral bands (Armon): preconventional → conventional → postconventional

Basic structure bands: sensorimotor · phantasmic-emotional · rep-mind · conop · formop · postformal

Correlative Basic Structures	Turner/Powell (social role-taking)	Cheryl Armon (Stages of the Good)	Peck (moral motivation)	Worldviews (Wilber) — name	Worldviews (Wilber) — general characteristics
matter -subatomic / -atomic / -molecular / -polymer					•undifferentiated, pleromatic
sensation	level and type of role-taking;			archaic	
perception					•hallucinatory wish fulfillment
exocept				archaic-magical	subject-object fusions "selfobject"
impulse/emotion			amoral-impulsive	magical	•egocentric, word magic, narcissistic; locus of magic power = ego
image					•omnipotence of ego challenged; security; ego omnipotence transferred to gods
symbol	identificatory			magic-mythic	
endocept	nonreflexive		expedient-self-protective	mythic	•concrete-literal myths
concept	identificatory	1. radical egoism		mythic (literal)	locus of magic power = deified Other
rule/role early	reflexive 3rd party	2. instrumental egoism	conformist	mythic	•rationalization of mythic structures
rule/role late	nonreflexive				
transition	3rd party reflexive	3. affective mutuality	(irrational-conscientious)	rational	•demythologizing, formalizing
formal early	interactive effect	4. individuality		rational	•static universal formalism
formal late		4/5. subjective relativism		formalism	•static systems/contexts
transition	interactive		rational-altruistic	pluralistic	•pluralistic systems, dynamic-
vision- logic early	empathy	5. autonomy		relativism	multiple contexts/histories
vision-logic middle	social genius	6. universal holism		holistic	•integrates multiple contexts, paradigmatic
vision-logic late				integralism	•cross-paradigmatic; dialectical developmentalism as World Process
psychic early (vision)				psychic (shamanic, yogic)	•union with World Process; nature mysticism; gross realm unity
psychic late					
subtle early (archetype) late				subtle (archetypal, saintly)	•union with creatrix of gross realm; deity mysticism; subtle realm unity
causal early				causal	•union with source of manifest realms; formless mysticism; causal unity
(formless) late				(formless, sage)	
nondual early / middle / late				nondual (siddha)	•union of form and formless, Spirit and World Process nondual mysticism

Chart 5c. The Self-Related Stages of Morals and Perspectives

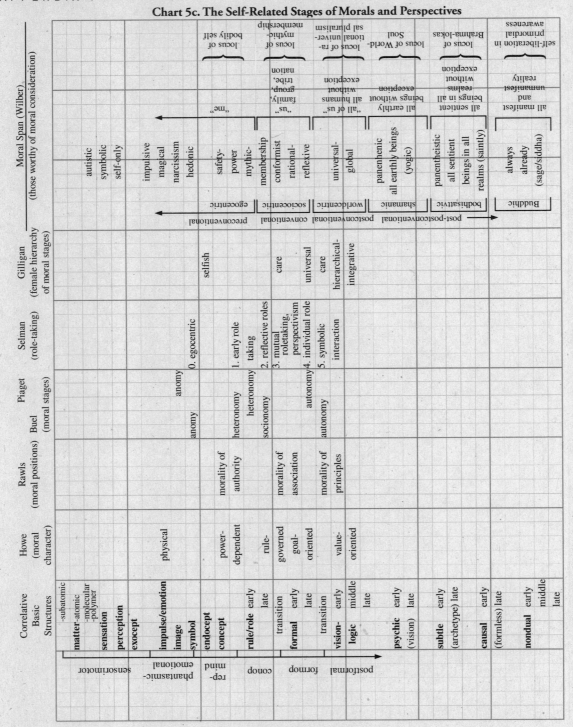

Chart 6a. Stages of Spirituality

Band	Correlative Basic Structures	Hazrat Inayat Khan (Sufism)	Mahamudra (stages of meditation)	Fowler (stages of faith)	Wilber	Underhill	Helminiak (spiritual development)	Funk (contact with Numinous)
sensorimotor	**matter** -subatomic -atomic -molecular -polymer	matter (nasut)						
sensorimotor	**sensation**	vegetable						
sensorimotor	**perception**	animal			archaic			
phantasmic-emotional	exocept	mundane-person		0. preverbal, undifferentiated	archaic-magical			libidinal, prepersonal
phantasmic-emotional	**impulse/emotion**	(bodily desires)			magical			
phantasmic-emotional	**image**			1. magical, projective	magical			
phantasmic-emotional	**symbol**							
rep-mind	endocept		concepts and beliefs of gross mind		magic-mythic			
rep-mind	concept	material-person		2. mythic-literal	mythic-literal	conceptual faith and beliefs	conformist	personal
conop	**rule/role** early	(earthly gain)			(mythic-membership)			
conop	late		right beliefs	3. conventional				
formop	transition		foundations					psychological
formop	**formal** early	artistic person		4. individual-reflexive	rational-universal		conscientious-conformist conscientious	
formop	late	(beyond conventions)						creative
formop	transition							
formop	**vision-** early	idealistic	universal-ethical practices	5. conjunctive faith	integral-			
postformal	**logic** middle	(universal principles)		6. universalizing	holistic (global)	contemplative illumination:	compassionate cosmic	(global)
postformal	late		**meditation:**	→				
postformal	**psychic** early	djinn (genius)	access **1. one-pointedness**		**nature mysticism** shamanic, yogic	**1. nature mysticism** union with stream of life		nature mysticism
postformal	(vision) late	vision mind	gross union		gross-realm unity	lateral expansion of csness		
postformal	**subtle** early	(malkut) soul (angelic)	subtle perception luminosity		**deity mysticism** luminosity, saintly	**2. metaphysical mysticism** recollection (archetypal)		archetypal, theistic mysticism
postformal	(archetype) late	akasha-archetypal arwah- divine luminosity			subtle-realm unity	luminosity		
postformal	**causal** early	wahdat-witness	**2. simplicity**		**formless mysticism**	contemplation-divine love		
postformal	(formless) late	djabrut-cessation formless	cessation emptiness		cessation causal unity	divine ignorance (cessation)		
postformal	**nondual** early	zat: absolute consciousness nondual	**3. one taste** unity form/formless **4. non-meditation**		**nondual mysticism** constant consciousness	**3. divine mysticism** - dark night - union		spirit, union with absolute
postformal	middle							
postformal	late							

401

Chart 6b. Stages of Spirituality

Developmental band	Correlative Basic Structures	Daniel Brown (crosscultural stages of meditation)	Muhyiddin Ibn 'Arabi (stations of zikr)	St. Palamas	traditional samadhis (highest contemplative states)	Highest Yoga Tantra — seven stages of practice	Highest Yoga Tantra — levels of csness	Highest Yoga Tantra — phenomenological signs of appearance
sensorimotor	subatomic							
sensorimotor	matter -atomic		mineral world				form (1st skandha)	(1st dissolves into 2nd:)
sensorimotor	-molecular -polymer		vegetal world				sensation (2nd)	mirage
sensorimotor	sensation							(2nd dissolves
sensorimotor	perception						perception-impulse (3rd)	into 3rd:) smoke
sensorimotor	exocept							
phantasmic-emotional	impulse/emotion		animal world				emotion-image (4th)	(3rd into 4th:) fireflies
phantasmic-emotional	image							
phantasmic-emotional	symbol							(4th into 5th:)
rep-mind	endocept						gross mental csness (5th)	flickering butterlamp
rep-mind	concept							
conop	rule/role early	• preliminary practices	surface signs					steady butterlamp
conop	late							
conop	transition		universal order					
formop	formal early	• concentration with support					80 gross mental conceptions (overall gross csness)	
formop	late	• transcending gross perception	integral ideas	vision	supramental mediative consciousness:			
formop	transition							
postformal	vision-logic early		intellect in holy forms	recollection				
postformal	middle					① physical (gross) transcendence — in central channel — winds dissolve: at heart		
postformal	late	• subtle-perception	vision-wholeness			② verbal (subtle) transcendence — at heart		
postformal	psychic (vision) early	• luminosity	ascending sights	divine light	savikalpa		(dissolution of gross csness:) subtle csness	clear autumn moonlight
postformal	late		divine light	theosis	luminosity, deity form archetypal form	③ mental (causal) transcendence — at drop in heart	white appearance (luminosity)	clear autumn sunlight
postformal	subtle (archetype) early	• insight	bliss			④ (impure illusory body)	red increase very subtle	
postformal	late		witness-totality	formless	nirvikalpa-cessation			
postformal	causal early	• cessation	gnosis	illumination	jnana-nirodh, nirvana post-nirvana stages:		(causal) csness black near-attainment (cessation)	thick blackness of autumn night
postformal	(formless) late	• advanced insight	a returned one		sahaja-one taste	5. actual clear light	clear-light	clear autumn dawn
postformal	nondual early	• Enlightenment: a,b,c			" -nonmeditation: bhava post-Enlightenment	6. learner's union	emptiness	
postformal	middle					7. Buddhahood		
postformal	late							

Chart 6c. Stages of Spirituality

Alexander (TM): transcendental csness · Witness · permanence · refined " · unity csness

St. Gregory Nyssa: darkness of sin · faith in God · light · "not seeing" · luminous · darkness

Yoga Sutras of Patanjali: cleansing, restraint, pranayana · recollection · dhyana · one-pointedness · subtle perception · luminosity · shining forth · oneness of buddhi · cessation (nirodh) · raincloud

St. Dionysius (pseudo): prayer of simplicity (vocal) · prayer of mind (subvocal) · (purification) prayer of recollection · (illumination) prayer of quiet (unification) · prayer of union · "glorious nothingness" · (cloud of unknowing)

Chirban (Eastern Orthodox Christianity): image—preliminary orientation · metanoia—turning toward spiritual · apatheia—detachment · purification · light-divine—luminosity · theosis—oneness with God

St. Teresa (seven stages of interior life): 1. humility · 2. practice, prayer · 3. exemplary life · 4. prayer of recollection, early visions · 5. prayer of union (ego dies, soul emerges), luminosity · 6. cessation – formless · 7. spiritual marriage

General Great Chain: matter · body · mind · soul · spirit

Correlative Basic Structures:
- sensorimotor: matter (-subatomic, -molecular, -polymer), sensation, perception
- phantasmic-emotional: except, impulse/emotion, image, symbol
- rep-mind: endocept, concept
- conop: rule/role early, late, transition
- formop: formal early, late, transition
- postformal: vision-logic early, middle, late
- psychic (vision) early, late
- subtle (archetype) early, late
- causal (formless) early, late
- nondual early, middle, late

Chart 7. Miscellaneous Developmental Lines

Correlative Basic Structures	Erotic relationships (Fortune)	Needs (Maslow)	Levels of "Food" (relational exchange) (Wilber)	Modal Experience (Chinen)	Empathy (Benack)	Gender Identity (Wilber)	Affect (Wilber)
matter -subatomic						• morphological-genetic givens	• reactivity
-atomic							
-molecular	physical					• undifferentiated	• sensations
-polymer							
sensation		physiological					• physiostates: touch, temperature, pleasure, pain
perception	instinctual		**material exchange** -food				
exocept		beginning of safety	-labor				
impulse/emotion	emotional		**emotional exchange** -sex			• differentiated basic-gender identity	• protoemotions: tension, fear, rage, satisfaction
image			-safety, power				
symbol		safety	-belongingness, care				• 2° emotions: anxiety, anger, wishing, liking, safety
endocept				1. enactment	**unwilling** to assume others' perspective	• gender conventionality	
concept	concrete, mental	belongingness	**mental exchange** -membership		**unable** to assume others' perspective	• gender consistency (norms)	• 3° emotions: love, joy, depression, hate, belongingness
rule/role early			discourse	2. reflection	**willing** to assume others' persp.		
late		self-esteem	-self-reflective exchange	3. representation	**able** to assume others' perspective		• 4° emotions: universal affect, global justice, care, compassion, all-
transition				4. pragmatic			
formal early	abstract, mental	self-actualization	-autonomous exchange	5. hermeneutic		• gender perspective	
late							
transition			exchange				
vision- early				6. attunement		• gender androgyny (trans-differentiated)	human love, world-centric altruism
logic middle			**soul exchange**				
late			-psychic vision				• awe, rapture, all-species love, compassion
psychic early (vision)	concrete, spirit	self-transcendence →	-God communion	7. enlightenment →		• archetypal gender union (tantra)	
late							• ananda, ecstasy love-bliss, saintly commitment
subtle early (archetype)			-God union				
late							• infinite freedom- release, boddhisattvic-compassion
causal early (formless)	pure, spirit		**spiritual exchange** -Godhead identity			• beyond gender	
late	spirit						
nondual early			-sahaja				• one taste
middle							
late							

sensorimotor — phantasmic-emotional — rep-mind — conop — formop — postformal

Chart 8. Miscellaneous

Correlative Basic Structures

- -subatomic
- **matter** -atomic -molecular -polymer
- **sensation**
- **perception**
- **exocept**
- **impulse/emotion**
- **image**
- **symbol**
- **endocept**
- **concept**
- **rule/role** early / late
- transition
- **formal** early / late
- transition
- **vision-** early
- **logic** middle / late
- **psychic** early (vision) late
- **subtle** early (archetype) late
- **causal** early (formless) late
- **nondual** early / middle / late

Bottom axis: sensorimotor | phantasmic-emotional | rep-mind | conop | formop | postformal

Universal Waves of development (H. Gardner)

- event structuring
- analog mapping — [preconventional]
- digital mapping
- notational systems
- symbolic flowering — [conventional]
- rules, regulations
- skill mastery — [conventional]
- self-critical
- relativism — [postconventional]
- integration of self and culture — [post-postconventional]

Art (Wilber)

- **sensorimotor** (initial aesthetic impact)
- **emotional-expressivist** (feeling-expression)
- **magical imagery** (e.g., Paleolithic cave art, dream imagery, surrealist)
- **mythological-literal** (e.g., concrete religious art, icons)
- **perspectival** — naturalistic, empirical-representational, impressionist, conceptual, formal
- **aperspectival** — cubist, abstract
- **symbolist** — fantastic realist, psychic perceptual
- **archetypal** (e.g., thangka, bhakti expressivist)
- **nondual** (e.g., Zen landscape)

Melvin Miller (Intermediate-level Worldviews)

teleological	ateleological	antiteleological
mythic		
theism	stoicism	mechanism
humanism	skepticism	nihilism
integrated theism	existentialism	pantheism

Chart 9a. Sociocultural Evolution

Lenski (techno-economic base)
- simple hunting and gathering
- advanced hunting and gathering
- simple horticultural
- advanced horticultural
- simple agrarian
- advanced agrarian
- industrial
- informational

Age
- Paleolithic
- Mesolithic
- Neolithic
- Copper
- Bronze
- Iron
- Enlightenment
- Globalization

Habermas (scare resource)
- power over nature (bodily security)
- legal security (law and order)
- value
- meaning

Jean Houston (G. Heard)
- constricted consciousness
- pre-individual
- proto-ind.
- mid-ind.
- individual
- post-individual

Habermas (epochs)
- **archaic** — familiazation of male
- **magical-animistic** — tribal kinship — preconventional law
- **mythological** — conventional law — early state
- **mythic-rational** — empire
- **rational-reflective** — nation-state — postconventional law
- **world citizens** — global

Major Epochs (Wilber) — Social
- **foraging** — tribes — organized hunt
- **horticultural** — village
- **agrarian** — early state
- **advanced ag.** — empire
- **industrial** — nation/state
- **informational** — planetary — global

Major Epochs (Wilber) — Cultural
- archaic
- magic-typhonic
- mythic-membership
- rational-egoic
- integral-centauric
- shaman
- saint
- sage
- siddha
- most advance in each:

Correlative Basic Structures
- **matter** — -subatomic / -atomic / -molecular / -polymer
- **sensation**
- **perception**
- **exocept**
- **impulse/emotion**
- **image**
- **symbol**
- **endocept**
- **concept**
- **rule/role** — early / late — transition
- **formal** — early / late — transition
- **vision-logic** — early / middle / late
- **psychic** — early / (vision) late
- **subtle** — early / (archetype) late
- **causal** — early / (formless) late
- **nondual** — early / middle / late

(cognitive line: sensorimotor → phantasmic-emotional → rep-mind → conop → formop → postformal)

Chart 9b. Sociocultural Evolution

Correlative Basic Structures	Sociocultural (Wilber)	Jean Gebser	A. Taylor (levels of social organization)	Jay Earley	Robert Bellah (evolution of religious systems)	Duane Elgin (era consciousness)
-subatomic						
matter -atomic						
-molecular						
-polymer						
sensation						
perception						
exocept	archaic — foraging tribes	archaic	S₁ – family, clan, band	1. tribal hunting magic	primitive	1. archaic humans (contracted consciousness)
impulse/emotion						2. hunter-gatherer (surface consciousness)
image	magic —	magic			archaic	
symbol	horticultural village		S₂ – tribe, territorial	2. horticulture, villages, mythology		3. agrarian (depth)
endocept	mythic — agrarian	mythic			historic	
concept	early state		S₃ – theocratic empires	3. empires, gods and heroes		
rule/role early	advanced ag. empire	mental		4. medieval	early-modern	4. urban-industrial (dynamic)
late	rational — industrial		S₄ – national state	5. modern, democracy, individualism	modern	FUTURE:
formal early	nation					
transition						
late		integral-aperspectival	S₅ – supra-national			
vision- early	centauric — informational			6. global consciousness →		5. global reconciliation (reflective)
transition	global					
logic early						
middle						
late						
psychic early						
(vision) late						6. global bonding (oceanic)
subtle early						
(archetype) late						7. global creativity (flow)
causal early						
(formless) late						8. global wisdom (integral)
nondual early						
middle						
late						

Cognitive line (bottom): sensorimotor · phantasmic-emotional · rep-mind · conop · formop · postformal →

Chart 10. Jürgen Habermas

Correlative Basic Structures		individual's identity	level of communication	idea of the good life	domain of validity	ethics
sensorimotor: —subatomic; **matter**-atomic, -molecular, -polymer; **sensation**; **perception**						
exocept						
phantasmic-emotional: **impulse/emotion**; **image**						
rep-mind: **symbol**	(bodyego)	natural identity				
conop: **endocept**; **concept**			actions and consequences of actions			
rule/role early / late	(persona)	role identity	roles	1. hedonism under obedience 2. hedonism under exchange	nature and social environment	naive hedonism
transition				3. concrete morality /primary groups 4. " /secondary groups	group of primary reference persons	specific order
formop: **formal** early / late	(ego)	ego identity	systems of norms	5. civil liberties, legal freedom	members of the political community all legal associates	rational natural law formalistic ethics
transition				6. moral freedom	all humans as private persons	
postformal: **vision-logic** early / middle / late	(centaur)		principles	7. political freedom	all humans as world citizens	universal ethics of speech
psychic early / late (vision)						
subtle early / late (archetype)						
causal early / late (formless)						
nondual early / middle / late						

Chart 11. James Mark Baldwin

cognitive band	Correlative Basic Structures	logical mode (levels of consciousness)	psychic objects	dualism	aesthetic stages	religious stages	ethical levels
sensorimotor	-subatomic						
	matter-atomic						
	-molecular						
	-polymer						
	sensation						
	perception	prelogical	sense	adualistic animistic			
phantasmic-emotional	**exocept**		memory	present vs. persisting	none	physical spontaneous (magical)	adual -projective -external necessity
	impulse/emotion						
	image			inner vs. outer			
rep-mind	**symbol**		fancy				
	endocept		play		play		
conop	**concept**	quasi-logical	substantive	mind vs. body	spontaneous		
	rule/role early		content	self vs. not self		intellectual ethical-1	
	late						
formop	transition						
	formal early	logical	judged-thought	truth vs. falsity	reflective →	ethical-2	dualistic -relativistic -instrumental
	late						
	transition						
postformal	**vision**- early	extra-logical	moral	good vs. bad		aesthetic-religious immediacy	ethical -ideal -synnomic
	middle						
	late						
	logic						
	psychic early	hyper-logical	aesthetic	pancalistic (nondual)			
	(vision) late						
	subtle early						
	(archetype) late						
	causal early						
	(formless) late						
	nondual early						
	middle						
	late						

Ken Wilber
Bibliography

1974

"The Spectrum of Consciousness," *Main Currents in Modern Thought,* November/
December 1974, vol. 31, no. 2.

"The Perennial Psychology and the Spectrum of Consciousness," *Human Dimensions,* Summer 1974, vol. 4, no. 2 [guest editor John White].

1975

"Psychologia Perennis: The Spectrum of Consciousness," *The Journal of Transpersonal Psychology,* vol. 7, no. 2, pp. 105–32.

"The Ultimate State of Consciousness," *Journal of Altered States of Consciousness,* 1975–76, vol. 2, no. 3 [revised as last chapter in *Eye to Eye,* 1983].

1976

"The Eternal Moment," *Science of Mind,* June 1976.

1977

The Spectrum of Consciousness (Wheaton, Ill.: A Quest Book, Theosophical Publishing House).

1978

"Spectrum Psychology, Part I: Transpersonal Developmental Psychology," *ReVision,* Spring 1978, vol. 1, no. 1, pp. 5–29.

"Spectrum Psychology, Part II: The Transpersonal Dynamic of Evolution," *ReVision,* Spring/Summer 1978, vol. 1, no. 2, pp. 5–33.

"Spectrum Psychology, Part III: Microgeny and the Tibetan Book of the Dead," *ReVision,* Summer/Fall 1978, vol. 1, no. 3/4, pp. 52–84.

"On Dreaming: The Other Side of You," *Foundation for Human Understanding,* vol. 1, no. 1.

"Projection," *Foundation for Human Understanding,* vol. 1, no. 2.

"A Working Synthesis of Transactional Analysis and Gestalt Therapy," *Psychotherapy: Theory, Research and Practice,* vol. 15, no. 1, pp. 68–79.

"Where It Was, I Shall Become," in *Beyond Health and Normality: An Exploration of Extreme Well-Being,* ed. by Roger Walsh and Deane H. Shapiro, Jr. (New York: Van Nostrand Reinhold), pp. 67–121.

"Some Remarks on the Papers Delivered at the Spiritual/Transpersonal Symposium," Annual Meeting of the American Psychological Association, *The Journal of Transpersonal Psychology,* vol. 11, no. 1.

1979

No Boundary: Eastern and Western Approaches to Personal Growth (Los Angeles: Center Publications).

"Spectrum Psychology, Part IV: Into the Transpersonal," *ReVision,* Winter/Spring 1979, vol. 2, no. 1, pp. 65–73.

"A Developmental View of Consciousness," *The Journal of Transpersonal Psychology,* vol. 11, no. 1, pp. 1–21 [expanded and revised as Chapter 3 and Chapter 4 of *Eye to Eye*].

"Eye to Eye: The Relationship Between Science, Reason, and Religion and Its Effect on Transpersonal Psychology," *ReVision,* Winter/Spring 1979, vol. 2, no. 1, pp. 3–25 [revised as Chapter 1 of *Eye to Eye*].

"Physics, Mysticism and the New Holographic Paradigm: A Critical Appraisal," *ReVision,* vol. 2, no. 2, pp. 43–55 [reprinted in *Holographic Paradigm,* 1982].

"On Heroes and Cults," *Vision Mound,* April 1979, vol. 2, no. 8, pp. 6–8.

"Development and Transcendence," *American Theosophist,* May 1, 1979.

"The Master-Student Relationship," *Foundation for Human Understanding,* vol. 2, no. 1.

"Are the Chakras Real?" in *Kundalini, Evolution, and Enlightenment,* ed. by John White (New York: Anchor Press/Doubleday), pp. 121–31.

"On Ego Strength and Egolessness," "Psychologia Perennis" in *The Meeting of the Ways,* ed. by John Welwood (New York: Schocken).

"The One Who Was to Come Is Always Already Here: A Short Appreciation of the Teaching of Bubba Free John," *Vision Mound,* May 1979, vol. 2, no. 9, pp. 28–29.

1980

The Atman Project: A Transpersonal View of Human Development (Wheaton, IL: A Quest Book, Theosophical Publishing House).

"The Pre/Trans Fallacy," *ReVision,* vol. 3, no. 2, pp. 51–72 [reprinted as Chapter 7 in *Eye to Eye*].

"Paradigms in Collision," with Roger Walsh, Duane Elgin, Frances Vaughan, "A Developmental Model of Consciousness," "Eye to Eye: Science and Transpersonal Psychology," "Two Modes of Knowing" in *Beyond Ego: Transpersonal Dimensions in Psychology,* ed. by Roger Walsh & Frances Vaughan (Los Angeles: Jeremy P. Tarcher).

"On Heroes and Cults," Foreword to *Scientific Proof of the Existence of God Will Soon Be Announced by the White House!* by Bubba Free John (Adi Da) (Clearlake, Calif.: Dawn Horse Press).

"Who Am I? Eastern and Western Approaches to Personal Growth," *Inner Paths,* March/April 1980, pp. 28–36.

1981

Up From Eden: A Transpersonal View of Human Evolution (Garden City, N.Y.: Anchor Press/Doubleday).

"Ontogenetic Development: Two Fundamental Patterns," *The Journal of Transpersonal Psychology,* vol. 13, no. 1, pp. 33–58.

"Republicans, Democrats and Mystics," *Association for Humanistic Psychology Newsletter,* Special Issue, November 1981, pp. 22–26 [last chapter in *Up from Eden*].

1982

The Holographic Paradigm and Other Paradoxes: Exploring the Leading Edge of Science, ed. by Ken Wilber (Boulder: Shambhala Publications), including "Introduction," "Physics, Mysticism, and the New Holographic Paradigm: A Critical Appraisal," "Reflections on the New Age Paradigm: A Conversation with Ken Wilber."

"Up From Eden: Ken Wilber Cracks Open the Creation/Evolution Debate: A New

Age Interview with Ken Wilber" by Rich Ingrasci, M.D., *New Age Journal,* April 1982, pp. 34–41/76–77 [cover story].

"The Problem of Proof," *ReVision,* Spring 1982, vol. 5, no. 1, pp. 80–100.

"The Pre/Trans Fallacy," *The Journal of Transpersonal Psychology,* vol. 22, no. 2, pp. 5–43.

"Odyssey: A Personal Inquiry into Humanistic and Transpersonal Psychology," *Journal of Humanistic Psychology,* Winter 1982, vol. 22, no. 1, pp. 57–90.

1983

A Sociable God: A Brief Introduction to a Transcendental Sociology (NY: McGraw-Hill).

Eye to Eye: The Quest for the New Paradigm (New York: Anchor Press/Doubleday).

"Kierkegaard's Passion," *ReVision,* Spring 1983, vol. 6, no. 1, pp. 81–85.

"The Neo-Perennial Philosophy," *The American Theosophist,* Special Fall Issue 1983, pp. 349–55 [reprinted in *The Quest,* 1992; now part of Chapter 2: "In a Modern Light: Integral Anthropology and the Evolution of Cultures" in *The Eye of Spirit,* 1997].

"In Praise of the Ego: An Uncommon Buddhist Sermon," *The Middle Way,* November 1983, vol. 58, no. 3, pp. 151–53.

"Sociocultural Evolution" [originally titled "Reply to Critics," it was written in 1983 and circulated privately, then finally published in *CW4* (Boston: Shambhala Publications, 1999))].

1984

Quantum Questions: Mystical Writings of the World's Great Physicists, edited by Ken Wilber (Boulder: Shambhala Publications, New Science Library) including "Of Shadows and Symbols" (Introduction).

A Sociable God: Towards a New Understanding of Religion (Boulder: Shambhala Publications, New Science Library) [reprint with new subtitle and publisher].

"The Developmental Spectrum and Psychopathology, Part I: Stages and Types of Pathology," *The Journal of Transpersonal Psychology,* vol. 16, no. 1, pp. 75–118.

"The Developmental Spectrum and Psychopathology, Part II: Treatment Modalities," *The Journal of Transpersonal Psychology,* vol. 16, no. 2, pp. 137–66.

"Sheldrake's Theory of Morphogenesis," *Journal of Humanistic Psychology,* Spring 1984, vol. 24, no. 2, pp. 107–15.

"Of Shadows and Symbols: Physics and Mysticism," *ReVision,* Spring 1984, vol. 7, no. 1, pp. 3–17.

"What Is Transpersonal Psychology?" *The Laughing Man,* vol. 5, no. 2, pp. 15–16.

"God, Evolution, and the Spectrum of Consciousness: An Interview with Ken

Wilber" by John White, *Science of Mind*, Part I: January 1984, pp. 9–15, Part II: February 1984, pp. 31–81.

1985

"On Heroes and Cults," *The Laughing Man*, vol. 6, no. 1 [reprint of 1979 Foreword].

"The Dawn Horse Testament: A Brief Appreciation," promotional endorsement for *The Dawn Horse Testament* by Da Free John (Adi Da), various sources.

1986

Transformations of Consciousness: Conventional and Contemplative Perspectives on Development with Jack Engler and Daniel P. Brown (Boston: Shambhala Publications), including "Introduction," "The Spectrum of Development," "The Spectrum of Psychopathology," and "Treatment Modalities."

1987

Spiritual Choices: The Problem of Recognizing Authentic Paths to Inner Transformation, ed. by Dick Anthony, Bruce Ecker, and Ken Wilber (New York: Paragon House).

The Great Chain of Being: A Modern Introduction to the Perennial Philosophy and the World's Great Mystical Traditions [unpublished 800-page manuscript mentioned in *Grace and Grit;* some chapters have appeared as articles in various magazines].

"The Pundit of Transpersonal Psychology," interview by Catherine Ingram, *Yoga Journal*, September/October 1987, no. 76, pp. 38–49 [cover story].

1988

"On Being a Support Person," *The Journal of Transpersonal Psychology*, vol. 20, no. 2, pp. 141–59.

"There Is No New Age: Baby Boomers, Narcissism and the 60's," *Vajradattu Sun*.

"Do We Make Ourselves Sick?," *New Age Journal*, September/October 1988, pp. 50–54/85–91.

1989

"Let's Nuke the Transpersonalists: A Response to Albert Ellis," *Journal of Counseling and Development*, February 1989, vol. 67, no. 6, pp. 332–35.

"Two Humanistic Psychologies? A Response," *Journal of Humanistic Psychology*, Spring 1989, vol. 29, no. 2, pp. 230–43.

"Paradigm Wars: An Interview with Ken Wilber," *The Quest,* Spring 1989, pp. 6–12.

"God Is so Damn Boring: A Response to Kirk Schneider," *Journal of Humanistic Psychology,* Fall 1989, vol. 29, no. 4, pp. 457–69.

"Reply to Schneider," *Journal of Humanistic Psychology,* Fall 1989, vol. 29, no. 4, pp. 493–500.

"Love Story," *New Age Journal,* July/August 1989, pp. 32–52 [cover story].

"Foreword" to *Yoga: The Technology of Ecstasy* by Georg Feuerstein (Los Angeles: Jeremy P. Tarcher).

"Foreword" to *Coming Home: The Experience of Enlightenment in Sacred Traditions* by Lex Hixon (Los Angeles: Jeremy P. Tarcher).

1990

Eye to Eye: The Quest for the New Paradigm, 2nd Edition (Boston: Shambhala Publications) [new chapter added: "In the Eye of the Artist: Art and the Perennial Philosophy"].

"Two Patterns of Transcendence: A Reply to Washburn," *Journal of Humanistic Psychology,* Summer 1990, vol. 30, no. 3, pp. 113–36 [reprinted as "A Unified Theory of Development" in *CW4,* 1999].

"Death, Rebirth, and Meditation," in *What Survives?: Contemporary Explorations of Life After Death,* ed. by Gary Doore (Los Angeles: Jeremy P. Tarcher).

"In the Eye of the Artist: Art and the Perennial Philosophy," in *Sacred Mirrors: The Visionary Art of Alex Grey* by Alex Grey (Rochester, Vt.: Inner Traditions International).

1991

Grace and Grit: Spirituality and Healing in the Life of Treya Killam Wilber (Boston: Shambhala Publications).

"Sex, Gender and Transcendence," *The Quest,* Summer 1991, pp. 41–49.

"Gender Wars: A Continuing Conversation on Ken Wilber's 'Sex, Gender and Transcendence,'" *The Quest,* Winter 1991, letters, pp. 4–12.

"Taking Responsibility for Your Shadow," in *Meeting the Shadow: The Hidden Power of the Dark Side of Human Nature,* by Connie Zweig & Jeremiah Abrams (Los Angeles: Jeremy P. Tarcher, A New Consciousness Reader).

1992

"There Are No Others to Save," in *The Way Ahead: A Visionary Perspective for the New Millennium,* ed. by Eddie and Debbie Shapiro (Rockport, Mass.: Element, Inc.), pp. 225–27.

"Two Modes of Knowing," *Mind Field: A Quarterly Source Journal for Consciousness,* Summer 1992, pp. 51–72.

"The Neo-Perennial Philosophy," *The Quest,* Autumn 1992, pp. 16–21 [originally published in 1983].

"Foreword" to *Lord of the Dance: The Autobiography of a Tibetan Lama* by Chagdud Tulku (Junction City, Calif.: Padma Publishing).

1993

The Spectrum of Consciousness, 2nd anniversary edition (Wheaton, IL: Quest Books, Theosophical Publishing House), with a new Foreword by John White [Wilber's literary agent].

"The Great Chain of Being," *Journal of Humanistic Psychology,* vol. 33, no. 3, pp. 52–65.

"Paths Beyond Ego in the Coming Decade," *ReVision,* Spring 1993, vol. 15, no. 4, pp. 188–92.

"Psychologia Perennis: The Spectrum of Consciousness," "The Spectrum of Transpersonal Development," "The Pre/Trans Fallacy," "The Spectrum of Pathologies," "The Spectrum of Therapies," "Eye to Eye: Science and Transpersonal Psychology," "The Great Chain of Being," "Paths Beyond Ego in the Coming Decades," in *Paths Beyond Ego: The Transpersonal Vision,* ed. by Roger Walsh & Frances Vaughan (Los Angeles: Jeremy P. Tarcher, A New Consciousness Reader).

Grace and Grit: Spirituality and Healing in the Life of Treya Killam Wilber, paperback edition (Boston: Shambhala Publications).

1994

"Stages of Meditation: An Interview with Ken Wilber," *The Quest,* Spring 1994, pp. 42–46.

"Foreword" to *Healing the Split: Madness or Transcendence?: A New Understanding of the Crisis and Treatment of the Mentally Ill* by John E. Nelson (Albany, N.Y.: SUNY Press).

1995

Sex, Ecology, Spirituality: The Spirit of Evolution (Boston: Shambhala Publications) [also known as *The Kosmos Trilogy: Volume 1*].

"An Informal Overview of Transpersonal Studies," *The Journal of Transpersonal Psychology,* vol. 27, no. 2.

"A Message to *Eurotas*," *Eurotas News,* Spring 1995, no. 2.

"The World According to Wilber," by David Guy, *New Age Journal,* August 1995, pp. 76–79.

"Don't Blame Men for the Patriarchy: A Conversation with Ken Wilber," *New Age Journal,* August 1995, pp. 79/136–40.

"Mind and the Heart of Emptiness: Reflections on Intellect and the Spiritual Path," *The Quest,* Winter 1995, pp. 16–22.

"Foreword" to *Shadows of the Sacred: Seeing Through Spiritual Illusions* by Frances Vaughan (Wheaton, Ill.: Quest Books).

1996

A Brief History of Everything (Boston: Shambhala Publications).

The Atman Project: A Transpersonal View of Human Development, 2nd edition reprint (Wheaton, Ill.: Quest Books, Theosophical Publishing House) with a new Foreword by Ken Wilber [now part of Chapter 1 of *The Eye of Spirit*].

Up From Eden: A Transpersonal View of Human Evolution, 2nd edition reprint, (Wheaton, Ill.: Quest Books, The Theosophical Publishing House) with a new Foreword by Ken Wilber [now part of Chapter 2 of *The Eye of Spirit*].

Eye to Eye: The Quest for the New Paradigm, 3rd edition, reprint paperback (Boston: Shambhala Publications) [removed chapter "In the Eye of the Artist" with new Preface by Ken Wilber and Foreword by Frances Vaughan].

"A More Integral Approach: A Response to the *ReVision* Authors," "Afterword," *ReVision,* Fall 1996, vol. 19, no. 2, pp. 10–34. [a response to critical articles in *ReVision,* Spring 1996, vol. 18, no. 4 and Summer 1996, vol. 19, no. 1].

"Transpersonal Art and Literary Theory," *The Journal of Transpersonal Psychology,* vol. 28, no. 1.

"How Shall We See Art?" an essay by Ken Wilber in *Andrew Wyeth: America's Painter* by Martha R. Severens (New York: Hudson Hills Press), pp. 109–39.

"How Big Is Our Umbrella?" *Noetic Sciences Review,* Winter 1996.

"Big Map: The Kosmos According to Ken Wilber," an interview by Robin Kornman in *Shambhala Sun,* September 1996, pp. 34–66 [cover article: "Ken Wilber and Other Big Thinkers"].

"Foreword" to *Textbook of Transpersonal Psychiatry and Psychology,* ed. by B. W. Scotton, A. B. Chinen, & J. R. Battista (New York: Basic Books).

1997

The Eye of Spirit: An Integral Vision for a World Gone Slightly Mad (Boston: Shambhala Publications).

"Transpersonal Hot Spots: Reflections on the New Editions of *Up From Eden, The*

Atman Project and *Eye to Eye*," *Journal of Humanistic Psychology,* Fall 1997,
vol. 37, no. 4.

"An Integral Theory of Consciousness," *Journal of Consciousness Studies,* vol. 4,
no. 1, pp. 71–92 [now reprinted in *CW7*].

"A Spirituality That Transforms," *What Is Enlightenment?,* Fall/Winter 1997,
Issue 12, pp. 22–32 [cover article with Georg Feuerstein].

"To See a World: Art and the I of the Beholder" [essay for art exhibition of Anselm
Kiefer, a major European painter].

"A Ticket to Athens: Pathways Exclusive Interview with Ken Wilber," by Richard G.
Young, Ph.D., *Pathways,* www.pathwayspublications.com.

"Bodhisattvas Are Going to Have to Become Politicians," *Eurotas News:* Newsletter of the European Transpersonal Association, no. 4 (interview by Frank
Visser).

"Foreword" to *Clinical Studies in Transpersonal Psychology* by Seymour Boorstein
(Albany, N.Y.: SUNY Press).

1998

The Marriage of Sense and Soul: Integrating Science and Religion (New York: Random House).

The Marriage of Sense and Soul: Integrating Science and Religion, audio tape read by
Denis deBoisblanc, unabridged (Audio Renaissance).

The Eye of Spirit: An Integral Vision for a World Gone Slightly Mad, paperback edition (Boston: Shambhala Publications).

"A More Integral Approach," in *Ken Wilber in Dialogue: Conversations with Leading Transpersonal Thinkers,* ed. by Donald Rothberg & Sean Kelly (Wheaton,
Ill.: Quest Books [reprint of 1996 *ReVision* article].

"Up Close and Transpersonal: Ken Wilber," interview by Mark Matousek, *Utne
Reader,* August 1998, pp. 51–55/106–7.

"Spiritual Diary," *Tikkun,* vol. 13, no. 5, pp. 37–44 [prepublication excerpt from
One Taste].

"Foreword" to *The Mission of Art* by Alex Grey (Boston: Shambhala Publications).

"Foreword" to *The Fabric of the Future: Women Visionaries Illuminate the Path to
Tomorrow,* ed. by M. J. Ryan (Berkeley: Conari Press).

1999

One Taste: The Journals of Ken Wilber (Boston: Shambhala Publications).

The Collected Works of Ken Wilber, Volumes One–Four (Boston: Shambhala Publications):

> CW1: *The Collected Works of Ken Wilber, Volume One* [*The Spectrum of Consciousness/No Boundary*/selected essays].
>
> CW2: *The Collected Works of Ken Wilber, Volume Two* ["A Personal Odyssey"/ *The Atman Project/ Up From Eden*].
>
> CW3: *The Collected Works of Ken Wilber, Volume Three* [*A Sociable God/Eye to Eye*].
>
> CW4: *The Collected Works of Ken Wilber, Volume Four* [*Transformations of Consciousness/Integral Psychology*/selected essays].

"An Approach to Integral Psychology," *The Journal of Transpersonal Psychology*, vol. 31, no. 2, pp. 109–36.

The Marriage of Sense and Soul: Integrating Science and Religion, paperback edition (New York: Random House).

2000

The Collected Works of Ken Wilber, Volumes Five–Eight (Boston: Shambhala Publications):

> CW5: *The Collected Works of Ken Wilber, Volume Five* [*Grace and Grit*].
>
> CW6: *The Collected Works of Ken Wilber, Volume Six* [*Sex, Ecology, Spirituality* (revised edition)].
>
> CW7: *The Collected Works of Ken Wilber, Volume Seven* [*A Brief History of Everything* (revised edition)/*The Eye of Spirit* (revised edition)].
>
> CW8: *The Collected Works of Ken Wilber, Volume Eight* [*The Marriage of Sense and Soul/One Taste*].

Integral Psychology: Consciousness, Spirit, Psychology, Therapy (Boston: Shambhala Publications) [originally part of *CW4*, 1999].

A Theory of Everything: An Integral Vision for Business, Politics, Science, and Spirituality (Boston: Shambhala Publications).

Grace and Grit: Spirituality in the Life and Death of Treya Killam Wilber, reprint paperback edition (Boston: Shambhala Publications).

Eye to Eye: The Quest for the New Paradigm, 3rd edition, revised paperback edition (Boston: Shambhala Publications).

Sex, Ecology, Spirituality: The Spirit of Evolution, 2nd edition, revised paperback (Boston: Shambhala Publications) [about fifty new pages and some diagrams].

A Brief History of Everything, 2nd edition, revised paperback (Boston: Shambhala Publications) [some new pages and diagrams].

One Taste: Daily Reflections on Integral Spirituality, reprint paperback edition (Boston: Shambhala Publications).

"Waves, Streams, States, and Self," *Journal of Consciousness Studies*, November/

December 2000, vol. 7, nos. 11–12 [new chapter added to revised edition of *The Eye of Spirit*].

"Integral Transformative Practice: In This World or Out of It," *What Is Enlightenment?* Fall/Winter 2000, issue 18, pp. 34–39/126–31.

"On Critics, Integral Institute, My Recent Writing, and Other Matters of Little Consequence: A Shambhala Interview with Ken Wilber," wilber.shambhala.com.

"Waves, Streams, States, and Self—a Summary of My Psychological Model (or, Outline of an Integral Psychology)," wilber.shambhala.com.

"Announcing the Formation of Integral Institute," (wilber.shambhala.com).

"Foreword" to *A Greater Psychology: An Introduction to Sri Aurobindo's Psychological Thought* by A. S. Dalal (New York: Jeremy P. Tarcher).

"Foreword" to *Putting on the Mind of Christ* by Jim Marion (Charlottesville, VA: Hampton Roads Publishing Company).

"Foreword" to *The Fabric of the Future: Women Visionaries of Today Illuminate the Path to Tomorrow* ed. by M. J. Ryan (Berkeley: Conari Press).

"Foreword" to *Drinking Lightning: Art, Creativity, and Transformation* by P. Rubinov-Jacobson (Boston: Shambhala Publications).

2001

Ken Wilber: Speaking of Everything, two-CD interview by Jordan Gruber for www.enlightenment.com.

"Do Critics Misrepresent My Position? A Test Case from a Recent Academic Journal," wilber.shambhala.com.

"The Deconstruction of the World Trade Center: A Date That Will Live in a Sliding Chain of Signifiers," wilber.shambhala.com.

"Introduction to 'The Deconstruction of the World Trade Center,' and Prologue to *Boomeritis,*" wilber.shambhala.com.

"On the Nature of a Post-Metaphysical Spirituality: Response to Habermas and Weis," wilber.shambala.com [original interview by Frank Visser and Edith Zundel in German, in *Transpersonale Psychologie und Psychotherapie,* ViaNova].

"To See a World: Some Technical Points," www.worldofkenwilber.com.

No Boundary: Eastern and Western Approaches to Personal Growth, reprint paperback edition (Boston: Shambhala Publications).

Quantum Questions: Mystical Writings of the World's Great Physicists, reprinted paperback edition (Boston: Shambhala Publications).

The Eye of Spirit: An Integral Vision for a World Gone Slightly Mad, revised paperback edition (Boston: Shambhala Publications) [revised from 2000 with new chapter: "Waves, Streams, States, and Self"].

A Theory of Everything: An Integral Vision for Business, Politics, Science, and Spirituality, reprint paperback edition (Boston: Shambhala Publications).

2002

Boomeritis: A Novel That Will Set You Free, June 2002 (Boston: Shambhala Publications) [originally written as nonfiction treatise subtitled: "The Extraordinary Emergence of an Integral Culture—and Its Many Obstacles," then subsequently rewritten as a postmodern fiction novel].

"Endnotes to *Boomeritis,*" wilber.shambhala.com.

"Interview with Ken Wilber: On the Release of *Boomeritis* and the Completion of Volume 3 of the Kosmos Trilogy," wilber.shambhala.com.

"Sidebars" to *Boomeritis,* wilber.shambhala.com.

- Sidebar A: "Who Ate Captain Cook? Integral Historiography in a Postmodern Age"
- Sidebar B: "The Many Names of the Levels of Consciousness"
- Sidebar C: "Orange and Green: Levels or Cousins?"
- Sidebar D: "Childhood Spirituality"
- Sidebar E: "The Genius Descartes Gets a Postmodern Drubbing"
- Sidebar F: "Participatory Samsara: The Green-Meme Approach to the Mystery of the Divine"
- Sidebar G: "States and Stages"
- Sidebar H: "Boomeritis Buddhism"
- Sidebar I: "Kosmic Karma"
- Sidebar J: "Integral Post-Metaphysics"
- Sidebar K: "Subtle Energies"

"The Guru and the Pandit: The Evolution of Enlightenment," Andrew Cohen and Ken Wilber in Dialogue, *What Is Enlightenment?,* Spring/Summer 2002, pp. 38–49, 136–43.

"The Guru and the Pandit: Breaking the Rules: Andrew Cohen and Ken Wilber in Dialogue," *What Is Enlightenment?,* Fall/Winter 2002.

The Kosmos Trilogy, Vol. 2: Excerpt A: "An Integral Age at the Leading Edge," wilber.shambhala.com.

The Kosmos Trilogy, Vol. 2: Excerpt B: "The Many Ways We Touch: Three Principles Helpful for Any Integrative Approach," (wilber.shambhala.com).

"Foreword" to *A Monk in the World: Cultivating a Spiritual Life* by Wayne Teasdale (New York: New World Library).

"Foreword" to *Living Enlightenment: A Call for Evolution Beyond Ego* by Andrew Cohen (Moksha Press).

"Foreword" to *Finding God Through Sex: A Spiritual Guide to Ecstatic Loving and Deep Passion for Men and Women* by David Deida (Plexus).

2003

Boomeritis: A Novel That Will Set You Free, reprint paperback edition (Boston: Shambhala Publications).

"Foreword" to *Spirit and Politics for the XXI Century,* ed. by Salvador Harguindey, including contributions by the Dalai Lama, Vaclav Havel, Raimon Panikkar, Allan Combs, Gregory Wilpert, Thomas Jordan, Michael McDermott, Mikhail Gorbachev, and Nelson Mandela.

"Foreword" to *Integral Medicine: A Noetic Reader* ed. by Marilyn Schlitz & Tina Hyman, including contributions by Larry Dossey, Roger Walsh, Michael Murphy, Ivan Illich, Eugene Taylor, and Lawrence LeShan.

FUTURE PROJECTS

Kosmic Karma and Creativity: Volume 2 of the Kosmos Trilogy (forthcoming) [originally Volume 3, tentatively titled "The Spirit of Post/Modernity," it became Volume 2 when completed in 2002 to supplement Wilber's critique of postmodernity and "boomeritis"; prepublication excerpts posted on Wilber websites].

Sex, God and Gender: The Ecology of Men and Women (now volume 3, originally volume 2 of *The Kosmos Trilogy*).

The Simple Feeling of Being: Embracing Your True Nature. Compiled and edited by Mark Palmer, Sean Harsens, Vipassana Esbjörn, and Adam Leonard (Boston, Shambhala Publications, 2004).

Notes

INTRODUCTION

1. Ken Wilber, *Grace and Grit*, p. 240.
2. "Everybody is right" is a phrase Wilber often uses, calling it "the essence of integral metatheory," describing the integral position which generally accepts the view that every discipline or worldview or intellectual position is "correct but partial," and thus each has something important to offer in any integrative synthesis. This generous and integrative stance is one that Wilber has adopted from his very first book to his most recent writings in the new millennium.
3. See Ken Wilber, "Personal Odyssey: A Personal Inquiry into Humanistic and Transpersonal Psychology," *Journal of Humanistic Psychology*, vol. 22, no. 1, winter 1982, p. 58. This valuable biographical essay was a major source for this Introduction and will henceforth appear referenced as "Ken Wilber, *Personal Odyssey*."
4. Ken Wilber, *Grace and Grit*, p. 12.
5. This is a translation of the first chapter of the Tao Te Ching by Lao Tzu that Wilber read at Duke, and which he presented in the opening page of *Personal Odyssey*, p. 57.
6. Ken Wilber, *Personal Odyssey*, pp. 58–59.
7. Ken Wilber, *Personal Odyssey*, p. 58, 60.
8. Ken Wilber, *Up From Eden*, p. 4.
9. Ken Wilber, *Collected Works*, vol. 8, p. 62, 29n.
10. Ken Wilber, *Personal Odyssey*, pp. 59–60.
11. The "four forces" of psychology are the principal paradigms of modern psychology. They are 1) Freudianism, 2) behaviorism, 3) humanistic, and 4) transpersonal.
12. Ken Wilber, *Personal Odyssey*, pp. 60–61.
13. Tony Schwartz, *What Really Matters* (1995), p. 364.

14. "Transcend-and-include" or "transcend-yet-include" is a fundamental operating principle of evolutionary development in the "nested hierarchy" (or holarchy) of the Kosmos. Thus Wilber identifies it as the dynamic or "secret impulse" of evolution. This principle was emphasized in particular from Wilber/Phase 2 onward.

15. *Kosmos* is an ancient Greek Pythagorean term that Wilber reintroduced in *Sex, Ecology, Spirituality* in order to signify that the whole universe is actually a pluridimensional or multilayered reality, not merely a material world, which in today's parlance is the common understanding of the word *cosmos*.

16. Ken Wilber, *Personal Odyssey,* p. 61.

17. Roger Walsh, Frances Vaughan, "The Worldview of Ken Wilber," *Journal of Humanistic Psychology,* vol. 34, no. 2, spring 1994, p. 19.

18. Ken Wilber, *Grace and Grit,* p. 13; *Collected Works,* vol. 3, pp. 19–20. The five books are *The Spectrum of Consciousness* (1977), *No Boundary* (1979), *The Atman Project* (1980), *Up From Eden* (1981), and *A Sociable God* (1983), as well as most of the essays for *Eye to Eye* (1983).

19. See Ken Wilber, *A Theory of Everything,* pp. 138–39: Integral transformative practice, or ITP, was pioneered by Michael Murphy, the founder of the Esalen Institute, and his colleague George Leonard, the *Look* magazine writer who coined the expression "human potential movement" in the early 1960s. See *The Future of the Body: Explorations into Me: Further Evolution of Human Nature* (LA: Tarcher, 1992) by Michael Murphy; *The Life We Are Given: A Long-Term Program for Realizing the Potential of Body, Mind, Heart, and Soul* (NY: Tarcher/Putnam, 1995) by George Leonard and Michael Murphy; and *Essential Spirituality: The 7 Central Practices to Awaken Heart and Mind* (NY: Wiley & Sons, 1999) by Roger Walsh.

20. Ken Wilber, *Eye to Eye,* pp. 235–36.

21. Ken Wilber, *One Taste,* p. 224.

22. Ken Wilber, *A Brief History of Everything,* p. 43.

23. It needs to be noted, however, that as much as Wilber was originally one of Adi Da's greatest champions, he has, especially since his Phase 4 period, distanced himself from the traditional approach—guru bhakti yoga—that Adi Da and his lineage have tended to promote. In other words, Wilber claims that this traditional yet esoteric approach or method does not adequately serve today's modern democratic culture of the scientific mind and emerging centaur (second-tier thinking).

24. Ken Wilber, *One Taste,* p. 69.

25. Ken Wilber, *Grace and Grit,* p. 246.

26. Ken Wilber, *The Marriage of Sense and Soul,* p. 92.

27. Ken Wilber, *Collected Works, vol. 3,* p. 1; also see *Collected Works, vol. 1,* p. vii; and *Collected Works, vol. 4,* p. 23, 6n.

28. Ken Wilber, *The Spectrum of Consciousness,* p. 19 (Wilber's italics).

29. John Rowan, *The Transpersonal Psychotherapy and Counseling* (London & NY: Routledge, 1993, 1998), p. 97.

30. Ken Wilber, *Personal Odyssey,* p. 80.
31. Ken Wilber, *Personal Odyssey,* p. 82.
32. Ken Wilber, *Personal Odyssey,* p. 83.
33. Ken Wilber, *Personal Odyssey,* p. 83.
34. Ken Wilber, *The Eye of Spirit,* p. 47.
35. Ken Wilber, *Personal Odyssey,* p. 84.
36. Wilber is not claiming, nor do I claim, that he is a fully enlightened being. Rather he has had a taste of the enlightened condition of consciousness, which is ultimately inherent in every being. Indeed, according to the wisdom traditions, there are many further transformations within enlightenment. It's important to point out that the wisdom traditions distinguish between a short, temporary or sudden experience of enlightenment and the final enlightenment, which must be integrated, and is lived constantly in every moment. Wilber's first major satori, on that day in 1978 was more or less temporary, thus he does not regard himself as fully enlightened.
37. In *The Spectrum of Consciousness* Wilber explains that the phrase "It is always already the case" is used extensively by Franklin Jones (now known as Adi Da) in *The Knee of Listening* (Los Angeles, Dawn Horse, 1973) to describe the ever-present nature of nondual consciousness, or enlightenment.
38. In Japanese, *ken* means "true nature"; *sho* means "direct seeing."
39. Ken Wilber, *Grace and Grit,* p. 169; this of course is a paradoxical joke between master and student since a satori, by definition, can be neither big nor small, for no type of polarity ultimately exists when the nondual is revealed.
40. Ken Wilber, in a personal communication to the author.
41. Ken Wilber, *Personal Odyssey,* p. 72. One of Wilber's inspirations for naming this subdivision of the transpersonal realms as psychic (or the way of the yogi), subtle (or the way of the saint), causal (or the way of the sage), and nondual (or the way of the siddha) comes from Adi Da (then Bubba Free John). (See *The Paradox of Instruction,* Clearlake, CA: Dawn Horse Press, 1977.)
42. Ken Wilber, *The Eye of Spirit,* p. 154.
43. Ken Wilber, *A Brief History of Everything,* p. 151.
44. Ken Wilber, *Sex, Ecology, Spirituality,* p. 206.
45. Ken Wilber, *Up From Eden,* p. 313.
46. Ken Wilber, *Up From Eden,* p. 3.
47. Ken Wilber, *Personal Odyssey,* p. 71.
48. See *Journal of Humanistic Psychology,* vol. 22, no. 1, winter 1982, or *Collected Works, vol. 2* (1999).
49. Ken Wilber, *Personal Odyssey,* p. 68: "[Crittenden] wanted to start a journal that was dedicated to such concerns as raised in *Spectrum,* and that was, in a sense, a cross between *Main Currents: Studies in Comparative Religion,* and *The Journal of Transpersonal Psychology.*"
50. "Holonic" is a Phase 4 term that Wilber uses to describe his "twenty tenets" (or evolutionary patterns) of holons, terminology borrowed from Arthur Koestler,

meaning "whole/part." Thus, for example, Tenet #1: "Reality as a whole is not composed of things or processes, but of holons." In this case, "holonic" refers to the fact that "reality is composed of holons within holons within holons indefinitely, with no discernible bottom or top. Even the entire universe right now is simply a part of the next moment's universe. Every whole is always a part, endlessly." (*Integral Psychology,* pp. 166–67)

51. Ken Wilber, in a personal communication to the author, June 13, 1998.
52. Ken Wilber, "Kierkegaard's Passion," *ReVision,* vol. 6, no. 1, spring 1983, p. 81.
53. Ken Wilber, *Collected Works,* vol. 5 (2000), p. ix.
54. Ken Wilber, *Grace and Grit,* p. 72.
55. A phrase of Adi Da's that touched and served the Wilbers during their difficult times, especially near Treya's death.
56. Huston Smith, *The World's Religions* (1958, 1991) p. 29.
57. Ken Wilber, "Mind and the Heart of Emptiness: Reflections on Intellect and the Spiritual Path," *The Quest,* winter 1995, p. 22.
58. Ken Wilber, *The Quest,* winter 1995, p. 22.
59. Ken Wilber, *A Brief History of Everything,* p. 72.
60. Ken Wilber, *Collected Works,* vol. 6, p. xii.
61. Ken Wilber, *A Theory of Everything,* p. 41.
62. *Flatland* is defined by Wilber as "the idea that the sensory and empirical and material world is the only world there is." (*A Brief History of Everything,* p. 11) It is a central metaphor he uses to critique the modern, scientific approach to existence. It is also the title to a famous Victorian classic, by Edwin A. Abbott, about a befuddled narrator who lives in a place of only two dimensions, though he has visited other places of only one dimension. Thus when he claims there's a third, and even fourth, dimension, his fellow Flatlanders became outraged, leading to his tragic fate. According to Wilber, "Flatland is simply the failure to grasp the entire spiral of development or the full spectrum of consciousness; the antidote to flatland is an integral vision, which is what *SES* attempts to provide." (*A Theory of Everything,* p. 41)
63. Ken Wilber, *Collected Works,* vol. 7, p. 43, 25n.
64. Ken Wilber, *Integral Psychology,* p. 189.
65. From Shambhalas Web site promotion for *A Theory of Everything:* "Who Is Ken Wilber, and Does He Really Understand Everything?" @www.Shambhala.com.
66. According to Wilber, as of 2002, *Kindred Visions* is indefinitely on hold owing to its immense size, thus it might appear on a Web site in the future. Nevertheless, the voluminous collection of essays is an excellent testimony to Wilber's worldwide influence.
67. The expression "I-I" actually has several meanings. It's a common phrase in Wilber's Phase 4 writings recalling Sri Ramana Maharshi, who, as Wilber explains, "refers to the Self by the name 'I-I,' since the Self is the simple Witness of even the

Ordinary 'I.' We are all, says Ramana, perfectly aware of the I-I, for we are all aware of our capacity to witness in the present moment." (*SES,* p. 306)

68. Ken Wilber, *A Theory of Everything,* p. 7.

69. *Centaur* comes from the Greek (a creature that's half horse, half human) and is one of Wilber's designations signifying the conscious integration of body and mind. The image had been previously used in psychology, by Hubert Benoit and E. H. Erikson, where the centauric self is defined as an integrated self or a self-actualized person, the epitome of personal ego evolution.

70. See Ken Wilber, *Integral Psychology,* pp. 12, 16, 27, 30, 47, 90, 128, 131, 145, 149, 153, 158.

71. Op. cit., p. 145.

Permissions

Index

Marx, Karl, 150

Maslow, Abraham, 6–7, 193, 204–5, 245, 332–33

Material Exchange, 157

Mature ego, 248

Mean green meme, 64, 305, 367

Meditation, 111–12, 213, 251, 280, 381

Meditative state, 318

Membership Self, 104–5, 137

Men's movement, 250

Mental

    -Egoic Period, 105–6, 140, 353

    -phenomenological inquiry, 179

    realm, 185, 292

    self, 206

Metabolism, 325

Microevolution, 231

Middle

    ego, 105–6

    Egoic Period, 140, 145–46

    stages of psyche, 181

    vision-logic, 327–28

The Middle Way, 39–40

Milarepa, 13

Millennials, 367

Mind, 335

Mind-body problem, 356–58

Modern

    heritage, 354

    physics, 198

Modernity, 269, 272, 283, 330, 333, 359

    dignity and disaster, 284–85

    integrating with premodern, 330–31

    pioneers of, 331–33

Modes of cognition, 170–71, *172*

Monological sciences, 180

Moral Development, 279

Morals, 342

Moses, 146

Most Advanced Mode, 135, 352

Motivation, 343

Murder, 136–37

Murphy, Michael, 51, 280

Mutual Exchange, 158

Mysticism, 116

Mythic

    epoch, 242–43, 353

    indissociation, 254

    -membership, 130–31, 327

    -rational epoch, 243

Nagarjuna, 13, 177, 264, 353

Narcissism, 207, 212, 337, 366–67, 382

Natural

    hierarchy, 352

    selection, 262

    state, 317–18

Nature, 261

    mysticism, 253–54, 353

Negation without preservation, 233

Negative assertions, 79

Neomammalian brain, 232

Neo-perennial philosophy, 278

"The Neo-Perennial Philosophy" (Wilber), 38–39

Nested hierarchy of organization, 165–66

New Age, 367, 382

New physics models, 184–86

New York Times, 43

The Next Development in Man (Whyte), 141–42

Nietzsche, Friedrich, 381

Nirmanakaya, 108, 129, 147, 157

No Boundary (Wilber), 18, 22, 24–27, 41, 378–79

    Chapter 1. Introduction: Who am I?, 92–93

    Chapter 2. Half of It, 93

About the Author

BRAD REYNOLDS did graduate work at the California Institute of Integral Studies (CIIS) before leaving to study under Ken Wilber for more than ten years. A longtime scholar of integral studies and the perennial philosophy, Reynolds is an independent writer and computer graphics artist living in the San Francisco Bay Area. (www.embracingreality.com)